D1432414

Northwestern University
STUDIES IN *Phenomenology &*
Existential Philosophy

The Crisis of European Sciences
and Transcendental Phenomenology

Edmund Husserl

Translated, with an Introduction, by

The Crisis
of European Sciences
and Transcendental
Phenomenology

An Introduction
to Phenomenological Philosophy

David Carr

NORTHWESTERN UNIVERSITY PRESS

EVANSTON   1970

Northwestern University Press
www.nupress.northwestern.edu

Originally published in German under the title *Die Krisis der europäischen Wissenschaften und die transzendentale Phänomenologie: Eine Einleitung in die phänomenologische Philosophie,* edited by Walter Biemel. Copyright © 1954 by Martinus Nijhoff, The Hague; second printing 1962. English translation and Translator's Introduction copyright © 1970 by Northwestern University Press. All rights reserved.

Printed in the United States of America

20   19   18   17   16   15   14

ISBN-13: 978-0-8101-0458-7
ISBN-10: 0-8101-0458-X

Library of Congress Catalog Card Number: 77-82511

∞ The paper used in this publication meets the minimum requirements of the American National Standard for Information Sciences—Permanence of Paper for Printed Library Materials, ANSI Z39.48-1992.

Contents

Translator's Introduction

ENGLISH-SPEAKING READERS of European phenomenology and existentialism are accustomed to references to Husserl's "great last work," *The Crisis of European Sciences and Transcendental Phenomenology* subtitled *An Introduction to Phenomenological Philosophy*. The work is known to be important both for its content and for the influence it has had on other philosophers. In it Husserl makes a last attempt (and since he began it in his mid-seventies he doubtless knew it would be his last attempt) to explain and ground his phenomenological philosophy. Only three other books had been published by Husserl since the *Logische Untersuchungen* of 1900–1901, and each was explicitly characterized by its author as an "introduction to phenomenology." [1] But this new "introduction," written in the

1. Both the first volume of the *Ideen zu einer reinen Phänomenologie und phänomenologischen Philosophie* (1913) and the *Méditations Cartésiennes* (published in French in 1931) had been subtitled "introductions" to phenomenology. Even the *Formale und transzendentale Logik* (Halle: Niemeyer, 1929) was described by Husserl as "eine Emporleitung zur transzendentalen Phänomenologie" (in a *Selbstanzeige* quoted by Eugen Fink in "Die Spätphilosophie Husserls in der Freiburger Zeit," *Edmund Husserl 1859–1959* [The Hague: Nijhoff, 1959], p. 105).

The *Ideen*, Volume I, edited by Walter Biemel, is Volume III (1950) in the *Husserliana* series, and *Cartesianische Meditationen und Pariser Vorträge*, edited by Stephan Strasser, is Volume I (1950). The series as a whole, titled *Husserliana: Edmund Husserl, Gesam-*

mid-1930's, differs radically from earlier ones; the author adopts a wholly new form, and his phenomenology takes on important new dimensions whose significance is still being disputed. Furthermore, he gives unmistakable and passionate expression, though in the most general terms, to his position on the turbulent events of the time.

What is usually not mentioned in passing references, however, is the fact that the work is incomplete and that the text available to us is not a finished version and in some places is almost fragmentary in character. For those who now turn for the first time, through this English translation, to the study of the *Crisis*, it is important to emphasize this incompleteness; the reader who approaches it as a finished book may well be disappointed.

1. Husserl's Work on the *Crisis*

The work on the theme of the *Crisis* seems to have begun sometime in 1934, and it continued until the summer of 1937 and the beginning of Husserl's terminal illness, to which he succumbed on April 27, 1938. The problem of the European "crisis" was much in the air during this period, for obvious reasons. Many people, notably the Nazis themselves, were convinced that Europe was confronted not merely with a political crisis but with a crisis of its very civilization. Philosophers felt called upon to examine the situation from their point of view. The beginnings of Husserl's explicit reflections on this subject seem to have been occasioned by an outside source. They are found in a letter dated August 30, 1934, to the International Congress of Philosophy at Prague. The organizing committee of the Congress had asked Husserl to comment on "the mission of philosophy in our time," and Husserl's letter was read in the session bearing that title. The letter contains many ideas and language similar to the first parts of the *Crisis* and states that "the grounding which would give effective force to what I have to say [on this subject] would require a substantial treatise." [2] Ac-

---

melte Werke, is edited by Herman L. van Breda and is published at The Hague by Martinus Nijhoff. Subsequent references to this series will be by volume numbers and dates and thereafter by titles of individual volumes.

2. The letter, which will be quoted more extensively below, is found in the *Actes du huitième Congrès Internationale de Philosophie à Prague, 2–7 Septembre 1934* (Prague, 1936), pp. XLI–XLV. The

cording to the recently published correspondence with Roman Ingarden, Husserl actually wrote a lengthy essay at this time to accompany his letter to Prague, but the essay was not read. Husserl describes it as a "hurriedly written (two weeks) outline of a historical interpretation of the origin of *our* guiding idea [*Zweckidee*] of philosophy." He writes that it has "given me to think" and that it "led to deep problems in the philosophy of history which truly disturb me." [3]

Then, in May, 1935, Husserl lectured in Vienna, following an invitation by the Vienna Kulturbund, on "Philosophy in the Crisis of European Mankind." [4] In November of the same year he lectured in Prague on "The Crisis of European Sciences and Psychology," and it was this series of lectures which served as the basis for the projected work. As a Jew who was denied any public platform in Germany, Husserl had to publish, as he had lectured, outside his own country. An international yearbook called *Philosophia*, edited by Arthur Liebert in Belgrade, arranged to publish the *Crisis* in installments. After his return from Prague, Husserl worked feverishly on the essay, and the first two parts of the present text were published in *Philosophia* in 1936. By the time Husserl became ill in 1937, the text of the third part was longer than that of the first two parts combined and was still not completed. Eugen Fink, who was Husserl's research assistant and worked closely with him during this period, had produced a typed version of Husserl's stenographic manuscript of Part III, and Husserl had gone over it, perhaps

---

public reading of the letter is reported in the "Feuilleton" of the *Frankfurter Zeitung*, October 2, 1934, and is confirmed by personal recollections of Professor Herbert Spiegelberg.

3. Edmund Husserl, *Briefe an Roman Ingarden* (The Hague: Nijhoff, 1968), p. 89 (Letter LXXIII of November 26, 1934; see also Letter LXX, p. 88).

4. For the rest of this account, unless otherwise indicated, see Walter Biemel's editor's introduction to the posthumous German edition of the *Crisis* (*Die Krisis der europäischen Wissenschaften und die transzendentale Phänomenologie: Eine Einleitung in die phänomenologische Philosophie, Husserliana*, Vol. VI [1954; 2nd printing, 1962]). I have not translated Biemel's introduction, primarily because it deals largely with the preparation and makeup of the German edition, from which this translated version differs in some details. The relation of this translation to the Biemel edition will be explained below.

In the following pages, references to the "*Krisis*" are to Biemel's German edition, while references to the "*Crisis*" are to the present volume.

more than once, making many changes and expressing much dissatisfaction with many parts of the text, indicating changes still to be made. The result was that the third part never reached the publisher in final form.[5] During this period Fink produced an outline, later approved by Husserl himself, for the completion of Part III and for two more parts in addition to the three already worked on.[6] We can see that the *Crisis* was to be an immense work, much longer than the present text. But no manuscript has been found for the conclusion of Part III or for the text of Parts IV and V.

2. The Text, the German Edition, and This Translation

Thus the *Crisis* cannot be regarded as a finished work in any sense of the word. Not only does it break off incompleted; the text we have is in very rough shape, and the ideas it presents flow unevenly. Needless repetitions occur, which might have been eliminated by a leisurely overview of the work. In many places the obvious is belabored, while other passages are among the most dense Husserl ever wrote. Often, intricate trains of thought are introduced which seem to refer to investigations already completed but for which the reader has not been prepared.

In his posthumous German edition of 1954, the editor, Walter Biemel, simply reproduced the published version of Parts I and II from *Philosophia;* the original manuscript had apparently been destroyed. But even these parts of the text give evidence of being patched together and hurriedly prepared, since they contain quite obvious repetitions and other purely textual or grammatical faults (cf. pp. 59, 97, below). And indeed, in certain correspondence during this period Husserl reveals that he added lengthy sections of a historical and critical nature to Part II even after it was in print, and he speaks of the feverishness of his

5. Stephan Strasser, in his introduction to the German edition of the *Cartesian Meditations* (p. xxx) says that Husserl "demanded the return" of the manuscript of Part III "that he had already sent to the publisher, in order to correct it." Biemel (*Krisis,* p. xvi) simply says that he "held [it] back because of plans for revision." It is likely (and a reported conversation with Fink confirms this) that Part IIIA was sent to the publisher and was then returned at Husserl's request. Husserl then began an introduction to a revised version of Part IIIA (see below, p. 102, note 1) but never completed the revision itself.

6. See Appendix X, p. 397, below.

work and the despair he must have caused his editor.[7] Thus, even though Parts I and II were published, their literary quality leaves something to be desired.

As for the third part, Biemel had to deal with a very difficult text, a typescript containing Husserl's corrections on almost every page, in both longhand and shorthand, and even some inserts by Fink. Inevitably, a heavy editorial hand was required in order to decide whether marginal notes should be inserted in the text—and, if so, where—or whether they should be reproduced as footnotes, etc. In the admirable scholarly fashion which is typical of *Husserliana* editions, Biemel has given a complete account in the *textkritischer Anhang* (pp. 517–43) of the variants, marginal notes, etc., involved in his preparation of the text.

This translation is based on Biemel's edition. However, in connection with Part III, puzzlement over the text drove me again and again to the *textkritischer Anhang* and from there to the original typescript in the Archives. In most cases my puzzlement simply remained, and I was filled with sympathy for Biemel's task and admiration for his work. I could not question his reading of Husserl's shorthand, of course, since I could not decipher it. In a few cases, however, I was forced to differ with his interpretation and to make changes. These few changes involve the position of inserted sentences, the character of interpolations, and the elimination of repetitions, and they are clearly indicated in my footnotes to the translation. These mark the extent to which my translation differs with the German edition as far as the text of the *Crisis* itself is concerned.[8]

7. Husserl remarks in one of his letters that the additions amounted to one and a half signatures—"almost a treatise in itself." Comparison of the *Crisis* with the original Prague lecture, of which a transcription has been made, suggests that the added section was the long § 9 on Galileo. (I am indebted to Professor Spiegelberg and the staff of the Husserl Archives at Louvain for allowing me to examine this transcription and certain late correspondence of Husserl.) It is interesting to speculate that the Galileo section might have resulted from a reported visit during this period by Husserl's friend and former student Alexander Koyré, who published his monumental *Etudes Galiléennes* in 1940. The striking similarity between Husserl's and Koyré's interpretation of the significance of Renaissance science is best seen in the latter's *From the Closed World to the Infinite Universe* (Baltimore: Johns Hopkins University Press, 1957).

8. A minor change involves Husserl's very extensive use of typographical emphasis (the German equivalent of italics). For better

Biemel's edition of the *Crisis*, however, is presented in a volume containing some other materials. These are writings of varying lengths and literary appearance, all having to do with the subjects covered in the *Crisis*. Most were written during the same period as the *Crisis*. While some are stylistically well formulated and even seem to indicate that they were meant for inclusion in the text (see, in particular, Appendixes V and VI, below), most are Husserl's famous *Forschungsmanuskripte*— Husserl thinking on paper, often in incomplete sentences, often expressing a view not his own without clearly indicating it, etc. Although I have used Biemel's edition of these texts, I have taken the liberty of presenting them in a different way in this volume. My reasons for doing this are the following:

First, Biemel adds one of these manuscripts to the text of the *Crisis* itself as "§ 73. Schlusswort" (*Krisis*, pp. 269 ff.). He justifies this (p. 519) by saying that the manuscript rounds out the interrupted text, has a summarizing character, and corresponds to the theme of the projected concluding part of the *Crisis* in Fink's outline. But several considerations speak against this choice. First, the manuscript in question (K III 6, pp. 150–56) bears the note "zu K I" after its title, which I take to mean "to *Krisis*, Part I," an interpretation borne out by its subject matter and phraseology. Second, the text differs drastically in both style and content from the preceding paragraphs, and it is disturbing to have it follow these, separated only by a paragraph title. In terms of its content it should at least be set off by itself and not be included in Part III B; as for its style, it is clearly a *Forschungsmanuskript* and should not be treated as part of a work meant for publication. Finally, it gives the impression, no matter how clearly it is marked, that the *Crisis* is completed when it is not. These considerations have led me to include this text in an appendix (Appendix IV) with other *Forschungsmanuskripte*.

Biemel then presents three *Abhandlungen* ("treatises"), the third of which is the important Vienna lecture. In my opinion, the first two of these texts do not rate the title *Abhandlungen* and should not be placed alongside the Vienna lecture. What distinguishes them seems to be the fact that they were found in typescript rather than shorthand and that they were written before 1930 and show the early development of some of the

---

conformity to English style I have been more restrained in the use of italics.

ideas in the *Crisis*. But their rough style clearly places them in the category of *Forschungsmanuskripte*, whereas the relatively polished literary presentation and the thematic importance of the Vienna lecture require its being placed in a class by itself. Consequently, I have presented the Vienna lecture by itself as Appendix I, while the two early manuscripts are placed at the beginning of Part II of the appendixes, where other *Forschungsmanuskripte* are found. They are followed by the manuscript referred to above as Biemel's *Schlusswort*, as it relates to Part I of the *Crisis*.

In his section of *Beilagen*, Biemel presents 29 items totaling 167 pages. These were selected from hundreds of pages of manuscripts from the period of the *Crisis*. All of those selected by Biemel are of interest to the serious Husserl scholar. But many, I feel, do not add significantly to material presented in the *Crisis* itself except by way of emphasis or expression, while some stand out as especially valuable supplements to the reading of the *Crisis*. For reasons of economy I have translated only a selection of Biemel's selection. I think that the needs of the English-speaking reader, seeking insight into this period of Husserl's thought, will be satisfied by this selection. Thus the makeup of this volume differs somewhat from that of Biemel's *Husserliana* edition.[9]

3. Problems of Translation

Translation always involves interpretation. Husserl is difficult to translate at the best of times. There is no concealing the fact that he is simply not a careful writer; he has little thought for literary niceties or for the capacity of his readers to take in interminable and complex sentences, and little thought, it must be said, even for terminological exactness and consistency. In the present case of a text that was for the most part still in the process of revision, and of purely private *Forschungsmanuskripte*, the problems are multiplied.

The ordinary problems are those of terminology and sentence structure. In the case of some writers who are careful in their use of technical terms, precisely defined in advance, it may be possible to devise a sort of one-to-one correspondence in

9. For readers seeking the German text of materials translated in the appendixes, the translator's notes refer to the original designations and the page numbers of the Biemel edition.

translation so that the reader will always know what German word is meant and so that a glossary of terms can be produced. Husserl was not such a writer; unlike Heidegger, for example, he was not attentive to language as a valuable tool to be carefully fashioned and put to use in communicating his ideas. His assumption is that terms, even those he invents, take on their own meanings in context and convey them adequately.[10] And when he does speak of terminology in general, it is usually to warn the reader that the phenomenologist's language must necessarily remain "in flux" and that a demand for mathematical exactness of definitions is totally inappropriate in phenomenology.[11] There is some consistency, of course, but on the whole the result is that each sentence must be translated almost *ad hoc,* much as one must translate ordinary (as opposed to technical) language, namely, on the assumption that words must be translated differently according to the context. Some translators have unfortunately seen their task as that of providing a kind of system for deciphering the German text, full of neologisms to correspond to every terminological nuance. The result is often that one has neither the German text, nor a readable translation, nor, most importantly, a comprehensible rendering of the *sense* of Husserl's work. This last is the primary responsibility of the translator which I have sought to fulfill. Naturally I have tried to be as consistent as possible, but this possibility is limited. Another tendency of overzealous translators has been to suppose that every noun must be translated by a noun. In the case of some of Husserl's lengthier noun compounds I have used a phrase instead of a noun. This may depart from the literal, but it better conveys the sense, in my opinion, than an outlandish neologism which must be explained at great length in a footnote.

I do not mean to suggest that I have been able to turn Husserl's labored German into a piece of felicitous English prose. On the contrary, precisely the need to replace nouns by phrases often results in very involved sentences. Also, it has not been possible to avoid completely some rather forbidding termi-

10. Cf. *Ideen,* Vol. I, § 66: "The words used may stem from ordinary language, being ambiguous and vague in their changing meaning. [But] as soon as they 'coincide' [*sich decken*] in the manner of immediate [*aktuell*] expression, with what is given intuitively, they take on a definite sense which is their immediate and clear sense *hic et nunc*" (my translation).

11. Cf. the remarks at the end of the Introduction to *Ideen,* Vol. I, and the note "zur Terminologie" at the end of §84 of the same work.

nological innovations. But the worst obstruction to readable style in this translation is Husserl's involved sentence construction. One speaks of a translator's "breaking down complex sentences," but this is easier said than done if one is to preserve the sense. I have done this as often as I could. But to make a subordinate clause, or especially one of those lengthy adjectival clauses Husserl is so fond of, into a separate sentence is to give it an importance it was not meant to have and thus really to violate the flow (if this is the word) of the text. Husserl wrote as most of us speak, with many asides, afterthoughts, and qualifications thrown in. This is a matter not just of style but of content, since it concerns the priority and subordination of ideas. The attempt to preserve this has, unfortunately, resulted in some rather long sentences.

The special problems of this translation are related to the state of the text described above. Probably because of the hurried way in which it was prepared, it contains numerous sentences which do not hang together logically or even grammatically. As an editor, Biemel was correct in presenting these sentences as they were, for the most part, leaving the reader to figure out what Husserl meant. A translator, however, should hardly try to render grammatical and logical nonsense in another language. Thus I have been forced to intervene in the text on some occasions, sometimes with bracketed words or phrases, sometimes by translating the sentence I thought Husserl must have *meant* to write, explaining the difficulty in a footnote. Thus the present translation is perhaps more of an "interpretation" than most.

Like most translators, of course, I have also used bracketed insertions of a less interpretative sort simply to clarify the text. Bracketed insertions made by Biemel in the German edition are identified as such in the notes.

The translator's notes deal primarily with terminology and other matters concerning the text. Occasional references are made to other works. In connection with Part III, I have mentioned or quoted some of Husserl's own marginal comments on the manuscript drawn from Biemel's critical apparatus and my own consultation of the original text. These will help the reader to appreciate the state of flux the work was in and to know what Husserl thought of some parts of it. In a few instances I have offered a brief paraphrase or commentary on passages I thought were unusually obscure.

My footnotes are numbered. Husserl's few notes are marked by asterisks.

4. The Significance of the *Crisis*

What distinguishes the *Crisis* from those works already known to English-speaking readers? We have noted that the work marks Husserl's last published attempt at an "introduction to phenomenology," a systematic, definitive presentation of the fundamentals of his method. A glance suffices to convince us, however, that by comparison to the other "introductions" available in English—the *Ideas,* Volume I, and the *Cartesian Meditations* [12]—the *Crisis* is radically different in format. Husserl's brief Preface to the original published version of Part I (see p. 3, note 1) makes this clear in a few words:

> The work that I am beginning with the present essay, and shall complete in a series of further articles in *Philosophia,* makes the attempt, by way of a teleological-historical reflection upon the origins of our critical scientific and philosophical situation, to establish the unavoidable necessity of a transcendental-phenomenological reorientation of philosophy. Accordingly, it becomes, in its own right, an introduction to transcendental phenomenology.

The earlier works mentioned above are both characterized explicitly by a "Cartesian" approach. In them, Husserl begins by inviting his readers to reflect upon the world and upon one's own consciousness of and thought about the world and to see that a certain new attitude, embodied in certain methodical procedures, will enable us to answer the questions of philosophy, to solve or dissolve its problems. Here, by contrast, Husserl announces "a teleological-historical reflection upon the origins of our critical scientific and philosophical situation." [13] True to his

12. *Ideas: General Introduction to Pure Phenomenology,* translated by W. R. Boyce Gibson (London: Allen & Unwin, 1931), and *Cartesian Meditations: An Introduction to Phenomenology,* translated by Dorion Cairns (The Hague: Nijhoff, 1960).

13. It is not only by contrast to these two earlier works that the *Crisis* is unusual. *Formale und transzendentale Logik* (1929), which Husserl also characterized as an introduction to phenomenology, does not share the Cartesian approach, but it takes up a much earlier theme, that of the *Logische Untersuchungen* (Halle: Niemeyer, 1900–1901; rev. ed., 1913). Such a comparison can also be made with other earlier "introductions" since published posthumously, notably *Die Idee der Phänomenologie,* a series of lectures from 1907 (*Husserliana,* Vol. II, edited by Walter Biemel [1950]; English translation, *The Idea of Phenomenology,* by William P. Alston and George Nakhnikian [The Hague: Nijhoff, 1964]), the *Encyclopaedia Britannica* article (14th ed.; London, 1927), and the Amsterdam lectures of 1928, the last two

word, he begins with an exposition of "the crisis of the sciences," which he interprets as an "expression of the radical life-crisis of European humanity" (Part I). Then, in search of the origins of this "critical situation," Husserl proceeds to a long discussion of Greek philosophy and mathematics, the rise of modern science with Galileo, and its philosophical interpretations from Descartes to Kant (Part II).

5. The Circumstances Surrounding the Writing of the *Crisis*

What could have motivated Husserl to take such a novel approach in his final attempt to present phenomenology? Certainly considerable importance must be attached to what we might call "external" considerations. It is well known that Husserl was always disappointed at the tendency of his students to go their own way, to embark upon fundamental revisions of phenomenology rather than engage in the communal task of concrete "research" based on principles laid down by Husserl. This situation was worse than ever at the end of his life; and while there is abundant evidence that Husserl was increasingly bitter toward the revisionists themselves, it is also clear that he held himself at least partly responsible for the fact that his phenomenology had not had the effect he desired. A new mode of presentation was called for.

In particular, Husserl's phenomenology was being eclipsed in both academic circles and the public mind by the increasingly popular *Existenzphilosophie* of Jaspers and Heidegger. Husserl had no kind words for this philosophy itself; but the *Crisis* and the Vienna lecture make clear his growing awareness of the profound malaise among the educated to which the existentialists were directly speaking. Husserl's bitterness, especially against his former protégé Heidegger (who, like many others, appropriated the term "phenomenology"), did not prevent him from seeing that existentialism had given needed expression to something real: a deeply felt lack of direction for man's existence as a whole, a sense of the emptiness of Europe's cultural values, a feeling of crisis and breakdown, the demand that philos-

---

published in *Phänomenologische Psychologie* (edited by Walter Biemel; *Husserliana*, IX [1962], 237–301 and 302–49, respectively). The last two begin with a discussion of psychology and are to that extent like Part IIIB of the *Crisis*. But all these lack the historical dimension which sets the tone for the *Crisis* as a whole.

ophy be relevant to life. And these texts are full of Husserl's tacit admissions that his philosophy had not seemed to speak to these needs. In describing the crisis itself, he refers to the "younger generation's" justified hostility toward the science of the nineteenth and twentieth centuries. "In our vital need—so we are told—this science has nothing to say to us" (*Crisis*, p. 6). Later Husserl sees this attitude applied—mistakenly, to be sure —to phenomenology's own emphasis on "rigorous science" and method: "This way of looking at it makes it appear as if, once again, a new, purely theoretical interest, a new 'science' with a new vocational technique, is to be established, carried on either as an intellectualistic game with very ideal pretensions or as a higher-level intellectual technique in the service of the positive sciences" (*ibid.*, p. 136). Again, in the Vienna lecture, he writes:

> Is it not the case that what we have presented here is something rather inappropriate to our time, an attempt to rescue the honor of rationalism, of "enlightenment," of an intellectualism which loses itself in theories alienated from the world . . . ? Does this not mean that we are being led again into the fateful error of believing that science makes men wise, that it is destined to create a genuine and contented humanity that is master of its fate? Who would still take such notions seriously today? (*ibid.*, Appendix I, pp. 289 f.).

Husserl was convinced that his philosophy was every bit as relevant to human problems as existentialism, and he is at pains to show this in the *Crisis*. This no doubt influenced his attention to the "crisis" theme itself, his emphasis on values, on the practical aspects of existence, on "life," and hence his borrowing of many terms made popular by existentialism (*Dasein, Existenz, existentiell*, etc.). But for Husserl, existentialism, whatever its value as an expression of man's problems and Europe's problems, was precisely a symptom and the farthest thing from a proper remedy. It attacked the old rationalism, with its sterile legacy of nineteenth-century positivism, simply by turning it upside down; it was "irrationalism" pure and simple, upon which Husserl makes his most vigorous attacks.[14]

14. Another threat to philosophy of which Husserl was aware was the logical positivism of the Vienna Circle, whose famous manifesto had been published in 1929. Husserl did not consider this a form of irrationalism and even saw it as an attempted "bulwark" against it; but he was hardly sympathetic to it: in a letter to Ingarden (*Briefe an Roman Ingarden*, p. 93) he wrote that against "irrationalistic skepticism" "the bulwark of mathematical positivism will not help for long,

But existentialism was not only symptomatic of Europe's problems; it was also symptomatic of the desperate and false solutions being accepted by society as a whole. The scope of Husserl's attacks on "irrationalism" makes it unmistakably clear that he had in mind not merely a philosophical "direction" that was fashionable among the educated. Antirationalism and anti-intellectualism were everywhere, and not merely "in the air"; they were explicit elements of Nazi ideology and propaganda. Husserl's blanket indictment gives expression to a clear link in his mind between philosophical antirationalism and political antirationalism. Heidegger's actual connection with the Nazis at one time during this period simply underlined in fact what for Husserl was a kinship in essence.

These strains in both the *Crisis* and the Vienna lecture are couched in the most general terms. Reasons of prudence alone would have dictated this, of course, but in any case Husserl's concern was not a political polemic but a sober philosophical diagnosis of the roots of the problem. His perhaps most explicit public remarks are contained in the open letter, mentioned above (note 2), to the Prague congress of 1934. Philosophy, he says there, is the "force which has transformed mere internationality through power into a completely new sort of internationality, and sustains it, namely a solidarity [*Verbundenheit*] through the spirit of autonomy." But the spirit of philosophy is hindered, he goes on, by skepticism and specialization:

> To this we must add the influence of great fateful events [*Schicksale*] that completely upset the international community insofar as, through them, the general faith in the idea and the practical ideal of Europe, that of a harmonious unity of the life of nations with its sources in the rational spirit, has been undermined.
>
> At present we are faced with the imminent danger of the extinction of philosophy in this sense, and with it necessarily the extinction of a Europe founded on the spirit of truth (p. XLIII).

6. Internal Significance of the Approach of the *Crisis*

But it is a mistake to suppose that Husserl's novel approach, his "teleological-historical reflection upon the origins of our critical scientific and philosophical situation," represents nothing but an attempt to respond to the particular situation of his place and

---

since people will ultimately discover that it is a sham philosophy and not a true philosophy."

time. If this were true, we might regard the "crisis" theme and the historical sections as a *pièce de circonstance*, to be set apart from the "systematic" introduction to phenomenology, i.e., from its true exposition and genuine grounding for all time. It is true that the historical considerations proper characterize only Parts I and II of the *Crisis* as it stands and that the longer Part III seeks "the way into" phenomenology through a reflection first upon the life-world (Part A) and then upon psychology (Part B). Thus the third part, even though it differs from earlier books in important ways, could still be described, like them, as a "reflection upon the world and upon one's own consciousness of and thought about the world." Husserl himself compared Parts I and II to an overture preparing for the "actual work (the opera itself)" to follow (see p. 102, note 1, below). Besides, the discussion of other philosophers and the history of philosophy, it might be argued, is not really new to Husserl. One recalls the 1910 article "Philosophy as Rigorous Science," [15] criticizing the current scene in philosophy; and even the early pages of the *Ideen* contain a critique of empiricism. Furthermore, like most philosophy professors, he often began his lecture courses with a historical account of views on the problem to be taken up, showing that earlier philosophers were unable to solve the problems he would proceed to solve by means of phenomenology. The lectures of 1923–24 on "first philosophy," with their long introductory "critical history of ideas," [16] are a good example of this. And there are many resemblances between this historical section and the one in the *Crisis*.

But even the most cursory comparison between the *Crisis* and these earlier writings makes it clear that the historical considerations of this work play a much more important role. Husserl does make the point, in the text in which the "overture" analogy occurs, that he has especially emphasized "certain prejudices" that are "dominant in our philosophical present" (*Krisis*, p. 438). He apologizes for this, in effect, noting that "philosophy is not a private matter" (p. 439) and must be directed at the contemporary world. But at the same time he explicitly insists that his historical reflections on philosophy are not "accidental"

15. "Philosophie als strenge Wissenschaft," *Logos*, I (1910–11), 289–341; English translation in Quentin Lauer, *Edmund Husserl: Phenomenology and the Crisis of Philosophy* (New York: Harper & Row, 1965), pp. 69–147.
16. *Erste Philosophie*, Part I: *Kritische Ideengeschichte*, edited by Rudolf Boehm, *Husserliana*, Vol. VII (1956).

aspects of his method "chosen for the sake of an impressive presentation" (p. 441). We must remember that the whole work is announced by reference to the "teleological-historical reflections" and that the introduction to phenomenology they present is called *eigenständig*—it stands on its own; furthermore, the work is thematically continuous in the sense that the discussions of Part III are explicitly set up and made possible by the earlier sections; finally, if we can regard Fink's plan for the continuation of the *Crisis* as authoritative, the fifth and concluding section of the work was to be entitled "the indispensable task of philosophy: the responsibility of humanity for itself" (see below, p. 400). Thus the *Crisis* was to end on the note with which it began, placing the whole work within the framework of the "teleological-historical reflections" referred to by Husserl in his Preface.

The work must be approached as a whole, then, and not divided into "purely introductory" and "systematic" parts. Only the particular features of the European "crisis" of Husserl's time can be set apart, perhaps; but even they are interwoven with general historical reflections on philosophy. And this is the work that Husserl regarded as his definitive exposition of phenomenology. Alfred Schutz reported that "in the last conversation which the writer had the good fortune of having with Husserl, he repeatedly designated this series of essays as the summary and the crowning achievement of his life work." [17] Now Husserl had said something very similar about the *Cartesian Meditations* while working on a version to be published in German. In a letter to Roman Ingarden dated March 19, 1930, he wrote:

> I . . . *should* . . . not postpone the German version of the *Cartesian Meditations*. For it will be the major work of my life, a basic outline of the philosophy that has accrued to me, a fundamental work of method and of philosophical problematics. At least for *me* [it will represent] a conclusion and ultimate clarity, which I can defend and with which I can die contented.[18]

Yet, only a few years later, Husserl had apparently abandoned the task of giving final form to the *Cartesian Meditations*, pinning his hopes instead on a work which was explicitly historical in its fundamental approach.

17. "Phenomenology and the Social Sciences," in *Philosophical Essays in Memory of Edmund Husserl*, edited by Marvin Farber (Cambridge, Mass.: Harvard University Press, 1940), p. 165.
18. *Briefe an Roman Ingarden*, p. 59.

It is important to realize the significance of this. In earlier works, discussions of other philosophers are not part of the introduction to phenomenology, strictly speaking, but form either a kind of "introduction to the introduction" or a series of asides. A constant strain throughout Husserl's career is his disdain for the tendency of some philosophers to conjure up a doctrine of their own simply by an ingenious dialectical combination of the doctrines of others. The true introduction to phenomenology—and thus to philosophy, for Husserl—is to be found precisely by turning *away* from the opinions of philosophers and by turning *toward* "the things themselves" (*zu den Sachen selbst!*). In the *Crisis,* by contrast, as stated in the Preface, the teleological-historical reflection serves "in its own right" as an introduction to phenomenology. That is, if we take the word *eigenständig* seriously, it is not in need of other elements to make it a true introduction. Furthermore, as Husserl indicates in the strongest possible terms,[19] this kind of introduction is not only one among other possible kinds of introduction to philosophy but is a necessary one and indeed the most fundamental one.

Thus while the notion of the European crisis itself, and Husserl's mention of its particular features, may represent the philosopher's response to his circumstances, the historical reflections undertaken in search of the origins of this crisis are seen as an essential part of the introduction to a genuine philosophy. This historical discussion, as is generally agreed, is one of the truly new elements in Husserl's philosophy which make their appearance in the *Crisis.* And the other innovation usually mentioned in this connection, the concept of the life-world, is so intimately bound up with this dimension that it must be considered as issuing directly from Husserl's historical reflections.

These two themes and their interconnection must be examined in order to assess the significance of the *Crisis* not merely as a document of its time but as a general statement of Husserl's phenomenology. Such an examination is all the more important in light of an opinion first expressed by Merleau-Ponty [20] and

19. See pp. 71 ff., below.
20. *Phénoménologie de la perception* (Paris: Gallimard, 1945), p. 61 n.: "It was in his last period that Husserl himself became fully conscious of what the return to the phenomenon meant and tacitly broke with the philosophy of essences." Merleau-Ponty gives repeated expression to this conviction in many of his writings, and the *Crisis* was one of the main texts on which his opinion was based. He was one of the first scholars outside Husserl's immediate circle to study Part

since taken up by many of his followers, the view that these new dimensions of the *Crisis* introduce elements into phenomenology that strain to the breaking point, whether he fully recognized it or not, Husserl's philosophical program and undermine the results of his earlier works. If this view is correct, it provides an answer to the question of why the German version of the *Cartesian Meditations* was abandoned and Husserl embarked on such an unusual approach at the end of his life.[21]

This is not the place to embark upon the full-scale examination that would be needed for evaluating this opinion. What we can do is bring out some of the problems raised by Husserl's new approach which might serve as perspectives from which to study the *Crisis*.

7. The Problem of History

What is the relation between phenomenology and history? In

III of the *Crisis*, having visited the new Husserl Archives in Louvain in April, 1939 (H. L. van Breda, "Maurice Merleau-Ponty et les Archives-Husserl à Louvain," *Revue de métaphysique et de morale*, LXVII [1962], 410–30). The influence of this text, especially its concept of the life-world, on Merleau-Ponty is well known.

21. My remark "whether he fully recognized it or not" should be underlined. Whatever the validity of Merleau-Ponty's view, it does not support the myth that Husserl explicitly gave up in despair the ideal of a rigorous science of philosophy, a myth often supported by quoting Husserl's statement "Philosophy as a rigorous science—the dream is over [*der Traum ist ausgeträumt*]." The text in which this phrase occurs appeared as a Beilage to the German edition of the *Crisis* and is translated below in Appendix IX, and it is clear from the context that Husserl was attributing this view to his age, not asserting it himself. Even Merleau-Ponty attributes to Husserl only a "tacit" break with his philosophy of essences. It is amazing that this passage should still be quoted as if it were Husserl's final assessment when the full text has been available since 1954 (see, e.g., Johannes-Jürgen Meister, *Wesen und Bewusstsein*, Inaugural Dissertation [Munich, 1967], p. 199). Ingarden claims to have heard it from Fink as Husserl's own opinion and repeated it as such in a memorial address in 1959. Yet it is no more borne out by letters to him than by the *Crisis* or the text in question, as he admits (*Briefe an Roman Ingarden*, p. 181). This fact, however, does not *refute* Merleau-Ponty's view as described above. One possibility is that Husserl developed a new idea of philosophical "science" that was radically different from or even incompatible with the earlier one; another is that the investigations of the *Crisis* and other manuscripts of the period *imply* a denial of scientific philosophy even though Husserl did not recognize it or would not admit it to himself.

presenting his "teleological-historical" treatise as being "in its own right" an introduction to phenomenology, did Husserl now believe that access to the genuine philosophical method could somehow proceed *without* recourse to the *Sachen selbst*? If this were the case, it would indeed constitute an abandonment of one of his firmest principles. A more appropriate interpretation, however, seems to be that the historical matters under discussion in the *Crisis,* or even the phenomenon of history generally in some sense, had come to be seen by Husserl as numbering among the *Sachen* to which we must turn in order to solve the problems of philosophy.

But what is Husserl's approach to the phenomenon of history? In search of the "origins of our critical scientific and philosophical situation," he discusses primarily the history of Western science and philosophy. But this raises the question of the point of view or "attitude"—to use a good Husserlian term—under which this discussion is conducted. If Husserl is simply engaging in a bit of intellectual history, he would seem to share the ontological commitment of the "natural attitude" involved in all normal historical inquiry by his own account, i.e., the concern with men who actually existed and in this case with their theories, which we believe they held on the basis of certain documentary evidence. How could such an investigation of history serve the purposes of an introduction to phenomenology? If it is, as Husserl suggests, really essential to such an introduction, it means that it is no longer sufficient simply to bracket the views of other philosophers and turn with an unprejudiced gaze to a reflection on consciousness. On the contrary, we must consider the views of others in great detail and in their historical sequence. And in doing so, rather than departing from the natural attitude, which is the *sine qua non* of all earlier approaches to phenomenology, we seem to be committed to a special version of it.

Of course we must remember that Husserl describes the *Crisis* as a *teleological*-historical reflection and that he places this reflection in a broad cultural context, explicitly denying that he is engaged merely in a bit of intellectual history. In both the *Crisis* and the Vienna lecture he speaks not only of philosophy but of the European spirit as such. "True," he says,

> universal philosophy, together with all the special sciences, makes up only a partial manifestation of European culture. Inherent in the sense of my whole presentation, however, is that this part is the

functioning brain, so to speak, on whose normal function the genuine, healthy European spiritual life depends.[22]

Philosophers do not think for themselves alone but are, in their philosophizing, "functionaries for mankind" (*Crisis*, p. 17). "The genuine spiritual struggles of European humanity as such take the form of struggles between the philosophies" (p. 15). With philosophy thus placed at the head of European culture, a teleological-historical reflection on philosophy becomes a teleological reflection on the history of the European spirit as such.

Hence the view of many commentators that "Husserl's history of philosophy is at the same time, even primarily, a philosophy of history." [23] "In this historical regress [Husserl] seeks to grasp the historical development [*Gewordenheit*] and its teleology: its inner driving force and lawfulness." [24]

Husserl does indeed speak in terms of a philosophy of history. What most commentators have failed to appreciate, however, is the possible anomaly this presents in the context of Husserl's earlier phenomenological program. If a treatise on the history of philosophy seems out of keeping with Husserl's phenomenological approach, a philosophy of history, at least in the most familiar sense of that term, seems even more so. By placing philosophy in the context of the European *Geist* as a whole with the function of reflecting its development, and by speaking repeatedly of the "teleology" of that development, Husserl has invited obvious comparison with Hegel. His use on several occasions of rather typical Hegelian turns of phrase [25] adds to the impression of a Hegelian influence on Husserl's later years, something that has not escaped the commentators. Is Husserl's philosophy of history to be understood after the model of Hegel's? Is Husserl concerned with revealing the "reason in history" by accounting for the actual cultural events of the past in terms of an overarching dynamic logic or design which renders these events necessary? After all, like Hegel, he seems to be speaking of the particular events of European history, to which he accords a special significance in relation to other civilizations, even though, unlike Hegel, he concentrates on philosophical events

22. Vienna Lecture, Appendix I, pp. 290 f., below.
23. Aron Gurwitsch, "The Last Work of Edmund Husserl," in *Studies in Phenomenology and Psychology* (Evanston: Northwestern University Press, 1966), p. 401.
24. Hubert Hohl, *Lebenswelt und Geschichte* (Freiburg and Munich: Alber, 1962), p. 21.
25. See especially Appendix IV, below.

alone. Are the philosophies under discussion presented as necessarily abstract and one-sided because they reflect an incomplete stage of the developing spirit? Does phenomenology represent the necessary culmination for which the generations of philosophers, unbeknown to themselves, have been steadily preparing the way?

Such an impression, it must be admitted, is often given by Husserl's writings of this period. But if this is really Husserl's intent, then it would appear that his earlier phenomenological approach has been discarded in favor of something very different indeed. To give a causal explanation of actual particular events in the past or present which shows why they must occur in the order in which they do occur is something the earlier phenomenological method is not designed to do and which it has no means of grounding. Nor would this seem to be affected by the fact that the particular events in question are mental or spiritual events and that the causality involved is final or teleological rather than efficient. Even Husserl's phenomenology of "internal time" or his "genetic phenomenology" are not explanations of any particular series of mental events. And to move to the explanation of such a series spanning a plurality of conscious subjects would be to enter the sphere of intersubjective or objective time. Such an explanation would constitute a science of fact rather than a science of essence, an account of why things are actual rather than how they are possible.

Not only would such a "philosophy of history" seem to find no justification in phenomenological terms; it might even directly contradict the results obtained by that method. Husserl's earlier account of reason [26] as the relation in consciousness between intention and self-evident fulfillment would be drastically transformed because the ego would be subjected in its quest to the order of world history lying outside it. The description of this objective order would be an objective account of the transcendent being to which consciousness is subject. This is the sense of Paul Ricoeur's question: "How can a philosophy of the *cogito*, of the radical return to the ego as the founder of all being, become capable of a philosophy of history?" [27] And a fortiori, how can

26. See "Reason and Reality," the fourth section of *Ideen*, Vol. I.
27. "Husserl and the Sense of History" in *Husserl: An Analysis of His Phenomenology* (Evanston: Northwestern University Press, 1967), p. 145. See *ibid.*, pp. 145–50, for an excellent account of "the opposition of transcendental phenomenology to historical considerations."

such a philosophy of history serve as an introduction "in its own right" to a transcendental phenomenology which bears any resemblance to Husserl's earlier philosophy?

Finally, how could such a "Hegelian" attitude toward history be compatible even with the "crisis" theme itself? The very idea of a true crisis of man, with the fate of the human spirit undecided and hanging in the balance, is unthinkable in the context of the Hegelian "theodicy." The failure of philosophy to fulfill its task for humanity at any given stage in history must be seen as only an apparent failure, the crisis as only an apparent crisis, whose purpose is to prepare for the necessary fulfillment which is to come. By insisting on the reality of the crisis as a turning point for man, Husserl is being consistent with the indeterminism he elsewhere attributes to consciousness in its relation to the world and to its own reason.

The fact is that the text of the *Crisis* itself does not adequately clear up these puzzles about the treatment of history. The question of historical genesis is explicitly banned from phenomenology per se in Husserl's writings up through the *Cartesian Meditations*. Yet in the *Crisis* it suddenly makes its appearance as something the author obviously thinks is important. At the same time, Husserl is apparently not simply adopting an approach he had earlier ruled out, for he repeatedly claims a new approach to the phenomenon of history. But what is this new approach? As Jacques Derrida says: "Though it is constantly *practiced* in the *Crisis* . . . itself, this new access to history is never *made a problem* there." [28]

Now Husserl was not unaware of the problem, as can be seen in many of the working manuscripts translated in this volume, some of which were tentatively meant for inclusion in the *Crisis*. But most of his remarks do little more than pose the problem: historical reflection is necessary; but what kind of reflection is it, and why and in what sense is it necessary? [29] Perhaps the most illuminating remarks are found in the text on "the origin of geometry" (Appendix VI, below). There he refers to his reflections on Galileo and the origins of modern physics as opening up "depth-problems" which throw a "clarifying light" on "our whole

28. Edmund Husserl, *L'Origine de la géométrie,* French translation, with an introduction by Jacques Derrida (Paris: Presses Universitaires de France, 1962), Translator's Introduction, p. 8. An English translation of Husserl's text is given in Appendix VI, below.

29. See Appendix IX, the title and *passim.* See also the last pages of Appendix V.

undertaking." "For, as will become evident here in connection with one example, our investigations are historical in an unusual sense, namely, in virtue of a thematic direction which opens up depth-problems quite unknown to ordinary history, problems which, [however,] in their own way, are undoubtedly historical problems." Thus "our problems and expositions concerning Galilean geometry take on an exemplary significance" (pp. 353 f., below). The key word here is "example." If Galileo, and indeed all the historical developments described by Husserl, have merely an "exemplary" function, they can be seen as serving an inquiry into the *essence* of history as such rather than one concerned with facts directly. And indeed, Husserl speaks of himself as seeking "what is essential to history" (p. 377) and of "methodically and systematically [bringing] to recognition the a priori of history" (Appendix V, p. 349). Thus his primary concern is man's *general* character of being historical, what has come to be called his "historicity."

Now this notion is clearly compatible with Husserl's earlier "eidetic" approach to the extent that it concerns not particular events but an essential trait of consciousness as such: its character of being laden in its relation to the world with preconceptions derived from its social milieu. A constant theme throughout the *Crisis* itself, the Vienna lecture, and the supplementary texts is the engagement of consciousness in the intersubjective community, its tacit acceptance of what Husserl calls the *Selbstverständlichkeiten* (what is "obvious," "taken for granted") of that community, and its motivation to action and thought in terms of the norms provided thereby. Husserl's description of social consciousness in the process of inheriting and handing-down amounts to a general theory of *tradition* or of the very *eidos* of history itself, which becomes an aspect of an eidetic theory of consciousness.

The concern with historicity might seem to reflect another aspect of Husserl's interaction with Heidegger, considering the importance of this concept in the later pages of *Sein und Zeit*.[30] Actually it represents Husserl's attempt to come to terms with an adversary of much longer standing, namely, the historicism he had attacked in "Philosophy as Rigorous Science." Dilthey is the key figure here rather than Heidegger. In fact, Dilthey is a commanding figure not only in Husserl's treatment of history

---

30. Husserl often uses the word *Geschichtlichkeit*, but only rarely in a sense that is comparable to Heidegger's use of the term.

but also in his section on psychology in Part III B of the *Crisis* and in other writings devoted to psychology in the later years.[31] While "Philosophy as Rigorous Science" was concerned with distinguishing phenomenology sharply from both psychology and *Geisteswissenschaft,* many of Husserl's later writings stress the affinities rather than the differences.

In this case Husserl could be seen as still trying to avoid the skeptical implications of historicism and *Weltanschauungsphilosophie* while according considerable legitimacy to their notion of the socially and historically conditioned character of consciousness. But this elevation of Husserl's treatment of history to the eidetic level does not remove all its problems. The question is whether he can accept what is good in historicism without being forced to accept the bad. This problem becomes acute in light of Husserl's admission, indeed his insistence, that historicity is a character not only of mores, religion, etc., but also of scientific thinking itself. In the section on Galileo (pp. 23 ff.) and in the manuscript on "The Origin of Geometry" (pp. 353 ff.) Husserl presents science as a historical process involving its own sort of *tradition,* its inherited way of looking at the world and its unquestioned assumptions about it derived from the past. Now philosophy, as Husserl presents it in the *Crisis* and the Vienna lecture, is science par excellence, the all-encompassing science of which all special sciences are branches. If historicity is really an essential trait of the scientific endeavor, what becomes of the ideal of "philosophy as a rigorous science," i.e., a science with no unquestioned assumptions, no unexamined tradition?

One implication of Husserl's new awareness of historicity seems clear, and it constitutes a significant innovation in phenomenological procedure. In *Ideen,* Volume I, Husserl refers to what he calls the "philosophical ἐποχή"—"not to be confused with [the ἐποχή] that shapes philosophy itself as a method, i.e., the phenomenological reduction"—and disposes of it in one sentence:

31. Those writings, including lectures on psychology from 1925 in which Dilthey is explicitly discussed as the true reformer of psychology, are presented in *Phänomenologische Psychologie* (see n. 13, above). Biemel's editor's introduction to that volume (pp. XVIII–XXI) gives excerpts from a letter in which Husserl denies that he was attacking Dilthey when he attacked historicism in "Philosophy as Rigorous Science"; but that article leaves little doubt that Husserl considered Dilthey's theory inadequate to overcome the skeptical implications of its treatment of history.

The philosophical ἐποχή. . . . expressly formulated, consists in this, that we completely abstain from judgment respecting the doctrinal content of all pre-existing philosophy, and conduct all our expositions within the framework of this abstention.[32]

If the notion of historicity, especially as it applies to philosophy itself, is to be taken seriously, then the "philosophical ἐποχή" would seem to be a much more difficult procedure, something that requires as much mental effort and explanation as the "phenomenological reduction" per se. Indeed, Husserl's entire treatment of the *facts* of Western philosophy could be seen as the attempt to accomplish what he *thought*, in the *Ideen*, had been done in one sentence.

But the paradox we are left with is this: If the notion of historicity is *really* taken seriously, how can such an attempt ever be successful?

8. The Problem of the Life-World

It is Husserl's reflections on "the origin of philosophy" in the Vienna lecture that provide the best direct link between the problem of historicity and that of the life-world, the subject of Part III A of the *Crisis*. And this problem raises similar difficulties for Husserl's program. Both the Vienna lecture and "The Origin of Geometry" complement the *Crisis* in important ways, and one wishes they could have been included in the body of the work itself. In this case Husserl's point is that it is not merely our various theoretical approaches to the world that derive from a tradition. The very notion or motive of approaching the world "theoretically" at all is itself a tradition, one whose origin we normally associate with the Greeks. In order to understand Galileo's accomplishment, for example, we must understand not only his inheritance of the "ready-made" science of geometry but also his inheritance of the very *idea* of science, the *task* of finding nonrelative truths about the world as such, the task the Greeks defined by distinguishing between "appearance" and "reality," between δόξα and ἐπιστήμη. What we associate with the "origin of philosophy" in Greece must be seen not as the presentation of a new hypothesis about the nature of the world but as a change in man's recognition of his relation to his surroundings, a change in his style of life which first made questions about the nature of the world "as such" possible. What this amounts to is not a

32. *Ideen*, Vol. I, pp. 40 f. and note.

change of doctrine, or even of method, but a change of *attitude*.

Now if the "theoretical attitude" of the Greeks is really new, it must be distinguished by reference to some prior attitude or style of life. This Husserl describes as the "natural primordial attitude," that of "original natural life" (*Crisis*, p. 281). Husserl uses the term "natural attitude" here, but he is clearly talking about something other than the "natural attitude" of *Ideen*, Volume I. There the natural attitude is explicitly described as a "theoretical" attitude [33]—it is the theory of naïve realism—while the attitude described here is precisely *not* directed essentially toward theory or *epistēmē*, toward the knowledge of the world as it is in itself. "Natural life," he says,

> can be characterized as a life naïvely, straightforwardly directed at the world, the world being always in a certain sense consciously present as a universal horizon without, however, being thematic as such. What is thematic is whatever one is directed toward. Waking life is always a directedness toward this or that, being directed toward it as an end or as means, as relevant and irrelevant, toward the interesting or the indifferent, toward the private or public, toward what is daily required or obtrusively new (*Crisis*, p. 281).

Husserl uses the term "natural" to refer to what is original and naïve, prior to critical reflection. While the "natural attitude" of the *Ideen* is perhaps "natural" to the theoretical orientation,[34] what is described here is "natural" to life itself, or rather waking life, i.e., consciousness. The naïve, pretheoretical life is not totally devoid of critical reflection, of course, but its criticism is always practical, relative to the end in view rather than to the goal of an absolute, nonrelative truth.

But Husserl means to do more than merely distinguish between the theoretical and pretheoretical attitudes. He tries to

33. *Ibid.*, p. 10.
34. The relation between the natural attitude of the *Ideen* and the pretheoretical attitude described here raises interesting problems. If the former is truly "theoretical" and is actually a sort of "naïve realism," perhaps it is nothing but the popularized version of the "objectivism" which Husserl describes in the *Crisis* as a peculiarly modern phenomenon. Thus it is not so much natural as historical, and the "suspension of the natural attitude" which forms the core of the *phenomenological* reduction in the *Ideen* now becomes part of the *philosophical* ἐποχή described above. The truly phenomenological reduction "that shapes philosophy itself as a method" is now no longer the suspension of any particular historical theoretical attitude but the bracketing of the theoretical attitude generally, so as to reveal the pretheoretical life and its life-world.

show the relation between them, preparing the way for the theory of the life-world that emerges in the *Crisis*. If one attitude is "natural" to consciousness, how do we characterize the emergence of the other? Husserl follows Plato and Aristotle in attributing the origin of philosophy to θαυμάζειν, simple wonder at things being the way they are. But while such wonder constitutes at most a recurring, fleeting pause in the natural course of life, the theoretical attitude reverses the priorities: the concern with "the way things are" which was intrusive and nonessential to natural life becomes the primary concern, while the nontheoretical life, which still remains, is subordinated to the theoretical life. "In other words," Husserl says, "man becomes a nonparticipating spectator, surveyor of the world; he becomes a philosopher" (Appendix I, p. 285, below).

Yet contained in this description of the emergence of the theoretical attitude, and developed at length in the *Crisis*, is a theory of its dependence upon the naïve attitude that precedes it. The naïve, pretheoretical life is engaged in the world, the milieu and horizon of its activity. The world with which the philosopher, the scientist, attempts to deal is this very world-horizon in which the naïve life runs its course. This is the life-world, which is always "already there," "pregiven," when theory begins its work. But the world's very pregivenness, the structure through which it envelops conscious life and provides the ground (*Boden*) on which it moves, is always presupposed by any theoretical activity.

The pretheoretical attitude of naïve world-life, and the life-world which is its horizon, are thus found to be prior to all theory, and not merely in the historical sense. In fact, they can be said to be *necessarily* prior historically because they are essentially prior at all times, even after the birth and elaborate development of the European theoretical spirit. Again Husserl's apparently historical reflections can be seen as issuing in a series of eidetic claims about conscious life and historicity generally.

The life-world's pretheoretical character, its pregivenness [*Vorgegebenheit*] in relation to theory, is the notion stressed by Husserl in his preoccupation with European science and its relation to man's crisis. But many other descriptions go to make up the sections on the life-world in this work, and there is some question whether all these descriptions operate on the same level and whether they are all compatible with one another. At times Husserl refers to the life-world as the "world of immediate experience," the *prepredicative* world described in *Formale und tran-*

szendentale Logik and *Erfahrung und Urteil*. Yet this world is also described as a cultural world, richly organized for practical ends and laden with *linguistic* tradition. Such a world could be pretheoretical but could hardly be described as prepredicative. And of course its very social or intersubjective character places it, on Husserl's earlier scheme, in a secondary position in regard to the immediate world of perception. Here it often seems, in keeping with Husserl's stress on historicity, that the individual's world of immediate experience, rather than grounding the cultural world, is determined by it.

And what of the life-world of those who live in the tradition of Western scientific theory? Husserl frequently insists that the theories of our scientific culture "flow into" the life-world; compounded of such theories, it forms the traditional *Boden* of both our theoretical and our extratheoretical life and is thus certainly pregiven. But in this case it could not be described as pretheoretical. This seems to contrast sharply with repeated descriptions of the life-world as one whose very essence is to envelop or underlie all theoretical interpretations of it.

These apparent inconsistencies make the concept of the life-world a difficult one to understand. Perhaps they are not insoluble and could be ironed out by a richer and many-leveled exposition of the notion. But in any case the life-world presents Husserl's phenomenological program with two overarching difficulties. One questions one of the most important aspects of Husserl's over-all theory, and the other threatens to undermine its claim to scientific rigor. In the first case, if we take seriously the "pregivenness" of the life-world, upon which the author repeatedly insists, Husserl's earlier idealism seems to be in difficulty. While the theoretically known world may depend on consciousness for its "constitution," the life-world seems to provide the given materials with which consciousness deals. If it is in turn to be dealt with in terms of transcendental constitution, as Husserl also insists, then it seems to lose precisely what was described as one of its essential features, its pregivenness. But in either case the second difficulty arises, namely, that the attempt to describe the life-world, as Husserl admits, is itself a theoretical activity, indeed, *theōria* of the highest order, phenomenology. But if every theoretical activity presupposes the structures of the life-world, this must also be true of phenomenology, which in this case cannot be without presuppositions. If phenomenology is to overcome this difficulty, there must be something special about it which distinguishes it sharply from all other theoretical activity, which Husserl would of course not deny. But then we must ask how it can be presented as the fulfillment of the sense implicit in all attempts at *theōria* since the Greeks, being thus placed on a continuum with other forms. The presupposition of the life-world is either essential to theoretical activity or it is not. Husserl must show how it is that phenomenology can fulfill the *telos* of all *theory* without being caught up in its *archē*, its rootedness in the life-world.

Husserl is not unaware of this issue; indeed, it is involved at every step of his attempt to give an adequate grounding to his philosophy. In fact, all the problems I have mentioned are seen and dealt with by Husserl, either in the *Crisis* itself or in the supplementary texts of the period. And I do not mean to suggest that it is impossible, as his critics claim, to resolve those problems in a way that is consistent with his earlier writings. What is clear, and what contributes to the importance and vitality of this unfinished work, is that Husserl had caught sight of new horizons at the end of his life; and here we find him passionately engaged in beginning philosophy again in an effort to understand them.

In preparing this translation I have had the assistance of many persons. Above all I am indebted to Professor Herbert Spiegelberg of Washington University for his advice and kind encouragement at every step of the way. Not only did he read my entire translation of the *Crisis* text itself with the utmost care, offering valuable suggestions on every page; he also provided me with much material from his ongoing historical researches which contributed to my understanding of the work and helped in preparing this introduction. I could not have hoped for a better aid in this project than one who combines a native understanding of the German language with great erudition in the subject matter and infinite patience.

I also wish to thank Professor James M. Edie, the associate editor of this series, for encouraging me to undertake the translation; Professor H. L. van Breda and the staff of the Husserl Archives at Louvain for permission to consult the extant manuscript of the *Crisis* and other manuscripts of the period and for additional materials that have come to me through Professor Spiegelberg; the New School for Social Research, and Professor Aron Gurwitsch in particular, for allowing me to examine some of its copies of the Husserl papers; and the Philosophy Department of Yale University for generously providing for much stenographic assistance, primarily in the person of Mrs. Nancy Kaplan. Valuable suggestions and corrections of English style have been made by Mr. David Hemmendinger, Mr. and Mrs. Allan H. Merrill, and my wife, Leslie, who also typed early versions of the translation.

DAVID CARR

Yale University
April, 1969

PART I

The Crisis of the Sciences as Expression of the Radical Life-Crisis of European Humanity

§ 1. *Is there, in view of their constant successes, really a crisis of the sciences?*

I EXPECT THAT AT THIS PLACE, dedicated as it is to the sciences, the very title of these lectures, "The Crisis of European Sciences and Psychology," [1] will incite controversy. A crisis of our sciences as such: can we seriously speak of it? Is not this talk, heard so often these days, an exaggeration? After all, the crisis of a science indicates nothing less than that its genuine scientific character, the whole manner in which it has set its task and developed a methodology for it, has become questionable. This may be true of philosophy, which in our time threatens to succumb to skepticism, irrationalism, and mysticism. The same may hold for psychology, insofar as it still makes philosophical claims rather than merely wanting a place among the positive sciences. But how could we speak straightforwardly and quite seriously of a crisis of the sciences in general—that is, also of the positive sciences, including pure mathematics and the exact natural sciences, which we can never cease to admire as models

---

1. This was the original title of the lecture series before the "Cercle philosophique de Prague pour les recherches sur l'entendement humain." In *Philosophia*, Vol. I, where Parts I and II of the *Crisis* were published, Husserl prefaced the text with the following remarks:

"The work that I am beginning with the present essay, and shall complete in a series of further articles in *Philosophia*, makes the attempt, by way of a teleological-historical reflection upon the origins of our critical scientific and philosophical situation, to establish the unavoidable necessity of a transcendental-phenomenological reorientation of philosophy. Accordingly, it becomes, in its own right, an introduction to transcendental phenomenology.

"The work has grown from the development of ideas that made up the basic content of a series of lectures I gave in November, 1935, in Prague (half in the hospitable rooms of the German university, half in those of the Czech university), following a kind invitation by the 'Cercle philosophique de Prague pour les recherches sur l'entendement humain.' "

The German text of this preface is given in *Krisis*, p. XIV, note 3. (In these footnotes, references to *Krisis* are to the German edition edited by Walter Biemel. See Translator's Introduction, note 4.)

of rigorous and highly successful scientific discipline? To be sure, they have proved to be changeable in the total style of their systematic theory-building and methodology. Only recently they overcame, in this respect, a threatening paralysis, under the title of classical physics—threatening, that is, as the supposed classical consummation of the confirmed style of centuries. But does the victorious struggle against the ideal of classical physics, as well as the continuing conflict over the appropriate and genuine form of construction for pure mathematics, mean that previous physics and mathematics were not yet scientific or that they did not, even though affected with certain unclarities or blind spots, obtain convincing insights within their own field of endeavor? Are these insights not compelling even for us who are freed from such blind spots? Can we not thus, placing ourselves back into the attitude of the classical theorists, understand completely how it gave rise to all the great and forever valid discoveries, together with the array of technical inventions which so deserved the admiration of earlier generations? Physics, whether represented by a Newton or a Planck or an Einstein, or whomever else in the future, was always and remains exact science. It remains such even if, as some think, an absolutely final form of total theory-construction is never to be expected or striven for.

The situation is clearly similar in regard to another large group of sciences customarily counted among the positive sciences,[2] namely, the concrete humanistic sciences, however it may stand with their controversial reference back to the ideal of exactness in the natural sciences—a difficulty, incidentally, which concerns even the relation of the biophysical ("concrete" natural-scientific) disciplines to those of the mathematically exact natural sciences. The scientific rigor of all these disciplines, the convincingness of their theoretical accomplishments, and their enduringly compelling successes are unquestionable. Only of psychology must we perhaps be less sure, in spite of its claim to be the abstract, ultimately explanatory, basic science of the concrete humanistic disciplines. But generally we let psychology stand, attributing its obvious retardation of method and accomplishment to a naturally slower development. At any rate, the contrast between the "scientific" character of this group of sciences and the "unscientific" character of philosophy is unmis-

2. As is usual in German, the term *Wissenschaften* is applied to the humanities as well as the natural and social sciences. The term "science" will be used in this inclusive sense, though I have sometimes translated *Geisteswissenschaften* as "humanistic disciplines."

takable. Thus we concede in advance some justification to the first inner protest against the title of these lectures from scientists who are sure of their method.

§ 2. *The positivistic reduction of the idea of science to mere factual science. The "crisis" of science as the loss of its meaning for life.*

IT MAY BE, HOWEVER, that motives arise from another direction of inquiry—that of the general lament about the crisis of our culture and the role here ascribed to the sciences—for subjecting the scientific character of all sciences to a serious and quite necessary critique without sacrificing their primary sense of scientific discipline, so unimpeachable within the legitimacy of their methodic accomplishments.

The indicated change in the whole direction of inquiry is what we wish, in fact, to undertake. In doing this we shall soon become aware that the difficulty which has plagued psychology, not just in our time but for centuries—its own peculiar "crisis" —has a central significance both for the appearance of puzzling, insoluble obscurities in modern, even mathematical sciences and, in connection with that, for the emergence of a set of world-enigmas which were unknown to earlier times. They all lead back to the *enigma of subjectivity* and are thus inseparably bound to the *enigma of psychological subject matter and method*. This much, then, as a first indication of the deeper meaning of our project in these lectures.

We make our beginning with a change which set in at the turn of the past century in the general evaluation of the sciences. It concerns not the scientific character of the sciences but rather what they, or what science in general, had meant and could mean for human existence.[1] The exclusiveness with which

1. *menschliches Dasein.* Husserl makes rather extensive use in this work of the word *Dasein* as applied specifically to man's existence. This is probably a conscious or unconscious concession to the popularity of Heidegger's work. His use of the term *Existenz* will be noted below (§ 5, note 1).

the total world-view of modern man, in the second half of the
nineteenth century, let itself be determined by the positive sciences and be blinded by the "prosperity" [2] they produced, meant
an indifferent turning-away from the questions which are decisive for a genuine humanity.[3] Merely fact-minded sciences make
merely fact-minded people. The change in public evaluation was
unavoidable, especially after the war, and we know that it has
gradually become a feeling of hostility among the younger generation. In our vital need—so we are told—this science has nothing to say to us. It excludes in principle precisely the questions
which man, given over in our unhappy times to the most portentous upheavals, finds the most burning: questions of the meaning or meaninglessness of the whole of this human existence. Do
not these questions, universal and necessary for all men, demand universal reflections and answers based on rational
insight? In the final analysis they concern man as a free, self-
determining being in his behavior toward the human and
extrahuman surrounding world [4] and free in regard to his capacities for rationally shaping himself and his surrounding world.
What does science have to say about reason and unreason or
about us men as subjects of this freedom? The mere science of
bodies clearly has nothing to say; it abstracts from everything
subjective. As for the humanistic sciences, on the other hand, all
the special and general disciplines of which treat of man's
spiritual [5] existence, that is, within the horizon of his historicity:
their rigorous scientific character requires, we are told, that the
scholar carefully exclude all valuative positions, all questions of
the reason or unreason of their human subject matter and its
cultural configurations. Scientific, objective truth is exclusively a
matter of establishing what the world, the physical as well as the
spiritual world, is in fact. But can the world, and human existence in it, truthfully have a meaning if the sciences recognize as

2. Husserl uses the English word.
3. *Menschentum.* Husserl uses this term and *Menschheit* indis-
tinguishably. The distinction made by Paul Ricoeur (*Husserl: An
Analysis of His Phenomenology* [Evanston: Northwestern University
Press, 1967], p. 159) seems to me to be unfounded, though I have
generally translated the latter as "mankind." Difficulty arises when
Husserl begins using *Menschheit* in the plural. See below, § 6, note 1.
4. *Umwelt.* "Surrounding world" will be used throughout.
5. *geistig.* The translating difficulties with *Geist* and its derivatives
are too well known to require comment. I have usually opted for
"spirit" as the least of several evils. Sometimes "mental" is used for
the adjectival form.

true only what is objectively established in this fashion, and if history has nothing more to teach us than that all the shapes of the spiritual world, all the conditions of life, ideals, norms upon which man relies, form and dissolve themselves like fleeting waves, that it always was and ever will be so, that again and again reason must turn into nonsense, and well-being into misery? [6] Can we console ourselves with that? Can we live in this world, where historical occurrence is nothing but an unending concatenation of illusory progress and bitter disappointment?

§ 3. *The founding of the autonomy of European humanity through the new formulation of the idea of philosophy in the Renaissance.*

IT WAS NOT ALWAYS THE CASE that science understood its demand for rigorously grounded truth in the sense of that *sort* of objectivity which dominates our positive sciences in respect to method and which, having its effect far beyond the sciences themselves, is the basis for the support and widespread acceptance of a philosophical and ideological positivism. The specifically human questions were not always banned from the realm of science; their intrinsic relationship to all the sciences —even to those of which man is not the subject matter, such as the natural sciences—was not left unconsidered. As long as this had not yet happened, science could claim significance—indeed, as we know, the major role—in the completely new shaping of European humanity which began with the Renaissance. Why science lost this leadership, why there occurred an essential change, a positivistic restriction of the idea of science—to understand this, according to its *deeper motives*,[1] is of great importance for the purpose of these lectures.

6. A paraphrase from *Faust,* Part I, line 1976: "Vernunft wird Unsinn, Wohltat Plage."
1. Husserl's use of *Motif, motivieren,* and *Motivation* is so important in this work that I have simply used "motive," "motivate," "motivation," etc., to translate them, even though Husserl's use often exceeds the bounds of standard English usage of these terms. It is hoped that Husserl's sense will emerge from the context.

In the Renaissance, as is well known, European humanity brings about a revolutionary change. It turns against its previous way of existing—the medieval—and disowns it, seeking to shape itself anew in freedom. Its admired model is ancient humanity. This mode of existence is what it wishes to reproduce in itself.

What does it hold to be essential to ancient man? After some hesitation, nothing less than the "philosophical" form of existence: freely giving oneself, one's whole life, its rule through pure reason or through philosophy. Theoretical philosophy is primary. A superior survey of the world must be launched, unfettered by myth and the whole tradition: universal knowledge, absolutely free from prejudice, of the world and man, ultimately recognizing in the world its inherent reason and teleology and its highest principle, God. Philosophy as theory frees not only the theorist but any philosophically educated person. And theoretical autonomy is followed by practical autonomy. According to the guiding ideal of the Renaissance, ancient man forms himself with insight through free reason. For this renewed "Platonism" this means not only that man should be changed ethically [but that] the whole human surrounding world, the political and social existence of mankind, must be fashioned anew through free reason, through the insights of a universal philosophy.

In accordance with this ancient model, recognized at first only by individuals and small groups, a theoretical philosophy should again be developed which was not to be taken over blindly from the tradition but must grow out of independent inquiry and criticism.

It must be emphasized here that the idea of philosophy handed down from the ancients is not the concept of present-day schoolbooks, merely comprising a group of disciplines; in the first centuries of the modern period—even though it changes not insignificantly as soon as it is taken up—it retains the formal meaning of the one all-encompassing science, the science of the totality of what is.[2] Sciences in the plural, all those sciences ever to be established or already under construction, are but dependent branches of the One Philosophy. In a bold, even extravagant, elevation of the meaning of universality, begun by Descartes, this new philosophy seeks nothing less than to encompass, in the

2. I have used "what is," "that which is," and sometimes "that which exists" to translate *Seiendes, das Seiende*, etc. This particular locution may be another result of Heidegger's influence.

unity of a theoretical system, all meaningful questions in a rigorous scientific manner, with an apodictically intelligible methodology, in an unending but rationally ordered progress of inquiry. Growing from generation to generation and forever, this one edifice of definitive, theoretically interrelated truths was to solve all conceivable problems—problems of fact and of reason, problems of temporality and eternity.

Thus the positivistic concept of science in our time is, historically speaking, a *residual concept*. It has dropped all the questions which had been considered under the now narrower, now broader concepts of metaphysics, including all questions vaguely termed "ultimate and highest." Examined closely, these and all the excluded questions have their inseparable unity in the fact that they contain, whether expressly or as implied in their meaning, the *problems of reason*—reason in all its particular forms. Reason is the explicit theme in the disciplines concerning knowledge (i.e., of true and genuine, rational knowledge), of true and genuine valuation (genuine values as values of reason), of ethical action (truly good acting, acting from practical reason); here reason is a title for "absolute," "eternal," "supertemporal," "unconditionally" valid ideas and ideals. If man becomes a "metaphysical" or specifically philosophical problem, then he is in question as a rational being; if his history is in question, it is a matter of the "meaning" or reason in history. The problem of God clearly contains the problem of "absolute" reason as the teleological source of all reason in the world—of the "meaning" of the world. Obviously even the question of immortality is a question of reason, as is the question of freedom. All these "metaphysical" questions, taken broadly—commonly called specifically philosophical questions—surpass the world understood as the universe of mere facts. They surpass it precisely as being questions with the idea of reason in mind. And they all claim a higher dignity than questions of fact, which are subordinated to them even in the order of inquiry. Positivism, in a manner of speaking, decapitates philosophy. Even the ancient idea of philosophy, as unified in the indivisible unity of all being, implied a meaningful order of being and thus of problems of being. Accordingly, metaphysics, the science of the ultimate and highest questions, was honored as the queen of the sciences; its spirit decided on the ultimate meaning of all knowledge supplied by the other sciences. This, too, was taken over by the reviving philosophy [of the Renaissance]; indeed, it even believed it had discovered the true, universal method through which such a systematic philosophy, culminating in metaphysics, could be constructed as a serious *philosophia perennis*.

In light of this we can understand the energy which animated all scientific undertakings, even the merely factual sciences of the lower level; in the eighteenth century (which called itself the philosophical century) it filled ever widening circles with enthusiasm for philosophy and for all the special sciences as its branches. Hence the ardent desire for learning, the zeal for a philosophical reform of education and of all of humanity's social and political forms of existence, which makes that much-abused Age of Enlightenment so admirable. We possess an undying testimony to this spirit in the glorious "Hymn to Joy" of Schiller and Beethoven. It is only with painful feelings that we can understand this hymn today. A greater contrast with our present situation is unthinkable.

§ 4. *The failure of the new science after its initial success; the unclarified motive for this failure.*

Now if the new humanity, animated and blessed with such an exalted spirit, did not hold its own, it must have been because it lost the inspiring belief in its ideal of a universal philosophy and in the scope of the new method. And such, indeed, was the case. It turned out that this method could bring unquestionable successes only in the positive sciences. But it was otherwise in metaphysics, i.e., in problems considered philosophical in the special sense—though hopeful, apparently successful beginnings were not lacking even here. Universal philosophy, in which these problems were related—unclearly—to the factual sciences, took the form of system-philosophies, which were impressive but unfortunately were not unified, indeed were mutually exclusive. If the eighteenth century still held the conviction of proceeding toward unity, of arriving at a critically unassailable edifice which grew theoretically from generation to generation, as was undisputedly the case in the universally admired positive sciences—this conviction could not survive for long. The belief in the ideal of philosophy and method, the guideline of all movements since the beginning of the modern era, began to waver; this happened not merely for the external motive that the contrast became monstrous between the repeated failures of metaphysics and the uninterrupted and ever increasing wave of theoretical and practical successes in the positive sciences. This much had its effect on outsiders as well as scientists, who, in the specialized business of the positive sciences, were fast becoming unphilosophical experts. But even among those theorists who were filled with the philosophical spirit, and thus were interested precisely in the highest metaphysical questions, a growing feeling of failure set in—and in their case because the most profound, yet quite *unclarified,* motives protested ever more loudly against the deeply rooted assumptions of the reigning ideal. There begins a long period, extending from Hume and Kant to our own time, of passionate struggle for a clear, reflective understanding of the true reasons for this centuries-old failure; it was a struggle, of course, only on the part of the few called and chosen ones; the mass of others quickly found and still find formulas with which to console themselves and their readers.

§ 5.   *The ideal of universal philosophy and the process of its inner dissolution.*

THE NECESSARY CONSEQUENCE was a peculiar change in the whole way of thinking. Philosophy became a problem for itself, at first, understandably, in the form of the [problem of the] possibility of a metaphysics; and, following what we said earlier, this concerned implicitly the meaning and possibility of the whole problematics of reason. As for the positive sciences, at first they were untouchable. Yet the problem of a possible metaphysics also encompassed *eo ipso* that of the possibility of the factual sciences, since these had their relational meaning—that of truths merely for areas of what is—in the indivisible unity of philosophy. *Can reason and that-which-is be separated, where reason, as knowing, determines what is?* This question suffices to make clear in advance that the whole historical process has a remarkable form, one which becomes visible only through an interpretation of its hidden, innermost motivation. Its form is not that of a smooth development, not that of a continual growth of lasting spiritual acquisitions or of a transformation of spiritual configurations—concepts, theories, systems—which can be explained by means of the accidental historical situations. A definite ideal of a universal philosophy and its method forms the beginning; this is, so to speak, the primal establishment of the philosophical modern age and all its lines of development. But instead of being able to work itself out in fact, this ideal suffers an inner dissolution. As against attempts to carry out and newly fortify the ideal, this dissolution gives rise to revolutionary, more or less radical innovations. Thus the problem of the genuine ideal of universal philosophy and its genuine method now actually becomes the innermost driving force of all historical philosophical movements. But this is to say that, ultimately, all modern sciences drifted into a peculiar, increasingly puzzling crisis with regard to the meaning of their original founding as branches of philosophy, a meaning which they continued to bear within themselves. This is a crisis which does not encroach upon the theoretical and practical successes of the special sciences; yet it shakes to the foundations the whole meaning of their truth. This is not just a matter of a special form of culture— "science" or "philosophy"—as one among others belonging to European mankind. For the primal establishment of the new philosophy is, according to what was said earlier, the primal establishment of modern European humanity itself—humanity which seeks to renew itself radically, as against the foregoing medieval and ancient age, precisely and only through its new philosophy. Thus the crisis of philosophy implies the crisis of all modern sciences as members of the philosophical universe: at first a latent, then a more and more prominent crisis of European humanity itself in respect to the total meaningfulness of its cultural life, its total "Existenz." [1]

Skepticism about the possibility of metaphysics, the collapse of the belief in a universal philosophy as the guide for the new man, actually represents a collapse of the belief in "reason," understood as the ancients opposed epistēmē to doxa. It is reason which ultimately gives meaning to everything that is thought to be, all things, values, and ends—their meaning understood as their normative relatedness to what, since the beginnings of phi-

1. Husserl uses the term made popular by Jaspers and Heidegger. This and existentiell are used in a rather loose and popular sense throughout this work.

losophy, is meant by the word "truth"—truth in itself—and correlatively the term "what is"—ὄντως ὄν. Along with this falls the faith in "absolute" reason, through which the world has its meaning, the faith in the meaning of history, of humanity, the faith in man's freedom, that is, his capacity to secure rational meaning for his individual and common human existence.

If man loses this faith, it means nothing less than the loss of faith "in himself," in his own true being. This true being is not something he always already has, with the self-evidence of the "I am," but something he only has and can have in the form of the struggle for his truth, the struggle to make himself true. True being is *everywhere* an ideal goal, a task of *epistēmē* or "reason," as opposed to being which through *doxa* is merely thought to be, unquestioned and "obvious." Basically every person is acquainted with this difference—one related to his true and genuine humanity—just as truth as a goal or task is not unknown to him even in everyday life—though here it is merely isolated and relative. But this prefiguration is surpassed by philosophy: in its first, original establishment, ancient philosophy, it conceives of and takes as its task the exalted idea of universal knowledge concerning the totality of what is. Yet in the very attempt to fulfill it, the naïve obviousness of this task is increasingly transformed—as one feels already in the opposition of the ancient systems—into unintelligibility. More and more the history of philosophy, seen from within, takes on the character of a struggle for existence, i.e., a struggle between the philosophy which lives in the straightforward pursuit of its task—the philosophy of naïve faith in reason—and the skepticism which negates or repudiates it in empiricist fashion. Unremittingly, skepticism insists on the validity of the factually experienced [*erlebte*] world, that of actual experience [*Erfahrung*],[2] and finds in it nothing of reason or its ideas. Reason itself and its [object,] "that which is," become more and more enigmatic—reason as giving, of itself, meaning to the existing world and, correlatively, the world as existing through reason—until finally the *consciously* recognized world-problem of the deepest essential interrelation between reason and what is in general, the *enigma of all enigmas*, has to become the actual theme of inquiry.

2. "Experience" will be used to translate *Erfahrung* unless otherwise indicated. *Erlebnis* and *erleben*, so important in Husserl's earlier writings, are seldom used in this text.

Our interest is confined here to the philosophical modern age.[3] But this is not merely a fragment of the greater historical phenomenon we have just described, that is, humanity struggling to understand itself (for this phrase expresses the whole phenomenon). Rather—as the reestablishment of philosophy with a new universal task and at the same time with the sense of a renaissance of ancient philosophy—it is at once a repetition and a universal transformation of meaning. In this it feels called to initiate a new age, completely sure of its idea of philosophy and its true method, and also certain of having overcome all previous naïvetés, and thus all skepticism, through the radicalism of its new beginning. But it is the fate of the philosophical modern age, laden with its own unnoticed naïvetés, that it has first to seek out, in the course of a gradual self-disclosure motivated by new struggles, the definitive idea of philosophy, its true subject matter and its true method; it has first to discover the genuine world-enigmas and steer them in the direction of a solution.

As men of the present, having grown up in this development, we find ourselves in the greatest danger of drowning in the skeptical deluge and thereby losing our hold on our own truth. As we reflect in this plight, we gaze backward into the history of our present humanity. We can gain self-understanding, and thus inner support, only by elucidating the unitary meaning which is inborn in this history from its origin through the newly established task [of the Renaissance], the driving force of all [modern] philosophical attempts.

§ 6. *The history of modern philosophy as a struggle for the meaning of man.*

IF WE CONSIDER the effect of the development of philosophical ideas on (nonphilosophizing) mankind as a whole, we must conclude the following:

Only an understanding from within of the movement of

---

3. This is true of the whole historical part of the *Crisis*. Part II begins with a study of Galileo. An important supplement to this text is provided by the Vienna lecture (see Appendix I, pp. 269 ff.), which treats of the beginnings of philosophy in the Greek context.

modern philosophy from Descartes to the present, which is coherent despite all its contradictions, makes possible an understanding of the present itself. The true struggles of our time, the
only ones which are significant, are struggles between humanity
which has already collapsed and humanity which still has roots
but is struggling to keep them or find new ones. The genuine
spiritual struggles of European humanity as such take the form
of struggles between the philosophies, that is, between the skeptical philosophies—or nonphilosophies, which retain the word
but not the task—and the actual and still vital philosophies. But
the vitality of the latter consists in the fact that they are struggling for their own true and genuine meaning and thus for the
meaning of a genuine humanity. To bring latent reason to the
understanding of its own possibilities and thus to bring to insight the possibility of metaphysics as a true possibility—this is
the only way to put metaphysics or universal philosophy on the
strenuous road to realization. It is the only way to decide
whether the *telos* which was inborn in European humanity at
the birth of Greek philosophy—that of humanity which seeks to
exist, and is only possible, through philosophical reason, moving
endlessly from latent to manifest reason and forever seeking its
own norms through this, its truth and genuine human nature—
whether this *telos*, then, is merely a factual, historical delusion,
the accidental acquisition of merely one among many other
civilizations [1] and histories,[2] or whether Greek humanity was not
rather the first breakthrough to what is essential to humanity as
such, its *entelechy*. To be human at all is essentially to be a
human being in a socially and generatively united civilization;
and if man is a rational being (*animal rationale*), it is only
insofar as his whole civilization is a rational civilization, that is,
one with a latent orientation toward reason or one openly oriented toward the entelechy which has come to itself, become
manifest to itself, and which now of necessity consciously di-
rects human becoming. Philosophy and science would ac-

1. *Menschheiten.* "Civilizations" comes closest to what Husserl
means when he uses this term in the plural. Clearly something similar
is implied when he qualifies it in the singular ("European humanity"
as opposed to Chinese, for example, or "present-day humanity"), but
here the use of "humanity" in English does not seem to violate its accepted meaning.

2. *Geschichtlichkeiten.* Husserl often uses *Geschichtlichkeit* in
this text in a sense which is almost indistinguishable from *Geschichte*.
Sometimes it denotes a particular line of historical development. Only
occasionally is "historicity" appropriate.

cordingly be the historical movement through which universal reason, "inborn" in humanity as such, is revealed.

This *would* be the case if the as yet unconcluded movement [of modern philosophy] had *proved* to be the entelechy, properly started on the way to pure realization, or if reason had in fact become manifest, fully conscious of itself in its own essential form, i.e., the form of a universal philosophy which grows through consistent apodictic insight and supplies its own norms through an apodictic method. Only then could it be decided whether European humanity bears within itself an absolute idea, rather than being merely an empirical anthropological type like "China" or "India"; it could be decided whether the spectacle of the Europeanization of all other civilizations bears witness to the rule of an absolute meaning, one which is proper to the sense, rather than to a historical non-sense, of the world.

We are now certain that the rationalism of the eighteenth century, the manner in which it sought to secure the necessary roots of European humanity, was *naïve*. But in giving up this naïve and (if carefully thought through) even absurd rationalism, is it necessary to sacrifice the *genuine* sense of rationalism? And what of the serious clarification of that naïveté, of that absurdity? And what of the rationality of that irrationalism which is so much vaunted and expected of us? Does it not have to convince us, if we are expected to listen to it, with rational considerations and reasons? Is its irrationality not finally rather a narrow-minded and bad rationality, worse than that of the old rationalism? Is it not rather the rationality of "lazy reason," which *evades* the struggle to clarify the ultimate data [*die letzten Vorgegebenheiten*] and the goals and directions which they alone can rationally and truthfully prescribe?

But enough of this. I have advanced too quickly, in order to make felt the incomparable significance attaching to the clarification of the deepest motives of this crisis—a crisis which developed very early in modern philosophy and science and which extends with increasing intensity to our own day.

§ 7.   *The project of the investigations of this work.*

BUT NOW *we ourselves*, we philosophers of the present —what can and must reflections of the sort we have just carried out mean *for us*? Did we just want to hear an academic oration?

Can we simply return again to the interrupted vocational work on our "philosophical problems," that is, each to the further construction of his own philosophy? Can we seriously do that when it seems certain that our philosophy, like that of all our fellow philosophers, past and present, will have its fleeting day of existence only among the flora of ever growing and ever dying philosophies?

Precisely herein lies our own plight—the plight of all of us who are not philosophical literati but who, educated by the genuine philosophers of the great past, live for truth, who only in this way are and seek to be in our own truth. But as philosophers of the present we have fallen into a painful existential contradiction. The faith in the possibility of philosophy as a task, that is, in the possibility of universal knowledge, is something we *cannot* let go. We *know* that we are *called* to this task as serious philosophers. And yet, how do we hold onto this belief, which has meaning only in relation to the single goal which is common to us all, that is, philosophy as such?

We have also become aware in the most general way [through the foregoing reflections] that human philosophizing and its results in the whole of man's existence mean anything but merely private or otherwise limited cultural goals. In *our* philosophizing, then—how can we avoid it?—we are *functionaries of mankind*. The quite personal responsibility of our own true being as philosophers, our inner personal vocation, bears within itself at the same time the responsibility for the true being of mankind; the latter is, necessarily, being toward a *telos* and can only come to realization, *if at all*, through philosophy—through *us, if* we are philosophers in all seriousness. Is there, in this existential "if," a way out? If not, what should we, who *believe*, do in order to *be able* to believe? We cannot seriously continue our previous philosophizing; it lets us hope only for philosophies, never for philosophy.

Our first historical reflection has not only made clear to us the actual situation of the present and its distress as a sober fact; it has also reminded us that we as philosophers are heirs of the past in respect to the goals which the word "philosophy" indicates, in terms of concepts, problems, and methods. What is clearly necessary (what else could be of help here?) is that we *reflect back,* in a thorough *historical* and *critical* fashion, in order to provide, *before all decisions,* for a radical self-understanding: we must inquire back into what was originally and always sought in philosophy, what was continually sought by all the philosophers and philosophies that have communicated with one another historically; but this must include a *critical* consideration of what, in respect to the goals and methods [of philosophy], is ultimate, original, and genuine and which, once seen, apodictically conquers the will.

How this is really to be carried out, and what this apodicticity could ultimately be which would be decisive for our existential being as philosophers, is at first unclear. In the following I shall attempt to show the paths that I myself have taken, the practicability and soundness of which I have tested for decades. From now on we proceed together, then, armed with the most skeptical, though of course not prematurely negativistic, frame of mind. We shall attempt to strike through the crust of the externalized "historical facts" of philosophical history, interrogating, exhibiting, and testing their inner meaning and hidden teleology. Gradually, at first unnoticed but growing more and more pressing, possibilities for a complete reorientation of view will make themselves felt, pointing to new dimensions. Questions never before asked will arise; fields of endeavor never before entered, correlations never before grasped or radically understood, will show themselves. In the end they will require that the total sense of philosophy, accepted as "obvious" throughout all its historical forms, be basically and essentially transformed. Together with the new task and its universal apodictic ground,[1] the *practical* possibility of a new philosophy will prove itself: through its execution. But it will also become apparent that all the philosophy of the past, though unbeknown to itself, was inwardly oriented toward this new sense of philosophy. In this regard, the tragic failure of modern psychology in particular, its contradictory historical existence, will be clarified and made understandable: that is, the fact that it had to claim (through its historically accumulated meaning) to be the basic philosophical science, while this produced the obviously paradoxical consequences of the so-called "psychologism."

I seek not to instruct but only to lead, to point out and describe what I see. I claim no other right than that of speaking according to my best lights, principally before myself but in the same manner also before others, as one who has lived in all its seriousness the fate of a philosophical existence.

1. *Boden.* "Ground" is always used to translate this word, unless otherwise indicated (e.g., *Grund*, in one of its senses). *Boden* is much used in connection with the concept of the life-world; it suggests nourishing soil and support, rather than a logical ground or cause.

PART II
Clarification of the Origin
of the Modern Opposition
between Physicalistic Objectivism
and Transcendental Subjectivism

§ 8. *The origin of the new idea of the universality of science in the reshaping of mathematics.*

THE FIRST THING we must do is understand the fundamental transformation of the idea, the task of universal philosophy which took place at the beginning of the modern age when the ancient idea was taken over. From Descartes on, the new idea governs the total development of philosophical movements and becomes the inner motive behind all their tensions.

The reshaping begins with prominent special sciences inherited from the ancients: Euclidean geometry and the rest of Greek mathematics, and then Greek natural science. In our eyes these are fragments, beginnings of our developed sciences. But one must not overlook here the immense change of meaning whereby *universal* tasks were set, primarily for mathematics (as geometry and as formal-abstract theory of numbers and magnitudes)—tasks of a style which was *new in principle,* unknown to the ancients. Of course the ancients, guided by the Platonic doctrine of ideas, had already idealized empirical numbers, units of measurement, empirical figures in space, points, lines, surfaces, bodies; and they had transformed the propositions and proofs of geometry into ideal-geometrical propositions and proofs. What is more, with Euclidean geometry had grown up the highly impressive idea of a systematically coherent deductive theory, aimed at a most broadly and highly conceived ideal goal, resting on "axiomatic" fundamental concepts and principles, proceeding according to apodictic arguments—a totality formed of pure rationality, a totality whose unconditioned truth is available to insight and which consists exclusively of unconditioned truths recognized through immediate and mediate insight. But Euclidean geometry, and ancient mathematics in general, knows only finite tasks, a finitely closed a priori. Aristotelian syllogistics belongs here also, as an a priori which takes precedence over all others. Antiquity goes this far, but never far enough to grasp the possibility of the infinite task which, for us, is linked as a matter

[21]

of course with the concept of geometrical space and with the concept of geometry as the science belonging to it. To ideal space belongs, for us, a universal, systematically coherent a priori, an infinite, and yet—in spite of its infinity—self-enclosed, coherent systematic theory which, proceeding from axiomatic concepts and propositions, permits the deductively univocal construction of any conceivable shape which can be drawn in space. What "exists" ideally in geometric space is univocally decided, in all its determinations, in advance. Our apodictic thinking, proceeding stepwise to infinity through concepts, propositions, inferences, proofs, only "discovers" what is already there, what in itself already exists in truth.

What is new, unprecedented, is the conceiving of this idea of a rational infinite totality of being with a rational science systematically mastering it. An infinite world, here a world of idealities, is conceived, not as one whose objects [1] become accessible to our knowledge singly, imperfectly, and as it were accidentally, but as one which is attained by a rational, systematically coherent method. In the infinite progression of this method, every object is ultimately attained according to its full being-in-itself [*nach seinem vollen An-sich-sein*].

But this is true not only in respect to ideal space. Even less could the ancients conceive of a similar but more general idea (arising from formalizing abstraction), that of a formal mathematics. Not until the dawn of the modern period does the actual discovery and conquest of the infinite mathematical horizons begin. The beginnings of algebra, of the mathematics of continua, of analytic geometry arise. From here, thanks to the boldness and originality peculiar to the new humanity, the great ideal is soon anticipated of a science which, in this new sense, is rational and all-inclusive, or rather the idea that the infinite totality of what is in general is intrinsically a rational all-encompassing unity that can be mastered, without anything left over, by a corresponding universal science. Long before this idea comes to maturity, it determines further developments as an unclear or half-clear presentiment. In any case it does not stop with the new mathematics. Its rationalism soon overtakes natural science and creates for it the completely new idea of *mathe-*

1. *Objekte.* There is no difference in meaning between *Objekt* and *Gegenstand* as Husserl uses these terms and hence no reason for following Dorion Cairns (*Cartesian Meditations* [The Hague: Martinus Nijhoff, 1960], translator's note 2, p. 3) in trying to distinguish them in translation.

matical natural science—Galilean science, as it was rightly called for a long time. As soon as the latter begins to move toward successful realization, the idea of philosophy in general (as the science of the universe, of all that is) is transformed.

§ 9.   *Galileo's mathematization of nature.*

FOR PLATONISM, the real [1] had a more or less perfect methexis in the ideal. This afforded ancient geometry possibilities of a primitive application to reality. [But] through Galileo's *mathematization of nature, nature itself* is idealized under the guidance of the new mathematics; nature itself becomes—to express it in a modern way—a mathematical manifold [*Mannigfaltigkeit*].

What is the meaning of this mathematization of nature? How do we reconstruct the train of thought which motivated it?

Prescientifically, in everyday sense-experience, the world is given in a subjectively relative way. Each of us has his own appearances; and for each of us they count as [*gelten als*] that which actually is. In dealing with one another, we have long since become aware of this discrepancy between our various ontic validities.[2] But we do not think that, because of this, there are many worlds. Necessarily, we believe in *the* world, whose things only appear to us differently but are the same. [Now] have we nothing more than the empty, necessary idea of things which

1. *das Reale.* I have used "real" almost exclusively for the German *real* and its derivatives. For Husserl this term refers to the spatio-temporal world as conceived by physics (or to the psychic when it is mistakenly conceived on the model of the physical). The more general *Wirklichkeit* has usually been translated by the etymologically correct term "actuality."

2. *Seinsgeltungen. Geltung* is a very important word for Husserl, especially in this text. It derives from *gelten*, which is best translated "to count (as such and such) (for me)," as in the previous sentence, or "to be accepted (as, etc.)" or "to have the validity (of such and such) (for me)." *Gültigkeit* is the more common substantive but is less current in Husserl. Thus "validity" ("our validities," etc.) seems an appropriate shortcut for such more exact but too cumbersome expressions as "that which counts (as)," "those things which we accept (as)," etc., in this case, "those things that we accept as existing." I have used "ontic" when Husserl compounds *Sein* with this and other words, e.g., *Seinssinn, Seinsgewissheit.*

exist objectively in themselves? Is there not in the appearances themselves a content we must ascribe to true nature? Surely this includes everything which pure geometry, and in general the mathematics of the pure form of space-time, teaches us, with the self-evidence of absolute, universal validity, about the pure shapes it can construct *idealiter*—and here I am describing, without taking a position, what was "obvious" [3] to Galileo and motivated his thinking.

We should devote a careful exposition to what was involved in this "obviousness" for Galileo and to whatever else was taken for granted by him in order to motivate the idea of a mathematical knowledge of nature in his new sense. We note that he, the philosopher of nature and "trail-blazer" of physics, was not yet a physicist in the full present-day sense; that his thinking did not, like that of our mathematicians and mathematical physicists, move in the sphere of symbolism, far removed from intuition; and that we must not attribute to him what, through him and the further historical development, has become "obvious" to us.

a. "Pure geometry."

Let us first consider "pure geometry," the pure mathematics of spatiotemporal shapes in general, pregiven [4] to Galileo as an old tradition, involved in a process of lively forward development —in other words, in generally the same way we still find it: [on the one hand] as a science of "pure idealities" which is, on the other hand, constantly being practically applied to the world of sense-experience. So familiar to us is the shift between a priori theory and empirical inquiry in everyday life that we usually tend not to separate the space and the spatial shapes geometry talks about from the space and spatial shapes of experiential actuality, as if they were one and the same. If geometry is to be understood as the foundation for the meaning [*Sinnesfundament*] of exact physics, however, we must be very precise here as elsewhere. In order to clarify the formation of Galileo's thought we must accordingly reconstruct not only what

3. *Selbstverständlichkeit* is another very important word in this text. It refers to what is unquestioned but not necessarily unquestionable. "Obvious" works when the word is placed in quotation marks, as it is here. In other cases I have used various forms of the expression "taken for granted."

4. *vorgegeben*. Implying "already there," as material to be worked with. This term is much used later on as applied to the life-world.

consciously motivated him. It will also be instructive to bring to light what was implicitly included in his guiding model of mathematics, even though, because of the direction of his interest, it was kept from his view: as a hidden, presupposed meaning it naturally had to enter into his physics along with everything else.

In the intuitively given surrounding world, by abstractively directing our view to the mere spatiotemporal shapes, we experience "bodies"—not geometrical-ideal bodies but precisely those bodies that we actually experience, with the content which is the actual content of experience. No matter how arbitrarily we may transform these bodies in fantasy, the free and in a certain sense "ideal" possibilities we thus obtain are anything but geometrical-ideal possibilities: they are not the geometrically "pure" shapes which can be drawn in ideal space—"pure" bodies, "pure" straight lines, "pure" planes, "pure" figures, and the movements and deformations which occur in the "pure" figures. Thus geometrical space does not mean anything like imaginable space or, generally speaking, the space of any arbitrarily imaginable (conceivable) world. Fantasy can transform sensible shapes only into other sensible shapes. Such shapes, in actuality or fantasy, are thinkable only in gradations: the more or less straight, flat, circular, etc.

Indeed, the things of the intuitively given surrounding world fluctuate, in general and in all their properties, in the sphere of the merely typical: their identity with themselves, their self-sameness and their temporally enduring sameness, are merely approximate, as is their likeness with other things. This affects all changes, and *their* possible samenesses and changes. Something like this is true also of the abstractly conceived shapes of empirically intuited bodies and their relations. This gradualness can be characterized as that of greater or less perfection. Practically speaking there is, here as elsewhere, a simple perfection in the sense that it fully satisfies special practical interests. But when interests change, what was fully and exactly satisfactory for one is no longer so for another; and of course there is a limit to what can be done by means of the normal technical capacity of perfecting, e.g., the capacity to make the straight straighter and the flat flatter. But technology progresses along with mankind, and so does the interest in what is technically more refined; and the ideal of prefection is pushed further and further. Hence we always have an open horizon of *conceivable* improvement to be further pursued.

Without going more deeply into the essential interconnections involved here (which has never been done systematically and is by no means easy), we can understand that, out of the praxis of perfecting, of freely pressing toward the horizons of *conceivable* perfecting "again and again," *limit-shapes* [5] emerge toward which the particular series of perfectings tend, as toward invariant and never attainable poles. If we are interested in these ideal shapes and are consistently engaged in determining them and in constructing new ones out of those already determined, we are "geometers." The same is true of the broader sphere which includes the dimension of time: we are mathematicians of the "pure" shapes whose universal form is the coidealized form of space-time. In place of real praxis—that of action or that of considering empirical possibilities having to do with actual and really [i.e., physically] possible empirical bodies—we now have an *ideal* praxis of "pure thinking" which remains exclusively within the realm of pure limit-shapes. Through a method of idealization and construction which historically has long since been worked out and can be practiced intersubjectively in a community, these limit-shapes have become acquired tools that can be used habitually and can always be applied to something new—an infinite and yet self-enclosed world of ideal objects as a field for study. Like all cultural acquisitions which arise out of human accomplishment, they remain objectively knowable and available without requiring that the formulation of their meaning be repeatedly and explicitly renewed. On the basis of sensible embodiment, e.g., in speech and writing, they are simply apperceptively [6] grasped and dealt with in our operations. Sensible "models" function in a similar way, including especially the drawings on paper which are constantly used during work, printed drawings in textbooks for those who learn by reading, and the like. It is similar to the way in which certain cultural objects (tongs, drills, etc.) are understood, simply "seen," with their specifically cultural properties, without any renewed process of making intuitive what gave such properties their true meaning. Serving in the methodical praxis of mathematicians, in this form of long-understood acquisitions, are

5. *Limesgestalten.* Husserl has in mind the mathematic concept of limit.
6. *apperzeptiv.* Husserl uses this term in the Leibnizian sense to denote a self-conscious act (but not necessarily an act of reflection) under a certain point of view or "attitude" (*Einstellung*), here the mathematical.

significations which are, so to speak, sedimented in their embodiments. And thus they make mental manipulation possible in the geometrical world of ideal objects. (Geometry represents for us here the whole mathematics of space-time.)

But in this mathematical praxis we attain what is denied us in empirical praxis: "exactness"; for there is the possibility of determining the ideal shapes in absolute identity, of recognizing them as substrates of absolutely identical and methodically, univocally determinable qualities. This occurs not only in particular cases, according to an everywhere similar method which, operating on sensibly intuitable shapes chosen at random, could carry out idealizations everywhere and originally create, in objective and univocal determinateness, the pure idealities which correspond to them. For this, [rather,] certain structures stand out, such as straight lines, triangles, circles. But it is possible—and this was the discovery which created geometry—using these elementary shapes, singled out in advance as universally available, and according to universal operations which can be carried out with them, to *construct* not only more and more shapes which, because of the method which produces them, are intersubjectively and univocally determined. For in the end the possibility emerges of producing constructively and univocally, through an a priori, all-encompassing systematic method, *all* possibly *conceivable* ideal shapes.

The geometrical methodology of operatively determining some and finally all ideal shapes, beginning with basic shapes as elementary means of determination, points back to the methodology of determination by surveying and measuring in general, practiced first primitively and then as an art in the prescientific, intuitively given surrounding world. The undertaking of such measurement has its obvious origin in the essential form of that surrounding world. The shapes in it that are sensibly experienceable and sensibly-intuitively conceivable, and the types [of shapes] that are conceivable at any level of generality, fade into each other as a continuum. In this continuity they fill out (sensibly intuited) space-time, which is their form. Each shape in this open infinitude, even if it is given intuitively in reality as a *fact*, is still without "objectivity"; it is not thus intersubjectively determinable, and communicable in its determinations, for everyone —for every other one who does not at the same time factually see it. This purpose [of procuring objectivity] is obviously served by the *art of measuring*. This art involves a great deal, of which the actual measuring is only the concluding part: on the one hand, for the bodily shapes of rivers, mountains, buildings, etc., which as a rule lack strictly determining concepts and names, it must create such concepts—first for their "forms" (in terms of pictured similarity), and then for their magnitudes and relations of magnitude, and also for the determinations of position, through the measurement of distances and angles related to known places and directions which are presupposed as being fixed. The art of measuring discovers *practically* the possibility of picking out as [standard] measures certain empirical basic shapes, concretely fixed on empirical rigid bodies which are in fact generally available; and by means of the relations which obtain (or can be discovered) between these and other body-shapes it determines the latter intersubjectively and in practice univocally—at first within narrow spheres (as in the art of surveying land), then in new spheres where shape is involved. So it is understandable how, as a consequence of the awakened striving for "philosophical" knowledge, knowledge which determines the "true," the objective being of the world, the empirical art of measuring and its empirically, practically objectivizing function, through a change from the practical to the theoretical interest, was idealized and thus turned into the purely geometrical way of thinking. The art of measuring thus becomes the trail-blazer for the ultimately universal geometry and its "world" of pure limit-shapes.

b. The basic notion of Galilean physics: nature as a mathematical universe.

The relatively advanced geometry known to Galileo, already broadly applied not only to the earth but also in astronomy, was for him, accordingly, already pregiven by tradition as a guide to his own thinking, which [then] related empirical matters to the mathematical ideas of limit. Also available to him as a tradition, of course—itself partially determined in the meantime by geometry—was the art of measuring, with its intention of ever increasing exactness of measurement and the resulting objective determination of the shapes themselves. If the empirical and very limited requirements of technical praxis had originally motivated those of pure geometry, so now, conversely, geometry had long since become, as "applied" geometry, a means for technology, a guide in conceiving and carrying out the task of systematically constructing a methodology of measurement for objectively determining shapes in constantly increasing "approximation" to the geometrical ideals, the limit-shapes.

For Galileo, then, this was given—and of course he, quite understandably, did not feel the need to go into the manner in which the accomplishment of idealization originally arose (i.e., how it grew on the underlying basis of the pregeometrical, sensible world and its practical arts) or to occupy himself with questions about the origins of apodictic, mathematical self-evidence. There is no need for that in the attitude of the geometer: one has, after all, studied geometry, one "understands" geometrical concepts and propositions, is familiar with methods of operation as ways of dealing with precisely defined structures and of making proper use of figures on paper ("models"). It did not enter the mind of a Galileo that it would ever become relevant, indeed of fundamental importance, to geometry, as a branch of a universal knowledge of what is (philosophy), to make geometrical self-evidence—the "how" of its origin—into a problem. For us, proceeding beyond Galileo in our historical reflections, it will be of considerable interest to see how a shift of focus became urgent and how the "origin" of knowledge had to become a major problem.

Here we observe the way in which geometry, taken over with the sort of naïveté of a priori self-evidence that keeps every normal geometrical project in motion, determines Galileo's thinking and guides it to the idea of physics, which now arises for the first time in his life-work. Starting with the practically understandable manner in which geometry, in an old traditional sphere, aids in bringing the sensible surrounding world to univocal determination, Galileo said to himself: Wherever such a methodology is developed, there we have also overcome the relativity of subjective interpretations which is, after all, essential to the empirically intuited world. For in this manner we attain an identical, nonrelative truth of which everyone who can understand and use this method can convince himself. Here, then, we recognize something that truly is—though only in the form of a constantly increasing approximation, beginning with what is empirically given, to the geometrical ideal shape which functions as a guiding pole.

However, all this *pure* mathematics has to do with bodies and the bodily world only through an abstraction, i.e., it has to do only with *abstract shapes* within space-time, and with these, furthermore, as purely "ideal" limit-shapes. *Concretely,* however, the actual and possible empirical shapes are given, at first in empirical sense-intuition, merely as "forms" of a "matter," of a sensible plenum; [7] thus they are given together with what shows itself, with its own gradations, in the so-called "specific" sense-qualities:* color, sound, smell, and the like.

To the concreteness of sensibly intuitable bodies, of their being in actual and possible experience, belongs also the fact that they are restricted by the [type of] changeability that is essential to them. Their changes of spatiotemporal position, or of form- or plenum-characteristics, are not accidental and arbitrary but depend on one another in sensibly *typical* ways. Such types of relatedness between bodily occurrences are themselves moments of everyday experiencing intuition. They are experienced as that which gives the character of *belonging together* to bodies which *exist together* simultaneously and successively, i.e., as that which *binds* their being [*Sein*] to their being-such [*Sosein*]. Often, though not always, we are clearly confronted in experience with the connected elements which make up these real-causal interdependencies. Where that is not the case, and

* It is a bad legacy of the psychological tradition since Locke's time that the sense-qualities of actually experienced bodies in the everyday, intuited surrounding world—colors, touch-qualities, smells, warmth, heaviness, etc., which are perceived as belonging to the bodies themselves, as their properties—are always surreptitiously replaced by the [so-called] "sense data" [*sinnliche Daten, Empfindungsdaten.* Both terms must be translated by the same expression.— TRANS.]; these are also indiscriminately called sense-qualities and, at least in general, are not at all differentiated from [properties as such]. Where a difference is felt, instead of thoroughly describing the peculiarities of this difference, which is quite necessary, one holds to the completely mistaken opinion (and we shall speak of this later) that "sense-data" constitute what is immediately given. What corresponds to them in the [perceived] bodies themselves is then ordinarily replaced by their mathematical-physical [properties]—when it is precisely the origin of the meaning [of these properties] that we are engaged in investigating. Here and everywhere we shall speak— giving faithful expression to actual experience—of *qualities* or *properties* of the bodies which are actually perceived through these properties. And when we characterize them as the *plena* of shapes, we also take these shapes to be "qualities" of the bodies themselves, indeed sense-qualities; except that, as αἰσθητὰ κοινά they are not related to sense-organs belonging to them alone, as are the αἰσθητὰ ἴδια.

7. *einer sinnlichen Fülle.* I have used the word *plenum* to translate this strange use of *Fülle*: the sensible content which "fills in" the shapes of the world, the "secondary qualities" that are left over after pure shape has been abstracted. Cf. the related but not identical use of *Fülle* in *Logische Untersuchung* VI, § 21.

where something happens which is strikingly new, we nevertheless immediately ask why and look around us into the spatiotemporal circumstances. The things of the intuited surrounding
world (always taken as they are intuitively there for us in everyday life and count as actual) have, so to speak, their "habits"—
they behave similarly under typically similar circumstances. If
we take the intuitable world as a whole, in the flowing present in
which it is straightforwardly there for us, it has even as a whole
its "habit," i.e., that of continuing habitually as it has up to now.
Thus our empirically intuited surrounding world has an *empirical over-all style.* However we may change the world in imagina-
tion or represent to ourselves the future course of the world,
unknown to us, in terms of its possibilities, "as it might be," we
necessarily represent it according to the style in which we have,
and up to now have had, the world. We can become explicitly
conscious of this style by reflecting and by freely varying these
possibilities. In this manner we can make into a subject of
investigation the invariant general style which this intuitive
world, in the flow of total experience, persistently maintains.
Precisely in this way we see that, universally, things and their
occurrences do not arbitrarily appear and run their course but
are *bound* a priori by this style, by the invariant form of the
intuitable world. In other words, through a *universal causal
regulation, all that is together in the world* has a universal
immediate or mediate way of *belonging together;* through this
the world is not merely a totality [*Allheit*] but an all-encompassing unity [*Alleinheit*], a *whole* (even though it is infinite). This
is self-evident a priori, no matter how little is actually experienced of the particular causal dependencies, no matter how little
of this is known from past experience or is prefigured about
future experience.

This universal causal style of the intuitively given surrounding world makes possible hypotheses, inductions, predictions
about the unknowns of its present, its past, and its future. In the
life of prescientific knowing we remain, however, in the sphere
of the [merely] approximate, the typical. How would a "philosophy," a scientific knowledge of the world, be possible if we were
to stop at the vague consciousness of totality whereby, amidst
the vicissitudes of temporary interests and themes of knowledge,
we are also conscious of the world as horizon? Of course we can,
as has been shown, also thematically reflect on this world-whole
and grasp its causal style. But we gain thereby only the empty,
general insight that any experienceable occurrence at any place

and at any time is causally determined. But what about the specifically determined world-causality, the specifically determined network of causal interdependencies that makes concrete all real events at all times? Knowing the world in a seriously scientific way, "philosophically," can have meaning and be possible only if a method can be devised of *constructing*, systematically and in a sense in advance, the world, the infinitude of causalities, starting from the meager supply of what can be established only relatively in direct experience, and of compellingly *verifying* this construction in spite of the infinitude [of experience]. How is this thinkable?

But here mathematics offers its services as a teacher. In respect to spatiotemporal shapes it had already blazed the trail, in two ways in fact. *First:* by idealizing the world of bodies in respect to what has spatiotemporal shape in this world, it created ideal objects. Out of the undetermined universal form of the life-world, space and time, and the manifold of empirical intuitable shapes that can be imagined into it, it made for the first time an objective world in the true sense—i.e., an infinite totality of ideal objects which are determinable univocally, methodically, and quite universally for everyone. Thus mathematics showed for the first time that an infinity of objects that are subjectively relative and are thought only in a vague, general representation is, through an a priori all-encompassing method, objectively determinable and can actually be thought as determined in itself or, more exactly, as an infinity which is determined, decided in advance, in itself, in respect to all its objects and all their properties and relations. It can be thought in this way, I said— i.e., precisely because it is constructible *ex datis* in its objectively true being-in-itself, through its method which is not just postulated but is actually created, apodictically generated.[8]

Second: coming into contact with the art of measuring and then guiding it, mathematics—thereby descending again from the world of idealities to the empirically intuited world—showed that one can universally obtain objectively true knowledge of a completely new sort about the things of the intuitively actual world, in respect to that aspect of them (which all things necessarily share) which alone interests the mathematics of shapes, i.e., a [type of] knowledge related in an approximating fashion to its own idealities. All the things of the empirically intuitable world have, in accord with the world-style, a bodily character,

8. Reading *erzeugte* for *erzeugende*.

are *res extensae,* are experienced in changeable collocations which, taken as a whole, have their total collocation; in these, particular bodies have their relative positions, etc. By means of pure mathematics and the practical art of measuring, one can produce, for everything in the world of bodies which is extended in this way, a completely new kind of inductive prediction; namely, one can "calculate" with compelling necessity, on the basis of given and measured events involving shapes, events which are unknown and were never accessible to direct measurement. Thus ideal geometry, estranged from the world, becomes "applied" geometry and thus becomes in a certain respect a general method of knowing the real.

But does not this manner of objectifying, to be practiced on one abstract aspect of the world, give rise to the following thought and the conjectural question:

Must not something similar be possible for the concrete world as such? If one is already firmly convinced, moreover, like Galileo—thanks to the Renaissance's return to ancient philosophy—of the possibility of philosophy as *epistēmē* achieving an objective science of the world, and if it had just been revealed that pure mathematics, applied to nature, consummately fulfills the postulate of *epistēmē* in its sphere of shapes: did not this also have to suggest to Galileo the idea of a nature which is constructively determinable in the same manner in all its *other aspects?*

But is this not possible only if the method of measuring through approximations and constructive determinations extends to *all* real properties and real-causal relations of the intuitable world, to everything which is ever experienceable in particular experiences? But how can we do justice to this general anticipation, [and] how can it become a practicable method for a concrete knowledge of nature?

The difficulty here lies in the fact that the material plena— the "specific" sense-qualities—which concretely fill out the spatio-temporal shape-aspects of the world of bodies *cannot,* in their own gradations, be *directly* treated as are the shapes themselves. Nevertheless, these qualities, and everything that makes up the concreteness of the sensibly intuited world, must count as manifestations of an "objective" world. Or rather, they must continue to count as such; because (such is the way of thinking which motivates the idea of the new physics) the certainty, binding us all, of one and the same world, the actuality which exists in itself, runs uninterrupted through all changes of subjective interpretation; all aspects of experiencing intuition manifest something of this world. It becomes attainable for our objective knowledge when those aspects which, like sensible qualities, are abstracted away in the pure mathematics of spatiotemporal form and its possible particular shapes, and are not themselves directly mathematizable, nevertheless become mathematizable *indirectly*.

c. The problem of the mathematizability of the "plena."

The question now is what an *indirect mathematization* would mean.

Let us first consider the more profound reason why a direct mathematization (or an analogue of approximative construction), in respect to the specifically sensible qualities of bodies, is impossible in principle.

These qualities, too, appear in gradations, and in a certain way measurement applies to them as to all gradations—we "assess" the "magnitude" of coldness and warmth, of roughness and smoothness, of brightness and darkness, etc. But there is no exact measurement here, no growth of exactness or of the methods of measurement. Today, when we speak of measuring, of units of measure, methods of measure, or simply of magnitudes, we mean as a rule those that are already related to idealities and are "exact"; so it is difficult for us to carry out the abstract isolation of the plena which is so necessary here: i.e., to consider —experimentally, so to speak—the world of bodies exclusively according to the "aspect" of those properties belonging under the title "specific sense-qualities," through a universal abstraction opposed to the one which gives rise to the universal world of shapes.

What constitutes "exactness"? Obviously, nothing other than what we exposed above: empirical measuring with increasing precision, but under the guidance of a world of idealities, or rather a world of certain particular ideal structures that can be correlated with given scales of measurement—such a world having been objectified in advance through idealization and construction. And now we can make the contrast clear in a word. We have not two but only *one* universal form of the world: not two but only *one geometry*, i.e., one of shapes, without having a second for plena. The bodies of the empirical-intuitable world are such, in accord with the world-structure belonging to this world–a priori, that each body has—abstractly speaking—an extension of its own and that all these extensions are yet shapes of the one total infinite extension of the world. As world, as the universal configuration of all bodies, it thus has a total form encompassing all forms, and *this* form is idealizable in the way analyzed and can be mastered through construction.

To be sure, it is also part of the world-structure that all bodies have their specific sense-qualities. But the qualitative configurations based purely on these are not analogues of spatiotemporal shapes, are not incorporated into a world-form peculiar to them. The limit-shapes of these qualities are not idealizable in an analogous sense; the measurement ("assessing") of them cannot be related to corresponding idealities in a constructible world already objectivized into idealities. Accordingly, the concept of "approximation" has no meaning here analogous to that within the mathematizable sphere of shapes—the meaning of an objectifying achievement.

Now with regard to the "indirect" mathematization of that aspect of the world which in itself has no mathematizable world-form: such mathematization is thinkable only in the sense that the specifically sensible qualities ("plena") that can be experienced in the intuited bodies are closely related in a quite peculiar and *regulated* way with the shapes that belong essentially to them. If we ask what is predetermined a priori by the universal world-form with its universal causality—i.e., if we consult the invariant, general style of being to which the intuited world, in its unending change, adheres: on the one hand the form of space-time is predetermined, and everything that belongs to it a priori (before idealization), as encompassing all bodies in respect to shape. It is further predetermined that, in each case of real bodies, factual shapes require factual plena and vice versa; that, accordingly, *this* sort of general causality obtains, binding together aspects of a *concretum* which are only abstractly, not really, separable. What is more, considering everything as a totality, there obtains a universal *concrete* causality. This causality contains the necessary anticipation that the intuitively given world can be intuited as a world only as an endlessly open horizon and hence that the infinite manifold of particular causalities can be anticipated only in the manner of a horizon and is not itself given. We are thus in any case, and a priori, certain, not only that the total shape-aspect of the world of bodies generally requires a plenum-aspect pervading all the shapes, but also that *every change,* whether it involves aspects of shape or of plenum, occurs according to certain causalities, immediate or mediate, which make it necessary. This is the extent, as we said, of the undetermined general anticipation a priori.

This is not to say, however, that the total behavior of plenum-qualities, in respect to what changes and what does not change, follows causal rules in such a way that this whole abstract aspect of the world is dependent in a consistent way on what occurs causally in the shape-aspect of the world. In other words, we do not have an a priori insight that every change of the specific qualities of intuited bodies which is experienced or is conceivable in actual or possible experience refers causally to occurrences in the abstract shape-stratum of the world, i.e., that every such change has, so to speak, a counterpart in the realm of shapes in such a way that any total change in the whole plenum has its causal counterpart in the sphere of shapes.

Put in this way, this conception might appear almost fantastic. Still, let us take into account the long-familiar idealization of the form of space-time with all its shapes, carried out (in large areas, though by no means completely) for thousands of years, together with the changes and configurations of change relating to this form. The idealization of the art of measurement was, as we know, included in this, not merely as the art of measuring things but as the art of empirical causal constructions (in which deductive inferences helped, of course, as they do in every art). The theoretical attitude and the thematization of pure idealities and constructions led to pure geometry (under which we include here all pure mathematics of shapes); and later—in the reversal which has by now become understandable—applied geometry (as we remember) arose, as the practical art of measuring, guided by idealities and the constructions ideally carried out with them: i.e., an objectification of the concrete causal world of bodies within corresponding limited spheres. As soon as we bring all this to mind, the conception proposed above, which at first appeared almost eccentric, loses its strangeness for us and takes on —thanks to our earlier scientific schooling—the character of something taken for granted. What we experienced, in prescientific life, as colors, tones, warmth, and weight belonging to the things themselves and experienced causally as a body's radiation of warmth which makes adjacent bodies warm, and the like, indicates in terms of physics, of course, tone-vibrations, warmth-vibrations, i.e., pure events in the world of shapes. This universal indication is taken for granted today as unquestionable. But if we go back to Galileo, as the creator of the conception which first made physics possible: what came to be taken for granted only through his deed could not be taken for granted by him. He took for granted only pure mathematics and the old familiar way of applying it.

If we adhere strictly to Galileo's motivation, considering the way in which it in fact laid the foundation for the new idea of physics, we must make clear to ourselves the *strangeness* of his basic conception in the situation of his time; and we must ask, accordingly, how he could hit upon this conception, namely, that everything which manifests itself as real through the specific sense-qualities must have its *mathematical index* in events belonging to the sphere of shapes—which is, of course, already thought of as idealized—and that there must arise from this the possibility of an *indirect* mathematization, in the fullest sense, i.e., it must be possible (though indirectly and through a particular inductive method) to construct *ex datis,* and thus to determine objectively, *all* events in the sphere of the plena. The whole of infinite nature, taken as a concrete universe of causality—for this was inherent in that strange conception—became [the object of] a *peculiarly applied mathematics.*

But first let us answer the question of what, in the pregiven world which was already mathematized in the old limited way, could have incited Galileo's basic conception.

d. The motivation of Galileo's conception of nature.

Now there were some occasions, rather scanty, to be sure, of manifold but disconnected experiences, within the totality of prescientific experience, which suggested something like the indirect quantifiability of certain sense-qualities and thus a certain possibility of characterizing them by means of magnitudes and units of measurement. Even the ancient Pythagoreans had been stimulated by observing the functional dependency of the pitch of a tone on the length of a string set vibrating. Many other causal relations of a similar sort were, of course, generally known. Basically, all concrete intuitively given events in the familiar surrounding world contain easily discernible dependencies of plenum-occurrences on those of the sphere of shapes. But there was generally no motive for taking an analytical attitude toward the nexus of causal dependencies. In their vague indeterminateness they could not incite interest. It was different in cases where they took on the character of a determinateness which made them susceptible to determining induction; and this leads us back to the measurement of plena. Not everything which concomitantly and visibly changed on the side of shapes was measurable through the old, developed measuring methods. Also, it was a long way from such experiences to the universal idea and hypothesis that all specifically qualitative events function as indices for precisely corresponding constellations and occurrences of shape. But it was not so far for the men of the Renaissance, who were inclined to bold generalizations everywhere and in whom such exuberant hypotheses immediately found a receptive audience. Mathematics as a realm of genuine objective knowledge (and technology under its direction)—that was, for Galileo and even before him, the focal point of "modern" man's guiding interest in a philosophical knowledge of the world and a rational praxis. There must be measuring methods for everything encompassed by geometry, the mathematics of shapes with its a priori ideality. And the whole concrete world must turn out to be a mathematizable and objective world if we pursue those individual experiences and actually measure everything about them which, according to the presuppositions, comes under applied geometry—that is, if we work out the appropriate method of measuring. If we do that, the sphere of the specifically qualitative occurrences must *also* be mathematized *indirectly*.

In interpreting what was taken for granted by Galileo, i.e., the universal applicability of pure mathematics, the following must be noted: In every application to intuitively given nature, pure mathematics must give up its abstraction from the intuited plenum, whereas it leaves intact what is idealized in the shapes (spatial shapes, duration, motion, deformation). But in one respect this involves the performance of coidealization of the sensible plena belonging to the shapes. The extensive and intensive infinity which was substructed through the idealization of the sensible appearances, going beyond all possibilities of actual intuition—separability and divisibility *in infinitum,* and thus everything belonging to the mathematical continuum—implies a substruction of infinities for the *plenum*-qualities which themselves are *eo ipso* cosubstructed. The whole concrete world of bodies is thus charged with infinities not only of shape but also of plena. But it must also be noted once again that the "indirect mathematizability" which is essential for the genuine Galilean conception of physics is not yet given thereby.

As far as we have come, only a general idea has been attained or, more precisely, a general hypothesis: that a universal inductivity [9] obtains in the intuitively given world, one which announces itself in everyday experiences but whose infinity is hidden.

To be sure, this inductivity was not understood by Galileo as a hypothesis. For him a physics was immediately almost as certain as the previous pure and applied mathematics. The hypothesis also immediately traced out for him [its own] path of realization (a realization whose success necessarily has the sense, in our eyes, of a *verification of the hypothesis*—this by no means obvious hypothesis related to the [previously] inaccessible factual structure of the concrete world).[10] What mattered for him first, then, was the attainment of farther reaching and ever more perfectible *methods* in order actually to develop, beyond those which had thus far in fact been developed, all the methods of measuring that were prefigured as ideal possibilities in the ideality of pure mathematics—to measure, for example, speeds and accelerations. But the pure mathematics of shapes itself required a richer development as constructive quantification— which later on led to analytic geometry. The task now was to grasp systematically, by means of these aids, the universal causality—or, as we may say, the peculiar universal inductivity—of the world of experience which was presupposed in the hypothesis. It is to be noted, [then,] that along with the new, concrete, and thus two-sided idealization of the world, which was involved in Galileo's hypothesis, the obviousness of a universal, exact causality was also given—a universal causality which is not, of course, first arrived at by induction through the demonstration of individual causalities but which precedes and guides all induction of particular causalities—this being true even of the concretely general, intuitable causality which makes up the concretely intuitable form of the world as opposed to particular, individual causalities experienceable in the surrounding world of life [*Lebensumwelt*].

This universal idealized causality encompasses all factual shapes and plena in their idealized infinity. Obviously, if the measurements made in the sphere of shapes are to bring about truly objective determinations, occurrences on the side of the plena must also be dealt with methodically. All the fully concrete

9. *eine universale Induktivität*, i.e., that all types of occurrence in the world are such as to be susceptible to induction.

10. "Our eyes," referring to us who are engaged in this historical reflection. Once we have removed our own prejudices, we see this as a strange hypothesis rather than simply taking it for granted.

things and occurrences—or rather the ways in which factual plena and shapes stand in causal relation—must be included in the method. The application of mathematics to plena of shape given in reality makes, because of the concreteness involved, causal presuppositions which must be brought to determinateness. How one should actually proceed here, how one should regulate methodically the work to be accomplished completely within the intuitively given world; how the factually accessible bodily data, in a world charged through hypothetical idealization with as yet unknown infinities, are to be brought to causal determination in *both* aspects;[11] how the hidden infinities in these data are to be progressively disclosed according to methods of measuring; how, through growing approximations in the sphere of shapes, more and more perfect indices of the qualitative plena of the idealized bodies become apparent; how the bodies themselves, as concrete, become determinable through approximations in respect to all their ideally possible occurrences: all this was a matter of *discovery* in physics. In other words, it was a matter for the passionate *praxis of inquiry* and not a matter for prior systematic reflection upon what is possible in principle, upon the essential presuppositions of a mathematical objectification which is supposed to be able to determine the concretely real within the network of universal concrete causality.

Discovery is really a mixture of instinct and method. One must, of course, ask whether such a mixture is in the strict sense philosophy or science—whether it can be knowledge of the world in the ultimate sense, the only sense that could serve us as a [genuine] understanding of the world and ourselves. As a discoverer, Galileo went directly to the task of realizing his idea, of developing methods for measuring the nearest data of common experience; and actual experience demonstrated (through a method which was of course not radically clarified) what his hypothetical anticipation in each case demanded; he actually found causal interrelations which could be mathematically expressed in "formulae."

The actual process of measuring, applied to the intuited data of experience, results, to be sure, only in empirical, inexact magnitudes and their quantities. But the art of measuring is, in itself, at the same time the art of pushing the exactness of measuring further and further in the direction of growing

11. I.e., the aspect of shape and the aspect of plenum.

perfection. It is an art not [only] in the sense of a finished method for completing something; it is at the same time a method for improving [this very] method, again and again, through the invention of ever newer technical means, e.g., instruments. Through the relatedness of the world, as field of application, to pure mathematics, this "again and again" acquires the mathematical sense of the *in infinitum,* and thus every measurement acquires the sense of an approximation to an unattainable but ideally identical pole, namely, one of the definite mathematical idealities or, rather, one of the numerical constructions belonging to them.

From the beginning, the whole method has a *general* sense, even though one always has to do with what is individual and factual. From the very beginning, for example, one is not concerned with the free fall of *this* body; the individual fact is rather an *example,* embedded from the start in the concrete totality of types belonging to intuitively given nature, in its empirically familiar invariance; and this is naturally carried over into the Galilean attitude of idealizing and mathematizing. The indirect mathematization of the world, which proceeds as a methodical objectification of the intuitively given world, gives rise to general numerical formulae which, once they are formed, can serve by way of application to accomplish the factual objectification of the particular cases to be subsumed under them. The formulae obviously express general causal interrelations, "laws of nature," laws of real dependencies in the form of the "functional" dependencies of numbers. Thus their true meaning does not lie in the pure interrelations between numbers (as if they were formulae in the purely arithmetical sense); it lies in what the Galilean idea of a universal physics, with its (as we have seen) highly complicated meaning-content, gave as a task to scientific humanity and in what the process of its fulfillment through successful physics results in—a process of developing particular methods, and mathematical formulae and "theories" shaped by them.

e. The verificational character of natural science's fundamental hypothesis.

According to our remark [above, pp. 38–39]—which of course goes beyond the problem of merely clarifying Galileo's motivation and the resulting idea and task of physics—the Galilean idea is a *hypothesis,* and a very remarkable one at that; and the actual natural science throughout the centuries of its verification is a correspondingly remarkable sort of verification. It is remarkable because the hypothesis, in spite of the verification, continues to be and is always a hypothesis; its verification (the only kind conceivable for it) is an endless course of verifications. It is the peculiar essence of natural science, it is a priori its way of being, to be unendingly hypothetical and unendingly verified. Here verification is not, as it is in all practical life, merely susceptible to possible error, occasionally requiring corrections. There is in every phase of the development of natural science a perfectly correct method and theory from which "error" is thought to be eliminated. Newton, the ideal of exact natural scientists, says "*hypotheses non fingo*," and implied in this is the idea that he does not miscalculate and make errors of method. In the total idea of an exact science, just as in all the individual concepts, propositions, and methods which express an "exactness" (i.e., an ideality)—and in the total idea of physics as well as the idea of pure mathematics—is embedded the *in infinitum,* the permanent form of that peculiar inductivity which first brought geometry into the historical world. In the unending progression of correct theories, individual theories characterized as "the natural science of a particular time," we have a progression of hypotheses which are in every respect hypotheses *and* verifications. In the progression there is growing perfection, and for all of natural science taken as a totality this means that it comes more and more to itself, to its "ultimate" true being, that it gives us a better and better "representation" ["*Vorstellung*"] of what "true nature" is. But true nature does not lie in the infinite in the same way that a pure straight line does; even as an infinitely distant "pole" it is an infinity of theories and is thinkable only as verification; thus it is related to an infinite historical process of approximation. This may well be a topic for philosophical thinking, but it points to questions which cannot yet be grasped here and do not belong to the sphere of questions we must now deal with. For our concern is to achieve complete clarity on the idea and task of a physics which in its Galilean form originally determined modern philosophy, [to understand it] as it appeared in Galileo's own motivation, and to understand what flowed into this motivation from what was traditionally taken for granted and thus remained an unclarified presupposition of meaning, as well as what was later added as seemingly obvious, but which changed its actual meaning.

In this connection it is not necessary to go more concretely into the first beginnings of the enactment of Galileo's physics and of the development of its method.

f. The problem of the sense of natural-scientific "formulae."

But one thing more is important for our clarification. The *decisive accomplishment* which, in accord with the total sense of natural-scientific method, makes determined, systematically ordered predictions immediately possible, going beyond the sphere of immediately experiencing intuitions and the possible experiential knowledge of the prescientific life-world, is the establishment of the actual correlation among the mathematical idealities which are hypothetically substructed in advance in undetermined generality but still have to be demonstrated in their determined form. If one still has a vivid awareness of this correlation in its original meaning, then a mere thematic focus of attention on this meaning is sufficient in order to grasp the ascending orders of *intuitions* (now conceived as approximations) indicated by the functionally coordinated quantities (or, more briefly, by the formulae); or rather one can, following these indications, bring the ascending orders of intuitions vividly to mind. The same is true of the coordination itself, which is expressed in functional forms; and thus one can outline the empirical regularities of the practical life-world which are to be expected. In other words, if one has the formulae, one already possesses, in advance, the practically desired prediction of what is to be expected with empirical certainty in the intuitively given world of concretely actual life, in which mathematics is merely a special [form of] praxis. Mathematization, then, with its realized formulae, is the achievement which is decisive for life.

Through these considerations we see that, from the very first conceiving and carrying-out of the method, the passionate interest of the natural scientist was concentrated on this decisive, fundamental aspect of the above-mentioned total accomplishment, i.e., on the *formulae*, and on the technical [12] method ("natural-scientific method," "method of the true knowledge of nature") of acquiring them and grounding them logically and compellingly for all. And it is also understandable that some

12. *kunstmässig,* i.e., having the character of a technique.

were misled into taking these formulae and their formula-meaning for the true being of nature itself.

This "formula-meaning" requires a more detailed clarification, now, in respect to the superficialization of meaning [13] which unavoidably accompanies the technical development and practice of method. Measurements give rise to numbers on a scale, and, in general propositions about functional dependencies of measured quantities, they result not in determined numbers but in numbers in general, stated in general propositions which express laws of functional dependencies. Here we must take into account the enormous effect—in some respects a blessing, in others portentous—of the algebraic terms and ways of thinking that have been widespread in the modern period since Vieta (thus since even before Galileo's time). Initially this means an immense extension of the possibilities of the arithmetic thinking that was handed down in old, primitive forms. It becomes free, systematic, a priori thinking, completely liberated from all intuited actuality, about numbers, numerical relations, numerical laws. This thinking is soon applied in all its extensions—in geometry, in the whole pure mathematics of spatiotemporal shapes—and the latter are thoroughly formalized algebraically for methodical purposes. Thus an "arithmetization of geometry" develops, an arithmetization of the whole realm of pure shapes (ideal straight lines, circles, triangles, motions, relations of position, etc.). They are conceived in their ideal exactness as measurable; the units of measurement, themselves ideal, simply have the meaning of spatiotemporal magnitudes.

This arithmetization of geometry leads almost automatically, in a certain way, to the emptying of its meaning. The actually spatiotemporal idealities, as they are presented firsthand [*originär*] in geometrical thinking under the common rubric of "pure intuitions," are transformed, so to speak, into pure numerical configurations, into algebraic structures. In algebraic calculation, one lets the geometric signification recede into the background as a matter of course, indeed drops it altogether; one calculates, remembering only at the end that the numbers signify magnitudes. Of course one does not calculate "mechanically," as in ordinary numerical calculation; one thinks, one

---

13. *Sinnesveräusserlichung*, literally, "externalization of meaning," but with the sense of rendering it superficial, separating it from its origin.

invents, one may make great discoveries—but they have acquired, unnoticed, a displaced, "symbolic" meaning. Later this becomes a fully conscious methodical displacement, a methodical transition from geometry, for example, to pure *analysis*, treated as a science in its own right; and the results achieved in this science can be applied to geometry. We must go into this briefly in more detail.

This process of method-transformation, carried out instinctively, unreflectively in the praxis of theorizing, begins in the Galilean age and leads, in an incessant forward movement, to the highest stage of, and at the same time a surmounting of, "arithmetization"; it leads to a completely universal "formalization." This happens precisely through an improvement and a broadening of the algebraic theory of numbers and magnitudes into a universal and thus purely formal "analysis," "theory of manifolds," "logistic"—words to be understood sometimes in a narrower, sometimes a broader, sense, since until now, unfortunately, there has been no unambiguous characterization of what in fact, and in a way practically understandable in mathematical work, a coherent mathematical field is. Leibniz, though far ahead of his time, first caught sight of the universal, self-enclosed idea of a highest form of algebraic thinking, a *mathesis universalis*, as he called it, and recognized it as a task for the future. Only in our time has it even come close to a systematic development. In its full and complete sense it is nothing other than a formal logic carried out universally (or rather to be carried out *in infinitum* in its own essential totality), a science of the forms of meaning of the "something-in-general" which can be constructed in pure thought and in empty, formal generality. On this basis it is a science of the "manifolds" which, according to formal elementary laws of the noncontradiction of these constructions, can be built up systematically as in themselves free of contradiction. At the highest level it is a science of the universe of the "manifolds" as such which can be conceived in this way. "Manifolds" are thus in themselves compossible totalities of objects in general, which are thought of as distinct only in empty, formal generality and are conceived of as defined by determinate modalities of the something-in-general. Among these totalities the so-called "definite" manifolds are distinctive. Their definition through a "complete axiomatic system" gives a special sort of totality in all deductive determinations to the formal substrate-objects contained in them. With this sort of totality, one can say, the formal-logical idea of a "world-in-general" is constructed. The "theory of manifolds" in the special sense is the universal science of the *definite* manifolds.*

g. The emptying of the meaning of mathematical natural science through "technization." [14]

This most extreme extension of the already formal but limited algebraic arithmetic has immediate applications, in its a priori fashion, within all "concretely material" [*konkret sachhaltige*] pure mathematics, the mathematics of "pure intuitions," and can thus be applied to mathematized nature; but it also has applications to itself, to previous algebraic arithmetic, and, again by extension, to all its own formal manifolds; in this way it is related back to itself. Like arithmetic itself, in technically developing its methodology it is drawn into a process of transformation, through which it becomes a sort of *technique;* that is, it becomes a mere art of achieving, through a calculating technique according to technical rules, results the genuine sense of whose truth can be attained only by concretely intuitive thinking actually directed at the subject matter itself. But now [only] those modes of thought, those types of clarity which are indispensable for a technique as such, are in action. One operates with letters and with signs for connections and relations ($+$, $\times$, $=$, etc.), according to *rules of the game* for arranging them together in a way essentially not different, in fact, from a game of cards or chess. Here the *original* thinking that genuinely gives meaning to this technical process and truth to the correct results (even the "formal truth" peculiar to the formal *mathesis universalis*) is excluded; in this manner it is also excluded in the formal theory of manifolds itself, as in the previous algebraic theory of number and magnitude and in all the other applications of what has been obtained by a technique, without recourse to the genuine scientific meaning; this includes also the application to geometry, the pure mathematics of spatiotemporal shapes.

* For a more exact exposition of the concept of the definite manifold see *Ideen zu einer reinen Phänomenologie und phänomenologischen Philosophie* (1913), pp. 135 ff. [i.e., § 72]. On the idea of the *mathesis universalis* see *Logische Untersuchungen*, Vol. I (1900; rev. ed., 1913) [§§ 60, 69, 70], and, above all, *Formale und transzendentale Logik* (Halle: Niemeyer, 1930) [§ 23].

14. *Technisierung,* i.e., the process of becoming a technique.

Actually the process whereby material mathematics is put into formal-logical form, where expanded formal logic is made self-sufficient as pure analysis or theory of manifolds, is perfectly *legitimate*, indeed necessary; the same is true of the technization which from time to time completely loses itself in merely technical thinking. But all this can and must be a method which is understood and practiced in a fully conscious way. It can be this, however, only if care is taken to avoid dangerous shifts of meaning by keeping always immediately in mind the original bestowal of meaning [*Sinngebung*] upon the method, through which it has the sense of achieving knowledge about the *world*. Even more, it must be freed of the character of an *unquestioned tradition* which, from the first invention of the new idea and method, allowed elements of obscurity to flow into its meaning.

Naturally, as we have shown, the *formulae*—those obtained and those to be obtained—count most for the predominant interest of the discovering scientist of nature. The further physics has gone in the actual mathematization of the intuited, pregiven nature of our surrounding world, the more mathematical-scientific propositions it has at its disposal, the further the instrument destined for it, the *mathesis universalis*, has been developed: the greater is the range of its possible deductive conclusions concerning new facts of quantified nature and thus the range of indicated corresponding verifications to be made. The latter devolve upon the experimental physicist, as does the whole work of ascending from the intuitively given surrounding world, and the experiments and measurements performed in it, to the ideal poles. Mathematical physicists, on the other hand, settled in the arithmetized sphere of space-time, or at the same time in the formalized *mathesis universalis*, treat the mathematical-physical formulae brought to them as special pure structures of the formal *mathesis*, naturally keeping invariant the constants which appear in them as elements of functional laws of factual nature. Taking into account all the "natural laws already proved or in operation as working hypotheses," and on the basis of the whole available formal system of laws belonging to this *mathesis*, they draw the logical consequences whose results are to be taken over by the experimenters. But they also accomplish the formation of the available logical possibilities for new hypotheses, which of course must be compatible with the totality of those accepted as valid at the time. In this way, they see to the preparation of those forms of hypotheses which now are the only ones admissible, as hypothetical possibilities for the interpretation of causal regular-

ities to be empirically discovered through observation and exper-
iment in terms of the ideal poles pertaining to them, i.e., in
terms of exact laws. But experimental physicists, too, are constantly oriented in their work toward ideal poles, toward
numerical magnitudes and general formulae. Thus in *all* natural-
scientific inquiry these are at the center of interest. All the
discoveries of the old as well as the new physics are discoveries
in the formula-world which is coordinated, so to speak, with
nature.

The formula-meaning of this world lies in idealities, while
the whole toilsome work of achieving them takes on the character of a mere pathway to the goal. And here one must take into
consideration the influence of the above-characterized technization of formal-mathematical thinking: the transformation of its
experiencing, discovering way of thinking, which forms, perhaps
with great genius, constructive theories, into a way of thinking
with transformed concepts, "symbolic" concepts. In this process
purely geometrical thinking is also depleted, as is its application
to factual nature in natural-scientific thinking. In addition, a
technization takes over all other methods belonging to natural
science. It is not only that these methods are later "mechanized."
To the essence of all method belongs the tendency to superficial-
ize itself in accord with technization. Thus natural science undergoes a many-sided transformation and covering-over of its
meaning. The whole cooperative interplay between experimental
and mathematical physics, the enormous intellectual work constantly accomplished here, takes place within a transformed
horizon of meaning. One is, of course, to some degree conscious
of the difference between τέχνη and science. But the reflection
back upon the actual meaning which was to be obtained for
nature through the technical method stops too soon. It no longer
reaches far enough even to lead back to the position of the idea
of mathematizing nature sketched out in Galileo's creative medi-
tation, to what was wanted from this mathematization by Galileo
and his successors and what gave meaning to their endeavors to
carry it out.

h. The life-world as the forgotten meaning-fundament of natural science.

But now we must note something of the highest importance
that occurred even as early as Galileo: the surreptitious substitution of the mathematically substructed world of idealities for the

only real world, the one that is actually given through perception, that is ever experienced and experienceable—our everyday life-world. This substitution was promptly passed on to his successors, the physicists of all the succeeding centuries.

Galileo was himself an heir in respect to pure geometry. The inherited geometry, the inherited manner of "intuitive" conceptualizing, proving, constructing, was no longer original geometry: in this sort of "intuitiveness" it was already empty of meaning. Even ancient geometry was, in its way, τέχνη, removed from the sources of truly immediate intuition and originally intuitive thinking, sources from which the so-called geometrical intuition, i.e., that which operates with idealities, has at first derived its meaning. The geometry of idealities was preceded by the practical art of surveying, which knew nothing of idealities. Yet such a pregeometrical achievement was a meaning-fundament for geometry, a fundament for the great invention of idealization; the latter encompassed the invention of the ideal world of geometry, or rather the methodology of the objectifying determination of idealities through the constructions which create "mathematical existence." It was a fateful omission that Galileo did not inquire back into the original meaning-giving achievement which, as idealization practiced on the original ground of all theoretical and practical life—the immediately intuited world (and here especially the empirically intuited world of bodies)—resulted in the geometrical ideal constructions. He did not reflect closely on all this: on how the free, imaginative variation of this world and its shapes results only in possible empirically intuitable shapes and not in exact shapes; on what sort of motivation and what new achievement was required for genuinely geometric idealization. For in the case of inherited geometrical method, these functions were no longer being *vitally* practiced; much less were they reflectively brought to theoretical consciousness as methods which realize the meaning of exactness from the inside. Thus it could appear that geometry, with its own immediately evident a priori "intuition" and the thinking which operates with it, produces a self-sufficient, absolute truth which, as such—"obviously"—could be applied without further ado. That this obviousness was an illusion —as we have pointed out above in general terms, thinking for ourselves in the course of our exposition of Galileo's thoughts— that even the meaning of the application of geometry has complicated sources: this remained hidden for Galileo and the ensuing period. Immediately with Galileo, then, begins the surreptitious substitution of idealized nature for prescientifically intuited nature.

Thus all the occasional (even "philosophical") reflections which go from technical [scientific] work back to its true meaning always stop at idealized nature; they do not carry out the reflection radically, going back to the ultimate purpose which the new science, together with the geometry which is inseparable from it, growing out of prescientific life and its surrounding world, was from the beginning supposed to serve: a purpose which necessarily lay *in* this prescientific life and was related to its life-world. Man (including the natural scientist), living in this world, could put all his practical and theoretical questions only to *it*—could refer in his theories only to it, in its open, endless horizons of things unknown. All knowledge of laws could be knowledge only of predictions, grasped as lawful, about occurrences of actual or possible experiential phenomena, predictions which are indicated when experience is broadened through observations and experiments penetrating systematically into unknown horizons, and which are verified in the manner of inductions. To be sure, everyday induction grew into induction according to scientific method, but that changes nothing of the essential meaning of the pregiven world as the horizon of all meaningful induction. It is this world that we find to be the world of all known and unknown realities. To it, the world of actually experiencing intuition, belongs the form of space-time together with all the bodily [*körperlich*] shapes incorporated in it; it is in this world that we ourselves live, in accord with our bodily [*leiblich*],[15] personal way of being. But here we find nothing of geometrical idealities, no geometrical space or mathematical time with all their shapes.

This is an important remark, even though it is so trivial. Yet this triviality has been buried precisely by exact science, indeed since the days of ancient geometry, through that substitution of a methodically idealized achievement for what is given immediately as actuality presupposed in all idealization, given by a [type of] verification which is, in its own way, unsurpassable. This actually intuited, actually experienced and experienceable world,

15. *Körper* means a body in the geometric or physical sense; *Leib* refers to the body of a person or animal. Where possible, I have translated *Leib* as "living body" (*Leib* is related to *Leben*); *Körper* is translated as "body" or sometimes "physical body." In cases where adjectival or adverbial forms are used, as here, it is sometimes necessary to insert the German words or refer to them in a footnote.

in which practically our whole life takes place, remains unchanged as what it is, in its own essential structure and its own
concrete causal style, whatever we may do with or without tech-
niques. Thus it is also not changed by the fact that we invent a
particular technique, the geometrical and Galilean technique
which is called physics. What do we actually accomplish through
this technique? Nothing but *prediction* extended to infinity. All
life rests upon prediction or, as we can say, upon induction. In
the most primitive way, even the ontic certainty[16] of any
straightforward experience is inductive. Things "seen" are always more than what we "really and actually" see of them.
Seeing, perceiving, is essentially having-something-itself
[*Selbsthaben*] and at the same time having-something-in-ad-
vance [*Vor-haben*], meaning-something-in-advance [*Vor-meinen*].
All praxis, with its projects [*Vorhaben*], involves inductions; it
is just that ordinary inductive knowledge (predictions), even if
expressly formulated and "verified," is "artless" compared to the
artful "methodical" inductions which can be carried to infinity
through the method of Galilean physics with its great productivity.

In geometrical and natural-scientific mathematization, in the
open infinity of possible experiences, we measure the life-world
—the world constantly given to us as actual in our concrete
world-life—for a well-fitting *garb of ideas*, that of the so-called
objectively scientific truths. That is, through a method which (as
we hope) can be really carried out in every particular and constantly verified, we first construct numerical indices for the
actual and possible sensible plena of the concretely intuited
shapes of the life-world, and in this way we obtain possibilities of
predicting concrete occurrences in the intuitively given life-
world, occurrences which are not yet or no longer actually given.
And this kind of prediction infinitely surpasses the accomplishment of everyday prediction.

Mathematics and mathematical science, as a garb of ideas,
or the garb of symbols of the symbolic mathematical theories,
encompasses everything which, for scientists and the educated
generally, *represents* the life-world, *dresses it up* as "objectively
actual and true" nature. It is through the garb of ideas that we
take for *true being* what is actually a *method*—a method which
is designed for the purpose of progressively improving, *in infinitum*, through "scientific" predictions, those rough predictions

16. *Seinsgewissheit,* i.e., certainty of being.

which are the only ones originally possible within the sphere of what is actually experienced and experienceable in the life-world. It is because of the disguise of ideas that the true meaning of the method, the formulae, the "theories," remained unintelligible and, in the naïve formation of the method, was *never* understood.

Thus no one was ever made conscious of the radical problem of *how* this sort of naïveté actually became possible and is still possible as a living historical fact; how a method which is actually directed toward a goal, the systematic solution of an endless scientific task, and which continually achieves undoubted results, could ever grow up and be able to function usefully through the centuries when no one possessed a real understanding of the actual meaning and the internal necessity of such accomplishments. What was lacking, and what is still lacking, is the actual self-evidence through which he who knows and accomplishes can give himself an account, not only of what he does that is new and what he works with, but also of the implications of meaning which are closed off through sedimentation or traditionalization, i.e., of the constant presuppositions of his [own] constructions, concepts, propositions, theories. Are science and its method not like a machine, reliable in accomplishing obviously very useful things, a machine everyone can learn to operate correctly without in the least understanding the inner possibility and necessity of this sort of accomplishment? But was geometry, was science, capable of being designed in advance, like a machine, without [17] an understanding which was, in a similar sense, complete—scientific? Does [18] this not lead to a *regressus in infinitum*?

Finally, does this problem not link up with the problem of the instincts in the usual sense? Is it not the problem of *hidden reason*, which knows itself as reason only when it has become manifest?

Galileo, the discoverer—or, in order to do justice to his precursors, the consummating discoverer—of physics, or physical nature, is at once a discovering and a concealing genius [*entdeckender und verdeckender Genius*]. He discovers mathematical nature, the methodical idea, he blazes the trail for the infinite number of physical discoveries and discoverers. By contrast to the universal causality of the intuitively given world (as

17. Reading *ohne ein* for *aus einem*.
18. Reading *führt* for *führte*.

its invariant form), he discovers what has since been called simply the law of causality, the "a priori form" of the "true" (idealized and mathematized) world, the "law of exact lawfulness" according to which every occurrence in "nature"— idealized nature—must come under exact laws. All this is discovery-concealment, and to the present day we accept it as straightforward truth. In principle nothing is changed by the supposedly philosophically revolutionary critique of the "classical law of causality" made by recent atomic physics. For in spite of all that is new, what is essential in principle, it seems to me, remains: namely, nature, which is in itself mathematical; it is given in formulae, and it can be interpreted only in terms of the formulae.

I am of course quite serious in placing and continuing to place Galileo at the top of the list of the greatest discoverers of modern times. Naturally I also admire quite seriously the great discoverers of classical and postclassical physics and their intellectual accomplishment, which, far from being merely mechanical, was in fact astounding in the highest sense. This accomplishment is not at all disparaged by the above elucidation of it as τέχνη or by the critique in terms of principle, which shows that the true meaning of these theories—the meaning which is genuine in terms of their origins—remained and had to remain hidden from the physicists, including the great and the greatest. It is not a question of a meaning which has been slipped in through metaphysical mystification or speculation; it is, rather, with the most compelling self-evidence, the true, the only real meaning of these theories, as opposed to the meaning of being a *method*, which has its own comprehensibility in operating with the formulae and their practical application, technique.

How what we have said up to now is still one-sided, and what horizons of problems, leading into new dimensions, have not been dealt with adequately—horizons which can be opened up only through a reflection on this life-world and man as its subject—can be shown only when we are much further advanced in the elucidation of the historical development according to its innermost moving forces.

i. Portentous misunderstandings resulting from lack of clarity about the meaning of mathematization.

With Galileo's mathematizing reinterpretation of nature, false consequences established themselves even beyond the realm of nature which were so intimately connected with this reinterpretation that they could dominate all further developments of views about the world up to the present day. I mean Galileo's famous doctrine of the merely subjective character of the specific sense-qualities,[19] which soon afterward was consistently formulated by Hobbes as the doctrine of the subjectivity of all concrete phenomena of sensibly intuitive nature and world in general. The phenomena are only in the subjects; they are there only as causal results of events taking place in true nature, which events exist only with mathematical properties. If the intuited world of our life is merely subjective, then all the truths of pre- and extrascientific life which have to do with its factual being are deprived of value. They have meaning only insofar as they, while themselves false, vaguely indicate an in-itself which lies behind this world of possible experience and is transcendent in respect to it.

In connection with this we arrive at a further consequence of the new formation of meaning, a self-interpretation of the physicists which grows out of this new formation of meaning as "obvious" and which was dominant until recently:

Nature is, in its "true being-in-itself," mathematical. The *pure* mathematics of space-time procures knowledge, with apodictic self-evidence, of a set of laws of this "in-itself" which are unconditionally, universally valid. This knowledge is immediate in the case of the axiomatic elementary laws of the a priori constructions and comes to be through infinite mediations in the case of the other laws. In respect to the space-time form of nature we possess the "innate" faculty (as it is later called) of knowing with definiteness true being-in-itself as mathematically ideal being (before all actual experience). Thus implicitly the space-time form is itself innate in us.

It is otherwise with the more concrete universal lawfulness of nature, although it, too, is mathematical through and through. It is inductively accessible a posteriori through factual experiential data. In a supposedly fully intelligible way, the a priori mathematics of spatiotemporal shapes is sharply distinguished from natural science which, though it applies pure mathematics, is inductive. Or, one can also say: the purely

19. This doctrine is perhaps best expressed in Galileo's *Il Saggiatore* (*The Assayer*). See *Discoveries and Opinions of Galileo*, trans. Stillman Drake (Garden City: Doubleday Anchor Original, 1957), pp. 274 ff.

mathematic relationship of ground and consequent is sharply distinguished from that of real ground and real consequent, i.e., that of natural causality.

And yet an uneasy feeling of obscurity gradually asserts itself concerning the relation between the mathematics of nature and the mathematics of spatiotemporal form, which, after all, belongs to the former, between the latter "innate" and the former "non-innate" mathematics. Compared to the absolute knowledge we ascribe to God the creator, one says to oneself, our knowledge in pure mathematics has only one lack, i.e., that, while it is always absolutely self-evident, it requires a systematic process in order to bring to realization as knowing, i.e., as explicit mathematics, all the shapes that "exist" in the spatiotemporal form. In respect to what exists concretely in nature, by contrast, we have no a priori self-evidence at all. The whole mathematics of nature, beyond the spatiotemporal form, we must arrive at inductively through facts of experience. But is nature in itself not thoroughly mathematical? Must it not also be thought of as a coherent mathematical system? Must it not be capable of being represented in a coherent mathematics of nature, precisely the one that natural science is always merely seeking, as encompassed by a system of laws which is "axiomatic" in respect of form, the axioms of which are always only hypotheses and thus never really attainable? Why is it, actually, that they are not? Why is it that we have no prospect of discovering nature's own axiomatic system as one whose axioms are apodictically self-evident? Is it because the appropriate innate faculty is lacking in us in a factual sense?

In the superficialized, more or less already technized meaning-pattern of physics and its methods, the difference in question was "completely clear": it is the difference between "pure" (a priori) and "applied" mathematics, between "mathematical existence" (in the sense of pure mathematics) and the existence of the mathematically formed real (i.e., that of which mathematical shape is a component in the sense of a real property). And yet even such an outstanding genius as Leibniz struggled for a long time with the problem of grasping the correct meaning of the two kinds of existence—i.e., universally the existence of the spatiotemporal form as purely geometrical and the existence of universal mathematical nature with its factual, real form—and of understanding the correct relation of each to the other.

The significance of these obscurities for the Kantian problem of synthetic judgments a priori and for his division between the synthetic judgments of pure mathematics and those of natural science will concern us in detail later [see below, § 25].

The obscurity was strengthened and transformed still later with the development and constant methodical application of pure formal mathematics. "Space" and the purely *formally* defined "Euclidean manifold" were confused; the *true axiom* (i.e., in the old, customary sense of the term), as an ideal norm with unconditional validity, grasped with self-evidence in pure geometric thought or in arithmetical, purely logical thought, was confused with the *inauthentic [uneigentliches]* "axiom"—a word which in the theory of manifolds signifies not judgments ("propositions") but forms of propositions as components of the definition of a "manifold" to be constructed formally without internal contradiction.

k. Fundamental significance of the problem of the origin of mathematical natural science.[20]

Like all the obscurities exhibited earlier, [the preceding] follow from the transformation of a formation of meaning which was originally vital, or rather of the originally vital consciousness of the task which gives rise to the methods, each with its special sense. The developed method, the progressive fulfillment of the task, is, as method, an art ($\tau\acute{\epsilon}\chi\nu\eta$) which is handed down; but its true meaning is not necessarily handed down with it. And it is precisely for this reason that a theoretical task and achievement like that of a natural science (or any science of the world)—which can master the infinity of its subject matter only through infinities of method [21] and can master the latter infinities only by means of a technical thought and activity which are empty of meaning—can only be and remain meaningful in a true and original sense *if* the scientist has developed in himself the ability to *inquire back* into the *original meaning* of all his meaning-structures and methods, i.e., into the *historical meaning of their primal establishment,* and especially into the meaning of all the *inherited meanings* taken over unnoticed in this primal establishment, as well as those taken over later on.

But the mathematician, the natural scientist, at best a highly brilliant technician of the method—to which he owes the discov-

20. There is no section "j." In German one does not distinguish between "i" and "j" in an enumeration of this sort.
21. I.e., the infinite pursuit of its method.

eries which are his only aim—is normally not at all able to carry out such reflections. In his actual sphere of inquiry and discovery he does not know at all that everything these reflections must clarify is even in *need* of clarification, and this for the sake of that interest which is decisive for a philosophy or a science, i.e., the interest in true knowledge of the *world itself, nature itself.* And this is precisely what has been lost through a science which is given as a tradition and which has become a τέχνη, insofar as this interest played a determining role at all in its primal establishment. Every attempt to lead the scientist to such reflections, if it comes from a nonmathematical, nonscientific circle of scholars, is rejected as "metaphysical." The professional who has dedicated his life to these sciences must, after all—it seems so obvious to him—know best what he is attempting and accomplishing in his work. The philosophical needs ("philosophicomathematical," "philosophicoscientific" needs), aroused even in these scholars by historical motives to be elucidated later, are satisfied by themselves in a way that is sufficient for them—but of course in such a way that the whole dimension which must be inquired into is not seen at all and thus not at all dealt with.

1. Characterization of the method of our exposition.

In conclusion let us say a word about the *method* we have followed in the very intricate considerations of this section, in the service of our over-all aim. The historical reflections we embarked upon, in order to arrive at the self-understanding which is so necessary in our philosophical situation, demanded clarity concerning the *origin of the modern spirit* and, together with that—because of the significance, which cannot be overestimated, of mathematics and mathematical natural science— clarity concerning the origin of these sciences. That is to say: clarity concerning the original motivation and movement of thought which led to the conceiving of their idea of nature, and from there to the movement of its realization in the actual development of natural science itself. With Galileo the idea in question appears for the first time, so to speak, as full-blown; thus I have linked all our considerations to his name, in a certain sense simplifying and idealizing the matter; a more exact historical analysis would have to take account of how much of his thought he owed to his "predecessors." (I shall continue, incidentally, and for good reasons, in a similar fashion.) In respect to the situation as he found it and to the way in which it had to motivate him and did motivate him according to his known pronouncements, much can be established immediately, so that we understand the beginning of the whole bestowal of meaning [*Sinngebung*] upon natural science. But in this very process we come upon the shifts and concealments of meaning of later and most recent times. For we ourselves, who are carrying out these reflections (and, as I may assume, my readers), stand under the *spell* of these times. Being caught up in them, we at first have no inkling of these shifts of meaning—we who all think we know so well what mathematics and natural science "are" and do. For who today has not learned this in school? But the first elucidation of the original meaning of the new natural science and of its novel methodical style makes felt something of the later shifts in meaning. And clearly they influence, or at least make more difficult, the analysis of the motivation [of science].

Thus we find ourselves in a sort of circle. The understanding of the beginnings is to be gained fully only by starting with science as given in its present-day form, looking back at its development. But in the absence of an understanding of the *beginnings* the development is mute as a *development of meaning*. Thus we have no other choice than to proceed forward and backward in a zigzag pattern; the one must help the other in an interplay. Relative clarification on one side brings some elucidation on the other, which in turn casts light back on the former. In this sort of historical consideration and historical critique, then, which begins with Galileo (and immediately afterward with Descartes) and must follow the temporal order, we nevertheless have constantly to make *historical leaps* which are thus not digressions but necessities. They are necessities if we take upon ourselves, as we have said, the task of self-reflection which grows out of the "breakdown" situation of our time, with its "breakdown of science" itself. Of first importance for this task, however, is the reflection on the original meaning of the new sciences, above all that of the exact science of nature; for the latter was and still is, through all its shifts of meaning and misplaced self-interpretations, of decisive significance (in a manner to be pursued further) for the becoming and being of the modern positive sciences, of modern philosophy, and indeed of the spirit of modern European humanity in general.

The following also belongs to the method: readers, especially those in the natural sciences, may have become irritated by the fact—it may appear to them almost as dilettantism—that no use has been made of the natural-scientific way of speaking. It has been consciously avoided. In the kind of thinking which everywhere tries to bring "original intuition" to the fore—that is, the pre- and extrascientific life-world, which contains within itself all actual life, including the scientific life of thought, and nourishes it as the source of all technical constructions of meaning—in this kind of thinking one of the greatest difficulties is that one must choose the naïve way of speaking of [everyday] life, but must also use it in a way which is appropriate for rendering evident what is shown.

It will gradually become clearer, and finally be completely clear, that the proper return to the naïveté of life—but in a reflection which rises above this naïveté—is the only possible way to overcome the philosophical naïveté which lies in the [supposedly] "scientific" character of traditional objectivistic philosophy. This will open the gates to the new dimension we have repeatedly referred to in advance.

We must add here that, properly understood, all our expositions are supposed to aid understanding only from the relative [perspective of our] position and that our expression of doubts, given in the criticisms [of Galileo, etc.] (doubts which we, living in the present, now carrying out our reflections, do not conceal), has the methodical function of preparing ideas and methods which will gradually take shape in us as results of our reflection and will serve to liberate us.[22] All reflection undertaken for "existential" reasons is naturally *critical*. But we shall not fail to bring to a reflective form of knowledge, later on, the basic meaning of the course of our reflections and our particular kind of critique.

22. This is a rough guess at a passage which is so obscure that I suspect something is missing (cf. Translator's Introduction, p. xviii). The sense, borne out by subsequent sentences, seems to be: In the historical but also critical reflections of this section, it is not yet clear (at least to the reader) *from what point of view* we are criticizing Galileo, Descartes, *et al.,* or where it will all lead. This point of view or attitude will gradually emerge as the phenomenological attitude which takes the form (in this case a historical-critical form) of liberating us from our prejudices.

§ 10. *The origin of dualism in the prevailing exemplary role of natural science.*
The rationality of the world more geometrico.

ONE BASIC ELEMENT of the novel conception of nature has yet to be brought to the fore. In his view of the world from the perspective of geometry, the perspective of what appears to the senses and is mathematizable, Galileo *abstracts* from the subjects as persons leading a personal life; he abstracts from all that is in any way spiritual, from all cultural properties which are attached to things in human praxis. The result of this abstraction is the things purely as bodies; but these are taken as concrete real objects, the totality of which makes up a world which becomes the subject matter of research. One can truly say that the idea of nature as a really self-enclosed world of bodies first emerges with Galileo. A consequence of this, along with mathematization, which was too quickly taken for granted, is [the idea of] a self-enclosed natural causality in which every occurrence is determined unequivocally and in advance. Clearly the way is thus prepared for dualism, which appears immediately afterward in Descartes.

In general we must realize that the conception of the new idea of "nature" as an encapsuled, really and theoretically self-enclosed world of bodies soon brings about a complete transformation of the idea of the world in general. The world splits, so to speak, into two worlds: nature and the psychic world, although the latter, because of the way in which it is related to nature, does not achieve the status of an independent world. The ancients had individual investigations and theories about bodies, but not a closed world of bodies as subject matter of a universal science of nature. They also had investigations of the human and the animal soul, but they could not have a psychology in the modern sense, a psychology which, because it had universal nature and a science of nature before it [as a model], could strive for a corresponding universality, i.e., within a similarly self-enclosed field of its own.

The splitting of the world and the transformation of its meaning were the understandable consequences of the exemplary role of natural-scientific method—or, to put it another way, natural-scientific rationality—a role which was indeed quite unavoidable at the beginning of the modern period. Implied in the mathematization of nature, as the idea and the task were understood, was the supposition of the coexistence of the infinite totality of its bodies in space-time as mathematically rational; though natural science, as inductive, could have only inductive access to interconnections which, in themselves, are mathematical. In any case, natural science possessed the highest rationality because it was guided by pure mathematics and achieved, through inductions, mathematical results. Should this not become the model of all genuine knowledge? Should knowledge, if it is to attain the status of a genuine science which goes beyond nature, not follow the example of natural science or, even better, that of pure mathematics, insofar as we have, perhaps, in other spheres of knowledge, the "innate" faculty of apodictic self-evidence through axioms and deductions? It is no wonder that we already find the idea of a universal mathematics in Descartes. Of course the weight of the theoretical and practical successes [of science], beginning immediately with Galileo, had its effect. Thus the world and, correlatively, philosophy, take on a completely new appearance. The world must, in itself, be a rational world, in the new sense of rationality taken from mathematics, or mathematized nature; correspondingly, philosophy, the universal science of the world, must be built up as a unified rational theory *more geometrico*.

§ 11. *Dualism as the reason for the incomprehensibility of the problems of reason; as presupposition for the specialization of the sciences; as the foundation of naturalistic psychology.*

Of course, if scientifically rational nature is a world of bodies existing in itself—which was taken for granted in the given historical situation—then the world-in-itself must, in a sense unknown before, be a peculiarly *split* world, split into nature-in-itself and a mode of being which is different from this: that which exists psychically. At first this was to introduce considerable difficulties, even in respect to the idea of God coming from religion, an idea which had by no means been given up. Was God not unavoidable as the principle of rationality? Does not rational being, even [merely] as nature, in order to be thinkable at all, presuppose rational theory and a subjectivity which accomplishes it? Does not nature, then, indeed the world-in-itself, presuppose God as reason existing absolutely? Does this not mean that, within being-in-itself, *psychic being* takes precedence as subjectivity existing purely for itself? It is, after all, subjectivity, whether divine or human.

In general, the separating-off of the psychic caused greater and greater difficulties whenever problems of reason made themselves felt. Of course it was only later that these difficulties became so pressing that they became the central theme of philosophy, in the great investigations on human understanding, in "critiques of reason." But the power of rationalistic motives was as yet unbroken; everywhere men proceeded, full of confidence, to carry through the rationalistic philosophy on all fronts. And they were not without success in acquiring undoubtedly valuable knowledge; even if this knowledge did "not yet" correspond to the ideal, it could be interpreted as a preliminary stage. Every establishment of a special science was now *eo ipso* guided by the idea of a rational theory, or of a *rational domain*, corresponding to it. The specialization of philosophy into particular sciences accordingly has a deeper meaning, one exclusively related to the modern attitude. The specializations of ancient scientists could not result in particular sciences in our sense. Galileo's natural science did not arise through a specialization. It was only the subsequent new sciences which by contrast specialized the idea of a rational philosophy motivated by the new natural science; it was from this idea that they received the momentum to make progress and conquer new domains, rationally closed special regions within the rational totality of the universe.

Naturally, as soon as Descartes had proclaimed the idea of a rational philosophy and the division of nature and spirit, a new psychology was an immediate requirement, and it already made its appearance in Descartes's contemporary, Hobbes. It was, as we have already indicated, a psychology of a sort completely unknown to earlier times, designed concretely as a psychophysical anthropology in the rationalistic spirit.

One should not be misled by the usual contrast between empiricism and rationalism. The naturalism of a Hobbes wants to be physicalism, and like all physicalism it follows the model of physical rationality.*

This is also true of the other sciences of the modern period, the biological, etc. The dualistic split, the consequence of the physicalistic conception of nature, brings about in them a development in the form of split disciplines. The biophysical sciences, those which at first concentrate, in a one-sided fashion, purely on what pertains to the physical body, still find it necessary to begin by grasping the concrete entities descriptively, analyzing and classifying them intuitively; but the physicalistic view of nature makes it obvious that a further-developed physics would in the end "explain" all these concrete entities in a physicalistically rational way. Thus the flourishing of the biophysical-descriptive sciences, especially in view of their occasional use of knowledge taken from physics, is considered a success of the scientific method, always interpreted in the sense of physics.

In regard to the soul, on the other hand, which is left over after the animal and the human bodies have been separated off as belonging inside the closed region of nature: here the exemplary role of physics' conception of nature, and of the scientific method, has the understandable effect—this since the time of Hobbes—that a type of being is ascribed to the soul which is similar in principle to that of nature; and to psychology is ascribed a progression from description to ultimate theoretical "explanation" similar to that of biophysics. This notwithstanding the Cartesian doctrine that bodily and psychic "substance" are separated by radically different attributes. This naturalization of the psychic comes down through John Locke to the whole modern period up to the present day. Locke's image of the *white paper* [1] is characteristic—the *tabula rasa* on which psychic data come and go, somehow ordered like the events of bodies in nature. This novel, physicalistically oriented naturalism is, in Locke, not yet consistently worked out, not thought through to the end as positivistic sensationalism. But it spreads rapidly, and in a way which is fateful for the historical development of all

---

* When I use the term "physicalism," here and elsewhere, I use it exclusively in the general sense which is understood throughout the course of our own investigations, i.e., to stand for philosophical errors resulting from misinterpretations of the true meaning of modern physics. Thus the word does not refer here specifically to the "physicalistic movement" ("Vienna Circle," "logical empiricism").

1. Husserl uses the English term.

philosophy. In any case, the new naturalistic psychology was from the beginning more than an empty promise; it enters the stage impressively, in great writings, claiming to give the lasting formulation of a universal science.

Borne by the same spirit, all the new sciences seem to succeed, even the highest, metaphysics. Where physicalistic rationalism could not be carried through in earnest, as precisely in the case of metaphysics, aid was sought in unclear qualifications, through the use of variations of Scholastic concepts. For the most part, in fact, the guiding sense of the new rationality was not precisely thought out, even though it was the driving force behind the movements. Its explication in more precise terms was itself a part of philosophy's intellectual labor up to the time of Liebniz and Christian Wolff. In Spinoza's *Ethica* we have a classical example of how the new naturalistic rationalism thought itself capable of creating *ordine geometrico* a systematic philosophy—metaphysics, a science of the ultimate and highest questions, questions of reason, but also questions of fact.

One must, of course, correctly understand Spinoza's historical meaning. It is a complete misunderstanding to interpret Spinoza according to what is visible on the surface of his "geometrical" method of demonstration. Beginning as a Cartesian, he is at first, of course, completely convinced that not only nature but the totality of being as such must be a coherent rational system. That was taken for granted in advance. The mathematical system of nature must be enclosed in the total system—but, as part of a system, the former cannot be self-sufficient. One cannot leave physics to the physicists as if it were truly a complete system and then entrust to psychological specialists the task of developing a rational system proper to the psychological arm of the dualism. God, the absolute substance, would also have to belong within the unity of the rational total system as a subject for theory. Spinoza is confronted with the task of discovering the postulated rational total system of what is—discovering first of all the conditions of its being thought in coherent fashion—and then of systematically realizing it through actual construction. It is only thus, through the deed, that the actual conceivability of a rational totality of being is established. Prior to this, in spite of the self-evidence this attitude found in the exemplary character of natural science, it was only a postulate; for the dualism of radically different "substances," with the one absolute and most real substance above them, the possibility of its being thought through was not at all clear. Of course, Spinoza was interested only in what was systematically general—his *Ethica* is the first universal ontology. Through it, he believed, the actual systematic meaning of existing natural science could be obtained, together with that of the psychology which was to be similarly constructed as a parallel to it. Without this meaning both remain incomprehensible.

⸙ §12. *Over-all characterization of modern physicalistic rationalism.*

PHILOSOPHY IN ITS ancient origins wanted to be "science," universal knowledge of the universe of what is; it wanted to be not vague and relative everyday knowledge—δόξα—but rational knowledge—ἐπιστήμη. But the true idea of rationality, and in connection with that the true idea of universal science, was not yet attained in ancient philosophy—such was the conviction of the founders of the modern age. The new ideal was possible only according to the model of the newly formed mathematics and natural science. It proved its possibility in the inspiring pace of its realization. What is the universal science of this new idea but—thought of as ideally completed—*omniscience?* This, then, is for philosophy truly a realizable, though infinitely distant, goal—not for the individual or a given community of researchers but certainly for the infinite progression of the generations and their systematic researches. The world is in itself a rational systematic unity—this is thought to be a matter of apodictic insight—in which each and every singular detail must be rationally determined. Its systematic form (the universal structure of its essence) can be attained, is indeed known and ready for us in advance, at least insofar as it is purely mathematical. Only its particularity remains to be determined; and unfortunately this is possible only through induction. This is the path— infinite, to be sure—to omniscience. Thus one lives in the happy certainty of a path leading forth from the near to the distant, from the more or less known into the unknown, as an infallible method of broadening knowledge, through which truly all of the totality of what is will be known as it is "in-itself"—in an infinite progression. To this always belongs another progression: that of approximating what is given sensibly and intuitively in the surrounding life-world to the mathematically ideal, i.e., the perfecting of the always merely approximate "subsumptions" of empirical data under the ideal concepts pertaining to them. This involves the development of a methodology, the refinement of measurements, the growing efficiency of instruments, etc.

Along with his growing, more and more perfect cognitive power over the universe, man also gains an ever more perfect mastery over his practical surrounding world, one which expands in an unending progression. This also involves a mastery over mankind as belonging to the real surrounding world, i.e., mastery over himself and his fellow man, an ever greater power over his fate, and thus an ever fuller "happiness"—"happiness" as rationally conceivable for man. For he can also know what is true in itself about values and goods. All this lies within the horizon of this rationalism as its obvious consequence for man. Man is thus truly an image of God. In a sense analogous to that in which mathematics speaks of infinitely distant points, straight lines, etc., one can say metaphorically that God is the "infinitely distant man." For the philosopher, in correlation with his mathematization of the world and of philosophy, has in a certain sense mathematically idealized himself and, at the same time, God.

There is no doubt that the new ideal of the universality and rationality of knowledge entails an enormous advance in the area in which it began, mathematics and physics—provided, of course, in accord with our earlier analysis, that it is brought to a correct understanding of itself and is kept free of all transformations of meaning. Is there in the history of the world anything more worthy of philosophical wonder than the discovery of infinite totalities of truth, realizable in infinite progress either purely (in pure mathematics) or in approximations (in inductive natural science)? Is it not almost a miracle, what was actually accomplished and continued to grow? The purely theoretical-technical accomplishment is a miracle, even if, through a transformation of meaning, it is taken for science itself. It is something else to ask *how far* the exemplary character of these sciences should be stretched and whether the philosophical reflections, which were said to be responsible for the new conceptions of the world and of world sciences, were at all adequate.

How little that was the case, even in respect to nature, was demonstrated (though only in most recent times) by the weakening of the firm belief that all natural science was ultimately physics—that the biological and all the concrete sciences of nature would, in the advance of their researches, resolve themselves more and more into physics. This belief was so weakened, in fact, that these sciences found it necessary to undertake reforms of method. Of course this did not take place on the basis of a fundamental *revision* of the ideas which originally established modern natural science and which became depleted in the process of becoming method.

§ 13. *The first difficulties of physicalistic naturalism in psychology: the incomprehensibility of functioning subjectivity.*

YET MUCH EARLIER than this, the dubious character of the mathematization of the world, or rather of the rationalization unclearly imitating it—philosophy *ordine geometrico*—made itself felt in the new *naturalistic psychology*. Its domain included, after all, the rational knowing activity and the knowledge of the philosophers, mathematicians, scientists of nature, etc., the activity in which the new theories developed as its intellectual constructions and which, as such, bore within itself the ultimate truth-meaning of the world. This caused such difficulties that in the case of Berkeley and Hume a paradoxical *skepticism* developed, one that was felt to be nonsense but was not properly understood [as such]. This directed itself at first precisely against the models of rationality, mathematics and physics, and even tried to invalidate their basic concepts, indeed even the sense of their domains (mathematical space, material nature) by calling them psychological fictions. In the case of Hume this skepticism was carried through to the end, to the uprooting of the whole ideal of philosophy, the whole manner in which the new sciences were scientific. Not only the modern philosophical ideal was affected—and this is of great significance—but the entire philosophy of the past, the very formulation of the task of philosophy as universal objective science. A paradoxical situation! Highly successful accomplishments, daily growing more numerous, at least in a large number of new sciences, were at hand. Those working in these sciences, and those carefully following and understanding them, experienced a kind of self-evidence neither they nor anyone could ignore. And yet this whole accomplishment, this very self-evidence, had become completely incomprehensible through a *certain new way of looking at it, from the viewpoint of psychology,* in whose domain the accomplishing activity took place. Even more than this: not only the new sciences and their world, the world interpreted as rational, were affected, but also everyday world-consciousness and world-life, the prescientific world in the everyday sense, the world within whose obvious validity of being the activities and dealings of men untouched by science take place —the world which is ultimately also that of the scientist, and not merely when he returns to everyday praxis.

[Even] the most radical skepticism of earlier times did not focus its attack on this world but only pointed to its relativity, in order to negate ἐπιστήμη and the world-in-itself substructed through it by philosophy. This was [the extent of] its agnosticism.

Thus world-enigmas now enter the stage, of a sort previously never imagined, and they bring about a completely new manner of philosophizing, the "epistemological" philosophy, that of the "theory of reason." Soon they also give rise to systematic philosophies with completely novel goals and methods. This greatest of all revolutions must be characterized as the transformation of scientific objectivism—not only modern objectivism but also that of all the earlier philosophies of the millennia—into a transcendental subjectivism.

§ 14 *Precursory characterization of objectivism and transcendentalism. The struggle between these two ideas as the sense of modern spiritual history.*

WHAT CHARACTERIZES OBJECTIVISM is that it moves upon the ground of the world which is pregiven, taken for granted through experience, seeks the "objective truth" of this world, seeks what, in this world, is unconditionally valid for every rational being, what it is in itself. It is the task of *epistēmē, ratio,* or philosophy to carry this out universally. Through these one arrives at what ultimately is; beyond this, no further questions would have a rational sense.

Transcendentalism, on the other hand, says: the ontic meaning [*Seinssinn*] of the pregiven life-world [1] is a *subjective structure* [*Gebilde*], it is the achievement of experiencing, prescientific life. In this life the meaning and the ontic validity [*Seinsgeltung*] of the world are built up—of that particular world, that is, which is actually valid for the individual experiencer. As for the "objectively true" world, the world of science, it is a structure at a higher level, built on prescientific experiencing and thinking, or rather on its accomplishments of validity [*Geltungsleistungen*]. Only a radical inquiry back into subjectivity—and specifically the subjectivity which *ultimately* brings about all world-validity, with its content and in all its prescientific and scientific modes, and into the "what" and the "how" of the rational accomplishments—can make objective truth comprehensible and arrive at the ultimate ontic meaning of the world. Thus it is not the being of the world as unquestioned, taken for granted, which is primary in itself; and one has not merely to ask what belongs to it objectively; rather, what is primary in itself is subjectivity, understood as that which naïvely pregives [2] the being of the world and then rationalizes or (what is the same thing) objectifies it.

Yet already one is threatened with absurdity here. For it first appears obvious that this subjectivity is man, i.e., psychological subjectivity. Mature transcendentalism protests against psychological idealism and, questioning objective science *as philosophy,* claims to have initiated a completely new sort of scientific procedure, the transcendental. Past philosophy had not even the slightest conception of a subjectivism in this transcendental style. Effective motives for the appropriate change of attitude were lacking, although such a change might have been conceivable from the direction of ancient skepticism, precisely through its anthropologistic relativism.

1. Husserl probably means to include Hume under transcendentalism, as is his usual practice. This sentence would not strictly apply to Kant, according to Husserl (cf. § 28, below), since Kant's transcendentalism did not penetrate to the role of the pregiven life-world in subjective life. In this sense Hume was for Husserl the more radical transcendental philosopher.

2. *vorgibt.* A peculiarly Husserlian twist: that which is (pre)given is (pre)given *by subjectivity* through its meaning-bestowing acts.

The whole history of philosophy since the appearance of "epistemology" and the serious attempts at a transcendental philosophy is a history of tremendous tensions between objectivistic and transcendental philosophy. It is a history of constant attempts to maintain objectivism and to develop it in a new form and, on the other side, of attempts by transcendentalism to overcome the difficulties entailed by the idea of transcendental subjectivity and the method it requires. The clarification of the origin of this internal split in the philosophical development, the analysis of the ultimate motives for this most radical transformation of the idea of philosophy, is of the utmost importance. It affords the first insight into the thoroughgoing *meaningfulness* [*Sinnhaftigkeit*] which unifies the whole movement of philosophical history in the modern period: a unity of purpose binding generations of philosophers together, and through this a direction for all the efforts of individual subjects and schools. It is a direction, as I shall try to show here, toward a *final form* of transcendental philosophy—as *phenomenology*. This also contains, as a suspended moment [*aufgehobenes Moment*], the *final form of psychology* which uproots the naturalistic sense of modern psychology.

§ 15. *Reflection on the method of our historical manner of investigation.*

THE TYPE OF INVESTIGATION that we must carry out, and which has already determined the style of our preparatory suggestions, is not that of a historical investigation in the usual sense. Our task is to make comprehensible the *teleology* in the historical becoming of philosophy, especially modern philosophy, and at the same time to achieve clarity about ourselves, who are the bearers of this teleology, who take part in carrying it out through our personal intentions. We are attempting to elicit and understand the *unity* running through all the [philosophical] projects of history that oppose one another and work together in their changing forms. In a constant critique, which always regards the total historical complex as a personal one, we are attempting ultimately to discern the historical task which we can acknowledge as the only one which is personally our own. This we seek to discern not from the outside, from facts, as if the temporal becoming in which we ourselves have evolved were merely an external causal series. Rather, we seek to discern it from the *inside*. Only in this way can we, who not only have a spiritual heritage but have become what we are thoroughly and exclusively in a historical-spiritual manner, have a task which is truly our own. We obtain it not through the critique of some present or handed-down system, of some scientific or prescientific *"Weltanschauung"* (which might as well be Chinese, in the end), but only through a critical understanding of the total unity of history —*our* history. For it has spiritual unity through the unity and driving force of the task which, in the historical process—in the thinking of those who philosophize for one another and with one another across time—seeks to move through the various stages of obscurity toward satisfying clarity until it finally works its way through to perfect insight. Then the task stands before us not merely as factually required but as a task *assigned* to us, the present-day philosophers. For we are what we are as functionaries of modern philosophical humanity; we are heirs and cobearers of the direction of the will which pervades this humanity; we have become this through a primal establishment which is at once a reestablishment [*Nachstiftung*] and a modification of the Greek primal establishment. In the latter lies the *teleological beginning*, the true birth of the European spirit as such.

This manner of clarifying history by inquiring back into the primal establishment of the goals which bind together the chain of future generations, insofar as these goals live on in sedimented forms yet can be reawakened again and again and, in their new vitality, be criticized; this manner of inquiring back into the ways in which surviving goals repeatedly bring with them ever new attempts to reach new goals, whose unsatisfactory character again and again necessitates their clarification, their improvement, their more or less radical reshaping—this, I say, is nothing other than the philosopher's genuine self-reflection on what he is *truly seeking*, on what is in him as a will coming *from* the will and *as* the will of his spiritual forefathers. It is to make vital again, in its concealed historical meaning, the sedimented conceptual system which, as taken for granted, serves as the ground of his private and nonhistorical work. It is to carry forward, through his own self-reflection, the self-reflection of his forebears and thus not only to reawaken the chain of thinkers, the social interrelation of their thinking, the community of their thought, and transform it into a living present for us but, on the basis of the *total unity* thus made present, to carry out a *responsible critique*, a peculiar sort of critique which has its ground in these historical, personal projects, partial fulfillments, and exchanges of criticism rather than in what is privately taken for granted by the present philosopher. If he is to be one who thinks for himself [*Selbstdenker*], an autonomous philosopher with the will to liberate himself from all prejudices, he must have the insight that all the things he takes for granted *are* prejudices, that all prejudices are obscurities arising out of a sedimentation of tradition—not merely judgments whose truth is as yet undecided [1]—and that this is true even of the great task and idea which is called "philosophy." All judgments which count as philosophical are related back to this task, this idea.

A historical, backward reflection of the sort under discussion is thus actually the deepest kind of self-reflection aimed at a self-understanding in terms of what we are truly seeking as the historical beings we are. Self-reflection serves in arriving at a decision; and here this naturally means immediately carrying on with the task which is most truly ours and which has now been clarified and understood through this historical self-reflection, the task set for us all in the present.

But to every primal establishment [*Urstiftung*] essentially belongs a final establishment [*Endstiftung*] assigned as a task to the historical process. This final establishment is accomplished when the task is brought to consummate clarity and thus to an apodictic method which, in every step of achievement, is a constant avenue to new steps having the character of absolute success, i.e., the character of apodictic steps. At this point philosophy, as an infinite task, would have arrived at its apodictic beginning, its horizon of apodictic forward movement. (It would, of course, be completely wrong to confuse the sense of the apodictic which is indicated here, and which is the most fundamental sense, with the usual sense taken from traditional mathematics.)

But we must be warned of a misunderstanding: Every historical philosopher performs his self-reflections, carries on his dealings with the philosophers of his present and past. He expresses himself about all this, fixes through these confrontations his own position, and thus creates a self-understanding of his own deeds in accord with the way his published theories have grown up within him in the consciousness of what he was striving for.

1. I.e., pre-judices (*Vor-Urteile*) in the literal sense.

But no matter how precisely we may be informed, through historical research, about such "self-interpretations" (even about those of a whole series of philosophers), we learn nothing in this way about what, through all these philosophers, "the point of it" ultimately was, in the hidden unity of intentional inwardness which alone constitutes the unity of history. Only in the final establishment is this revealed; only through it can the unified directedness of all philosophies and philosophers open up. From here elucidation can be attained which enables us to understand past thinkers in a way that they could never have understood themselves.

This makes it clear that the peculiar truth of such a "teleological consideration of history" can never be decisively refuted by citing the documented "personal testimony" of earlier philosophers. This truth is established only in the self-evidence of a critical over-all view which brings to light, behind the "historical facts" of documented philosophical theories and their apparent oppositions and parallels, a meaningful, final harmony.

§ 16. *Descartes as the primal founder not only of the modern idea of objectivistic rationalism but also of the transcendental motif which explodes it.*

WE SHALL NOW BEGIN actually to carry out the clarification of the unifying sense of the modern philosophical movements. Here the particular role assigned to the development of the new psychology will soon become evident. To this end we must go back to the primally founding genius of all modern philosophy, Descartes. After Galileo had carried out, slightly earlier, the primal establishment of the new natural science, it was Descartes who conceived and at the same time set in systematic motion the new idea of universal philosophy: in the sense of mathematical or, better expressed, physicalistic, rationalism—philosophy as "universal mathematics." And immediately it had a powerful effect.

This does not mean, then (in accord with our exposition above), that he had fully and systematically thought out this idea in advance, much less that his contemporaries and successors, constantly guided by it in the sciences, had it in mind in explicit form. For this it would have been necessary to have the higher systematic development of pure mathematics under the new idea of universality which appears in its first, relative maturity in Leibniz (as *mathesis universalis*) and which is now, in more mature form, still a subject of lively research as the mathematics of definite manifolds. Like all historical ideas that result in great developments, those in the new mathematics, the new natural science, and the new philosophy live in very diverse noetic modes in the consciousness of the persons who function as the bearers of their development: sometimes they strive forward like instincts, without these persons having any ability to give an account of where they are going; sometimes they are the results of a more or less clear realization, as plainly and simply grasped goals, possibly crystallizing into ever more precise goals through repeated consideration. On the other hand, there are modes in which these ideas become leveled down, are made unclear when ideas are taken over which have been made precise in another area and now take on different kinds of vagueness (we have already learned to understand this kind of thing): ideas emptied [of meaning] which have been obscured and have become mere word-concepts; ideas burdened, through attempts at exposition, with false interpretations, etc. In spite of all this, they are driving forces in the development. And the ideas which interest us here also have their effect on those who are not trained in mathematical thinking. It is well to take note of this when one speaks of the power of the new idea of philosophy, having its effect throughout the whole modern period in all sciences and culture, as it was first grasped and mastered in a relatively stable way by Descartes.

But it was not merely in the inauguration of this idea that Descartes was the founding father of the modern period. It is highly remarkable at the same time that it was he, in his *Meditations*—and precisely in order to provide a radical foundation for the new rationalism and then *eo ipso* for dualism—who accomplished the primal establishment of ideas which were destined, through their own historical effects (as if following a hidden teleology of history), to explode this very rationalism by uncovering its hidden absurdity. Precisely those ideas which were supposed to ground this rationalism as *aeterna veritas* bear within themselves a *deeply hidden sense,* which, once brought to the surface, completely uproots it.

§ 17. *Descartes's return to the* ego cogito. *Exposition of the sense of the Cartesian* epochē.

LET US CONSIDER the progress of the first two Cartesian meditations from a perspective which allows its general structures to come to the fore—the progress to the *ego cogito,* the *ego* of the *cogitationes* of the various *cogitata.* This beloved examination question for philosophical children, then, shall be our subject. In truth, there is in these first meditations a depth which is so difficult to exhaust that even Descartes was unable to do it, to the extent that he let slip away the great discovery he had in his hands. Even today, and perhaps especially today, everyone who would think for himself ought, it seems to me, to study these first meditations in the utmost depth, not being frightened off by the appearance of primitiveness, by the well-known use of the new ideas for the paradoxical and basically wrong proofs of the existence of God, or by many other obscurities and ambiguities —and also not being too quickly comforted by one's own refutations. It is with good reasons that I now devote considerable space to my attempt at a careful exposition, not repeating what Descartes said, but extracting what was really involved in his thinking and then separating what he became conscious of from what was concealed from him, or rather what was smuggled into his ideas, because of certain things—of course very natural things—taken for granted. These were not merely remains of Scholastic traditions, not merely accidental prejudices of his time, but were *things taken for granted throughout the millennia* which can be overcome only by clarifying and thinking through to the end what was original in Descartes's thought.

Philosophical knowledge is, according to Descartes, *absolutely grounded* knowledge; it must stand upon a foundation of immediate and apodictic knowledge whose self-evidence excludes all conceivable doubt. Every step of mediate knowledge must be able to attain the same sort of self-evidence. A survey of his hitherto existing convictions, acquired or taken over, shows him that doubts or possibilities of doubt arise on all sides. In this situation it is unavoidable that he, and anyone who seriously seeks to be a philosopher, begin with a sort of *radical, skeptical epochē* which places in question all his hitherto exist- ing convictions, which forbids in advance any judgmental use of them, forbids taking any position as to their validity or invalid- ity. Once in his life every philosopher must proceed in this way; if he has not done it, and even already has "his philosophy," he must still do it. Prior to the epochē "his philosophy" is to be treated like any other prejudice. The "Cartesian epochē" has in truth a hitherto unheard-of radicalism, for it encompasses ex- pressly not only the validity of all previous *sciences*—even math- ematics, which claims apodictic self-evidence, is not excluded— but even the validity of the pre- and extrascientific *life-world*, i.e., the world of sense-experience constantly pregiven as taken for granted unquestioningly and all the life of thought which is nourished by it—the unscientific and finally even the scientific. The lowest stratum of all objective knowledge, the cognitive ground of all hitherto existing sciences, all sciences of "the" world, is, we can say, for the first time called into question in the manner of a "critique of knowledge." It is experience in the usual sense which is thus called into question, "sense" experience— and its correlate, the world itself, as that which has sense and being for us in and through this experience, just as it is con- stantly valid for us, with unquestioned certainty, as simply there [*vorhanden*], having such and such a content of particular real objects [*Realitäten*], and which is occasionally devaluated as doubtful or as invalid illusion only in individual details. But from this point on, even all the accomplishments of meaning and validity which are founded on experience are called into question. Indeed, this is the historical beginning, as we have already said, of a "critique of knowledge," and specifically a radical critique of objective knowledge.

It must be recalled again that the ancient skepticism begun by Protagoras and Gorgias calls into question and denies *epi- stēmē*, i.e., scientific knowledge of what is in-itself, but that it does not go beyond such agnosticism, beyond the denial of the rational substructions of a "philosophy" which, with its supposed truths-in-themselves, assumes a rational in-itself and believes itself capable of attaining it. [According to skepticism] "the" world is not rationally knowable; human knowledge cannot ex- tend beyond the subjective-relative appearances. Starting from this point (for example, from Gorgias' ambiguous proposition "There is nothing"), it might have been possible to push radi- calism farther; but in reality it never came to this. The skepticism which was negativistically oriented toward the practical and ethical (political) lacked, even in all later times, the original Cartesian motif: that of pressing forward through the hell of an unsurpassable, quasi-skeptical epochē toward the gates of the heaven of an absolutely rational philosophy, and of constructing the latter systematically.

But how is this epochē supposed to accomplish this? If it puts out of play, with one blow, all knowledge of the world, in all its forms, including those of the straightforward experience of the world, and thus loses its grasp on the being of the world, how is it that precisely through the epochē a primal ground of immediate and apodictic self-evidences should be exhibited? The answer is: If I refrain from taking any position on the being or nonbeing of the world, if I deny myself every ontic validity related to the world, not *every* ontic validity is prohibited for me within this epochē. I, the ego [1] carrying out the epochē, am not included in its realm of objects but rather—if I actually carry out the epochē radically and universally—am excluded in principle. I am necessary as the one carrying it out. It is precisely herein that I find just the apodictic ground I was seeking, the one which absolutely excludes every possible doubt. No matter how far I may push my doubt, and even if I try to think that everything is dubious or even in truth does not exist, it is absolutely self-evident that I, after all, would still exist as the doubter and negator of everything. Universal doubt cancels itself. Thus, during the universal epochē, the absolutely apodictic self-evidence "I am" is at my disposal. But within this self-evidence a great deal is comprised. A more concrete version of the self-evident statement *sum cogitans* is: *ego cogito—cogitata qua cogitata.* This takes in all *cogitationes,* individual ones as well as their flowing synthesis into the universal unity of one *cogitatio* in which, as *cogitatum,* the world and what I have variously attributed to it in thought had and still has ontic validity for me —except that now, *as* one who is philosophizing, I may no longer straightforwardly effect these validities and use them as knowledge in the natural way. Standing above them all in my posture of epochē I may no longer take part in performing them. Thus my whole life of acts—experiencing, thinking, valuing, etc.—remains, and indeed flows on; but what was before my eyes in that life as "the" world, having being and validity for me,

1. I have usually translated both *das Ego* and *das Ich* as "the ego," since Husserl makes no distinction between these terms. Occasionally I have used "the 'I.'"

has become a mere "phenomenon," and this in respect to all determinations proper to it. In the epochē, all these determinations, and *the world itself,* have been transformed into my *ideae;* they are inseparable components of my *cogitationes,* precisely as their *cogitata.* Thus here we would have, included under the title "ego," an absolutely apodictic sphere of being rather than merely the one axiomatic proposition *ego cogito* or *sum cogitans.*

But something else, something especially remarkable, must be added. Through the epochē I have penetrated into the sphere of being which is prior in principle to everything which conceivably has being for me, and to all its spheres of being—as their absolutely apodictic presupposition. Or, what for Descartes counts as the same thing: I, the ego performing the epochē, am the only thing that is absolutely indubitable, that excludes in principle every possibility of doubt. Whatever else enters the stage as apodictic, as, for example, mathematical axioms, certainly does leave open possibilities of doubt and thus also the conceivability of their being false. The latter is excluded, and the claim to apodicticity justified, only with the success of an indirect and absolutely apodictic grounding which traces these things back to that sole absolute, primal self-evidence from which all scientific knowledge must—if a philosophy is to be possible—be derived.

§ 18. *Descartes's misinterpretation of himself.*
The psychologistic falsification of the
pure ego attained through the epochē.

HERE WE MUST BRING UP certain things about which we have deliberately been silent in the exposition up to now. Thereby a hidden double meaning of Descartes's ideas will become evident: there arise two possible ways of taking these ideas, developing them, and setting scientific tasks; whereas for Descartes only *one* of these was obvious from the start. Thus the sense of his presentations is factually (i.e., as his own sense) unambiguous; but unfortunately this unambiguousness stems from the fact that he does not actually carry through the original radicalism of his ideas, that he does not actually subject to the epochē (or "bracket") all his prior opinions, the world in all respects, that he, obsessed by his goal, does not draw out precisely what is most significant in what he gained through the "ego" of the epochē, so as to unfold, purely in connection with this ego, a philosophical θαυμάζειν. In comparison with what such an unfolding could yield, indeed very soon, everything new in what Descartes actually brought to light was in a certain sense superficial, in spite of its originality and widespread effects. In addition, it loses its value by Descartes's own interpretation of it. Namely: in wonder over this ego, first discovered in the epochē, he himself asks what *kind* of an ego it is, whether the ego is the human being, the sensibly intuited human being of everyday life. Then he excludes the living body—this, like the sensible world in general, falls under the epochē—and thus the ego becomes determined, for Descartes, as *mens sive animus sive intellectus*.

But here we have several questions. Is not the epochē related to the totality of what is pregiven to me (who am philosophizing) and thus related to the whole world, including all human beings, and these not only in respect to their bodies? Is it not thus related to me as a *whole* man as I am valid for myself in my natural possession of the world [*Welthabe*]? Is Descartes here not dominated in advance by the Galilean certainty of a universal and absolutely pure world of physical bodies, with the distinction between the merely sensibly experienceable and the mathematical, which is a matter of pure thinking? Does he not already take it for granted that sensibility points to a realm of what is in-itself, but that it can deceive us; and that there must be a rational way of resolving this [deception] and of knowing what is in-itself with mathematical rationality? But is all this not at once bracketed with the epochē, indeed even as a possibility? It is obvious that Descartes, in spite of the radicalism of the presuppositionlessness he demands, has, in advance, a *goal* in relation to which the breakthrough to this "ego" is supposed to be the *means*. He does not see that, by being convinced of the possibility of the goal and of this means, he has already left this radicalism behind. It is not achieved by merely deciding on the epochē, on the radical withholding of [judgment on] all that is pregiven, on all prior validities of what is in the world; the epochē must seriously *be* and *remain* in effect. The ego is not a residuum of the world but is that which is absolutely apodictically posited; and this is made possible only through the epochē, only through the "bracketing" of the *total* world-validity; and it is the only positing thus made possible. The *soul*, however, is the *residuum of a previous abstraction* of the pure physical body, and according to this abstraction, at least apparently, is a complement of this body. But this abstraction (and we must not overlook this) occurs not in the epochē but in the natural scientist's or psychologist's way of looking at things, on the natural ground of the world as pregiven and taken for granted. We shall have occasion to speak again about these abstractions and about the appearance of their obviousness. Here it suffices to be clear about the fact that in the foundation-laying reflections of the *Meditations*—those in which the epochē and its ego are introduced—a break of consistency occurs when this ego is identified with the pure soul. The whole gain, the great discovery of this ego, loses its value through an absurd misconstruction: a pure soul has no meaning at all in the epochē, unless it is as "soul" in "brackets," i.e., as mere "phenomenon" no less than the living body. One should not overlook, [by the way,] the *new* concept of "phenomenon" which arises for the first time with the Cartesian epochē.

We can see how difficult it is to maintain and use such an unheard-of change of attitude as that of the radical and universal epochē. Right away "natural common sense," some aspect of the naïve validity of the world, breaks through at some point and adulterates the new kind of thinking made possible and necessary in the epochē. (Whence also the naïve objections of almost all my philosophical contemporaries to my "Cartesianism" or to the "phenomenological reduction" for which I have prepared the way through this presentation of the Cartesian epochē.) This nearly ineradicable naïveté is also responsible for the fact that for centuries almost no one took exception to the "obviousness" of the possibility of inferences from the ego and its cognitive life to an "outside," and no one actually raised the question of whether, in respect to this egological sphere of being, an "outside" can have any meaning at all—which of course turns this ego into a paradox, the greatest of all enigmas. Yet perhaps a great deal, indeed everything for a philosophy, turns upon this enigma; and perhaps the way in which Descartes himself was shaken by the discovery of this ego is significant as an indication to us lesser spirits that something truly great, indeed of the greatest magnitude, is announced in it, something which should one day emerge, through all the errors and confusions, as the "Archimedean point" of any genuine philosophy.

The new motif of returning to the ego, once it had entered history, revealed its inner strength through the fact that in spite of falsifications and obfuscations it introduced a new philosophical age and implanted within it a new *telos*.

§ 19. *Descartes's obtrusive interest in objectivism as the reason for his self-misinterpretation.*

FOR DESCARTES, the *Meditations* work themselves out in the portentous form of a substitution of one's own psychic ego for the [absolute] ego, of psychological immanence for egological immanence, of the evidence of psychic, "inner," or "self-perception" for egological self-perception; and this is also their continuing historical effect up to the present day. Descartes himself really believes he is able to establish the dualism of finite substances by way of inferences to what transcends his own soul, mediated through the first inference to the transcendence of God. Likewise he thinks he is solving the problem which is meaningful for his absurd attitude and which returns later, in a modified form, in Kant: the problem of how the rational structures engendered in my reason (my own *clarae et distinctae perceptiones*)—those of mathematics and mathematical natural science—can claim an objectively "true," a metaphysically transcendent validity. What the modern period calls the theory of the understanding or of reason—in the pregnant sense "critique of reason," transcendental problematics—has the roots of its meaning in the Cartesian *Meditations*. The ancient world was not acquainted with this sort of thing, since the Cartesian epochē and its ego were unknown. Thus, in truth, there begins with Descartes a completely new manner of philosophizing which seeks its ultimate foundations in the subjective. That Descartes, however, persists in pure objectivism in spite of its subjective grounding was possible only through the fact that the *mens*, which at first stood by itself in the epochē and functioned as the absolute ground of knowledge, grounding the objective sciences (or, universally speaking, philosophy), appeared at the same time to *be* grounded along with everything else as a legitimate subject matter *within* the sciences,[1] i.e., in psychology. Descartes

1. Reading *denselben* for *derselben*.

does not make clear to himself that the ego, his ego deprived of its worldly character [*entweltlicht*] through the epochē, in whose functioning *cogitationes* the world has all the ontic meaning it can ever have for him, *cannot possibly* turn up as subject matter *in* the world, since everything that is of the *world* derives its meaning precisely *from these functions*—including, then, one's own psychic being, the ego in the usual sense. Even more inaccessible to him, and naturally so, was the consideration that the ego as it is disclosed in the epochē, existing for itself, is as yet not at all "an" ego which can have other or many fellow egos outside itself. It remained hidden from Descartes that all such distinctions as "I" and "you," "inside" and "outside," first "constitute" themselves in the absolute ego. Thus it is understandable why Descartes, in his haste to ground objectivism and the exact sciences as affording metaphysical, absolute knowledge, does not set himself the task of systematically investigating the pure ego —consistently remaining within the epochē—with regard to what acts, what capacities, belong to it and what it brings about, as intentional accomplishment, through these acts and capacities. Since he does not stop here, the immense set of problems cannot reveal itself to him, i.e., those of beginning with the world as a "phenomenon" in the ego and systematically inquiring back, to find out which of the actually demonstrable immanent accomplishments of the ego have given the world its ontic meaning. An analysis of the ego as *mens* was obviously for *him* a matter for a future objective psychology.

§20. *"Intentionality" in Descartes.*

ACCORDINGLY, the foundation-laying first meditations were actually a piece of psychology; but one element in them remains to be brought out expressly as highly significant, though completely undeveloped: *intentionality*, which makes up the essence of egological life. Another word for it is *cogitatio, having something consciously* [*etwas bewussthaben*], e.g., in experiencing, thinking, feeling, willing, etc.; for every *cogitatio* has its *cogitatum*. Each is in the broadest sense an act of believing [*ein Vermeinen*] and thus there belongs to each some mode of certainty—straightforward certainty, surmise, holding-to-be-probable, doubting, etc. In connection with these there are the distinctions between confirmation and disconfirmation or true and false. We can already see that the problem entitled "intentionality" contains within itself, inseparably, the problems of the understanding or of reason. To be sure, there is no question of a true presentation and treatment of the subject of intentionality [in Descartes]. On the other hand, the whole supposed founding of the new universal philosophy on the ego must be characterized as a "theory of knowledge," i.e., a theory of how the ego, in the intentionality of its reason (through acts of reason) brings about *objective* knowledge. For Descartes, of course, this means knowledge which metaphysically transcends the ego.

§ 21. *Descartes as the starting point of two lines of development, rationalism and empiricism.*

IF WE NOW FOLLOW the lines of development which proceeded from Descartes, one, the "rationalistic," leads through Malebranche, Spinoza, Leibniz, and the Wolff school to Kant, the turning point. Here the spirit of the new kind of rationalism, as implanted by Descartes, thrusts forward enthusiastically and unfolds in great systems. Here the conviction reigns, then, that through the method of *mos geometricus* an absolutely grounded, universal knowledge of the world, thought of as a transcendent "in-itself," can be realized. Precisely against this conviction, against the new science as having such scope as to extend to something "transcendent," indeed finally against this "transcendent" itself, English empiricism reacts—even though it is likewise strongly influenced by Descartes. But it is a reaction similar to that of ancient skepticism against the systems of rational philosophy of its time. The new skeptical empiricism already sets in with Hobbes. Of greater interest for us, however, because of its immense effect on psychology and the theory of knowledge, is Locke's critique of the understanding, together with its subsequent continuations in Berkeley and Hume. This line of development is especially significant in that it is an essential segment of the historical path on which the psychologically adulterated transcendentalism of Descartes (if we may already so call his original turn to the ego) seeks, through unfolding its consequences, to work its way through to the realization of its untenability and, from there, to a transcendentalism which is more genuine and more conscious of its true meaning. The primary and historically most important thing here was the self-revelation of empirical psychologism (of the sensationalistic, naturalistic cast) as an intolerable absurdity.

§ 22. *Locke's naturalistic-epistemological psychology.*

IT IS IN THE EMPIRICIST development, as we know, that the new psychology, which was required as a correlate to pure natural science when the latter was separated off, is brought to its first concrete execution. Thus it is concerned with investigations of introspective psychology in the field of the soul, which has now been separated from the body, as well as with physiological and psychophysical explanations. On the other hand, this psychology is of service to a theory of knowledge which, compared with the Cartesian one, is completely new and very differently worked out. In Locke's great work this is the actual intent from the start. It offers itself as a new attempt to accomplish precisely what Descartes's *Meditations* intended to accomplish: an epistemological grounding of the objectivity of the objective sciences. The skeptical posture of this intent is evident from the beginning in questions like those of the scope, the extent, and the degrees of certainty of human knowledge. Locke senses nothing of the depths of the Cartesian epochē and of the reduction to the ego. He simply takes over the ego as soul, which becomes acquainted, in the self-evidence of self-experience, with its inner states, acts, and capacities. Only what inner self-experience shows, only our own "ideas," are immediately, self-evidently given. Everything in the external world is inferred.

What comes first, then, is the internal-psychological analysis purely on the basis of the inner experience—whereby use is made, quite naïvely, of the experiences of other human beings and of the conception of self-experience as what belongs to *me, one human being* among human beings; that is, the objective validity of inferences to others is used; just as, in general, the whole investigation proceeds as an objective psychological one, indeed even has recourse to the physiological—when it is precisely all this objectivity, after all, which is in question.

The actual problem of Descartes, that of transcending egological (interpreted as internal-psychological) validities, including all manners of inference pertaining to the external world, the question of how these, which are, after all, themselves *cogitationes* in the encapsuled soul, are able to justify [assertions about] extrapsychic being—these problems disappear in Locke or turn into the problem of the psychological genesis of the real experiences of validity or of the faculties belonging to them. That sense-data, extracted from the arbitrariness of their production, are affections from the outside and announce bodies in the external world, is not a problem for him but something taken for granted.

Especially portentous for future psychology and theory of knowledge is the fact that Locke makes no use of the Cartesian first introduction of the *cogitatio* as *cogitatio* of *cogitata*—that is, intentionality; he does not recognize it as a subject of investigation (indeed the most authentic subject of the foundation-laying investigations). He is blind to the whole distinction. The soul is something self-contained and real by itself, as is a body; in naïve naturalism the soul is now taken to be like an isolated space, like a writing tablet, in his famous simile, on which psychic data come and go. This data-sensationalism, together with the doctrine of outer and inner sense, dominates psychology and the theory of knowledge for centuries, even up to the present day; and in spite of the familiar struggle against "psychic atomism," the basic sense of this doctrine does not change. Of course one speaks quite unavoidably, [even] in the Lockean terminology, of perceptions, representations "of" things, or of believing "in something," willing "something," and the like. But no consideration is given to the fact that in the perceptions, in the experiences of consciousness themselves, that of which we are conscious is included *as such*—that the perception is *in itself* a perception *of* something, of "this tree."

How is the life of the soul, which is through and through a life of consciousness, the intentional life of the ego, which has objects of which it is conscious, deals with them through knowing, valuing, etc.—how is it supposed to be seriously investigated if intentionality is overlooked? How can the problems of reason be attacked at all? Can they be attacked at all as psychological problems? In the end, behind the psychological-epistemological problems, do we not find the problems of the "ego" of the Cartesian epochē, touched upon but not grasped by Descartes? Perhaps these are not unimportant questions, which give a direction in advance to the reader who thinks for himself. In any case they are an indication of what will become a serious problem in later parts of this work, or rather will serve as a way to a philosophy which can really be carried through "without prejudice," a philosophy with the most radical grounding in its setting of problems, in its method, and in work which is systematically accomplished.

It is also of interest that the Lockean skepticism in respect to the rational ideal of science, and its limitation of the scope of the new sciences (which are supposed to retain their validity), leads to a new sort of agnosticism. It is not that the possibility of science is completely denied, as in ancient skepticism, although again unknowable things-in-themselves are assumed. [But] our human science depends exclusively on our representations and concept-formations; by means of these we may, of course, make inferences extending to what is transcendent; but in principle we cannot obtain actual representations of the things-in-themselves, representations which adequately express the proper essence of these things. We have adequate representations and knowledge only of what is in our own soul.

§ 23. *Berkeley. David Hume's psychology as fictionalistic theory of knowledge: the "bankruptcy" of philosophy and science.*

LOCKE'S NAÏVETÉS and inconsistencies lead to a rapid further development of his empiricism, which pushes toward a paradoxical idealism and finally ends in a consummated absurdity. The foundation continues to be sensationalism and what appears to be obvious, i.e., that the sole indubitable ground of all knowledge is self-experience and its realm of immanent data. Starting from here, Berkeley reduces the bodily things which appear in natural experience to the complexes of sense-data themselves through which they appear. No inference is thinkable, [according to Berkeley,] through which conclusions could be drawn from these sense-data about anything but other such data. It could only be inductive inference, i.e., inference growing out of the association of ideas. Matter existing in itself, a *je ne sais quoi,* according to Locke, is [for Berkeley] a philosophical invention. It is also significant that at the same time he dissolves the manner in which rational natural science builds concepts and transforms it into a sensationalistic critique of knowledge.

In this direction, Hume goes on to the end. All categories of objectivity—the scientific ones through which an objective, extrapsychic world is thought in scientific life, and the prescientific ones through which it is thought in everyday life—are fictions. First come the mathematical concepts: number, magnitude, continuum, geometrical figure, etc. *We* would say that they are methodically necessary idealizations of what is given intuitively. For Hume, however, they are fictions; and the same is true, accordingly, of the whole of supposedly apodictic mathematics. The origin of these fictions can be explained perfectly well psychologically (i.e., in terms of immanent sensationalism), namely, through the immanent lawfulness of the associations and the relations between ideas. But even the categories of the prescientific world, of the straightforwardly intuited world— those of corporeity (i.e., the identity of persisting bodies supposedly found in immediate, experiencing intuition), as well as the supposedly experienced identity of the person—are nothing but fictions. We say, for example, "that" tree over there, and distinguish from it its changing manners of appearing [*Erscheinungsweisen*]. But immanently, psychically, there is nothing there but these "manners of appearing." These are complexes of data, and again and again other complexes of data— "bound together," regulated, to be sure, by association, which explains the illusion of experiencing something identical. The same is true of the person: an identical "I" is not a datum but a ceaselessly changing bundle of data. Identity is a psychological fiction. To the fictions of this sort also belongs causality, or necessary succession. Immanent experience exhibits only a *post hoc.* The *propter hoc,* the necessity of the succession, is a fictive misconstruction. Thus, in Hume's *Treatise,* the world in general, nature, the universe of identical bodies, the world of identical persons, and accordingly also objective science, which knows these in their objective truth, are transformed into fiction. To be consistent, we must say: reason, knowledge, including that of true values, of pure ideals of every sort, including the ethical— all this is fiction.

This is indeed, then, a bankruptcy of objective knowledge. Hume ends up, basically, in a solipsism. For how could inferences from data to other data ever reach beyond the immanent sphere? Of course, Hume did not ask the question, or at least did not say a word, about the status of the reason—Hume's—which established this theory as truth, which carried out these analyses of the soul and demonstrated these laws of association. How do rules of associative ordering "bind"? Even if we knew about them, would not that knowledge itself be another datum on the tablet?

Like all skepticism, all irrationalism, the Humean sort cancels itself out. Astounding as Hume's genius is, it is the more regrettable that a correspondingly great philosophical ethos is not joined with it. This is evident in the fact that Hume takes care, throughout his whole presentation, blandly to disguise or interpret as harmless his absurd results, though he does paint a picture (in the final chapter of Volume I of the *Treatise*) of the immense embarrassment in which the consistent theoretical philosopher gets involved. Instead of taking up the struggle against absurdity, instead of unmasking those supposedly obvious views upon which this sensationalism, and psychologism in general, rests, in order to penetrate to a coherent self-understanding and a genuine theory of knowledge, he remains in the comfortable and very impressive role of academic skepticism. Through this attitude he has become the father of a still effective, unhealthy positivism which hedges before philosophical abysses, or covers them over on the surface, and comforts itself with the successes of the positive sciences and their psychologistic elucidation.

§ 24. *The genuine philosophical motif hidden in the absurdity of Hume's skepticism: the shaking of objectivism.*

LET US STOP FOR A MOMENT. Why does Hume's *Treatise* (in comparison to which the *Essay Concerning Human Understanding* is badly watered down) represent such a great historical event? What happened there? The Cartesian radicalism of presuppositionlessness, with the goal of tracing genuine scientific knowledge back to the ultimate sources of validity and of grounding it absolutely upon them, required reflections directed toward the subject, required the regression to the knowing ego in his immanence. No matter how little one may have approved of Descartes's epistemological procedure, one could no longer escape the necessity of this requirement. But was it possible to improve upon Descartes's procedure? Was his goal, that of grounding absolutely the new philosophical rationalism, still attainable after the skeptical attacks? Speaking in favor of this from the start was the immense force of discoveries in mathematics and natural science that were proceeding at breakneck speed. And so all who themselves took part in these sciences through research or study were already certain that its truth, its method, bore the stamp of finality and exemplariness. And now empiricist skepticism brings to light what was already present in the Cartesian fundamental investigation but was not worked out, namely, that all knowledge of the world, the prescientific as well as the scientific, is an enormous enigma. It was easy to follow Descartes, when he went back to the apodictic ego, in interpreting the latter as *soul,* in taking the primal self-evidence to be the self-evidence of "inner perception." And what was more plausible than the way in which Locke illustrated the reality of the detached soul and the history [*Geschichtlichkeit*] running its course within it, its internal genesis, by means of the "white paper" [1] and thus naturalized this reality? But now, could the "idealism" of Berkeley and Hume, and finally skepticism with all its absurdity, be avoided? What a paradox! Nothing could cripple the peculiar force of the rapidly growing and, in their own accomplishments, unassailable exact sciences or the belief in their truth. And yet, as soon as one took into account that they are the accomplishments of the consciousness of knowing subjects, their self-evidence and clarity were transformed into incomprehensible absurdity. No offense was taken if, in Descartes, immanent sensibility engendered pictures of the world; but in Berkeley this sensibility engendered the *world of bodies itself;* and in Hume the entire soul, with its "impressions" and "ideas," the forces belonging to it, conceived of by analogy to physical forces, its laws of association (as parallels to the law of gravity!), engendered the whole world, the *world itself*, not merely something like a picture—though, to be sure, this product was

1. Husserl uses the English term.

merely a fiction, a representation put together inwardly which was actually quite vague. And this is true of the world of the rational sciences as well as that of *experientia vaga*.

Was there not, here, in spite of the absurdity which may have been due to particular aspects of the presuppositions, a hidden and unavoidable truth to be felt? Was this not the revelation of a *completely new way* of assessing the objectivity of the world and its whole ontic meaning and, correlatively, that of the objective sciences, a way which did not attack their [2] own validity but did attack their philosophical or metaphysical claim, that of absolute truth? Now at last it was possible and necessary to become aware of the fact—which had remained completely unconsidered in these sciences—that the life of consciousness is a life of *accomplishment:* the accomplishment, right or wrong, of ontic meaning, even sensibly intuited meaning, and all the more of scientific meaning. Descartes had not pondered the fact that, just as the sensible world, that of everyday life, is the *cogitatum* of sensing *cogitationes,* so the scientific world is the *cogitatum* of scientific *cogitationes;* and he had not noticed the circle in which he was involved when he presupposed, in his proof of the existence of God, the *possibility* of inferences transcending the ego, when this possibility, after all, was supposed to be established only through this proof. The thought was quite remote from him that the whole world could itself be a *cogitatum* arising out of the universal synthesis of the variously flowing *cogitationes* and that, on a higher level, the rational accomplishment of the scientific *cogitationes,* built upon the former ones, could be constitutive of the scientific world. But was this thought not suggested, now, by Berkeley and Hume—under the presupposition that the absurdity of their empiricism lay only in [a belief] that was *supposedly obvious,* through which immanent reason had been driven out in advance? Through Berkeley's and Hume's revival and radicalization of the Cartesian fundamental problem, "dogmatic" objectivism was, from the point of view of our critical presentation, *shaken* to the foundations. This is true not only of the *mathematizing objectivism,* so inspiring to people of the time, which actually ascribed to the world itself a mathematical-rational in-itself (which we copy, so to speak, better and better in our more or less perfect theories); it was also true of the *general objectivism* which had been dominant for millennia.

2. Reading *deren* for *dessen.*

§ 25.   *The "transcendental" motif in rationalism: Kant's conception of a transcendental philosophy.*

As is known, Hume has a particular place in history also because of the turn he brought about in the development of Kant's thinking. Kant himself says, in the much-quoted words, that Hume roused him from his dogmatic slumbers and gave his investigations in the field of speculative philosophy a different direction. Was it, then, the historical mission of Kant to experience the shaking of objectivism, of which I just spoke, and to undertake in his transcendental philosophy the solution of the task before which Hume drew back? The answer must be negative. It is a new sort of transcendental subjectivism which begins with Kant and changes into new forms in the systems of German idealism. Kant does not belong to the development which expands in a continuous line from Descartes through Locke, and he is not the successor of Hume. His interpretation of the Humean skepticism and the way in which he reacts against it are determined by his own provenance in the Wolffian school. The "revolution of the way of thinking" motivated by Hume's impulse is not directed against empiricism but against post-Cartesian rationalism's way of thinking, whose great consummator was Leibniz and which was given its systematic textbook-like presentation, its most effective and by far most convincing form, by Christian Wolff.

First of all, what is the meaning of the "dogmatism," taken quite generally, that Kant uproots? Although the *Meditations* continued to have their effect on post-Cartesian philosophy, the passionate radicalism which drove them was not passed on to Descartes's successors. They were quite prepared to accept what Descartes only wished to establish, and found so hard to establish, by inquiring back into the ultimate source of all knowledge: namely, the absolute metaphysical validity of the objective sciences, or, taking these together, of philosophy as the one objective universal science; or, what comes to the same thing, the right of the knowing ego to let its rational constructs, in virtue of the self-evidences occurring in its *mens,* count as nature with a meaning transcending this ego. The new conception of the world of bodies, self-enclosed as nature, and the natural sciences related to them, the correlative conception of the self-enclosed souls and the task, related to them, of a new psychology with a rational method according to the mathematical model—all this had established itself. In every direction rational philosophy was under construction; of primary interest were discoveries, theories, the rigor of their inferences, and correspondingly the general problem of method and its perfection. Thus knowledge was very much discussed, and from a scientifically general point of view. This reflection on knowledge, however, was not *transcendental reflection* but rather a reflection on the *praxis of knowledge* and was thus similar to the reflection carried out by one who works in any other practical sphere of interest, the kind which is expressed in the general propositions of a *technology.* It is a matter of what we are accustomed to call logic, though in a traditional, very narrow, and limited sense. Thus we can say quite correctly (broadening the meaning): it is a matter of a logic as a theory of norms and a technology[1] with the fullest universality, to the end of attaining a universal philosophy.

The thematic direction was thus twofold: on the one hand, toward a systematic universe of "logical laws," the theoretical totality of the truths destined to function as norms for all judgments which shall be capable of being objectively true—and to this belongs, in addition to the old formal logic, also arithmetic, all of pure analytic mathematics, i.e., the *mathesis universalis* of Leibniz, and in general everything that is purely a priori.

On the other hand, the thematic direction was toward general considerations about those who make judgments as those striving for objective truth: how they are to make normative use of those laws so that the self-evidence through which a judgment is certified as objectively true can appear, and similarly about the ways and temptations of failure, etc.

Now clearly, in all the laws which are in the broader sense "logical," beginning with the principle of noncontradiction, *metaphysical truth* was contained *eo ipso.* The systematically worked-out theory of these laws had, of itself, the meaning of a general ontology. What happened here scientifically was the work of pure reason operating exclusively with concepts innate in the knowing soul. That these concepts, that logical laws, that

1. *Kunstlehre.* See Husserl's discussion of logic as a *Kunstlehre* in *Logische Untersuchungen,* Vol. I, Chapters I and II.

pure rational lawfulness in general contained metaphysical-objective truth was "obvious." Occasionally appeal was made to God as a guarantee, in remembrance of Descartes, with little concern for the fact that it was rational metaphysics which first had to establish God's existence.

Over against the faculty of pure a priori thinking, that of pure reason, stood that of sensibility, the faculty of outer and inner experience. The subject, affected in outer experience from "outside," thereby becomes certain of affecting objects, but in order to know them in their truth he needs pure reason, i.e., the system of norms in which reason displays itself, as the "logic" for all true knowledge of the objective world. Such is the [typical rationalist] conception.

As for Kant, who had been influenced by empiricist psychology: Hume had made him sensitive to the fact that between the pure truths of reason and metaphysical objectivity there remained a gulf of incomprehensibility, namely, as to how precisely these truths of reason could really guarantee the knowledge of things. Even the model rationality of the mathematical natural sciences was transformed into an enigma. That it owed its rationality, which was in fact quite indubitable—that is, its method—to the normative a priori of pure logicomathematical reason, and that the latter, in its disciplines, exhibited an unassailable pure rationality, remained unquestioned. Natural science is, to be sure, not purely rational insofar as it has need of outer experience, sensibility; but everything in it that is rational it owes to pure reason and its setting of norms; only through them can there be rationalized experience. As for sensibility, on the other hand, it had generally been assumed that it gives rise to the merely sensible data, precisely as a result of affection from the outside. And yet one acted as if the experiential world of the prescientific man—the world not yet logicized by mathematics—was the world pregiven by mere sensibility.

Hume had shown that we naïvely read causality into this world and think that we grasp necessary succession in intuition. The same is true of everything that makes the body of the everyday surrounding world into an identical thing with identical properties, relations, etc. (and Hume had in fact worked this out in detail in the *Treatise*, which was unknown to Kant). Data and complexes of data come and go, but the thing, presumed to be simply experienced sensibly, is not something sensible which persists through this alteration. The sensationalist thus declares it to be a fiction.

He is substituting, *we* shall say, mere sense-data for perception, which after all places *things* (everyday things) before our eyes. In other words, he overlooks the fact that mere sensibility, related to mere data of sense, cannot account for objects of experience. Thus he overlooks the fact that these objects of experience point to a hidden mental accomplishment and to the problem of what kind of an accomplishment this can be. From the very start, after all, it must be a kind which enables [the objects of] prescientific experience, through logic, mathematics, mathematical natural science, to be knowable with objective validity, i.e., with a necessity which can be accepted by and is binding for everyone.

But Kant says to himself: undoubtedly things appear, but only because the sense-data, already brought together in certain ways, in concealment, through a priori forms, are made logical in the course of their alteration—without any appeal to reason as manifested in logic and mathematics, without its being brought into normative function. Now is this quasilogical [function] something that is psychologically accidental? If we think of it as absent, can a mathematics, a logic of nature, ever have the possibility of knowing objects through mere sense-data?

These are, if I am not mistaken, the inwardly guiding thoughts of Kant. Kant now undertakes, in fact, to show, through a regressive procedure, that if common experience is really to be experience of *objects of nature,* objects which can really be knowable with objective truth, i.e., scientifically, in respect to their being and nonbeing, their being-such and being-otherwise [*So- und Andersbeschaffensein*], then the intuitively appearing world must already be a construct of the faculties of "pure intuition" and "pure reason," the same faculties that express themselves in explicit thinking in mathematics and logic.

In other words, reason has a *twofold* way of functioning and showing itself. One way is its systematic self-exposition, self-revelation in free and pure mathematizing, in the practice of the pure mathematical sciences. Here it presupposes the forming character of "pure intuition," which belongs to sensibility itself. The objective result of both faculties is pure mathematics as theory. The other way is that of reason constantly functioning in concealment, reason ceaselessly rationalizing sense-data and always having them as already rationalized. Its objective result is the sensibly intuited world of objects—the empirical presupposition of all natural-scientific thinking, i.e., the thinking which, through manifest mathematical reason, consciously gives norms to the experience of the surrounding world. Like the intuited world of bodies, the whole world of natural science (and with it the dualistic world which can be known scientifically) is a subjective construct of our intellect; only the material of the sense-data arises from a transcendent affection by "things in themselves." The latter are in principle inaccessible to (objective-scientific) knowledge. For according to this theory, man's science, as an accomplishment bound by the interplay of the subjective faculties "sensibility" and "reason" (or, as Kant says here, "understanding"), cannot explain the origin, the "cause," of the factual manifolds of sense-data. The ultimate presuppositions of the possibility and actuality of objective knowledge cannot be objectively knowable.

Whereas natural science had pretended to be a branch of philosophy, the ultimate science of what is, and had believed itself capable of knowing, through its rationality, what is in itself, beyond the subjectivity of the factualities of knowledge, for Kant, now, *objective science*, as an accomplishment remaining within subjectivity, is separated off from his *philosophical* theory. The latter, as a theory of the accomplishments necessarily carried out within subjectivity, and thus as a theory of the possibility and scope of objective knowledge, reveals the naïveté of the supposed rational philosophy of nature-in-itself.

We know how this critique is for Kant nevertheless the beginning of a philosophy in the old sense, for the universe of being, thus extending even to the *rationally* unknowable in-itself —how, under the titles "critique of practical reason" and "critique of judgment," he not only limits philosophical claims but also believes he is capable of opening ways toward the "scientifically" unknowable in-itself. Here we shall not go into this. What interests us now is—speaking in formal generality—that Kant, reacting against the data-positivism of Hume (as he understands it) outlines a great, systematically constructed, and *in a new way* still scientific philosophy in which the Cartesian turn to conscious subjectivity works itself out in the form of a transcendental subjectivism.[2]

Irrespective of the truth of the Kantian philosophy, about which we need not pass judgment here, we must not pass over the fact that Hume, as he is understood by Kant, is not the real Hume.

2. See note 4 in this section.

Kant speaks of the "Humean problem." What is the actual problem, the one which drives Hume *himself*? We find it when we transform Hume's skeptical theory, his total claim, back into his *problem*, extending it to those consequences which do not quite find their complete expression in the theory—although it is difficult to suppose that a genius with a spirit like Hume's did not see these consequences, which are not expressly drawn and not theoretically treated. If we proceed in this way, we find nothing less than this universal problem:

How is the *naïve obviousness* of the certainty of the world, the certainty in which we live—and, what is more, the certainty of the *everyday* world as well as that of the sophisticated theoretical constructions built upon this everyday world—to be made comprehensible? [3]

What is, in respect to sense and validity, the "objective world," objectively true being, and also the objective truth of science, once we have seen universally with Hume (and in respect to nature even with Berkeley) that "world" is a validity which has sprung up within subjectivity, indeed—speaking from my point of view, who am now philosophizing—one which has sprung up within *my* subjectivity, with all the content it ever counts as having for me?

The *naïveté* of speaking about "objectivity" without ever considering subjectivity as experiencing, knowing, and actually concretely accomplishing, the *naïveté* of the scientist of nature or of the world in general, who is blind to the fact that all the truths he attains as objective truths and the objective world itself as the substratum of his formulae (the everyday world of experience as well as the higher-level conceptual world of knowledge) are his own *life-construct* developed within himself—this naïveté is naturally no longer possible as soon as *life* becomes the point of focus. And must this liberation not come to anyone who seriously immerses himself in the *Treatise* and, after unmasking Hume's naturalistic presuppositions, becomes conscious of the power of his motivation?

But how is this most radical subjectivism, which subjectivizes the world itself, comprehensible? The world-enigma in the deepest and most ultimate sense, the enigma of a world whose being is being through subjective accomplishment, and this with

3. Husserl plays on words: how is the naïve *Selbstverständlichkeit* of our certainty of the world to be transformed into a true *Verständlichkeit*?

the self-evidence that another world cannot be at all conceivable
—that, and nothing else, is *Hume's problem.*

Kant, however, for whom, as can easily be seen, so many
presuppositions are "obviously" valid, presuppositions which in
the Humean sense are included within this world-enigma, never
penetrated to the enigma itself. For his set of problems stands on
the ground of the rationalism extending from Descartes through
Leibniz to Wolff.

In this way, through the problem of rational natural science
which primarily guides and determines Kant's thinking, we seek
to make understandable Kant's position, so difficult to interpret,
in relation to his historical setting. What particularly interests us
now—speaking first in formal generality—is the fact that in
reaction to the Humean data-positivism, which in his fictionalism gives up philosophy as a science, a great and systematically
constructed scientific philosophy appears for the *first time since
Descartes*—a philosophy which must be called *transcendental
subjectivism.*[4]

§ 26. *Preliminary discussion of the concept of the "transcendental" which guides us here.*

I SHOULD LIKE TO NOTE the following right away: the
expression "transcendental philosophy" has been much used
since Kant, even as a general title for universal philosophies
whose concepts are oriented toward those of the Kantian type. I
myself use the word "transcendental" *in the broadest sense* for
the original motif, discussed in detail above, which through
Descartes confers meaning upon all modern philosophies, the
motif which, in all of them, seeks to come to itself, so to speak
—seeks to attain the genuine and pure form of its task and its
systematic development. It is the motif of inquiring back into the
ultimate source of all the formations of knowledge, the motif of
the knower's reflecting upon himself and his knowing life in

4. This sentence is almost identical to the sentence indicated by
note 2 above, which gives a good indication of the rough state of the
missing MS, even though it was submitted and published in *Philosophia.* See Translator's Introduction, p. xviii.

which all the scientific structures that are valid for him occur purposefully, are stored up as acquisitions, and have become and continue to become freely available. Working itself out radically, it is the motif of a universal philosophy which is grounded purely in this source and thus ultimately grounded. This source bears the title *I-myself*, with all of my actual and possible knowing life and, ultimately, my concrete life in general. The whole transcendental set of problems circles around the relation of *this*, my "I"—the "ego"—to what it is at first taken for granted to be—my soul—and, again, around the relation of this ego and my conscious life to the *world* of which I am conscious and whose true being I know through my own cognitive structures.

Of course this most general concept of the "transcendental" cannot be supported by documents; it is not to be gained through the internal exposition and comparison of the individual systems. Rather, it is a concept acquired by pondering the coherent history of the entire philosophical modern period: the concept of its task which is demonstrable only in this way, lying within it as the driving force of its development, striving forward from vague *dynamis* towards its *energeia*.

This is only a preliminary indication, which has already been prepared to a certain extent by our historical analysis up to this point; our subsequent presentations are to establish the justification for our kind of "teleological" approach to history and its methodical function for the definitive construction of a transcendental philosophy which satisfies its most proper meaning. This preliminary indication of a radical transcendental subjectivism will naturally seem strange and arouse skepticism. I welcome this, *if* this skepticism bespeaks, not the prior resolve of rejection, but rather a free withholding of any judgment.

§ 27. *The philosophy of Kant and his followers seen from the perspective of our guiding concept of the "transcendental." The task of taking a critical position.*

RETURNING AGAIN TO KANT: his system can certainly be characterized, in the general sense defined, as one of "transcendental philosophy," although it is far from accomplishing a truly radical grounding of philosophy, the totality of all sciences. Kant never permitted himself to enter the vast depths of the Cartesian fundamental investigation, and his own set of problems never caused him to seek in these depths for ultimate groundings and decisions. Should I, in the following presentations, succeed—as I hope—in awakening the insight that a transcendental philosophy is the more genuine, and better fulfills its vocation as philosophy, the more radical it is and, finally, that it comes to its actual and true existence, to its actual and true beginning, only when the philosopher has penetrated to a clear understanding of himself as the subjectivity functioning as primal source, we should still have to recognize, on the other hand, that Kant's philosophy is on the *way* to this, that it is in accord with the formal, general sense of a transcendental philosophy in our definition. It is a philosophy which, in opposition to prescientific and scientific objectivism, goes back to knowing subjectivity as the primal locus of all objective formations of sense and ontic validities, undertakes to understand the existing world as a structure of sense and validity, and in this way seeks to set in motion an essentially new type of scientific attitude and a new type of philosophy. In fact, if we do not count the negativistic, skeptical philosophy of a Hume, the Kantian system is the first attempt, and one carried out with impressive scientific seriousness, at a truly universal transcendental philosophy meant to be a *rigorous science* in a sense of scientific rigor which has only now been discovered and which is the only genuine sense.

Something similar holds, we can say in advance, for the great continuations and revisions of Kantian transcendentalism in the great systems of German Idealism. They all share the basic conviction that the objective sciences (no matter how much they, and particularly the exact sciences, may consider themselves, in virtue of their obvious theoretical and practical accomplishments, to be in possession of the only true method and to be treasure houses of ultimate truths) are not seriously sciences at all, not cognitions ultimately grounded, i.e., not ultimately, theoretically responsible for themselves—and that they are not, then, cognitions of what exists in ultimate truth. This can be accomplished [according to German Idealism] only by a transcendental-subjective method and, carried through as a system, transcendental philosophy. As was already the case with Kant, the opinion is not that the self-evidence of the positive-scientific method is an illusion and its accomplishment an illusory accomplishment but rather that this self-evidence is itself a *problem;* that the objective-scientific method rests upon a never questioned, deeply concealed subjective ground whose philosophical elucidation will for the first time reveal the true meaning of the accomplishments of positive science and, correlatively, the true ontic meaning of the objective world—precisely as a transcendental-subjective meaning.

Now in order to be able to understand the position of Kant and of the systems of transcendental idealism proceeding from him, within modern philosophy's teleological unity of meaning, and thus to make progress in our own self-understanding, it is necessary to critically get closer to the style of Kant's scientific attitude and to clarify the lack of radicalism we are attacking in his philosophizing. It is with good reason that we pause over Kant, a significant turning point in modern history. The critique to be directed against him will reflect back and elucidate all earlier philosophical history, namely, in respect to the general meaning of scientific discipline which all earlier philosophies strove to realize—as the only meaning which lay and could possibly lie within their spiritual horizon. Precisely in this way a more profound concept—the most important of all—of "objectivism" will come to the fore (more important than the one we were able to define earlier), and with it the genuinely radical meaning of the opposition between objectivism and transcendentalism.

Yet, over and above this, the more concrete critical analyses of the conceptual structures of the Kantian turn, and the contrast between it and the Cartesian turn, will set in motion our own concurrent thinking in such a way as to place us, gradually and of its own accord, before the *final turn* and the final decisions. We ourselves shall be drawn into an inner transformation through which we shall come face to face with, to *direct experience* of, the long-felt but constantly concealed dimension of the "transcendental." The ground of experience, opened up in its infinity, will then become the fertile soil of a methodical working philosophy, with the self-evidence, furthermore, that all conceivable philosophical and scientific problems of the past are to be posed and decided by starting from this ground.

PART III

The Clarification of the Transcendental Problem and the Related Function of Psychology[1]

1. The appendix to the German edition contains a manuscript entitled "Foreword to the Continuation of the *Crisis*," which begins with the following paragraph:

"Herewith appears, unfortunately very much delayed, the continuation of this work which was begun in the first volume of *Philosophia* with two introductory sections. Insurmountable inhibitions, the effects of my faltering health, forced me to neglect drafts which were long since ready. With this there arose a pause which is dangerous for the understanding of the teleological-historical way attempted here to the conception of the idea and method of transcendental phenomenology. The resulting situation has become somewhat similar to that which would arise if the presentation of a great musical work were to break off with the conclusion of the overture, and indeed in such a way that the actual work (the opera itself) to which it points the way, and which it has created a vital readiness to understand, was then to be performed sometime later without repetition of the overture" (*Krisis*, p. 435).

The rest of this "Foreword" (some 11 pages) reveals that it was destined for a revision of Part III which was never made. It gives reasons for postponing the further critique of Kant promised at the end of Part II in favor of a nonhistorical exposition, presumably that of the life-world; whereas the extant version of Part III does deal with Kant at the beginning. It is for this reason that I have not included a full translation of this text. Some interesting passages are quoted in the Translator's Introduction, pp. xxviii f. (See also p. xviii, note 5.)

A.

The Way into Phenomenological Transcendental Philosophy by Inquiring back from the Pregiven Life-World

§ 28. *Kant's unexpressed "presupposition": the surrounding world of life, taken for granted as valid.*

KANT IS CERTAIN that his philosophy will bring the dominant rationalism to its downfall by exhibiting the inadequacy of its foundations. He rightly reproaches rationalism for neglecting questions which should have been its fundamental questions; that is, it had never penetrated to the subjective structure of our world-consciousness prior to and within scientific knowledge and thus had never asked how the world, which appears straightforwardly to us men, and to us as scientists, comes to be knowable a priori—how, that is, the exact science of nature is possible, the science for which, after all, pure mathematics, together with a further pure a priori, is the instrument of all knowledge which is objective, [i.e.,] unconditionally valid for everyone who is rational (who thinks logically).

But Kant, for his part, has no idea that in his philosophizing he stands on unquestioned presuppositions and that the undoubtedly great discoveries in his theories are there only in concealment; that is, they are not there as finished results, just as the theories themselves are not finished theories, i.e., do not have a definitive scientific form. What he offers demands new work and, above all, critical analysis. An example of a great discovery—a merely preliminary discovery—is the "understanding" which has, in respect to nature, two functions: [1] understanding interpreting itself, in explicit self-reflection, as normative laws, and, on the other hand, understanding ruling in concealment, i.e., ruling as constitutive of the always already developed and always further developing meaning-configuration "intuitively given surrounding world." This discovery could never be actually grounded or even be fully comprehensible in the manner of the Kantian theory, i.e., as a result of his merely regressive method. In the "transcendental deduction" of the first edition of the *Critique of Pure Reason* Kant makes an approach to a direct grounding, one which descends to the original sources, only to break off again almost at once without arriving at the genuine problems of foundation which are to be opened up from this supposedly psychological side.

We shall begin our considerations by showing that Kant's inquiries in the critique of reason have an unquestioned ground of presuppositions which codetermine the meaning of his questions. Sciences to whose truths and methods Kant attributes actual validity become a problem, and with them the spheres of being [*Seinssphären*] themselves to which these sciences refer. They become a problem in virtue of certain questions which take knowing subjectivity, too, into account, questions which find their answer in theories about transcendentally forming subjectivity, about the transcendental achievements of sensibility, of the understanding, etc., and, on the highest level, theories about functions of the "I" of "transcendental apperception." What had become an enigma, the achievement of mathematical natural science and of pure mathematics (in our broadened sense) as its logical method, was supposed to have been made comprehensible through these theories; but the theories also led to a revolutionary reinterpretation of the actual ontic meaning of nature as the world of possible experience and possible knowledge and thus correlatively to the reinterpretation of the actual truth-meaning of the sciences concerned.

Naturally, from the very start in the Kantian manner of posing questions, the everyday surrounding world of life is presupposed as existing—the surrounding world in which all of us (even I who am now philosophizing) consciously have our existence; here are also the sciences, as cultural facts in this world, with their scientists and theories. In this world we are objects among objects in the sense of the life-world, namely, as being

1. Reading ". . . ist der hinsichtlich der Natur doppelt fungierende Verstand. . . ."

here and there, in the plain certainty of experience, before anything that is established scientifically, whether in physiology,
psychology, or sociology. On the other hand, we are subjects for
this world, namely, as the ego-subjects experiencing it, contem-
plating it, valuing it, related to it purposefully; for us this surrounding world has only the ontic meaning given to it by our
experiencings, our thoughts, our valuations, etc.; and it has the
modes of validity (certainty of being, possibility, perhaps illusion, etc.) which we, as the subjects of validity, at the same time
bring about or else possess from earlier on as habitual acquisitions and bear within us as validities of such and such a content
which we can reactualize at will. To be sure, all this undergoes
manifold alterations, whereas "the" world, as existing in a unified way, persists throughout, being corrected only in its content.

Clearly the content-alteration of the perceived object, being
change or motion perceived as belonging to the object itself, is
distinguished with self-evidence from the alteration of its manners of appearing (e.g., the perspectives, the near and far
appearances) through which something objective of this type exhibits itself as being itself present. We see this in the change of
[our] attitude. [If we are] directed straightforwardly toward the
object and what belongs to it, [our] gaze passes through the
appearances toward what continuously appears through their
continuous unification: the object, with the ontic validity of the
mode "itself present." In the reflective attitude, [by contrast,] we
have not a one but a manifold. Now the sequence of the appearances themselves is thematic, rather than what appears in them.
Perception is the primal mode of intuition [*Anschauung*]; it
exhibits with primial originality, that is, in the mode of self-pres-
ence. In addition, there are other modes of intuition which in
themselves consciously have the character of [giving us] modifications of this "itself there" as themselves present. These are
presentifications, modifications of presentations; [2] they make us
conscious of the modalities of time, e.g., not that which *is*-itself-
there but that which *was*-itself-there or that which is in the
future, that which *will-be*-itself-there. Presentifying intuitions
"recapitulate"—in certain modifications belonging to them—all
the manifolds of appearance through which what is objective
exhibits itself perceptively. Recollecting intuition, for example,

2. *Vergegenwärtigungen*, i.e., modifications of *Gegenwärtigun-
gen*. The former are explicit acts of rendering consciously present
that which is not "itself present," as in the case of recollection or imag-
ination.

shows the object as having-been-itself-there, recapitulating the perspectivization and other manners of appearing, though in recollective modifications. I am now conscious of this perspectivization as one which has been, a sequence of subjective "exhibitions of," having-been in my earlier ontic validities.

Here we can now clarify the very limited justification for speaking of a sense-world, a world of sense-intuition, a sensible world of appearances. In all the verifications of the life of our natural interests, which remain purely in the life-world, the return to "sensibly" experiencing intuition plays a prominent role. For everything that exhibits itself in the life-world as a concrete thing obviously has a bodily character, even if it is not a mere body, as, for example, an animal or a cultural object, i.e., even if it also has psychic or otherwise spiritual properties. If we pay attention now purely to the bodily aspect of the things, this obviously exhibits itself perceptively only in seeing, in touching, in hearing, etc., i.e., in visual, tactual, acoustical, and other such aspects. Obviously and inevitably participating in this is our living body, which is never absent from the perceptual field, and specifically its corresponding "organs of perception" (eyes, hands, ears, etc.). In consciousness they play a constant role here; specifically they function in seeing, hearing, etc., together with the ego's motility belonging to them, i.e., what is called kinesthesis. All kinestheses, each being an "I move," "I do," [etc.] are bound together in a comprehensive unity—in which kinesthetic holding-still is [also] a mode of the "I do." Clearly the aspect-exhibitions of whatever body is appearing in perception, and the kinestheses, are not processes [simply running] alongside each other; rather, they work together in such a way that the aspects have the ontic meaning of, or the validity of, aspects of the body only through the fact that they are those aspects continually required by the kinestheses—by the kinesthetic-sensual total situation in each of its working variations of the total kinesthesis by setting in motion this or that particular kinesthesis—and that they correspondingly fulfill the requirement.

Thus sensibility, the ego's active functioning of the living body or the bodily organs, belongs in a fundamental, essential way to all experience of bodies. It proceeds in consciousness not as a mere series of body-appearances, as if these in themselves, through themselves alone and their coalescences, were appearance of bodies; rather, they are such in consciousness only in combination with the kinesthetically functioning living body [*Leiblichkeit*], the ego functioning here in a peculiar sort of activity and habituality. In a quite unique way the living body is constantly in the perceptual field quite immediately, with a completely unique ontic meaning, precisely the meaning indicated by the word "organ" (here used in its most primitive sense), [namely, as] that through which I exist in a completely unique way and quite immediately as the ego of affection and actions, [as that] in which I hold sway [3] quite immediately, kinesthetically—articulated into particular organs through which I hold sway, or potentially hold sway, in particular kinestheses corresponding to them. And this "holding-sway," here exhibited as functioning in all perception of bodies—the familiar, total system of kinestheses available to consciousness—is actualized in the particular kinesthetic situation [and] is perpetually bound to a [general] situation in which bodies appear, i.e., that of the field of perception. To the variety of appearances through which a body is perceivable as this one-and-the-same body correspond, in their own way, the kinestheses which belong to this body; as these kinestheses are allowed to run their course, the corresponding required appearances must show up in order to be appearances of this body at all, i.e., in order to be appearances which exhibit in themselves this body with its properties.

Thus, purely in terms of perception, physical body and living body [*Körper und Leib*] [4] are essentially different; living body, that is, [understood] as the only one which is actually given [to me as such] in perception: my own living body. How the consciousness originates through which my living body nevertheless acquires the ontic validity of one physical body among others, and how, on the other hand, certain physical bodies in my perceptual field come to count as living bodies, living bodies of "alien" ego-subjects—these are now necessary questions.

In our reflections we confined ourselves to the perceiving consciousness of things, to one's own perceiving of them, to my perceptual field. Here my own living body alone, and never an alien living body, can be perceived *as* living; the latter is per-

3. *walten.* "Holding sway" is somewhat awkward in English, but it seems to best approximate Husserl's use of this archaic term. The latter is often used in religious language (*Gottes Walten*) to signify God's rule and power over the world and his intervention in its affairs. The English "wield" is related to it but is transitive. Husserl uses the term primarily in connection with the living body (unlike Heidegger, who resurrected it for a different purpose), meaning one's "wielding" of the body and its organs so as to have some control of one's surroundings.

4. See § 9, note 15.

ceived only as a physical body. In my perceptual field I find myself holding sway as ego through my organs and generally through everything belonging to me as an ego in my ego-acts and faculties. However, though the objects of the life-world, if they are to show their very own being, necessarily show themselves as physical bodies, this does not mean that they show themselves only in this way; and [similarly] we, though we are related through the living body to all objects which exist for us, are not related to them solely as a living body. Thus if it is a question of objects in the perceptual field, we are perceptually also in the field; [5] and the same is true, in modification, of every intuitive field, and even of every nonintuitive one, since we are obviously capable of "representing" to ourselves everything which is nonintuitively before us (though we are sometimes temporally limited in this). [Being related] "through the living body" clearly does not mean merely [being related] "as a physical body"; rather, the expression refers to the kinesthetic, to functioning as an ego in this peculiar way, primarily through seeing, hearing, etc.; and of course other modes of the ego belong to this (for example, lifting, carrying, pushing, and the like).

But being an ego through the living body [*die leibliche Ichlichkeit*] is of course not the only way of being an ego, and none of its ways can be severed from the others; throughout all their transformations they form a unity. Thus we are concretely in the field of perception, etc., and in the field of consciousness, however broadly we may conceive this, through our living body, but not only in this way, as full ego-subjects, each of us as the full-fledged "I-the-man." Thus in whatever way we may be conscious of the world as universal horizon, as coherent universe of existing objects, we, each "I-the-man" and all of us together, belong to the world as living with one another in the world; and the world is our world, valid for our consciousness as existing precisely through this "living together." We, as living in wakeful world-consciousness, are constantly active on the basis of our passive having of the world; it is from there, by objects pregiven in consciousness, that we are affected; it is to this or that object that we pay attention, according to our interests; with them we deal actively in different ways; through our acts they are "thematic" objects. As an example I give the observant explication of the properties of something which appears perceptively, or our activity of combining, relating, actively identifying and distin-

5. I.e., as a physical body (*Körper*).

guishing, or our active evaluation, our projection of plans, our active realization of the planned means and ends.

As subjects of acts (ego-subjects) we are directed toward thematic objects in modes of primary and secondary, and perhaps also peripheral, directedness. In this preoccupation with the objects the acts themselves are not thematic. But we are capable of coming back and reflecting on ourselves and our current activity: it now becomes thematic and objective through a new act, the vitally functioning one, which itself is now unthematic.

The consciousness of the world, then, is in constant motion; we are conscious of the world always in terms of some object-content or other, in the alteration of the different ways of being conscious (intuitive, nonintuitive, determined, undetermined, etc.) and also in the alteration of affection and action, in such a way that there is always a total sphere of affection and such that the affecting objects are now thematic, now unthematic; here we also find ourselves, we who always and inevitably belong to the affective sphere, always functioning as subjects of acts but only occasionally being thematically objective as the object of preoccupation with ourselves.

Obviously this is true not only for me, the individual ego; rather we, in living together, have the world pregiven in this "together," as the world valid as existing for us and to which we, together, belong, the world as world for all, pregiven with this ontic meaning. Constantly functioning in wakeful life, we also function together, in the manifold ways of considering, together, objects pregiven to us in common, thinking together, valuing, planning, acting together. Here we find also that particular thematic alteration in which the we-subjectivity, somehow constantly functioning, becomes a thematic object, whereby the acts through which it functions also become thematic, though always with a residuum which remains unthematic—remains, so to speak, anonymous—namely, the reflections which are functioning in connection with this theme.*

* Naturally all activity, and thus also this reflecting activity, gives rise to its habitual acquisitions. In observing, we attain habitual knowledge, acquaintance with the object which exists for us in terms of its previously unknown characteristics—and the same is true of self-knowledge through self-observation. In the evaluation of ourselves and the plans and actions related to ourselves and our fellows, we likewise attain self-values and ends concerning ourselves [which become] our habitually persisting validities. But all knowledge in general, all value-validities and ends in general, are, as having been

Considering ourselves in particular as the scientists that we here factually find ourselves to be, what corresponds to our particular manner of being as scientists is our present functioning in the manner of scientific thinking, putting questions and answering them theoretically in relation to nature or the world of the spirit; and [the latter are] at first nothing other than the one or the other aspect of the life-world which, in advance, is already valid, which we experience or are otherwise conscious of either prescientifically or scientifically. Cofunctioning here are the other scientists who, united with us in a community of theory, acquire and have the same truths or, in the communalization of accomplishing acts, are united with us in a critical transaction aimed at critical agreement. On the other hand, we can be for others, and they for us, mere objects; rather than being together in the unity of immediate, driving, common theoretical interest, we can get to know one another observingly, taking note of others' acts of thought, acts of experiencing, and possibly other acts as objective facts, but "disinterestedly," without joining in performing these acts, without critically assenting to them or taking exception to them.

Naturally, all these things are the most obvious of the obvious. Must one speak about them, and with so much ado? In life certainly not. But not as a philosopher either? Is this not the opening-up of a realm, indeed an infinite realm, of always ready and available but never questioned ontic validities? Are they not *constant presuppositions* of scientific and, at the highest level, philosophical thinking? Not, however, that it would or could ever be a matter of utilizing these ontic validities in their objective truth.

It belongs to what is taken for granted, prior to all scientific thought and all philosophical questioning, that the world is—always is in advance—and that every correction of an opinion, whether an experiential or other opinion, presupposes the already existing world, namely, as a horizon of what in the given case is indubitably valid as existing, and presupposes within this horizon something familiar and doubtlessly certain with which that which is perhaps canceled out as invalid came into conflict. Objective science, too, asks questions only on the ground of this world's existing in advance through prescientific life. Like all praxis, objective science presupposes the being of this world, but

---

acquired through our activity, at the same time persisting properties of ourselves as ego-subjects, as persons, and can be found in the reflective attitude as making up our own being.

it sets itself the task of transposing knowledge which is imperfect and prescientific in respect of scope and constancy into perfect knowledge—in accord with an idea of a correlative which is, to be sure, infinitely distant, i.e., of a world which in itself is fixed and determined and of truths which are *idealiter* scientific ("truths-in-themselves") and which predicatively interpret this world. To realize this in a systematic process, in stages of perfection, through a method which makes possible a constant advance: this is the task.

For the human being in his surrounding world there are many types of praxis, and among them is this peculiar and historically late one, theoretical praxis. It has its own professional methods; it is the art of theories, of discovering and securing truths with a certain new ideal sense which is foreign to prescientific life, the sense of a certain "final validity," "universal validity."

Here we have again offered an example of exhibiting what is "obvious," but this time in order to make clear that in respect to all these manifold validities-in-advance, i.e., "presuppositions" of the philosopher, there arise questions of being in a new and immediately highly enigmatic dimension. These questions, too, concern the obviously existing, ever intuitively pregiven world; but they are not questions belonging to that professional praxis and $\tau \epsilon \chi \nu \eta$ which is called objective science, not questions belonging to that art of grounding and broadening the realm of objectively scientific truths about this surrounding world; rather, they are questions of how the object, the prescientifically and then the scientifically true object, stands in relation to all the subjective elements which everywhere have a voice in what is taken for granted in advance.

§ 29. *The life-world can be disclosed as a realm of subjective phenomena which have remained "anonymous."*

WHEN WE PROCEED, philosophizing with Kant, not by starting from his beginning and moving forward in his paths but by inquiring back into what was thus taken for granted (that of which Kantian thinking, like everyone's thinking, makes use as

unquestioned and available), when we become conscious of it as
"presuppositions" and accord these their own universal and theoretical interest, there opens up to us, to our growing astonishment, an infinity of ever new phenomena belonging to a new
dimension, coming to light only through consistent penetration
into the meaning- and validity-implications of what was thus
taken for granted—an infinity, because continued penetration
shows that every phenomenon attained through this unfolding
of meaning, given at first in the life-world as obviously existing,
itself contains meaning- and validity-implications whose exposition leads again to new phenomena, and so on. These are purely
subjective phenomena throughout, but not merely facts involving psychological processes of sense-data; rather, they are mental [geistige] processes which, as such, exercise with essential
necessity the function of constituting forms of meaning
[Sinnesgestalten]. But they constitute them in each case out of
mental "material" which [itself] proves in turn, with essential
necessity, to be mental form, i.e., to be constituted; just as any
newly developed form [of meaning] is destined to become material, namely, to function in the constitution of [some new] form.

No objective science, no psychology—which, after all,
sought to become the universal science of the subjective—and
no philosophy has ever made thematic and thereby actually
discovered this realm of the subjective—not even the Kantian
philosophy, which sought, after all, to go back to the subjective
conditions of the possibility of an objectively experienceable and
knowable world. It is a realm of something subjective which is
completely closed off within itself, existing in its own way, functioning in all experiencing, all thinking, all life, thus everywhere
inseparably involved; yet it has never been held in view, never
been grasped and understood.

Does philosophy fulfill the sense of its primal establishment
as the universal and ultimately grounding science if it leaves this
realm to its "anonymity"? Can it do this, can any science do this
which seeks to be a branch of philosophy, i.e., which would
tolerate no presuppositions, no basic sphere of beings beneath
itself of which no one knows, which no one interrogates scientifically, which no one has mastered in a knowing way? I called the
sciences in general branches of philosophy, whereas it is such a
common conviction that the objective, the positive, sciences
stand on their own, are self-sufficient in virtue of their supposedly fully grounding and thus exemplary method. But in the end
is not the teleological unifying meaning running through all

attempted systems in the whole history of philosophy that of achieving a breakthrough for the insight that science is only possible at all as universal philosophy, the latter being, in all the sciences, yet a single science, possible only as the totality of all knowledge? And did this not imply that they all repose upon *one* single ground [*Grund*], one to be investigated scientifically in advance of all the others? And can this ground be, I may add, any other than precisely that of the anonymous subjectivity we mentioned? But one could and can realize this only when one finally and quite seriously inquires into that which is *taken for granted*, which is presupposed by all thinking, all activity of life with all its ends and accomplishments, and when one, by consistently interrogating the ontic and validity-meaning of these ends and accomplishments, becomes aware of the inviolable unity of the complex of meaning and validity running through all mental accomplishments. This applies first of all to all the mental accomplishments which we human beings carry out in the world, as individual, personal, or cultural accomplishments. Before all such accomplishments there has always already been a universal accomplishment, presupposed by all human praxis and all prescientific and scientific life. The latter have the spiritual acquisitions of this universal accomplishment as their constant substratum, and all their own acquisitions are destined to flow into it. We shall come to understand that the world which constantly exists for us through the flowing alteration of manners of givenness is a universal mental acquisition, having developed as such and at the same time continuing to develop as the unity of a mental configuration, as a meaning-construct [*Sinngebilde*]—as the construct of a universal, ultimately functioning [1] subjectivity. It belongs essentially to this world-constituting accomplishment that subjectivity objectifies itself as human subjectivity, as an element of the world. All objective consideration of the world is consideration of the "exterior" and grasps only "externals," objective entities [*Objektivitäten*]. The radical consideration of the world is the systematic and purely internal consideration of the subjectivity which "expresses" [or "externalizes"] [2] itself in the exterior. It is like the unity of a living organism, which one can certainly consider and dissect from the outside but which one can understand only if one goes back to its hidden roots and systematically pursues the life

1. *letztfungierende*, i.e., functioning at the ultimate or deepest level.
2. *der sich selbst im Aussen "äussernden" Subjektivität.*

which, in all its accomplishments, is in them and strives upward from them, shaping from within. But is this not simply a metaphor? Is it not in the end our human being, and the life of consciousness belonging to it, with its most profound world-problematics, which is the place where all problems of living inner being and external exhibition are to be decided?

§ 30. *The lack of an intuitive exhibiting method as the reason for Kant's mythical constructions.*

THERE IS SOME COMPLAINT about the obscurities of the Kantian philosophy, about the incomprehensibility of the evidences of his regressive method, his transcendental-subjective "faculties," "functions," "formations," about the difficulty of understanding what transcendental subjectivity actually is, how its function, its accomplishment, comes about, how this is to make all objective science understandable. And in fact Kant does get involved in his own sort of mythical talk, whose literal meaning points to something subjective, but a mode of the subjective which we are in principle unable to make intuitive to ourselves, whether through factual examples or through genuine analogy. If we try to do it with the intuitively negotiable meaning to which the words refer, we find ourselves in the psychological sphere of the human person, the soul. But then we remember the Kantian doctrine of inner sense, according to which everything that can be exhibited in the self-evidence of inner experience has already been formed by a transcendental function, that of temporalization [*Zeitigung*]. But how are we supposed to arrive at a clear meaning for concepts of something transcendentally subjective, out of which the scientifically true world constitutes itself as objective "appearance," if we cannot give to "inner perception" some meaning other than the psychological one—if it is not a truly apodictic meaning which ultimately furnishes the experiential ground (a ground like that of the Cartesian *ego cogito*), [available to us] through a type of experience which is not Kantian scientific experience and does not have the certainty of objective being in the sense of science, as in physics, but is a truly apodictic certainty, that of a universal ground which finally can be exhibited as the apodictically necessary and ultimate

ground of all scientific objectivity and makes the latter understandable? This is where the source of all ultimate concepts of
knowledge must lie; here is the source of essential, general
insights through which any objective world can become scientifically understandable and through which an absolutely self-sup-
porting philosophy can achieve systematic development.

Perhaps a deeper critique could show that Kant, though he
attacks empiricism, still remains dependent upon this very empiricism in his conception of the soul and the range of tasks of a
psychology, that what counts for him as the soul is the soul
which is made part of nature and conceived of as a component
of the psychophysical human being within the time of nature,
within space-time. Hence the transcendentally subjective could
certainly not be [identical with] the psychic. But is truly apodictic inner perception (self-perception reduced to the truly apodictic) to be identified with the self-perception of this naturalized
soul, with its [supposed] self-evidence of the "writing tablet" and
its data and even of its faculties as the powers ascribed to it in
the manner of natural powers? Because he understands inner
perception in this empiricist, psychological sense and because,
warned by Hume's skepticism, he fears every recourse to the
psychological as an absurd perversion of the genuine problem of
the understanding, Kant gets involved in his mythical concept-
formation. He forbids his readers to transpose the results of his
regressive procedure into intuitive concepts, forbids every attempt to carry out a progressive construction which begins with
original and purely self-evident intuitions and proceeds through
truly self-evident individual steps. His transcendental concepts
are thus unclear in a quite peculiar way, such that for reasons of
principle they can never be transposed into clarity, can never be
transformed into a formation of meaning which is direct and
procures self-evidence.

The clarity of all [these] concepts and problems posed would
have been quite different if Kant, instead of being a child of his
time, completely bound by its naturalistic psychology (as patterned after natural science and as its parallel), had tackled in a
truly radical way the problem of a priori knowledge and its
methodical function in rational objective knowledge. This would
have required a fundamentally and essentially different regressive method from that of Kant, which rests on those unquestioned assumptions: not a mythically, constructively inferring
[*schliessende*] method, but a thoroughly intuitively disclosing
[*erschliessende*] method, intuitive in its point of departure and in

everything it discloses—even though the concept of intuitiveness may have to undergo a considerable expansion in comparison to the Kantian one, and indeed even though intuition, here, may lose its usual sense altogether through a new attitude, taking on only the general sense of original self-exhibition, but precisely only within the new sphere of being.

Thus one must quite systematically inquire back into those things taken for granted which, not only for Kant but for all philosophers, all scientists, make up an unspoken ground [Grund] of their cognitive accomplishments, hidden in respect to its deeper mediating functions. Further, there must be a systematic disclosure of the intentionality which vitally holds sway and is sedimented in this ground—in other words, there must be a genuine, i.e., an "intentional analysis" of mental being in its absolute ultimate peculiarity and of that which has come to be in and through the mind, an analysis which does not permit the reigning psychology to substitute for it a realistic [reale] analysis of a naturalistically conceived soul, [which would be] alien to the essence of the mental.*

§ 31. *Kant and the inadequacy of the psychology of his day. The opaqueness of the distinction between transcendental subjectivity and soul.*

IN ORDER TO MAKE palpably understandable what is concretely meant here and in this way to illuminate the situation which was peculiarly opaque to that whole historical epoch, we

* Yet this [fault] does not lie in [a psychological] beginning. [In fact,] the first thing Kant [should have done, if he] had taken the everyday world as the world of human consciousness, was to pass through psychology—but a psychology which allowed the subjective experiences of world-consciousness actually to come to expression as they showed themselves experientially. This would have been possible if Descartes's seminal hints about *cogitata qua cogitata* had been brought to germination as intentional psychology instead of being overlooked by the dominant Lockean philosophy. [This note derives from a stenographic marginal comment, and Biemel's version of the first two sentences makes little sense. I have given what I hope is an understandable interpretation.—TRANS.]

shall initiate a reflection which admittedly belongs to a very late fulfillment of the sense of the historical process.

The pregiven point of departure for all the enigmas of knowledge was that of the development of a modern philosophy in accord with its own peculiar rationalistic ideal of science (systematically expanding itself into its special sciences). This thrust in the development of sometimes clearly successful, sometimes hopefully attempted special sciences was suddenly checked. In the construction of one of these sciences, psychology, enigmas emerged which put all of philosophy in question.

Naturally, the psychology of Locke—with the natural science of a Newton before it as a model—found particularly interesting subjects for study in the merely subjective aspects of the appearances (which had been maligned since Galileo) and likewise generally in everything coming from the subjective side that interfered with rationality: the lack of clarity in concepts, the vagueness of judgmental thinking, the faculties of the understanding and of reason in all their forms. It was, of course, a matter of the human being's faculties for psychic accomplishments—precisely those accomplishments which were supposed to procure genuine science and with it a genuine practical life of reason. Thus, questions of the essence and the objective validity of purely rational knowledge, of logical and mathematical knowledge, and the peculiar nature of natural-scientific and metaphysical knowledge belong in this sphere. Looked at in this general way, was this not actually required? Without doubt it was right and a good thing that Locke understood the sciences as psychic accomplishments (though he also directed his gaze too much at what occurs in the individual soul) and everywhere posed questions of origin. After all, accomplishments can be understood only in terms of the activity that accomplishes them. To be sure, in Locke this was done with a superficiality, an unmethodical confusion, and indeed even a naturalism that resulted precisely in Humean fictionalism.

Thus, obviously, Kant could not simply go back and take up the psychology of Locke. But was it for this reason correct to drop the general idea of the Lockean—the psychological-epistemological—approach? Was not every question inspired by Hume first and quite correctly to be taken as a psychological question? If rational science becomes a problem, if the claim of the purely a priori sciences to have unconditional objective validity, and thus to be the possible and necessary method for rational sciences of fact, becomes a problem, it should first be taken into consideration (as we emphasized above) that science in general is a human accomplishment, an accomplishment of human beings who find themselves in the world, the world of general experience, [and that it is] one among other types of practical accomplishments which is aimed at spiritual structures of a certain sort called theoretical. Like all praxis, this one is related, in a sense which is its own and of which the practitioner of it is conscious, to the pregiven world of experience and at the same time takes its ordered place within this world. Thus enigmas about how a spiritual accomplishment comes to pass can be clarified, one will say, only through psychological demonstrations, and they remain thus within the pregiven world. If Kant, on the other hand, in the questions he posed and in his regressive method, also naturally makes use of the pregiven world but at the same time constructs a transcendental subjectivity through whose concealed transcendental functions, with unswerving necessity, the world of experience is formed, he runs into the difficulty that a particular quality of the human soul (which itself belongs to the world and is thus presupposed with it) is supposed to accomplish and to have already accomplished a formative process which shapes this whole world. But as soon as we distinguish this transcendental subjectivity from the soul, we get involved in something incomprehensibly mythical.

§ 32. *The possibility of a hidden truth in Kant's transcendental philosophy: the problem of a "new dimension." The antagonism between the "life of the plane" and the "life of depth."*

WERE THE KANTIAN THEORY nevertheless to contain some truth, a truth to be made actually accessible to insight—which is indeed the case—it would be possible only through the fact that the transcendental functions which are supposed to explain the above-mentioned enigmas concerning objectively valid knowledge belong to a dimension of the living spirit that had to remain hidden, because of very natural inhibitions, from humanity and even from the scientists of the ages—whereas this dimension *can* be made accessible to scientific understanding, through a method of disclosure appropriate to it, as a realm of experiential and theoretical self-evidence. The fact that this dimension remained hidden through the ages, the fact that, even after it made itself felt, it never aroused a habitual and consistent theoretical interest, can (and will) be explained by displaying a peculiar antagonism between the entry into this dimension and the preoccupations involved in all the interests which make up the naturally normal human world-life.

Since this is to be a matter of spiritual functions which exercise their accomplishments in all experiencing and thinking, indeed in each and every preoccupation of the human world-life, functions through which the world of experience, as the constant horizon of existing things, values, practical plans, works, etc., has meaning and validity for us, it would certainly be understandable that all objective sciences would lack precisely the knowledge of what is most fundamental, namely, the knowledge of what could procure meaning and validity for the theoretical constructs of objective knowledge and [which] thus first gives them the dignity of a knowledge which is ultimately grounded.

This schema for a possible clarification of the problem of objective science reminds us of Helmholtz' well-known image of the plane-beings, who have no idea of the dimension of depth, in which their plane-world is a mere projection. Everything of which men—the scientists and all the others—can become conscious in their natural world-life (experiencing, knowing, practically planning, acting) as a field of external objects—as ends, means, processes of action, and final results related to these objects—and on the other hand, also, in self-reflection, as the spiritual life which functions thereby—all this remains on the "plane," which is, though unnoticed, nevertheless only a plane within an infinitely richer dimension of depth. But this [image] is universally valid whether it concerns a life which is merely practical in the usual sense or a theoretical life, [i.e.,] scientific experiencing, thinking, planning, acting, or scientific experiential data, ideas, goals of thinking, premises, true results.

This explanatory schema, of course, leaves several pressing questions open. How could the development of the positive sciences purely upon the "plane" appear for so long in the form of a superabundant success? Why was it so late before, in the need for complete transparency in its methodical accomplishments, the difficulties, indeed incomprehensibilities, announced themselves, such that not even the most painstaking construction of logical technique could improve the situation? Why did the later attempts at an "intuitionistic" deepening, which in fact touched upon the higher dimension, and all efforts to clarify the situation in this way not lead to unanimously accepted, truly compelling scientific results? It is *not* the case that this is a matter of merely turning our gaze toward a sphere which up to now has simply not been noticed but which is accessible without further effort to theoretical experience and experiential knowledge. Everything experienceable in this way is the object and domain of possible positive knowledge; it lies on the "plane," in the world of actual and possible experience, experience in the natural sense of the word. We shall soon understand what extraordinary difficulties —grounded in the essence of the matters involved—greeted the methodical efforts actually to approach the depth-sphere, to approach first of all the possibility of its pure grasp of itself in the manner of experiencing proper to it; and it will become clear thereby how great the antagonism is between the "patent" life of the plane and the "latent" life of depth. Of course the power of historical prejudices also plays a constant role here, especially of those which, coming from the origin of the modern positive sciences, dominate us all. It is of the very essence of such prejudices, drilled into the souls even of children, that they are concealed in their immediate effects. The abstract general will to be without prejudice changes nothing about them.

Nevertheless, these are the slightest difficulties compared to those which have their ground in the essence of the new dimension and its relation to the old familiar field of life. Nowhere else is the distance so great from unclearly arising needs to goal-determined plans, from vague questionings to first working problems—through which actual working science first begins. Nowhere else is it so frequent that the explorer is met by logical ghosts emerging out of the dark, formed in the old familiar and effective conceptual patterns, as paradoxical antinomies, logical absurdities. Thus nowhere is the temptation so great to slide into logical aporetics and disputation, priding oneself on one's scientific discipline, while the actual substratum of the work, the phenomena themselves, is forever lost from view.

All this will be confirmed as I now leave the reference to Kant behind and attempt to show, to those willing to understand, one of the paths I have actually taken; *as* a path actually taken, it offers itself as one that can at any time be taken again. Indeed, it is a path which at every step allows just this self-evidence to be renewed and tested as apodictic, i.e., the self-evidence of a path capable of being taken repeatedly at will and capable of being followed further at will in repeatedly verifiable experiences and cognitions.

§ 33. *The problem of the "life-world" as a partial problem within the general problem of objective science.*

BRIEFLY REMINDING OURSELVES of our earlier discussions, let us recall the fact we have emphasized, namely, that science is a human spiritual accomplishment which presupposes as its point of departure, both historically and for each new student, the intuitive surrounding world of life, pregiven as existing for all in common. Furthermore, it is an accomplishment which, in being practiced and carried forward, continues to presuppose this surrounding world as it is given in its particularity to the scientist. For example, for the physicist it is the world in which he sees his measuring instruments, hears time-beats, estimates visible magnitudes, etc.—the world in which, furthermore, he knows himself to be included with all his activity and all his theoretical ideas.

When science poses and answers questions, these are from the start, and hence from then on, questions resting upon the ground of, and addressed to, the elements of this pregiven world in which science and every other life-praxis is engaged. In this life-praxis, knowledge, as prescientific knowledge, plays a constant role, together with its goals, which are in general satisfactorily achieved in the sense which is intended and in each case usually in order to make practical life possible. But a new civilization (philosophical, scientific civilization), rising up in Greece, saw fit to recast the idea of "knowledge" and "truth" in natural existence and to ascribe to the newly formed idea of "objective truth" a higher dignity, that of a norm for all knowledge. In relation to this, finally, arises the idea of a universal science encompassing all possible knowledge in its infinity, the bold guiding idea of the modern period. If we have made this clear to ourselves, then obviously an explicit elucidation of the objective validity and of the whole task of science requires that we first inquire back into the pregiven world. It is pregiven to us all quite naturally, as persons within the horizon of our fellow men, i.e., in every actual connection with others, as "the" world common to us all. Thus it is, as we have explained in detail, the constant ground of validity, an ever available source of what is taken for granted, to which we, whether as practical men or as scientists, lay claim as a matter of course.

Now if this pregiven world is to become a subject of investigation in its own right, so that we can arrive, of course, at scientifically defensible assertions, this requires special care in preparatory reflections. It is not easy to achieve clarity about what kind of peculiar scientific and hence universal tasks are to be posed under the title "life-world" and about whether something philosophically significant will arise here. Even the first attempt to understand the peculiar ontic sense of the life-world, which can be taken now as a narrower, now as a broader one, causes difficulties.

The manner in which we here come to the life-world as a subject for scientific investigation makes this subject appear an ancillary and partial one within the full subject of objective science in general. The latter has become generally, that is, in all its particular forms (the particular positive sciences), incomprehensible as regards the possibility of its objective accomplishment. If science becomes a problem in this way, then we must withdraw from the operation of it and take up a standpoint above it, surveying in generality its theories and results in the systematic context of predicative thoughts and statements, and on the other side we must also survey the life of acts practiced by working scientists, working with one another—their setting of goals, their termination in a given goal, and the terminating self-evidence. And what also comes under consideration here is precisely the scientists' repeated recourse, in different general manners, to the life-world with its ever available intuited data; to this we can immediately add the scientists' statements, in each case simply adapted to this world, statements made purely descriptively in the same prescientific manner of judging which is proper to the "occasional" [1] statements of practical, everyday life. Thus the problem of the life-world, or rather of the manner in which it functions and must function for scientists, is only a

1. *okkasionelle*. A term from the second of the *Logische Untersuchungen*, § 26 (1913 ed., Vol. II, p. 81): an expression is "essentially subjective and occasional" if its actual meaning depends "on the occasion [*Gelegenheit*], the person speaking, and his situation."

partial subject within the above-designated whole of objective science (namely, in the service of its full grounding).

It is clear, however, that prior to the general question of its function for a self-evident grounding of the objective sciences there is good reason to ask about the life-world's own and constant ontic meaning for the human beings who live in it. These human beings do not always have scientific interests, and even scientists are not always involved in scientific work; also, as history teaches us, there was not always in the world a civilization that lived habitually with long-established scientific interests. The life-world was always there for mankind before science, then, just as it continues its manner of being in the epoch of science. Thus one can put forward by itself the problem of the manner of being of the life-world; one can place oneself completely upon the ground of this straightforwardly intuited world, putting out of play all objective-scientific opinions and cognitions, in order to consider generally what kind of "scientific" tasks, i.e., tasks to be resolved with universal validity, arise in respect to this world's own manner of being. Might this not yield a vast theme for study? Is it not the case that, in the end, through what first appears as a special subject in the theory of science, that "third dimension" is opening up, immediately destined in advance to engulf the whole subject matter of objective science (as well as all other subject matters on the "plane")? At first this must appear peculiar and unbelievable. Many paradoxes will arise; yet they will be resolved. What imposes itself here and must be considered before everything else is the correct comprehension of the essence of the life-world and the method of a "scientific" treatment appropriate to it, from which "objective" scientific treatment, however, is excluded.

§ 34. *Exposition of the problem of a science of the life-world.*

a. The difference between objective science and science in general.

Is not the life-world as such what we know best, what is always taken for granted in all human life, always familiar to us in its typology through experience? Are not all its horizons of the unknown simply horizons of what is just incompletely known, i.e., known in advance in respect of its most general typology? For prescientific life, of course, this type of acquaintance suffices, as does its manner of converting the unknown into the known, gaining "occasional" knowledge on the basis of experience (verifying itself internally and thereby excluding illusion) and induction. This suffices for everyday praxis. If, now, something more can be and is to be accomplished, if a "scientific" knowledge is supposed to come about, what can be meant other than what objective science has in view and does anyway? Is scientific knowledge as such not "objective" knowledge, aimed at a knowledge substratum which is valid for everyone with unconditioned generality? And yet, paradoxically, we uphold our assertion and require that one not let the handed-down concept of objective science be substituted, because of the century-old tradition in which we have all been raised, for the concept of science in general.

The [1] title "life-world" makes possible and demands perhaps various different, though essentially interrelated, scientific undertakings; and perhaps it is part of genuine and full scientific discipline that we must treat these all together, though following their essential order of founding, rather than treating, say, just the one, the objective-logical one (this particular accomplishment within the life-world) by itself, leaving the others completely out of scientific consideration. There has never been a scientific inquiry into the way in which the life-world constantly functions as subsoil, into how its manifold prelogical validities act as grounds for the logical ones, for theoretical truths.[2] And perhaps the scientific discipline which this life-world as such, in its universality, requires is a peculiar one, one which is precisely not objective and logical but which, as the ultimately grounding one, is not inferior but superior in value. But how is this completely different sort of scientific discipline, for which the objective sort has always been substituted up to now, to be realized? The idea of objective truth is predetermined in its whole meaning by the contrast with the idea of the truth in pre- and extra-scientific life. This latter truth has its ultimate and deepest source of verification in experience which is "pure" in the sense

1. This whole paragraph is crossed out in the MS.
2. This sentence was added by Fink. It does not seem to fit in, and it breaks the continuity between the preceding and following sentences.

designated above, in all its modes of perception, memory, etc. These words, however, must be understood actually as prescientific life understands them; thus one must not inject into them, from current objective science, any psychophysical, psychological interpretation. And above all—to dispose of an important point right away—one must not go straight back to the supposedly immediately given "sense-data," as if *they* were immediately characteristic of the purely intuitive data of the life-world. What is actually first is the "merely subjective-relative" intuition of prescientific world-life. For us, to be sure, this "merely" has, as an old inheritance, the disdainful coloring of the δόξα. In prescientific life itself, of course, it has nothing of this; there it is a realm of good verification and, based on this, of well-verified predicative cognitions and of truths which are just as secure as is necessary for the practical projects of life that determine their sense. The disdain with which everything "merely subjective and relative" is treated by those scientists who pursue the modern ideal of objectivity changes nothing of its own manner of being, just as it does not change the fact that the scientist himself must be satisfied with this realm whenever he has recourse, as he unavoidably must have recourse, to it.

b. The use of subjective-relative experiences *for* the objective sciences, and the science *of* them.

The sciences build upon the life-world as taken for granted in that they make use of whatever in it happens to be necessary for their particular ends. But to use the life-world in this way is not to know it scientifically in its own manner of being. For example, Einstein uses the Michelson experiments and the corroboration of them by other researchers, with apparatus copied from Michelson's, with everything required in the way of scales of measurement, coincidences established, etc. There is no doubt that everything that enters in here—the persons, the apparatus, the room in the institute, etc.—can itself become a subject of investigation in the usual sense of objective inquiry, that of the positive sciences. But Einstein could make no use whatever of a theoretical psychological-psychophysical construction of the objective being of Mr. Michelson; rather, he made use of the human being who was accessible to him, as to everyone else in the prescientific world, as an object of straightforward experience, the human being whose existence, with this vitality, in these activities and creations within the common life-world, is always the presupposition for all of Einstein's objective-scientific lines of inquiry, projects, and accomplishments pertaining to Michelson's experiments. It is, of course, the one world of experience, common to all, that Einstein and every other researcher knows he is in as a human being, even throughout all his activity of research. [But] precisely this world and everything that happens in it, used as needed for scientific and other ends, bears, on the other hand, for every natural scientist in his thematic orientation toward its "objective truth," the stamp "merely subjective and relative." The contrast to this determines, as we said, the sense of the "objective" task. This "subjective-relative" is supposed to be "overcome"; one can and should correlate with it a hypothetical being-in-itself, a substrate for logical-mathematical "truths-in-themselves" that one can approximate through ever newer and better hypothetical approaches, always justifying them through experiential verification. This is the one side. But while the natural scientist is thus interested in the objective and is involved in his activity, the subjective-relative is on the other hand still functioning for him, not as something irrelevant that must be passed through but as that which ultimately grounds the theoretical-logical ontic validity for all objective verification, i.e., as the source of self-evidence, the source of verification. The visible measuring scales, scale-markings, etc., are used as actually existing things, not as illusions; thus that which actually exists in the life-world, as something valid, is a premise.

c. Is the subjective-relative an object for psychology?

Now the question of the manner of being of this subjective sphere, or the question of the science which is to deal with it in its own universe of being, is normally disposed of by the natural scientist by referring to psychology. But again one must not allow the intrusion of what exists in the sense of objective science when it is a question of what exists in the life-world. For what has always gone under the name of psychology, at any rate since the founding of modern objectivism regarding knowledge of the world, naturally has the meaning of an "objective" science of the subjective, no matter which of the attempted historical psychologies we may choose. Now in our subsequent reflections the problem of making possible an objective psychology will have to become the object of more detailed discussions. But first we must grasp clearly the contrast between objectivity and the subjectivity of the life-world as a contrast which determines the fundamental sense of objective-scientific discipline itself, and we must secure this contrast against the great temptations to misconstrue it.

d. The life-world as universe of what is intuitable in principle; the "objective-true" world as in principle nonintuitable "logical" substruction.

Whatever may be the chances for realizing, or the capacity for realizing, the idea of objective science in respect to the mental world (i.e., not only in respect to nature), this idea of objectivity dominates the whole *universitas* of the positive sciences in the modern period, and in the general usage it dominates the meaning of the word "science." This already involves a naturalism insofar as this concept is taken from Galilean natural science, such that the scientifically "true," the objective, world is always thought of in advance as nature, in an expanded sense of the word. The contrast between the subjectivity of the life-world and the "objective," the "true" world, lies in the fact that the latter is a theoretical-logical substruction, the substruction of something that is in principle not perceivable, in principle not experienceable in its own proper being, whereas the subjective, in the life-world, is distinguished in all respects precisely by its being actually experienceable.*

The life-world is a realm of original self-evidences.[3] That which is self-evidently given is, in perception, experienced as

* In life the verification of being, terminating in experience, yields a full conviction. Even when it is inductive, the inductive anticipation is of a possible experienceability which is ultimately decisive. Inductions can be verified by other inductions, working together. Because of their anticipations of experienceability, and because every direct perception itself includes inductive moments (anticipation of the sides of the object which are not yet experienced), everything is contained in the broader concept of "experience" or "induction." [Cf. p. 51, above].

3. Husserl's use of *Evidenz* does not permit of its always being translated in the same way. But when used in its most special or technical sense, as it is here, "self-evidence" is better than simply "evidence." As can be seen from the context here, it means "self-

"the thing itself," [4] in immediate presence, or, in memory, remembered as the thing itself; and every other manner of intuition is a presentification of the thing itself. Every mediate cognition belonging in this sphere—broadly speaking, every manner of induction—has the sense of an induction of something intuitable, something possibly perceivable as the thing itself or remadeable as having-been-perceived, etc. All conceivable verification leads back to these modes of self-evidence because the "thing itself" (in the particular mode) lies in these intutitions themselves as that which is actually, intersubjectively experienceable and verifiable and is not a substruction of thought; whereas such a substruction, insofar as it makes a claim to truth, can have actual truth only by being related back to such self-evidences.

It is of course itself a highly important task, for the scientific opening-up of the life-world, to bring to recognition the primal validity of these self-evidences and indeed their higher dignity in the grounding of knowledge compared to that of the objective-logical self-evidences. One must fully clarify, i.e., bring to ultimate self-evidence, how all the self-evidence of objective-logical accomplishments, through which objective theory (thus mathematical and natural-scientific theory) is grounded in respect of form and content, has its hidden sources of grounding in the ultimately accomplishing life, the life in which the self-evident givenness of the life-world forever has, has attained, and attains anew its prescientific ontic meaning. From objective-logical self-evidence (mathematical "insight," natural-scientific, positive-scientific "insight," as it is being accomplished by the inquiring and grounding mathematician, etc.), the path leads back, here, to the primal self-evidence in which the life-world is ever pregiven.

One may at first find strange and even questionable what has been simply asserted here, but the general features of the contrast among levels of self-evidence are unmistakable. The empiricist talk of natural scientists often, if not for the most part, gives the impression that the natural sciences are based on the

___

givenness"; whereas the English word "evidence" usually has a very different meaning, that of something testifying to the existence of something else (e.g., evidence in a trial).

4. "*es selbst*." The use of the word "thing" in this expression is not out of place as long as Husserl is talking about perception. But in another context that which is "itself" given might not be a "thing"; it could be an ideal state of affairs, for example in mathematical or logical intuition.

experience of objective nature. But it is not in this sense true that these sciences are experiential sciences, that they follow experience in principle, that they all begin with experiences, that all their inductions must finally be verified through experiences; rather, this is true only in that other sense whereby experience [yields] a self-evidence taking place purely in the life-world and as such is the source of self-evidence for what is objectively established in the sciences, the latter never themselves being experiences of the objective. The objective is precisely never experienceable as itself; and scientists themselves, by the way, consider it in this way whenever they interpret it as something metaphysically transcendent, in contrast to their confusing empiricist talk. The experienceability of something objective is no different from that of an infinitely distant geometrical construct and in general no different from that of all infinite "ideas," including, for example, the infinity of the number series. Naturally, "rendering ideas intuitive" in the manner of mathematical or natural-scientific "models" is hardly intuition of the objective itself but rather a matter of life-world intuitions which are suited to make easier the conception of the objective ideals in question. Many [such] conceptual intermediaries are often involved, [especially since] the conception itself does not always occur so immediately, cannot always be made so self-evident in its way, as is the case in conceiving of geometrical straight lines on the basis of the life-world self-evidence of straight table-edges and the like.

As can be seen, a great deal of effort is involved here in order to secure even the presuppositions for a proper inquiry, i.e., in order first to free ourselves from the constant misconstructions which mislead us all because of the scholastic dominance of objective-scientific ways of thinking.

e. The objective sciences as subjective constructs—those of a particular praxis, namely, the theoretical-logical, which itself belongs to the full concreteness of the life-world.

If the contrast [under discussion] has been purified, we must now do justice to the essential interrelatedness [of the elements contrasted]: objective theory in its logical sense (taken universally: science as the totality of predicative theory, of the system of statements meant "logically" as "propositions in themselves," "truths in themselves," and in this sense logically joined) is rooted, grounded in the life-world, in the original self-evidences belonging to it. Thanks to this rootedness objective science has a constant reference of meaning to the world in which we always live, even as scientists and also in the total community of scientists—a reference, that is, to the general life-world. But at the same time, as an accomplishment of scientific [5] persons, as individuals and as joined in the community of scientific activity, objective science itself belongs to the life-world. Its theories, the logical constructs, are of course not things in the life-world like stones, houses, or trees. They are logical wholes and logical parts made up of ultimate logical elements. To speak with Bolzano, they are "representations-in-themselves" ["*Vorstellungen an sich*"] "propositions in themselves," inferences and proofs "in themselves," ideal unities of signification whose logical ideality is determined by their *telos*, "truth in itself."

But this or any other ideality does not change in the least the fact that these are human formations, essentially related to human actualities and potentialities, and thus belong to this concrete unity of the life-world, whose concreteness thus extends farther than that of "things." Exactly the same thing is true, correlative to this, of scientific activities—those of experiencing, those of arriving at logical formations "on the basis of" experience—activities through which these formations appear in original form and original modes of variation in the individual scientists and in the community of scientists: the original status of the proposition or demonstration dealt with by all.

But here we enter an uncomfortable situation. If we have made our contrast with all necessary care, then we have two different things: life-world and objective-scientific world, though of course [they are] related to each other. The knowledge of the objective-scientific world is "grounded" in the self-evidence of the life-world. The latter is pregiven to the scientific worker, or the working community, as ground; yet, as they build upon this, what is built is something new, something different. If we cease being immersed in our scientific thinking, we become aware that we scientists are, after all, human beings and as such are among the components of the life-world which always exists for us, ever pregiven; and thus all of science is pulled, along with us, into the

5. The text reads "prescientific persons," which must be a mistake.

—merely "subjective-relative"—life-world. And what becomes of the objective world itself? What happens to the hypothesis of being-in-itself, related first to the "things" of the life-world, the "objects," the "real" bodies, real animals, plants, and also human beings within the "space-time" of the life-world—all these concepts being understood, now, not from the point of view of the objective sciences but as they are in prescientific life?

Is it not the case that this hypothesis, which in spite of the ideality of scientific theories has direct validity for the scientific subjects (the scientists as human beings), is but *one* among the many practical hypotheses and projects which make up the life of human beings in this life-world—which is at all times consciously pregiven to them as available? Do not all goals, whether they are "practical" in some other, extrascientific sense or are practical under the title of "theory," belong *eo ipso* to the unity of the life-world, if only we take the latter in its complete and full concreteness?

On the other hand, we have seen also that the propositions, the theories, the whole edifice of doctrine in the objective sciences are structures attained through certain activities of scientists bound together in their collaborative work—or, to speak more exactly, attained through a continued building-up of activities, the later of which always presuppose the results of the earlier. And we see further that all these theoretical results have the character of validities for the life-world, adding themselves as such to its own composition and belonging to it even before that as a horizon of possible accomplishments for developing science. The concrete life-world, then, is the grounding soil [*der gründende Boden*] of the "scientifically true" world and at the same time encompasses it in its own universal concreteness. How is this to be understood? How are we to do justice systematically—that is, with appropriate scientific discipline—to the all-encompassing, so paradoxically demanding, manner of being of the life-world?

We are posing questions whose clarifying answers are by no means obvious. The contrast and the inseparable union [we have been exploring] draw us into a reflection which entangles us in more and more troublesome difficulties. The paradoxical interrelationships of the "objectively true world" and the "life-world" make enigmatic the manner of being of both. Thus [the idea of a] true world in any sense, and within it our own being, becomes an enigma in respect to the sense of this being. In our attempts to attain clarity we shall suddenly become aware, in the face of emerging paradoxes, that all of our philosophizing up to now has been without a ground. How can we now truly become philosophers?

We cannot escape the force of this motivation. It is impossible for us to evade the issue here through a preoccupation with aporia and argumentation nourished by Kant or Hegel, Aristotle or Thomas.

f. The problem of the life-world not as a partial problem but rather as a universal problem for philosophy.

Of course, it is a new sort of scientific discipline that is required for the solution of the enigmas which now disquiet us: it is not mathematical, nor logical at all in the historical sense; it cannot already have before it, as an available norm, a finished mathematics, logic, or logistic, since these are themselves objective sciences in the sense which is presently problematical and, as included in the problem, cannot be presuppositions used as premises. At first, as long as one only makes contrasts, is only concerned with oppositions, it could appear that nothing more than or different from objective science is needed, just as everyday practical life undertakes its rational reflections, both particular and general, without needing a science for them. It just *is* this way, a fact familiar to all, unthinkingly accepted rather than being formulated as a fundamental fact and thought through as a subject for thinking in its own right—namely, that there are two sorts of truth: on the one side, everyday practical situational truths, relative, to be sure, but, as we have already emphasized, exactly what praxis, in its particular projects, seeks and needs; on the other side there are scientific truths, and their grounding leads back precisely to the situational truths, but in such a way that scientific method does not suffer thereby in respect to its own meaning, since it wants to use and must use precisely these truths.

Thus it could appear—if one allows oneself to be carried along by the thoughtless naïveté of life even in the transition from the extralogical to the logical, to the objective-scientific praxis of thinking—that a separate investigation under the title "life-world" is an intellectualistic enterprise born of a mania, peculiar to modern life, to theorize everything. But, on the other hand, it has at least become apparent that we cannot let the matter end with this naïveté, that paradoxical enigmas announce themselves here: merely subjective relativity is supposedly overcome by objective-logical theory, yet the latter belongs, as the theoretical praxis of human beings, to the merely subjective and relative and at the same time must have its premises, its sources of self-evidence, in the subjective and relative. From here on this much is certain: that all problems of truth and of being, all methods, hypotheses, and results conceivable for these problems—whether for worlds of experience or for metaphysical higher worlds—can attain their ultimate clarity, their evident sense or the evidence of their nonsense, only through this supposed intellectualistic hypertrophy. This will then include, certainly, all ultimate questions of legitimate sense and of nonsense in the busy routine of the "resurrected metaphysics" that has become so vocal and so bewitching of late.

Through this last series of considerations the magnitude, the universal and independent significance, of the problem of the life-world has become intelligible to us in an anticipatory insight. In comparison with this the problem of the "objectively true" world or that of objective-logical science—no matter how pressing it may repeatedly become, and properly so—appears now as a problem of secondary and more specialized interest. Though the peculiar accomplishment of our modern objective science may still not be understood, nothing changes the fact that it is a validity for the life-world, arising out of particular activities, and that it belongs itself to the concreteness of the life-world. Thus in any case, for the sake of clarifying this and all other acquisitions of human activity, the concrete life-world must first be taken into consideration; and it must be considered in terms of the truly concrete universality whereby it embraces, both directly and in the manner of horizons, all the built-up levels of validity acquired by men for the world of their common life and whereby it has the totality of these levels related in the end to a world-nucleus to be distilled by abstraction, namely, the world of straightforward intersubjective experiences. To be sure, we do not yet know how the life-world is to become an independent, totally self-sufficient subject of investigation, how it is supposed to make possible scientific statements—which as such, after all, must have their own "objectivity," even if it is in a manner different from that of our sciences, i.e., a necessary validity to be appropriated purely methodically, which we and everyone can verify precisely through this method. We are absolute beginners, here, and have nothing in the way of a logic designed to provide norms; we can do nothing but reflect, engross ourselves in the still not unfolded sense of our task, and thus secure, with the utmost care, freedom from prejudice, keeping our undertaking free of alien interferences (and we have already made several important contributions to this); and this, as in the case of every new undertaking, must supply us with our method. The clarification of the sense of the task is, indeed, the self-evidence of the goal *qua* goal; and to this self-evidence belongs essentially the self-evidence of the possible "ways" to it. The intricacy and difficulty of the preliminary reflections which are still before us will justify themselves, not only because of the magnitude of the goal, but also because of the essential strangeness and precariousness of the ideas which will necessarily become involved.

Thus what appeared to be merely a problem of the fundamental basis of the objective sciences or a partial problem within the universal problem of objective science has indeed (just as we announced in advance that it would) proven to be the genuine and most universal problem. It can also be put this way: the problem first appears as the question of the relation between objective-scientific thinking and intuition; it concerns, on the one hand, then, logical thinking as the thinking of logical thoughts, e.g., the physicist's thinking of physical theory, or purely mathematical thinking, in which mathematics has its place as a system of doctrine, as a theory. And, on the other hand, we have intuiting and the intuited, in the life-world prior to theory. Here arises the ineradicable illusion of a pure thinking which, unconcerned in its purity about intuition, already has its self-evident truth, even truth about the world—the illusion which makes the sense and the possibility, the "scope," of objective science questionable. Here one concentrates on the separateness of intuiting and thinking and generally interprets the nature of the "theory of knowledge" as theory of science, carried out in respect to two correlative sides [6] (whereby science is always understood in terms of the only concept of science available, that of objective science). But as soon as the empty and vague notion of intuition—instead of being something negligible and insignificant compared to the supremely significant logical sphere in which one supposedly already has genuine truth—has become the problem of the life-world, as soon as the magnitude and difficulty of this investigation take on enormous proportions as one seriously penetrates it, there occurs the great transforma-

6. I.e., the subjective and the objective.

tion of the "theory of knowledge" and the theory of science whereby, in the end, science as a problem and as an accomplishment loses its self-sufficiency and becomes a mere partial problem.

What we have said also naturally applies to logic, as the a priori theory of norms for everything "logical"—in the overarching sense of what is logical, according to which logic is a logic of strict objectivity, of objective-logical truths. No one ever thinks about the predications and truths which precede science, about the "logic" which provides norms within this sphere of relativity, or about the possibility, even in the case of these logical structures conforming purely descriptively to the life-world, of inquiring into the system of principles that give them their norms a priori. As a matter of course, traditional objective logic is substituted as the a priori norm even for this subjective-relative sphere of truth.

§ 35. *Analysis of the transcendental epochē. First step: The epochē of objective science.*

BECAUSE OF THE PECULIAR nature of the task which has arisen for us, the method of access to the new science's field of work—which must be attained before the working problems of the science are given—is articulated into a multiplicity of steps, each of which has, in a new way, the character of an epochē, a withholding of natural, naïve validities and in general of validities already in effect. The first necessary epochē, i.e., the first methodical step, has already come into view through the preliminary reflections hitherto carried out. But an explicit, universal formulation is needed. Clearly required before everything else is the epochē in respect to all objective sciences. This means not merely an abstraction from them, such as an imaginary transformation, in thought, of present human existence, such that no science appeared in the picture. What is meant is rather an epochē of all participation in the cognitions of the objective sciences, an epochē of any critical position-taking which is interested in their truth or falsity, even any position on their guiding idea of an objective knowledge of the world. In short, we carry out an epochē in regard to all objective theoretical interests, all aims and activities belonging to us as objective scientists or even simply as [ordinary] people desirous of [this kind of] knowledge.

Within this epochē, however, neither the sciences nor the scientists have disappeared for us who practice the epochē. They continue to be what they were before, in any case: facts in the unified context of the pregiven life-world; except that, because of the epochē, we do not function as sharing these interests, as coworkers, etc. We establish in ourselves just one particular habitual direction of interest, with a certain vocational attitude, to which there belongs a particular "vocational time." [1] We find the same thing here as elsewhere: when we actualize one of our habitual interests and are thus involved in our vocational activity (in the accomplishment of our work), we assume a posture of epochē toward our other life-interests, even though these still exist and are still ours. Everything has "its propér time," and in shifting [activities] we say something like: "Now it is time to go to the meeting, to the election," and the like.

In a special sense, of course, we call science, art, military service, etc., our "vocation," but as normal human beings we are constantly (in a broadened sense) involved in many "vocations" (interested attitudes) at the same time: we are at once fathers, citizens, etc. Every such vocation has its time of actualizing activities. Accordingly, this newly established vocational interest, whose universal subject matter is called the "life-world," finds its place among the other life-interests or vocations and it has "its proper time" within the one personal time, the form of the various exercised vocational times.

Of course, to equate the new science in this way with all "bourgeois" [bürgerliche] vocations, or even with the objective sciences, is a sort of trivialization, a disregard for the greatest value-distinction there can be between sciences. Understood in this way, it was so happily criticized by the modern irrationalistic philosophers. This way of looking at it makes it appear as if, once again, a new, purely theoretical interest, a new "science" with a new vocational technique, is to be established, carried on either as an intellectualistic game with very ideal pretensions or as a higher-level intellectual technique in the service of the positive sciences, useful for them, while they themselves, in turn, have their only real value in their usefulness for life. One is powerless against the misrepresentations of hurried readers and listeners who in the end hear only what they want to hear; but in any case they are part of the indifferent mass audience of the

1. *Berufszeit*, colloq., "working hours." But I have translated it literally as "vocational time" in order to preserve the notion of *Beruf*, a "calling."

philosopher. The few, for whom one [really] speaks, will know how to restrain such a suspicion, especially after what we have said in earlier lectures. They will at least wait to see where our path leads them.

There are good reasons for my stressing so sharply the vocational character of even the "phenomenologist's" attitude. One of the first things to be described about the epochē in question is that it is a habitual epochē of accomplishment, one with periods of time in which it results in work, while other times are devoted to other interests of work or play; furthermore, and most important, the suspension of its accomplishment in no way changes the interest which continues and remains valid within personal subjectivity—i.e., its habitual directedness toward goals which persist as its validities—and it is for this very reason that it can be actualized again and again, at different times, in this identical sense. This by no means implies, however, that the life-world epochē—to which further significant moments belong, as we shall show—means no more for human existence, practically and "existentially," than the vocational epochē of the cobbler, or that it is basically a matter of indifference whether one is a cobbler or a phenomenologist, or, also, whether one is a phenomenologist or a positive scientist. Perhaps it will even become manifest that the total phenomenological attitude and the epochē belonging to it are destined in essence to effect, at first, a complete personal transformation, comparable in the beginning to a religious conversion, which then, however, over and above this, bears within itself the significance of the greatest existential transformation which is assigned as a task to mankind as such.

§ 36 *How can the life-world, after the epochē of the objective sciences, become the subject matter of a science? The distinction in principle between the objective-logical a priori and the a priori of the life-world.*

IF OUR INTEREST is exclusively in the "life-world," we must ask: Has the life-world, through the epochē in respect to

objective science, already been laid open as a universal scientific
subject matter? * Do we already have thereby, the subject matter for statements that are generally valid scientifically, statements about facts that are to be established scientifically? How
do we have the life-world as a universal field, fixed in advance, of
such establishable facts? It is the spatiotemporal world of things
as we experience them in our pre- and extrascientific life and as
we know them to be experienceable beyond what is [actually]
experienced. We have a world-horizon as a horizon of possible
thing-experience [*Dingerfahrung*]. Things: that is, stones, animals, plants, even human beings and human products; but everything here is subjective and relative, even though normally,
in our experience and in the social group united with us in the
community of life, we arrive at "secure" facts; within a certain
range this occurs of its own accord, that is, undisturbed by any
noticeable disagreement; sometimes, on the other hand, when it

* First let us recall that what we call science is, within the constantly valid world, as life-world, a particular type of purposeful
activities and purposeful accomplishments like all human vocations
in the usual sense of the word; to this sphere also belong those practical intentions of a higher level which do not involve types of vocation
or goal-oriented interrelations and accomplishments at all, the more
or less isolated, incidental, more or less fleeting interests. All these
are, from the human point of view, peculiarities of human life and of
human habitualities, and they all lie within the universal framework
of the life-world into which all accomplishments flow and to which
all human beings and all accomplishing activities and capacities
always belong. Of course, the new theoretical interest in the universal
life-world itself, in its own manner of being, requires a certain epochē
in regard to all these interests, i.e., in regard to the pursuit of our
ends, in regard to all the criticism, always belonging to the purposeful life, of the means and the goals or ends themselves, e.g., whether
we should factually persist in them, whether certain paths should be
taken as general directives, etc. Living toward our ends, which are
valid for us habitually, we do, of course, live in the horizon of the life-
world, no matter which ends are "having their turn"; everything that
happens and develops here exists in the life-world and in the manner
of the life-world; but being oriented toward what exists within the
life-world is not the same as focusing on the [life-world] as the universal horizon, not the same as making thematic the end in view *as*
a being within this horizon, the newly thematic life-world. Thus the
first thing we must do is refrain from the pursuit of all scientific and
other interests. But the epochē alone is not enough: even all setting
of ends, all projecting, presupposes something worldly; the *wherewith*,
i.e., the life-world, is given prior to all ends. [This last sentence is only
a rough guess at the sense of this somewhat garbled stenographic
note.—TRANS.]

is of practical importance, it occurs in a purposive knowing process, i.e., with the goal of [finding] a truth which is secure for our purposes. But when we are thrown into an alien social sphere, that of the Negroes in the Congo, Chinese peasants, etc., we discover that their truths, the facts that for them are fixed, generally verified or verifiable, are by no means the same as ours. But if we set up the goal of a truth about the objects which is unconditionally valid for all subjects, beginning with that on which normal Europeans, normal Hindus, Chinese, etc., agree in spite of all relativity—beginning, that is, with what makes objects of the life-world, common to all, identifiable for them and for us (even though conceptions of them may differ), such as spatial shape, motion, sense-quality, and the like—then we are on the way to objective science. When we set up this objectivity as a goal (the goal of a "truth in itself") we make a set of hypotheses through which the pure life-world is surpassed. We have precluded *this* [type of] "surpassing" through the first epochē (that which concerns the objective sciences), and now we have the embarrassment of wondering what else can be undertaken scientifically, as something that can be established once and for all and for everyone.

But this embarrassment disappears as soon as we consider that the life-world does have, in all its relative features, a *general structure*. This general structure, to which everything that exists relatively is bound, is not itself relative. We can attend to it in its generality and, with sufficient care, fix it once and for all in a way equally accessible to all. As life-world the world has, even prior to science, the "same" structures that the objective sciences presuppose in their substruction of a world which exists "in itself" and is determined through "truths in themselves" (this substruction being taken for granted due to the tradition of centuries); these are the same structures that they presuppose as a priori structures and systematically unfold in a priori sciences, sciences of the *logos*, the universal methodical norms by which any knowledge of the world existing "in itself, objectively" must be bound. Prescientifically, the world is already a spatio-temporal world; to be sure, in regard to this spatiotemporality there is no question of ideal mathematical points, of "pure" straight lines or planes, no question at all of mathematically infinitesimal continuity or of the "exactness" belonging to the sense of the geometrical a priori. The bodies familiar to us in the life-world are actual bodies, but not bodies in the sense of physics. The same thing is true of causality and of spatiotemporal infinity. [These] categorical features of the life-world have the same names but are not concerned, so to speak, with the theoretical idealizations and the hypothetical substructions of the geometrician and the physicist. As we already know, physicists, who are men like other men, who know themselves as living in the life-world, the world of their human interests, have, under the title of physics, a particular sort of questions and (in a broader sense) practical projects directed toward the things of the life-world, and their "theories" are the practical results. Just as other projects, practical interests, and their realizations belong to the life-world, presuppose it as ground, and enrich it with their activity, so it is with science, too, as a human project and praxis. And this includes, as we have said, everything objectively a priori, with its necessary reference back to a corresponding a priori of the life-world. This reference-back is one of a founding of validity [*Geltungsfundierung*]. A certain idealizing accomplishment is what brings about the higher-level meaning-formation and ontic validity of the mathematical and every other objective a priori on the basis of the life-world a priori. Thus the latter ought first to become a subject of scientific investigation in its peculiarity and purity, and then one ought to set the systematic task of understanding how, on this basis and in what manners of new meaning-formation, the objective a priori comes about as a mediated theoretical accomplishment. What is needed, then, would be a systematic division of the universal structures—universal life-world a priori and universal "objective" a priori—and then also a division among the universal inquiries according to the way in which the "objective" a priori is grounded in the "subjective-relative" a priori of the life-world or how, for example, mathematical self-evidence has its source of meaning and source of legitimacy in the self-evidence of the life-world.

This consideration has a particular interest for us even though we have already detached our problem of a science of the life-world from the problem of objective science in that we, caught up through our schooling in the traditional objectivistic metaphysics, at first have no means of access whatever to the idea of a universal a priori belonging purely to the life-world. What we need first is a separation in principle of the latter from the objective a priori which is [always] immediately substituted for it. It is this very separation that is effected by the first epochē of all objective sciences, if we understand it also as the epochē of all objective a priori sciences and make it complete through the considerations we have just carried out. The latter provide us, in addition, with the fundamental insight that the universal a priori of the objective-logical level—that of the mathematical sciences and all others which are a priori in the usual sense—is grounded in a universal a priori which is in itself prior, precisely that of the pure life-world. Only through recourse to this a priori, to be unfolded in an a priori science of its own, can our a priori sciences, the objective-logical ones, achieve a truly radical, a seriously scientific, grounding, which under the circumstances they absolutely require.

Here we can also say: The supposedly completely self-sufficient logic which modern mathematical logicians [*Logistiker*] think they are able to develop, even calling it a truly scientific philosophy, namely, as the universal, a priori, fundamental science for all objective sciences, is nothing but naïveté. Its self-evidence lacks scientific grounding in the universal life-world a priori, which it always presupposes in the form of things taken for granted, which are never scientifically, universally formulated, never put in the general form proper to a science of essence. Only when this radical, fundamental science exists can such a logic itself become a science. Before this it hangs in mid-air, without support, and is, as it has been up to now, so very naïve that it is not even aware of the task which attaches to every objective logic, every a priori science in the usual sense, namely, that of discovering how this logic itself is to be grounded, hence no longer "logically" but by being traced back to the universal prelogical a priori through which everything logical, the total edifice of objective theory in all its methodological forms, demonstrates its legitimate sense and from which, then, all logic itself must receive its norms.

Yet this insight surpasses the interest in the life-world which governs us now; for this, as we have said, all that counts is the distinction in principle between the objective-logical and the life-world a priori; and the purpose of this is to be able to set in motion a radical reflection upon the great task of a pure theory of essence of the life-world.

§ 37.   *The formal and most general structures of the life-world: thing and world on the one side, thing-consciousness on the other.*

IF WE SEEK OUT, simply looking around us, what is formal and general, what remains invariant in the life-world throughout all alterations of the relative, we involuntarily stop at what alone determines for us in life the sense of talking about the world: the world is the universe of things, which are distributed within the world-form of space-time and are "positional" in two senses (according to spatial position and temporal position) —the spatiotemporal *onta*. Here would thus be found the task of a life-world ontology, understood as a concretely general doctrine of essence for these *onta*. For our interest in the present context it suffices to have indicated this. Rather than spend our time here, we prefer to move on to a task which is much greater, as will soon be seen—one which in fact encompasses such a doctrine. In order to prepare the way for this new subject of investigation, which also essentially concerns the life-world but is not ontological, we shall undertake a general reflection—we, that is, as waking, living human beings in the life-world (and thus naturally within the epochē regarding all interference of positive scientific discipline).

This general reflection will at the same time have the function of making evident an essential distinction among the possible ways in which the pregiven world, the ontic universe [*das ontische Universum*], can become thematic for us. Calling to mind what has repeatedly been said: the life-world, for us who wakingly live in it, is always already there, existing in advance for us, the "ground" of all praxis whether theoretical or extratheoretical. The world is pregiven to us, the waking, always somehow practically interested subjects, not occasionally but always and necessarily as the universal field of all actual and possible praxis, as horizon. To live is always to live-in-certainty-of-the-world. Waking life is being awake to the world, being constantly and directly "conscious" of the world and of oneself as living *in* the world, actually experiencing [*erleben*] and actually effecting the ontic certainty of the world. The world is pregiven thereby, in every case, in such a way that individual things are given. But there exists a fundamental difference between the way we are conscious of the world and the way we are conscious of things or objects (taken in the broadest sense, but still purely in the sense of the life-world), though together the two make up an inseparable unity. Things, objects (always understood purely in the sense of the life-world), are "given" as being valid for us in each case (in some mode or other of ontic certainty) but in principle only in such a way that we are conscious of them as things or objects *within the world-horizon*. Each one is something, "something of" the world of which we are constantly conscious as a horizon. On the other hand, we are conscious of this horizon only as a horizon for existing objects; without particular objects of consciousness it cannot be actual [*aktuell*]. Every object has its possible varying modes of being valid, the modalizations of ontic certainty. The world, on the other hand, does not exist as *an* entity, as an object, but exists with such uniqueness that the plural makes no sense when applied to it. Every plural, and every singular drawn from it, presupposes the world-horizon. This difference between the manner of being of an object in the world and that of the world itself obviously prescribes fundamentally different correlative types of consciousness for them.

§ 38.   *The two possible fundamental ways of making the life-world thematic: the naïve and natural straightforward attitude and the idea of a consistently reflective attitude toward the "how" of the subjective manner of givenness of life-world and life-world objects.*

THESE MOST GENERAL features of waking life make up the formal framework within which it now becomes possible to distinguish the different ways this life is carried on, though in all cases the world is pregiven and, within this horizon, objects are given. These ways result in the different manners, we could also say, in which we are awake to the world and to the objects in the world. The first, the naturally normal one which absolutely must precede the others not for accidental but for essential reasons, is that of straightforwardly living toward whatever objects are given, thus toward the world-horizon, in normal, unbroken constancy, in a synthetic coherence running through all acts. This normal, straightforward living, toward whatever objects are given, indicates that all our interests have their goals in objects. The pregiven world is the horizon which includes all our goals, all our ends, whether fleeting or lasting, in a flowing but constant manner, just as an intentional horizon-consciousness implicitly "encompasses" [everything] in advance. We, the subjects, in our normal, unbroken, coherent life, know no goals which extend beyond this; indeed we have no idea that there could be others. All our theoretical and practical themes, we can also say, lie always within the normal coherence of the life-horizon "world." World is the universal field into which all our acts, whether of experiencing, of knowing, or of outward action, are directed. From this field, or from objects in each case already given, come all affections, transforming themselves in each case into actions.

Yet there can be a completely different sort of waking life involved in the conscious having of the world. It would consist in a transformation of the thematic consciousness of the world which breaks through the normality of straightforward living. Let us direct our attention to the fact that in general the world or, rather, objects are not merely pregiven to us all in such a way that we simply have them as the substrates of their properties but that we become conscious of them (and of everything ontically meant) through subjective manners of appearance, or manners of givenness, without noticing it in particular; in fact we are for the most part not even aware of it at all. Let us now shape this into a new universal direction of interest; let us establish a consistent universal interest in the "how" of the manners of givenness and in the *onta* themselves, not straightforwardly but rather as objects in respect to their "how"—that is, with our interest exclusively and constantly directed toward *how*, throughout the alteration of relative validities, subjective appearances, and opinions, the coherent, universal validity *world—the* world—comes into being for us; how, that is, there arises in us the constant consciousness of the universal existence, of the universal horizon, of real, actually existing objects, each of which we are conscious of only through the alterations of our relative conceptions [*Auffassungen*] of it, of its manners of appearing, its modes of validity, even when we are conscious of it in particularity as something simply being there.

In this total change of interest, carried out with a new consistency founded on a particular resolve of the will, we notice that we acquire a number of never thematically investigated types, not only of individual things but also of syntheses, in an inseparable synthetic totality which is constantly produced by intentionally overlapping horizon-validities; and the latter influence each other reciprocally in the form of corroborating verifications of existence, or refuting cancelings-out, or other modalizations. This is the essential character of the synthetic totality in which we can take possession of something previously completely unknown, something never envisioned or grasped as a task for knowledge; this is the universal accomplishing life in which the world comes to be as existing for us constantly in flowing particularity, constantly "pregiven" to us. We can also say: this is the synthetic totality in which we now discover, for the first time, that and how the world, as correlate of a discoverable universe of synthetically connected accomplishments, acquires its ontic meaning and its ontic validity in the totality of its ontic [*ontische*] structures.

But here we do not need to go into more detailed expositions, into everything that can become thematic. What is essential for us here is the distinction between the two types of investigation,[1] each regarded as a universal investigation.

The natural life, whether it is prescientifically or scientifically, theoretically or practically interested, is life within a universal unthematic horizon. This horizon is, in the natural attitude, precisely the world always pregiven as that which exists. Simply living on in this manner, one does not need the word "pregiven"; there is no need to point out that the world is constantly actuality for us. All natural questions, all theoretical and practical goals taken as themes—as existing, as perhaps existing, as probable, as questionable, as valuable, as project, as action and result of action—have to do with something or other within the world-horizon. This is true even of illusions, nonactualities, since everything characterized through some modality

1. This could refer either to the "two ways of making the life-world thematic" (cf. section heading) or to the investigation of the "how" of the objects *vs.* the investigation of the subjective syntheses.

of being is, after all, related to actual being. For, in advance, "world" has the meaning "the universe of the 'actually' existing actualities": not the merely supposed, doubtful, or questionable actualities but the actual ones, which as such have actuality for us only in the constant movement of corrections and revisions of validities [*Umgeltungen von Geltungen*]—all this considered as the anticipation of an ideal unity.

Instead of persisting in this manner of "straightforwardly living into the world," let us attempt a universal change of interest in which the new expression "pregivenness of the world" becomes necessary because it is the title for this differently directed and yet again universal theme of the manners of pregivenness. In other words, nothing shall interest us but precisely that subjective alteration of manners of givenness, of manners of appearing and of the modes of validity in them, which, in its constant process, synthetically connected as it incessantly flows on, brings about the coherent consciousness of the straightforward "being" of the world.

Among the objects of the life-world we also find human beings, with all their human action and concern, works and suffering, living in common in the world-horizon in their particular social interrelations and knowing themselves to be such. All this, too, then, shall be included as we carry out our new universal direction of interest. A coherent theoretical interest shall now be directed exclusively toward the universe of the subjective, in which the world, in virtue of the universality of synthetically bound accomplishments in this universe, comes to have its straightforward existence for us. In the natural and normal world-life this subjective manifold constantly goes on, but there it remains constantly and necessarily concealed. How, by what method, is it to be revealed? Can it be shown to be a self-enclosed universe with its own theoretical and consistently maintained inquiry, revealing itself as the all-encompassing unity of ultimately functioning and accomplishing subjectivity which is to account for the existence of the world—the world for us, our natural life-horizon? If this is a legitimate and a necessary task, its execution implies the creation of a new science of a peculiar sort. In opposition to all previously designed objective sciences, which are sciences on the ground of the world, this would be a science of the universal *how* of the pregivenness of the world, i.e., of what makes it a universal ground for any sort of objectivity. And included in this is the creation of a science of the ultimate grounds [*Gründe*] which supply the true force of all objective grounding, the force arising from its ultimate bestowal of meaning.

Our historically motivated path, moving from the interpretation of the interplay of problems between Hume and Kant, has now led us to the postulate of clarifying the pregiven world's character of universally "being the ground" for all objective sciences and—what followed of itself—for all objective praxis; it has led us, then, to the postulate of that novel universal science of subjectivity as pregiving the world. We shall now have to see how we can fulfill this postulate. We notice thereby that the first step which seemed to help at the beginning, that epochē through which we freed ourselves from all objective sciences as grounds of validity, by no means suffices. In carrying out this epochē, we obviously continue to stand on the ground of the world; it is now reduced to the life-world which is valid for us prescientifically; it is just that we may use no sort of knowledge arising from the sciences as premises, and we may take the sciences into consideration only as historical facts, taking no position of our own on their truth.

But nothing about this affects our interested looking-around in the prescientifically intuited world or our paying attention to its relative features. In a certain way, concern with this sort of thing belongs continually even to [one type of] objective investigation, namely, that of the historians, who must, after all, reconstruct the changing, surrounding life-worlds of the peoples and periods with which they deal. In spite of this, the pregiven world is still valid as a ground [for them] and has not been transposed into the universe of the purely subjective, a universal framework in its own right, which is our concern now.

The same thing holds [even] if we take as our subject of investigation, in the unity of a systematic survey, all [historical] periods and peoples and finally the entire spatiotemporal world, paying constant attention to the relativity of the surrounding life-worlds of particular human beings, peoples, and periods as mere matters of fact. It is clear that the same thing is true of this world survey, in the form of an iterated synthesis of relative, spatiotemporal life-worlds, that is true of a survey of one such life-world individually. It is taken one part at a time and then, at a higher level, one surrounding world, one temporal period, at a time; each particular intuition [yields] an ontic validity, whether in the mode of actuality or possibility. As each intuition occurs, it presupposes others having objective validity—presupposes for us, the observers, the general ground of the validity of the world.

§ 39. *The peculiar character of the transcendental epochē as a total change of the natural attitude of life.*

Now, HOW CAN the pregivenness of the life-world become a universal subject of investigation in its own right? Clearly, only through a *total change* of the natural attitude, such that we no longer live, as heretofore, as human beings within natural existence, constantly effecting the validity of the pregiven world; rather, we must constantly deny ourselves this. Only in this way can we arrive at the transformed and novel subject of investigation, "pregivenness of the world as such": the world purely and exclusively *as*—and in respect to *how*—it has meaning and ontic validity, and continually attains these in new forms, in our conscious life. Only thus can we study what the world is as the ground-validity for natural life, with all its projects and undertakings, and, correlatively, what natural life and its subjectivity *ultimately* are, i.e., purely as the subjectivity which functions here in effecting validity. The life which effects world-validity in natural world-life does not permit of being studied from within the attitude of natural world-life. What is required, then, is a *total* transformation of attitude, a *completely unique, universal epochē.*

§ 40. *The difficulties surrounding the genuine sense of performing the total epochē. The temptation to misconstrue it as a withholding of all individual validities, carried out step by step.*

THE UNIVERSALITY of the epochē in regard to the totality of natural and normal life does indeed have an incomparable, peculiar character, and as such it is at first open to question in several respects. From the start it is not clear how it is to be carried out in such a way as to be capable of the methodical accomplishment expected of it, which in turn, in view of its generality, is still in need of clarification. Here many tempting blind alleys offer themselves, as we shall find out, i.e., ways of understanding the performance of the epochē which surely do not lead to the goal—as we can make evident to ourselves in advance.

In order to gain a conception of how this total transformation of attitude is to be carried out, let us consider again the style of natural, normal life. There we move in a current of ever new experiences, judgments, valuations, decisions. In each of these acts the ego is directed toward *objects* in its surrounding world, dealing with them in one way or another. It is of them that we are conscious in these acts themselves, sometimes simply as actual, sometimes in modalities of actuality (for example, as possible, as doubtful, etc.). None of these acts, and none of the validities involved in them, is isolated: in their intentions they necessarily imply an infinite horizon of inactive [*inaktuelle*] validities which function with them in flowing mobility. The manifold acquisitions of earlier active life are not dead sediments; even the background (for example, that of the perceptual field), of which we are always concurrently conscious but which is momentarily irrelevant and remains completely unnoticed, still functions according to its implicit validities. All things of this sort, even though they are momentarily not actualized, are in a constant motion involving modes of being awakened, immediately or mediately, and modes of affecting the ego and possibly passing over into active apperception, intervening as validities in the complex of acts. Thus the particular object of our active consciousness, and correlatively the active, conscious having of it, being directed toward it, and dealing with it—all this is forever surrounded by an atmosphere of mute, concealed, but cofunctioning validities, a *vital horizon* into which the active ego can also direct itself voluntarily, reactivating old acquisitions, consciously grasping new apperceptive ideas, transforming them into intuitions. Because of this constantly flowing *horizonal character,* then, every straightforwardly performed validity in natural world-life always presupposes validities extending back, immediately or mediately, into a necessary subsoil of obscure but occasionally available reactivatable validities, all of which together, including the present acts, make up a single indivisible, interrelated complex of life.

This consideration is of significance for the clarification of how the universal epochē is to be performed. We see, namely, that as an abstention from performing validity, carried out in individual steps, it cannot lead to the goal.

The abstention from performing individual validities (similar to the way this occurs in a critical attitude, caused by theoretical or practical demands) only creates for each instance a new mode of validity on the natural ground of the world; and the situation is not improved if we wish to exercise, through an anticipatory, universal resolve, the abstention from the performance, one by one, of all validities, even to infinity, i.e., in respect to all of one's own or alien validities which from now on could ever suggest themselves.

Instead of this universal abstention in individual steps, a completely different sort of universal epochē is possible, namely, one which puts out of action, with one blow, the total performance running through the whole of natural world-life and through the whole network (whether concealed or open) of validities—precisely that total performance which, as the coherent "natural attitude," makes up "simple" "straightforward" ongoing life. Through the abstention which inhibits this whole hitherto unbroken way of life a complete transformation of all of life is attained, a thoroughly new way of life. An attitude is arrived at which is *above* the pregivenness of the validity of the world, *above* the infinite complex whereby, in concealment, the world's validities are always founded on other validities, *above* the whole manifold but synthetically unified flow in which the world has and forever attains anew its content of meaning and its ontic validity. In other words, we thus have an attitude *above* the universal conscious life (both individual-subjective and intersubjective) through which the world is "there" for those naïvely absorbed in ongoing life, as unquestionably present, as the universe of what is there,[1] as the field of all acquired and newly established life-interests. They are all put out of action in advance by the epochē, and with them the whole natural ongoing life which is directed toward the actualities of "the" world.

It is to be noted also that the present, the "transcendental" epochē is meant, of course, as a habitual attitude which we resolve to take up once and for all. Thus it is by no means a temporary act, which remains incidental and isolated in its various repetitions. And again, everything we said about the earlier

1. *als fraglos vorhandene, als Universum der Vorhandenheiten.*

epochē, in comparing it with vocational attitudes, still holds: during "vocational time," while it does put all other interests "out of play," it by no means gives up their manner of being as belonging to us (or our own manner of being as those who are "interested"), as if we were to sacrifice them or even reconsider whether or not they should continue to be upheld. But we must also not forget what was said as a protest against a degrading equation [of this] with other vocations and what was said about the possibility of radically changing all human existence through this epochē which reaches into its philosophical depths.

§ 41. *The genuine transcendental epochē makes possible the "transcendental reduction"— the discovery and investigation of the transcendental correlation between world and world-consciousness.*

WE PERFORM THE epochē—we who are philosophizing in a new way—as a transformation of the attitude which precedes it not accidentally but essentially, namely, the attitude of natural human existence which, in its total historicity, in life and science, was never before interrupted. But it is necessary, now, to make really transparent the fact that we are not left with a meaningless, habitual abstention; rather, it is through this abstention that the gaze of the philosopher in truth first becomes fully free: above all, free of the strongest and most universal, and at the same time most hidden, internal bond, namely, of the pregivenness of the world. Given in and through this liberation is the discovery of the universal, absolutely self-enclosed and absolutely self-sufficient correlation between the world itself and world-consciousness. By the latter is meant the conscious life of the subjectivity which effects the validity of the world, the subjectivity which always has the world in its enduring acquisitions and continues actively to shape it anew. And there results, finally, taken in the broadest sense, the absolute correlation between beings of every sort and every meaning, on the one hand, and absolute subjectivity, as constituting meaning and ontic validity in this broadest manner, on the other hand. What must be shown in particular and above all is that through the epochē a new way of experiencing, of thinking, of theorizing, is opened to the philosopher; here, situated *above* his own natural being and *above* the natural world, he loses nothing of their being and their objective truths and likewise nothing at all of the spiritual acquisitions of his world-life or those of the whole historical communal life; he simply forbids himself—as a philosopher, in the uniqueness of his direction of interest—to continue the whole natural performance of his world-life; that is, he forbids himself to ask questions which rest upon the ground of the world at hand, questions of being, questions of value, practical questions, questions about being or not-being, about being valuable, being useful, being beautiful, being good, etc. All natural interests are put out of play. But the world, exactly as it was for me earlier and still is, as my world, our world, humanity's world, having validity in its various subjective ways, has not disappeared; it is just that, during the consistently carried-out epochē, it is under our gaze purely as the correlate of the subjectivity which gives it ontic meaning, through whose validities [1] the world "is" at all.

This is not a "view," an "interpretation" bestowed upon the world. Every view about . . . , every opinion about "the" world, has its ground in the pregiven world. It is from this very ground that I have freed myself through the epochē; I stand *above* the world, which has now become for me, in a quite peculiar sense, a *phenomenon*.

§ 42. *The task of concretely plotting ways in which the transcendental reduction can actually be carried out.*

BUT HOW IS THE indicated accomplishment, made possible by the epochē—we call it the "transcendental reduction"—and how is the scientific task which is thus opened up to be made understandable in more concrete terms? [We are referring to the] accomplishment of a reduction of "the" world to the transcendental phenomenon "world," a reduction thus also to its

1. Reading *Geltungen* for *Gelten*.

correlate, transcendental subjectivity, in and through whose "conscious life" the world, valid for us straightforwardly and naïvely prior to all science, attains and always has attained its whole content and ontic validity. How can we make it more concretely understandable that the reduction of mankind to the phenomenon "mankind," which is included as part of the reduction of the world, makes it possible to recognize mankind as a self-objectification of transcendental subjectivity which is always functioning ultimately and is thus "absolute"? How does it become possible, thanks to the epochē, to display this subjectivity in its accomplishment, in its transcendental "conscious life," extending into hidden subsoils, in the distinct manners in which it "brings about," within itself, the world as ontic meaning? How can we bring this to light with self-evidence, not inventing or mythically constructing? If this is a matter of a new sort of scientific discipline, of a new sort of theoretical questioning and resolving of questions, then the ground for these questions, too, must be prepared. Natural questions about the world have their ground in the pregiven world as the world of actual and possible experiences. And the gaze made free by the epochē must likewise be, in its own way, an experiencing gaze. [But] the accomplishment of the total transformation of attitude must consist in the fact that the infinity of actual and possible world-experience transforms itself into the infinity of actual and possible "transcendental experience," in which, as a first step, the world and the natural experience of it are experienced as "phenomenon."

But how do we begin this, and how do we progress? How, at first concretely feeling our way, do we attain our first results, even if only as material for new reflections through which the method of systematic progressive work and, at the same time, the genuine and pure sense of our whole project and the quite peculiar character of this new scientific discipline will become fully clear? The following reflections will show how much such material is needed when we no longer move on the old familiar ground of the world but rather stand, through our transcendental reduction, only at the gate of entrance to the realm, never before entered, of the "mothers of knowledge"; [1] they will show how great the temptation is, here, to misunderstand oneself and how much—indeed, ultimately, the actual success of a transcendental philosophy—depends upon self-reflective clarity carried to its limits.

1. Cf. *Faust*, Part II, line 6216.

§ 43. *Characterization of a new way to the reduction, as contrasted with the "Cartesian way."*

WE WISH TO PROCEED, here, by beginning anew, starting purely from natural world-life, and by asking after the *how* of the world's pregivenness. At first we understand the question of the world's pregivenness just as it arises within the natural attitude and is understandable by all: namely, as the pregivenness of the world of existing things through the constant alteration of relative manners of givenness, the world just as it essentially, always, obviously exists for us, throughout the whole of naturally flowing life, with an inexhaustible plenitude of what is taken for granted and constantly underlies the alteration of subjective appearances and validities. As such we now consistently make the world our subject of investigation, i.e., as the ground of all our interests and life-projects, among which the theoretical projects of the objective sciences make up only a particular group. But the latter is now to be in no way privileged as it was when it motivated our inquiries earlier. In this manner, then, let our subject now be not the world simply, but the world exclusively as it is constantly pregiven to us in the alteration of its manners of givenness.

At this point novel and ever broadening systematic tasks are opened up within a universal epoché which at first offers itself quite obviously as an immediate necessity. In systematically carrying out the epoché, or reduction, understood in this way, however, we find that in all the tasks it sets it requires a clarification and a transformation of its meaning if the new science is to become capable of being executed in a really concrete way and without absurdity; or if—what amounts to the same thing—it is actually to accomplish a reduction to the absolutely ultimate grounds [*Gründe*] and to avoid unnoticed, nonsensical admixtures of naturally naïve prior validities. Thus we arrive once again at the transcendental epoché which was introduced in advance in our previous presentation in a general way. But now it has not only been enriched by the samples of significant insights attained along the way; it has also attained a self-understanding in principle which procures for these insights and for the epochē itself their ultimate meaning and value.

I note in passing that the much shorter way to the transcendental epochē in my *Ideas toward a Pure Phenomenology and Phenomenological Philosophy,* which I call the "Cartesian way" (since it is thought of as being attained merely by reflectively engrossing oneself in the Cartesian epochē of the *Meditations* while critically purifying it of Descartes's prejudices and confusions), has a great shortcoming: while it leads to the transcendental ego in one leap, as it were, it brings this ego into view as apparently empty of content, since there can be no preparatory explication; so one is at a loss, at first, to know what has been gained by it, much less how, starting with this, a completely new sort of fundamental science, decisive for philosophy, has been attained. Hence also, as the reception of my *Ideas* showed, it is all too easy right at the very beginning to fall back into the naïve-natural attitude—something that is very tempting in any case.[1]

§ 44. *The life-world as subject matter for a theoretical interest determined by a universal epochē in respect to the actuality of the things of the life-world.*

LET US BEGIN our new way by devoting an exclusive, consistently theoretical interest to the "life-world" as the general "ground" of human world-life and, specifically, to just the way in which it fulfills this general "ground" function. Since we seek in vain in world literature for investigations that could serve as preparatory studies for us—investigations which might have understood this task as that of a science in its own right (a peculiar science, to be sure, since it concerns the disparaged δόξα, which now suddenly claims the dignity of a foundation for science,

1. It is to be remembered that the German version of the *Cartesian Meditations* had never been released for publication by Husserl. These remarks support the theory that Husserl had given up the project of a final version of the *Meditations* altogether in favor of the *Crisis* as the definitive introduction to phenomenology.

ἐπιστήμη)—we ourselves must make a completely new beginning. As is the case with all undertakings which are new in principle, for which not even an analogy can serve as guide, this beginning takes place with a certain unavoidable naïveté. In the beginning is the deed.[1] It makes the still insecure project more definite and at the same time clearer and clearer by means of samples of successful execution. After this, reflection on method is required (as the second step) which expressly delimits the general sense of such a project, the extent to which it can be fulfilled, and the scope of what has already been accomplished in aspiring to it.

We wish, then, to consider the surrounding life-world concretely, in its neglected relativity and according to all the manners of relativity belonging essentially to it—the world in which we live intuitively, together with its real entities [Realitäten]; but [we wish to consider them] as they give themselves to us at first in straightforward experience, and even [consider] the ways in which their validity is sometimes in suspense (between being and illusion, etc.). Our exclusive task shall be to comprehend precisely this style, precisely this whole merely subjective and apparently incomprehensible "Heraclitean flux." Thus we are not concerned with whether and what the things, the real entities of the world, actually are (their being actual, their actually being such and such, according to properties, relations, interconnections, etc.); we are also not concerned with what the world, taken as a totality, actually is, what in general belongs to it in the way of a priori structural lawfulness or factual "natural laws." We have nothing like this as our subject matter. Thus we exclude all knowledge, all statements about true being and predicative truths for it, such as are required in active life for its praxis (i.e., situational truths); but we also exclude all sciences, genuine as well as pseudosciences, with their knowledge of the world as it is "in itself," in "objective truth." Naturally, in the present thematic sphere, we also take no part in all the interests which set any kind of human praxis in motion, especially since the latter, because of its rootedness in the already existing world, is always at the same time interested in the true existence or the nonexistence of the things with which it deals.

This involves a type of universal epochē, then, which serves here only to isolate the subject matter of subsequent investigations, of whose possible results, by the way, we still have no conception. The motivation arising out of the need to clarify the

1. *Faust*, Part I, line 1237: "Im Anfang war die Tat."

obvious accomplishments of the positive sciences originally required this topic. But we have already detached ourselves from
this motivation. Deeper reflections are required in order to understand how this topic can become an independent task, a field
of working problems.

§ 45.   *Beginnings of a concrete exposition of what
is given in sense-intuition purely as such.*

ONE OF OUR FIRST steps will have to be that of filling in
the empty generality of our theme. As fully "disinterested" [1]
spectators (in the indicated sense of the epochē) of the world
purely as subjective-relative world (the one in which our whole
everyday communal life—our efforts, concerns, and accomplishments—takes place), let us now take a first, naïve look around;
our aim shall be, not to examine the world's being and being-
such, but to consider whatever has been valid and continues to
be valid for us as being and being-such in respect to *how* it is
subjectively valid, how it looks, etc.

For example, there are various individual things of experience at any given time; I focus on one of them. To perceive it,
even if it is perceived as remaining completely unchanged, is
something very complex: it is to see it, to touch it, to smell it, to
hear it, etc.; and in each case I have something different. What
is seen in seeing is in and for itself other than what is touched in
touching. But in spite of this I say: it is the same thing; it is only
the manners of its sensible exhibition, of course, that are different. If I remain purely within the realm of seeing, I find new
differences, arising in very manifold form in the course of any
normal seeing, which, after all, is a continuous process; each
phase is itself a seeing, but actually what is seen in each one is
something different. I express this somewhat in the following
way: the pure thing seen, what is visible "of" the thing, is first of
all a surface, and in the changing course of seeing I see it now
from this "side," now from that, continuously perceiving it from
ever differing sides. But in them *the* surface exhibits itself to me
in a continuous synthesis; each side is for consciousness a man-

1. Reading *uninteressierte* for *uninteressierter.*

ner of exhibition *of* it. This implies that, while the surface is immediately given, I mean more than it offers. Indeed, I have ontic certainty of this thing [as that] to which all the sides at once belong, and in the mode in which I see it "best." Each side gives me something *of* the seen thing. In the continuous alteration of seeing, the side just seen [2] ceases being actually still seen, but it is "retained" and "taken" together with those retained from before; and thus I "get to know" the thing. Similar observations should be developed at length in respect to nearness and farness.

Even if I stop at perception, I still have the full consciousness of the thing, just as I already have it at the first glance when I see it as this thing. In seeing I always "mean" it with all the sides which are in no way given to me, not even in the form of intuitive, anticipatory presentifications. Thus every perception has, "for consciousness," a *horizon* belonging to its object (i.e., whatever is meant in the perception).

But considered more exactly, what we have displayed so far, i.e., what I attribute to the thing itself—for example, its seen, colored shape in the alteration of near-and-far orientation—is again something which exhibits itself in manifold ways. I am speaking now of the alteration of *perspectives*. The perspectives of the shape and also of its color are different, but each is in this new way an *exhibiting of*—*of* this shape, *of* this color. Something similar to this can be studied in every modality of the sense-perception (touching, hearing, etc.) *of* the same thing. In the course of alteration they all play their role as exhibitings, now being interrupted, now beginning again; they offer many types of manifolds of exhibitings, appearances, each of which functions precisely as an exhibiting *of*. In running their course they function in such a way as to form a sometimes continuous and sometimes discrete synthesis of identification or, better, of *unification*. This happens not as a blending of externals; rather, as bearers of "sense" in each phase, as meaning something, the perspectives combine in an advancing *enrichment of meaning* and a *continuing development of meaning*, such that what no longer appears is still valid as retained and such that the prior meaning which anticipates a continuous flow, the expectation of "what is to come," is straightway fulfilled and more closely determined. Thus everything is taken up into the unity of validity or into the *one, the* thing. For now, this rough beginning of a description must suffice.

2. Reading *die eben gesehene* for *eben die gesehene*.

§ 46. *The universal a priori of correlation.*

As soon as we begin to be on the lookout for things or objects in the life-world, not in order to know them as what they [really] are but rather in order to inquire into the modes of their subjective manners of givenness, i.e., into *how* an object—in our example a perceived object—exhibits itself as being and being-such, we enter a realm of more and more involved and very remarkable expositions. Ordinarily we notice nothing of the whole subjective character of the manners of exhibiting "of" the things, but in reflection we recognize with astonishment that essential correlations obtain here which are the component parts of a farther-reaching, universal a priori. And what remarkable "implications" appear, ones that can even be quite immediately, descriptively displayed. As it was already pointed out briefly above: I am directly conscious of the thing existing there, yet changing from moment to moment I have the experience [*Erlebnis*] [of an] "exhibiting of," although the latter, with its remarkable "of," becomes visible only in reflection. Implied in the particular perception of the thing is a whole "horizon" of nonactive [*nichtaktuelle*] and yet cofunctioning manners of appearance and syntheses of validity.

Every first description here is of necessity rough, and soon one is faced with the enigmas caused by this implication of nonactive manifolds of appearances, without which no things, no world of experience, would be given to us. And soon we are also faced with the difficulties of concretely unfolding this a priori of correlation. The latter can be displayed only in relativity, in an unfolding of horizons in which one soon realizes that unnoticed limitations, horizons which have not been felt, push us on to inquire into new correlations inseparably bound up with those already displayed. For example, we involuntarily begin such an "intentional analysis" of perception by giving privileged status to a thing at rest, remaining qualitatively unchanged. But the things of the perceptual surrounding world give themselves only temporarily in this way, and soon the intentional problem of motion and change arises. But was such a beginning, with the unchanged thing at rest, actually only accidental? Does the privileged status of rest not itself have a motive in the necessary course of such investigations? Or, to look at the matter from another and very important side: involuntarily, we began with the intentional analysis of *perception* (purely as perception of its perceived object) and in fact gave privileged status thereby to intuitively given *bodies*. Might this not also point to essential necessities? The world exists as a temporal, a spatiotemporal, world in which each thing has its bodily extension and duration and, again in respect to these, its position in universal time and in space. It is as such that we are ever conscious of the world in waking consciousness, as such that it is valid as universal horizon. Perception is related only to the *present*. But this present is always meant as having an endless *past* behind it and an open *future* before it. We soon see that we need the intentional analysis of recollection as the original manner of being conscious of the past; but we also see that such an analysis presupposes in principle that of perception, since memory, curiously enough, implies having-perceived. If we consider perception abstractly, by itself, we find its intentional accomplishment to be presentation, making something present: the object gives itself as "there," originally there, present. But in this presence, as that of an extended and enduring object, lies a continuity of what I am still conscious of, what has flowed away and is no longer intuited at all, a continuity of "retentions"—and, in the other direction, a continuity of "protentions." Yet this is not, like memory in the usual sense of intuitive "recollection," a phenomenon which openly, so to speak, plays a part in object- and world-apperception. And thus the different modes of presentification in general enter into the universal investigation we are undertaking here, namely, that of inquiring consistently and exclusively after the *how* of the world's manner of givenness, its open or implicit "intentionalities." In displaying these, we must say to ourselves again and again that without them the objects and the world would not be there for us and that the former exist for us only with the meaning and the mode of being that they receive in constantly arising or having arisen out of those subjective *accomplishments*.

§ 47. *Indication of further directions of inquiry:
the basic subjective phenomena of kinesthesis,
alteration of validity, horizon-consciousness,
and the communalization of experience.*

BUT FIRST IT WILL be necessary to continue our groping
entrance into this unknown realm of subjective phenomena and
to carry out several further expositions, which will be understandably still rough and in many respects still imperfectly determined. Let us again give a privileged status to perception.
Previously our gaze was directed at the multiplicity of side-exhib-
itings of one and the same thing and to the alteration of near
and far perspectives. We soon note that these systems of "exhibiting of" are related back to correlative multiplicities of kinesthetic processes having the peculiar character of the "I do," "I
move" (to which even the "I hold still" must be added). The kinestheses are different from the movements of the living body
which exhibit themselves merely as those of a physical body,
yet they are somehow one with them, belonging to one's own
living body with its two-sided character (internal kinestheses,
external physical-real movements). If we inquire into this "belonging," we notice that in each case "my living body" requires
particular and extensive descriptions, that it has its special peculiarities in the manner of exhibiting itself in multiplicities.
    Another extraordinarily important thematic direction has
not yet been named; it is characterized by the phenomenon of
the *alteration of validity*—for example, the alteration of being
into illusion. In continuous perception a thing is there for me in
the straightforward ontic certainty of immediate presence—
though I must add: normally; for only when, giving my kinestheses free play, I experience concurrent exhibitings as belonging to it is the consciousness sustained of the one thing in
actual presence, exhibiting itself in manifold fashion as itself.
But if I ask what is implied in the fact that the thing-exhibitings
belong to the altering kinestheses, I recognize that a hidden
intentional "if-then" relation is at work here: the exhibitings
must occur in a certain systematic order; it is in this way that
they are indicated in advance, in expectation, in the course of a

harmonious perception. The actual kinestheses here lie within the system of kinesthetic capacity, which is correlated with the system of possible following events harmoniously belonging to it. This is, then, the intentional background of every straightforward ontic certainty of a presented thing.[1]

Often, however, a break in this harmony occurs: being is transformed into illusion or simply into being doubtful, being merely possible, being probable, being after all not completely illusory, etc. The illusion is undone through "correction," through changing the sense in which the thing had been perceived. It is easy to see that the change of apperceptive sense takes place through a change of the expectation-horizon of the multiplicities anticipated as normal (i.e., as running on harmoniously). For example, one saw a man, but then, upon touching him, had to reinterpret him as a mannequin (exhibiting itself visually as a man).

When our interest is turned in this direction, unexpectedly manifold phenomena can be noticed in every perception, and not only in connection with the individual thing. For consciousness the individual thing is not alone; the perception of a thing is perception of it within a *perceptual field*. And just as the individual thing in perception has meaning only through an open horizon of "possible perceptions," insofar as what is actually perceived "points" to a systematic multiplicity of all possible perceptual exhibitings belonging to it harmoniously, so the thing has yet another horizon: besides this "internal horizon" it has an "external horizon" precisely as a thing within a *field of things;* and this points finally to the whole "world as perceptual world." The thing is one out of the total group of simultaneously actually perceived things; but this group is not, for us, for consciousness, the world; rather, the world exhibits itself in it; such a group, as the momentary field of perception, always has the character for us of a *sector "of"* the world, of the universe of things for possible perceptions. Such, then, at any time, is the present world; it exhibits itself to me in every case through a nucleus of "original presence" (this designates the continuously subjective character of what is directly perceived as such) as well as through its internal and external horizon-validities.

In our—or, for each of us, my [2]—waking life, the world is

1. Cf. the similar passage on pp. 106 f., above.
2. *in unserem, je-meinem*—a very Heideggerian turn of phrase.

always perceived in this way; it always flows on in the unity of my perceptual conscious life; yet it does so in remarkable fashion, such that, in individual details, a harmonious flow of the preindicated multiplicities, which results in the consciousness of the straightforward existence of the thing in question, does not always occur. Ontic certainty, which involves an anticipatory certainty of bringing the appropriate multiplicities harmoniously into a fulfilling flow in the course of further perception through a voluntary direction of the kinestheses, is often not sustained; and yet a *harmony in the total perception* of the world is always sustained through a correction which actually constantly functions along with it. This includes, for example, the correction involved in seeing something close up, whereby what was seen from afar is determined more precisely and thus at the same time corrected (e.g., what was an undifferentiated red at a distance shows itself from close up to be spotted).

But instead of inquiring further in the sphere of our own intuitions, let us turn our attention to the fact that in our continuously flowing world-perceiving we are not isolated but rather have, within it, contact with other human beings. Each one has his perceptions, his presentifications, his harmonious experiences, devaluation of his certainties into mere possibilities, doubts, questions, illusions. But in *living with one another* each one can take part in the life of the others. Thus in general the world exists not only for isolated men but for the community of men; and this is due to the fact that even what is straightforwardly perceptual is communalized.

In this communalization, too, there constantly occurs an alteration of validity through reciprocal correction. In reciprocal understanding, my experiences and experiential acquisitions enter into contact with those of others, similar to the contact between individual series of experiences within my (one's own) experiential life; and here again, for the most part, intersubjective harmony of validity occurs, [establishing what is] "normal" in respect to particular details, and thus an intersubjective unity also comes about in the multiplicity of validities and of what is valid through them; here again, furthermore, intersubjective discrepancies show themselves often enough; but then, whether it is unspoken and even unnoticed, or is expressed through discussion and criticism, a unification is brought about or at least is certain in advance as possibly attainable by everyone. All this takes place in such a way that in the consciousness of each individual, and in the overarching community consciousness which has grown up through [social] contact, one and the same world achieves and continuously maintains constant validity as the world which is in part already experienced and in part the open horizon of possible experiences for all; it is the world as the universal horizon, common to all men, of actually existing things. Each individual, as a subject of possible experiences, has his experiences, his aspects, his perceptual interconnections, his alteration of validity, his corrections, etc.; and each particular social group has its communal aspects, etc. Here again, properly speaking, each individual has his experienced things, that is, if we understand by this what in particular is valid for him, what is seen by him and, through the seeing, is experienced as straightforwardly existing and being-such. But each individual "knows" himself to be living within the horizon of his fellow human beings, with whom he can enter into sometimes actual, sometimes potential contact, as they also can do (as he likewise knows) in actual and potential living together. He knows that he and his fellows, in their actual contact, are related to the same experienced things in such a way that each individual has different aspects, different sides, perspectives, etc., of them but that in each case these are taken from the same total system of multiplicities of which each individual is constantly conscious (in the actual experience of the same thing) as the horizon of possible experience of this thing. If one attends to the distinction between things as "originally one's own" and as "empathized" from others, in respect to the *how* of the manners of appearance, and if one attends to the possibility of discrepancies between one's own and empathized views, then what one actually experiences *originaliter* as a perceptual thing is transformed, for each of us, into a mere "representation of" ["*Vorstellung von*"], "appearance of," the one objectively existing thing. From the synthesis these have taken on precisely the new sense "appearance of," and as such they are henceforth valid. "The" thing itself is actually that which no one experiences as really seen, since it is always in motion, always, and for everyone, a unity for consciousness of the openly endless multiplicity of changing experiences and experienced things, one's own and those of others. The cosubjects of this experience themselves make up, for me and for one another, an openly endless horizon of human beings who are capable of meeting and then entering into actual contact with me and with one another.

§ 48. *Anything that is—whatever its meaning and to whatever region it belongs—is an index of a subjective system of correlations.*

IN THIS EXCLUSIVE concentration on the multiplicities of subjective manners of appearing through which the world is pregiven to us, we arrive, again and again—even though we have really considered only the world of perception, indeed only its corporeal features—at the insight that we are not dealing merely with contingent matters of fact. Rather, no conceivable human being, no matter how different we imagine him to be, could ever experience a world in manners of givenness which differ from the incessantly mobile relativity we have delineated in general terms, i.e., as a world pregiven to him in his conscious life and in community with fellow human beings. The fact which is naïvely taken for granted, that each person sees things and the world in general as they appear to him, concealed, as we now realize, a great horizon of remarkable truths whose uniqueness and systematic interconnection never entered the philosophical purview. The correlation between world (the world of which we always speak) and its subjective manners of givenness never evoked philosophical wonder (that is, prior to the first breakthrough of "transcendental phenomenology" in the *Logical Investigations*), in spite of the fact that it had made itself felt even in pre-Socratic philosophy and among the Sophists— though here only as a motive for skeptical argumentation. This correlation never aroused a philosophical interest of its own which could have made it the object of an appropriate scientific attitude. Philosophers were confined by what was taken for granted, i.e., that each thing appeared differently in each case to each person.

But as soon as we begin to examine carefully the *how* of the appearance of a thing in its actual and possible alteration and to pay consistent attention to the correlation it involves between *appearance* and *that which appears as such,* and if we consider the alteration as an alteration of validity for the intentionality occurring in the ego-subjects and their communalization, we are forced to recognize a fixed typology with ever widening ramifications. It applies not only to perceiving, to bodies, and to the penetrable depths of immediate sensibility but to any and every entity within the spatiotemporal world and to its subjective manners of givenness. Everything thus stands in correlation with its own manners of givenness, which are by no means merely sensible in character, within a possible experience; and everything has its modes of validity and its particular manners of synthesis. Experience, self-evidence, is not an empty generality but is differentiated according to the species, genera, and regional categories of what is and also according to all spatiotemporal modalities. Whatever exists, whether it has a concrete or abstract, real or ideal, meaning, has its manners of self-givenness and, on the side of the ego, its manners of intention in modes of validity; to this belong the manners of the subjective variation of these modes in syntheses of individual-subjective and intersubjective harmony and discrepancy. We also foresee (as even the first trials made clear in a preliminary way) that this confusingly manifold typology of correlations, comprising further differentiations at every turn, is not a mere though generally established fact but rather that the factual indicates an essential necessity which, with the proper method, can be translated into essential generalities, into an immense system of novel and highly astounding a priori truths. No matter where we turn, every entity that is valid for me and every conceivable subject as existing in actuality is thus correlatively—and with essential necessity—an index of its systematic multiplicities. Each one indicates an ideal general set of actual and possible experiential manners of givenness, each of which is an appearance of this one entity, such that every actual concrete experience brings about, from this total multiplicity, a harmonious flow of manners of givenness which continuously fulfills the experiencing intention.*

* The first breakthrough of this universal a priori of correlation between experienced object and manners of givenness (which occurred during work on my *Logical Investigations* around 1898) affected me so deeply that my whole subsequent life-work has been dominated by the task of systematically elaborating on this a priori of correlation. The further course of the reflections in this text will show how, when human subjectivity was brought into the problems of correlation, a radical transformation of the meaning of these problems became necessary which finally led to the phenomenological reduction to absolute, transcendental subjectivity.

The first, though still unclarified, emergence of the phenomenological reduction occurred several years after the publication of the

The total multiplicity of manners of givenness, however, is a horizon of possibly realizable processes, as opposed to the actual process, and as such it belongs to each experience, or rather to the intention which is operative within it. For each subject this intention is the *cogito;* the manners of givenness (understood in the widest sense) make up its *cogitatum* according to the "what" and the "how," and the manners of givenness in turn bring to "exhibition" the one and the same entity which is their unity.

§49. *Preliminary concept of transcendental constitution as "original formation of meaning." The restricted character of the exemplary analyses carried out so far; an indication of further horizons of exposition.*

WE SEE HOW FAR we must take all this when we realize that, while we are dealing with the total intentional accomplishment, having many levels, of the subjectivity in question, it is not that of the isolated subject. We are dealing, rather, with the entire intersubjectivity which is brought together in the accomplishment—and here the concepts of "what is," of "manners of givenness," of "syntheses," etc., are repeatedly relativized. Again and again we realize that, beginning with the superficially visible, the manners of appearing belonging to the unifying multiplicities are themselves unities of multiplicities which lie deeper and which constitute them through appearances, so that we are led back to an obscure horizon—which, however, can still be

---

Logical Investigations (1900–1901); the first attempt at a systematic introduction to the new philosophy of the transcendental reduction appeared in 1913 as a fragment (Volume I of *Ideas toward a Pure Phenomenology and Phenomenological Philosophy*).

Contemporary philosophy of the decades since then—even that of the so-called phenomenological schools—preferred to persist in the old philosophical naïveté. To be sure, the first breakthroughs of such a radical change, a total transformation of the whole natural manner of life, were difficult to present adequately, especially since certain considerations, which will become understandable in the following, constantly give rise to misinterpretations resulting from relapses into the natural attitude.

opened up through methodical regressive inquiry. All the levels and strata through which the syntheses, intentionally overlapping as they are from subject to subject, are interwoven form a universal unity of synthesis; through it the objective universe comes to be—the world which is and *as* it is concretely and vividly given (and pregiven for all possible praxis). In this regard we speak of the "intersubjective constitution" of the world, meaning by this the total system of manners of givenness, however hidden, and also of modes of validity for egos; through this constitution, if we systematically uncover it, the world as it is for us becomes understandable as a structure of meaning formed out of elementary intentionalities. The being of these intentionalities themselves is nothing but one meaning-formation operating together with another, "constituting" new meaning through synthesis. And meaning is never anything but meaning in modes of validity, that is, as related to intending ego-subjects which effect validity. Intentionality is the title which stands for the only actual and genuine way of explaining, making intelligible. To go back to the intentional origins and unities of the formation of meaning is to proceed toward a comprehension which, once achieved (which is of course an ideal case), would leave no meaningful question unanswered. But every serious and genuine move from a "ready-made entity" back to its intentional origins gives us, in respect to those strata already uncovered and the clarification of what is accomplished in them, an understanding which, though merely relative, is yet an actual understanding as far as it goes.

What we dealt with in the manner of examples was naturally only a beginning, in fact a beginning of the clarification of merely the world of perception, which is itself, taken as a whole, only a "stratum." The world is a spatiotemporal world; spatiotemporality (as "living," not as logicomathematical) belongs to its own ontic meaning as life-world. Our focus on the world of perception (and it is no accident that we begin here) gives us, as far as the world is concerned, only the temporal mode of the present; this mode itself points to its horizons, the temporal modes of past and future. Recollection, above all, exercises the intentional function of forming the meaning of the past—apart from the fact that perception itself, as the "flowing-static" present, is constituted only through the fact that the static "now" (as a deeper intentional analysis shows) has a horizon with two differently structured sides, known in intentional language as a continuum of retentions and protentions. These first prefigurations of temporalization and time, however, remain in the background. In the recollection founded upon them we have before us, in original intuition, a past—a present which has passed. It too has "being": it has its multiplicities of manners of givenness, its manners of coming to original self-givenness (to immediate self-evidence) as what has passed. Likewise, in expectation or anticipatory recollection, again understood as an intentional modification of perception (the future is a present-to-come), is found the meaning-formation from which arises the ontic meaning of that which is in the future. And the deeper structure of this can be revealed in more detail. This represents the beginnings of new dimensions of temporalization, or of time and its time content—quite apart from the fact (which is not to be elucidated here) that the constitution of every level and sort of entity is a temporalization which gives to each distinctive meaning of an entity in the constitutive system its own temporal form, whereas only through the all-inclusive, universal synthesis which constitutes the world do all these times come together synthetically into the unity of one time. One thing more should be pointed out: in the elucidation of the accomplishment of the intentional syntheses, privileged status is given to the clarification of the syntheses of continuity (for example, the one contained in the flowing unity of perception); these serve as a ground for elucidating on a higher level the discrete syntheses. I give as an example [of the latter] the identification of something perceived as the same thing that, according to recollection, was there before. This rerecognition, its exposition through the continuity of recollection, the corresponding deeper analyses of these "obvious" matters—all this leads to difficult investigations.

Here, as everywhere, we can investigate first only what is nearest to our comprehension. But it should be clear from the preceding that as soon as one has progressed far enough in the reorientation of the epochē to see the purely subjective in its own self-enclosed pure context as intentionality and to recognize it as the function of forming ontic meaning, the theoretical interest grows quickly, and one becomes more astonished at each step by the endless array of emerging problems and important discoveries to be made. To be sure, one is soon beset by extraordinary difficulties: that of preserving the pure frame of mind, of finding one's way in an unknown world, where all the concepts, all the ways of thinking and scientific methods based on the natural world, as well as all the logical methods of objective science, are of no help; and that of bringing about a novel and yet scientific way of thinking through the required method which is developing in a precursory way. In truth, this is a whole world—and if we could equate this subjectivity with the ψυχή of Heraclitus, his saying would doubtless be true of it: "You will never find the boundaries of the soul, even if you follow every road; so deep is its ground." [1] Indeed, every "ground" [Grund] that is reached points to further grounds, every horizon opened up awakens new horizons, and yet the endless whole, in its infinity of flowing movement, is oriented toward the unity of one meaning; not, of course, in such a way that we could ever simply grasp and understand the whole; rather, as soon as one has fairly well mastered the universal form of meaning-formation, the breadths and depths of this total meaning, in its infinite totality, take on valuative [axiotische] dimensions: there arise problems of the totality as that of a universal reason. Yet all this is far from the beginner; he starts by exhibiting only a few interconnections, and only gradually does he learn to discover the essential order of the work to be done or (what amounts to the same thing) to do justice to those important considerations which, in the course of exhibiting and describing, are belatedly recognized as determining everything else. Here we can only sketch them in broad outlines.

§ 50. *First ordering of all working problems under the headings* ego—cogito—cogitatum.

WHEN WE TAKE AN INTEREST in the subjective-relative life-world, what first arrests our gaze is, naturally: appearance and that which appears; and we remain at first in the sphere of the intuitively given, i.e., the sphere of the modes of experience. The nonintuitive manners of being conscious and their relatedness back to possibilities of intuition remain unconsidered. So we pursue the synthesis through which the manifold appearances bear within themselves "that which is" as their "object-pole." The latter is in the appearances not as a component part

1. Husserl slightly misquotes Diels's version of Fragment 45: the last phrase reads "so tiefen Sinn hat sie" (rather than *Grund*). Cf. *Die Fragmente der Vorsokratiker*, ed. W. Kranz, 12th ed. (Dublin and Zurich: Weidman, 1966), p. 161.

[*reell*] but intentionally, as that *of which* each, in its own way, is an appearance. A thing, for example, in the harmonious synthesis of unification, is just this one thing, showing itself one side at a time, revealing its identical being through its properties, which are exhibited in different perspectives. In terms of intentionality, anything straightforwardly experienced as a "this-here," as a thing, is an index of its manners of appearing, which become intuitable (or experienceable, in their own peculiar way) when our gaze is reflectively turned. All the above considerations, of course, touch upon the ego in passing, but the ego ultimately claims its right as the subject matter of a far-reaching investigation in its own right, namely, as the *performer* (also identical, in its own way) *of all validities,* the intending ego, directed toward the unity-pole "through" the alterations of the many-leveled manners of appearing. That is, it is directed toward its sought-after goal (its project [*Vorhabe*]), which is meant in advance with greater or less clarity and distinctness, which fulfills itself, being and becoming, phase by phase—fulfilling the *ego's* intention. At the same time the ego—as the *ego-pole*—continuously carries out a retaining function such that, while it actively explicates the object through its properties (i.e., its particular "is"-qualities, which give it its particularity), it does not let what has been explicated *originaliter* sink away into nothingness as perception proceeds but rather holds it in its meaning grasp even though it is now unperceived. Everything is centered in the ego-pole, including the modalization of the ontic certainties—"crossing out" what is illusory, attending to the decision about uncertainties, doubt, etc. *Affections,* on the other hand, go toward the ego-pole; they attract the ego with greater or less insistence, possibly motivating it to turn to them in a truly active way. These and similar matters point to special analyses in depth of the ego as ego-pole.

Accordingly we have, in the Cartesian manner of speaking, the three headings, *ego–cogitatio–cogitata:* the ego-pole (and what is peculiar to its identity), the subjective, as appearance tied together synthetically, and the object-poles. These are different directions our analyses can take, and to them correspond different aspects of the general notion of intentionality: direction toward something, appearance of something, and something, an objective something, *as* the unity in its appearances toward which the intention of the ego-pole, through these appearances, is directed. Although these headings are inseparable from one another, one must pursue them one at a time and in an order opposite to that suggested by the Cartesian approach. First comes the straightforwardly given life-world, taken initially as it is given perceptually: as "normal," simply there, unbroken, existing in pure ontic certainty (undoubted). When the new direction of interest is established, and thus also its strict epochē, the life-world becomes a first intentional heading, an *index* or *guideline* for inquiring back into the multiplicities of manners of appearing and their intentional structures. A further shift of direction, at the second level of reflection, leads to the ego-pole and what is peculiar to its identity. Let us here point out only what is most important, the most general aspect of the ego's form, namely, the peculiar temporalization by which it becomes an enduring ego, constituting itself in its time-modalities: the same ego, now actually present, is in a sense, in every past that belongs to it, another—i.e., as that which was and thus is not now—and yet, in the continuity of its time it is one and the same, which is and was and has its future before it. The ego which is present now, thus temporalized, has contact with its past ego, even though the latter is precisely no longer present: it can have a dialogue with it and criticize it, as it can others.

Now everything becomes complicated as soon as we consider that subjectivity is what it is—an ego functioning constitutively —only within intersubjectivity. From the "ego" perspective this means that there are new themes, those of the synthesis applying specifically to ego and other-ego (each taken purely as ego): the I-you-synthesis and, also, the more complicated we-synthesis. In a certain sense this is also a temporalization, namely, that of the simultaneity of the ego-poles or, what amounts to the same thing, that of the constitution of the personal horizon (pure ego-horizon) in which every ego knows itself to be. It is universal sociality (in this sense, "mankind"), the "space" of all ego-subjects. But the synthesis of intersubjectivity, of course, covers everything else as well: the intersubjectively identical life-world-for-all serves as an intentional "index" for the multiplicities of appearance, combined in intersubjective synthesis, through which all ego-subjects (and not merely each through the multiplicities which are peculiar to him individually) are oriented toward a common world and the things in it, the field of all the activities united in the general "we," etc.

§ 51. *The task of an "ontology of the life-world."*

BUT ALL THIS—and this is what makes scientific discipline, description, phenomenological-transcendental truth possible—is pervaded by a set of fixed types which, as we have said, is one of essential types and can be methodically encompassed as a pure a priori. Here it is remarkable, and philosophically very important, that this also applies to the first of our topics, the life-world, constituted throughout all its relative aspects as a unity, the universe of life-world objects. Even without any transcendental interest—that is, within the "natural attitude" (in the language of transcendental philosophy the naïve attitude, prior to the epochē)—the life-world could have become the subject matter of a science of its own, an ontology of the life-world purely as experiential world (i.e., as the world which is coherently, consistently, harmoniously intuitable in actual and possible experiencing intuition). For our part we, who up to now have constantly carried out our systematic reflections within the reorientation of the transcendental epochē, can at any time restore the natural attitude and, within it, inquire after the invariant structures of the life-world.

The world of life, which as a matter of course takes up into itself all practical structures (even those of the objective sciences as cultural facts, though we refrain from taking part in their interests), is, to be sure, related to subjectivity throughout the constant alteration of its relative aspects. But however it changes and however it may be corrected, it holds to its essentially lawful set of types, to which all life, and thus all science, of which it is the "ground," remain bound. Thus it also has an ontology to be derived from pure self-evidence.

We have already spoken of the possibility and the significance of such an ontology of the life-world on the natural ground, i.e., outside the transcendental horizon of interest, and we shall have occasion to speak of it again in another connection. We must keep firmly in mind the fact that this ontology's own sense of an a priori science contrasts sharply with that of the tradition. We must never ignore the fact that modern philosophy, with its objective sciences, is guided by a constructive concept of a world which is true in itself, one substructed in mathematical form, at least in respect to nature. Modern philosophy's concept of an a priori science, which is ultimately a universal mathematics (logic, logistic), cannot therefore have the dignity of actual self-evidence, i.e., the dignity of essential insight obtained from direct self-giving (experiencing intuition), much as it would like to claim this for itself.

If we return again, after this reminder, to the transcendental attitude, i.e., the epochē, the life-world transforms itself, within our transcendental-philosophical framework, into the mere transcendental "phenomenon." It remains thereby in its own essence what it was before, but now it proves to be a mere "component," so to speak, within concrete transcendental subjectivity; and correspondingly its a priori shows itself to be a "stratum" within the universal a priori of the transcendental [in general]. To be sure, words taken from the sphere of the natural world, such as "component" and "stratum," are dangerous, and the necessary transformation of their sense must therefore be noticed. Within the epochē we are free consistently to direct our gaze exclusively at this life-world or at its a priori essential forms; on the other hand, by correspondingly shifting our gaze we can direct it at the correlates which constitute its "things" or thing-forms, i.e., at the multiplicities of manners of givenness and their correlative essential forms. Further, we can also consider the subjects and communities of subjects, which function in all this, with regard to the essential ego-forms belonging to them. In the alteration of these partial attitudes, which are founded upon one another—whereby the attitude focused upon life-world phenomena serves as point of departure, namely, as transcendental guideline for correlative attitudes on higher levels—the universal task of inquiry, that of the transcendental reduction, is brought to realization.

§ 52. *The emergence of paradoxical enigmas. The necessity of new radical reflections.*

THE FIRST SURVEY of the pure problems of correlation, which opened up to us the reorientation from the life of natural interest in the world into the attitude of the "disinterested" spectator, has resulted, though with a certain naïveté and thus preliminarily, in an abundance of obviously very strange insights which, if they were perfectly secured methodically, would imply a radical reshaping of our whole way of looking at the world. For purposes of thus securing our method, a reflection is required concerning the ground of ultimate presuppositions in which all these problems are rooted and from which, then, their theoretical decisions ultimately take their meaning. But immediately we become involved in great difficulties, in unexpected and at first insoluble paradoxes, which place our whole undertaking in question—and this in spite of the self-evidences which offered themselves to us and which we cannot simply give up out of hand. Perhaps only a new inquiry back into the ground of *this* knowledge (as opposed to the inquiry back into the ground of objective knowledge) will lead to the clarification and thus the corresponding limitation of its true sense. In the study of correlation our constant theme was the world and mankind as the subjectivity which, in community, intentionally brings about the accomplishment of world-validity. Our epochē (the one determining our present investigation) denied us all natural world-life and its worldly interests. It gave us a position above these. Any interest in the being, actuality, or nonbeing of the world, i.e., any interest theoretically oriented toward knowledge of the world, and even any interest which is practical in the usual sense, with its dependence on the presuppositions of its situational truths, is forbidden; this applies not only to the pursuit, for ourselves, of our own interests (we who are philosophizing) but also to any participation in the interests of our fellow men —for in this case we would still be interested indirectly in existing actuality. No objective truth, whether in the prescientific or the scientific sense, i.e., no claim about objective being, ever enters our sphere of scientific discipline, whether as a premise or as a conclusion. Here we could discover a first difficulty. Are not we also doing science? Are we not establishing truths about true being? Are we not entering upon the dangerous road of double truth? Can there be, next to objective truth, yet a second truth, the subjective? The answer, of course, is as follows: it is precisely the result of inquiry within the epochē—a strange but self-evident result, which can be ultimately clarified only through our present reflection—that the natural, objective world-life is only a particular mode of the transcendental life which forever constitutes the world, [but] in such a way that transcendental subjectivity, while living on in this mode, has not become conscious of the constituting horizons and never can become aware of them. It lives in "infatuation," so to speak, with the poles of unity without being aware of the constituting multiplicities belonging essentially to them—for this, precisely, would require a complete reorientation and reflection. Objective truth belongs exclusively within the attitude of natural human world-life. It arises originally out of the needs of human praxis as the intent to secure what is straightforwardly given as existing (the object-pole anticipated in ontic certainty as persisting) against the possible modalizations of certainty. In the reorientation of the epochē nothing is lost, none of the interests and ends of world-life, and thus also none of the ends of knowledge. But for all these things their essential subjective correlates are exhibited, and thus the full and true ontic meaning of objective being, and thus of all objective truth, is set forth. Philosophy as universal *objective* science—and this is what all philosophy of the ancient tradition was—together with all the objective sciences, is not universal science at all. It brings into its sphere of inquiry only the constituted object-poles and remains blind to the full concrete being and life that constitutes them transcendentally. But, as we said, though we shall hold onto this as truth, we must still carry out a final clarification of its meaning.

A second difficulty emerges. The epochē in respect to all natural human life-interests appears to be a turning-away from them (which is, by the way, one of the most common misunderstandings of the transcendental epochē). But if it were meant in this way, there would be no transcendental inquiry. How could we take perception and the perceived, memory and the remembered, the objective and every sort of verification of the objective, including art, science, and philosophy, as a transcendental theme without living through these sorts of things as éxamples and indeed with [their] full self-evidence? This is, in fact, quite true. Thus in a certain sense the philosopher within the epochē must also "naturally live through" the natural life; yet the epochē effects an immense difference in that it changes the entire manner of investigation and, furthermore, reshapes the goal of knowledge in the whole of its ontic meaning. In straightforward natural life all purposes *terminate* in "the" world and all knowledge *terminates* in what actually exists as secured by verification. The world is the open universe, the horizon of "termini," the universal field of what exists which is presupposed by all praxis and is continually enriched by its results. Thus the world is the totality of what is taken for granted as verifiable; it is "there" through an aiming [*Abzielung*] and is the ground for ever

new aimings at what is—what "actually" is. In the epochē, however, we go back to the *subjectivity* which ultimately aims, which
already has results, already has the world through previous aims
and their fulfillment; and [we go back] to the ways in which this
subjectivity has, "has brought about," and continues to shape the
world through its concealed internal "method." The interest of
the phenomenologist is not aimed at the ready-made world or at
external, purposeful activity in it, which itself is something
"constituted." The phenomenologist carries out every sort of
praxis, either actually or in sympathetic understanding, but not
in such a way that its fulfilling "end" is his end, the one in which
he terminates. Rather, he takes being-an-end as such, this living
toward goals in world-life and terminating in them, as the subject of his own investigation in respect to the subjective aspects
pervading them; and thus the naïve ontic meaning of the world
in general is transformed for him into the meaning "system of
poles for a transcendental subjectivity," which "has" a world and
real entities within it, just as it has these poles, by constituting
them. This is obviously something fundamentally different from
the transformation of "ends" into "means," into premises for new
worldly ends, a transformation which remains within the world
itself.

What has been said here presupposes that one is fully clear
about our way of explicating intentional life, through the
epochē, as accomplishing life, and that one has first achieved the
insight that even in the most straightforward perception, and
likewise in every consciousness of something having the simple,
straightforward validity of existence, there lies an aiming, one
that is realized in the harmoniousness of ever new ontic validities (those of the manners of givenness themselves) and, in the
case of intuition, realizes the "thing itself." No matter what
variations we may find in intentionality as we proceed on from
its first exhibition in the ways of being actually directed toward
objects, they are all variational forms of accomplishments which
are ultimately those of the ego.

A third difficulty is that we cannot see how, in the epochē,
the "Heraclitean flux" of constituting life can be treated descriptively in its individual facticity. Here we are guided by the
distinction common in objective world-science between descriptive sciences—which, on the basis of experience, describe and
classify factual existence and sketch out inductive generalities
within intuitive experience so as to establish such existence for
everyone who has the same experience—and sciences of laws,

the sciences of unconditional generalities. Still, whatever the status of this objective difference, no real difficulty results for us, since it would be illegitimate to make demands on the transcendental sphere which originate in the sphere of objectivity. It is, however, correct that there can be no analogue to an empirical science of fact, no "descriptive" science of transcendental being and life understood as an inductive science based on experience alone, in the sense of establishing *individual* transcendental correlations as they factually occur and disappear. Not even the single philosopher by himself, within the epochē, can hold fast to anything in this elusively flowing life, repeat it with always the same content, and become so certain of its this-ness and its being-such that he could describe it, document it, so to speak (even for his own person alone), in definitive statements. But the full concrete facticity of universal transcendental subjectivity can nevertheless be scientifically grasped in another good sense, precisely because, truly through an eidetic method, the great task can and must be undertaken of investigating the essential form of the transcendental accomplishments in all their types of individual and intersubjective accomplishments, that is, the total essential form of transcendentally accomplishing subjectivity in all its social forms. The fact is here, as belonging to its essence, and it is determinable only *through* its essence; there is no way of documenting it empirically in a sense analogous to what is done in the objective sphere through inductive experience.

§ 53. *The paradox of human subjectivity: being a subject for the world and at the same time being an object in the world.*

BUT NOW A TRULY serious difficulty arises which assails our whole undertaking and the sense of its results and indeed necessitates a reshaping of both. By virtue of our present method of epochē, everything objective is transformed into something subjective. Clearly this cannot be meant in such a way that through this method the existing world and the human world-representation are set over against each other and that, on the ground of the world, taken for granted as actually existing, we inquire into the subjective, i.e., into the psychic occurrences in men through which they gain experience of the world, everyday or scientific opinions about the world, their particular sensible and conceptual "world-pictures." Scientific discipline for us is not that of the psychologist. Through the radical epochē every interest in the actuality or nonactuality of the world (in all modalities, thus including possibility and conceivability, as well as the decidability of this sort of thing) is put out of play. By the same token, we are not concerned here with any scientific psychology and its problems. For the latter the world, presupposed by it as unquestionably existing, is the ground; and it is precisely this ground that the epochē has taken from us. And in the pure attitude focused upon correlations, created by the epochē, the world, the objective, becomes itself something subjective. In this attitude, paradoxically, even the "subjective" is relativized, namely, in the following way. The world (called "transcendental phenomenon" in the transformed attitude) is from the start taken only as a correlate of the subjective appearances, views, subjective acts and capacities through which it constantly has, and ever attains anew, its changeable [but] unitary sense. Now if the inquiry gets underway, proceeding from the world (which already has merely the manner of being of a unity of meaning) back to the essential forms of these "appearances and views" of it, the latter count as its "subjective manners of givenness." If, then, through yet another reflection and regressive inquiry the ego-poles and everything about them of a specifically ego-character become the subject of essential inquiry, they now become, in a new and still higher sense, the subjective aspect of the world and also of its manners of appearing. But within the epochē a universal concept of the subjective encompasses everything: ego-pole and universe of ego-poles, multiplicities of appearance or object-poles and the universe of object-poles.

But precisely here lies the difficulty. Universal intersubjectivity, into which all objectivity, everything that exists at all, is resolved, can obviously be nothing other than mankind; and the latter is undeniably a component part of the world. How can a component part of the world, its human subjectivity, constitute the whole world, namely, constitute it as its intentional formation, one which has always already become what it is and continues to develop, formed by the universal interconnection of intentionally accomplishing subjectivity, while the latter, the subjects accomplishing in cooperation, are themselves only a partial formation within the total accomplishment?

The subjective part of the world swallows up, so to speak, the whole world and thus itself too. What an absurdity! Or is this a paradox which can be sensibly resolved, even a necessary one, arising necessarily out of the constant tension between the power of what is taken for granted in the natural objective attitude (the power of "common sense")[1] and the opposed attitude of the "disinterested spectator"? The latter is, to be sure, extremely difficult to carry out in a radical way, since it is constantly threatened by misunderstandings. Furthermore, by carrying out the epochē the phenomenologist by no means straightway commands a horizon of obviously possible new projects; a transcendental field of work does not immediately spread before him, preformed in a set of obvious types. The world is the sole universe of what is pregiven as obvious. From the beginning the phenomenologist lives in the paradox of having to look upon the obvious as questionable, as enigmatic, and of henceforth being unable to have any other scientific theme than that of transforming the universal obviousness of the being of the world —for him the greatest of all enigmas—into something intelligible.[2] If the paradox just developed were insoluble, it would mean that an actually universal and radical epochē could not be carried out at all, that is, for the purposes of a science rigorously bound to it. If the disinterestedness and the epochē were merely those of the psychologist, to which no one objects since they move on the ground of the world, then anything that is really tenable about our insights would be reduced to objective-psychological essential insights, though of a new style. But can we be content with this? Can we be satisfied simply with the notion that human beings are *subjects for the world* (the world which for consciousness is their world) and at the same time are objects in this world? As scientists, can we content ourselves with the view that God created the world and human beings within it, that he endowed the latter with consciousness and reason, that is, with the capacity for knowledge, the highest instance of which is scientific knowledge? For the naïveté that belongs to the essence of positive religion this may be undoubted truth and remain a truth forever, even though the philosophers cannot be content with such naïveté. The enigma of the creation and that of God himself are essential component parts of positive religion. For the philosopher, however, this, and also the

1. Husserl uses the English term.
2. I.e., of transforming this *Selbstverständlichkeit* into a *Verständlichkeit*.

juxtaposition "subjectivity *in* the world as object" and at the same time "conscious subject *for* the world," contain a necessary theoretical question, that of understanding how this is possible. The epochē, in giving us the attitude *above* the subject-object correlation which belongs to the world and thus the attitude of focus upon the *transcendental subject-object correlation,* leads us to recognize, in self-reflection, that the world that exists for us, that is, our world in its being and being-such, takes its ontic meaning entirely from our intentional life through a priori types of accomplishments that can be exhibited rather than argumentatively constructed or conceived through mythical thinking.

One can make no headway with this, and with the profound difficulties contained in it, if one hastily overlooks it and spares oneself the trouble of making consistent regressive inquiries and investigations or if one adduces arguments from the workshops of past philosophers, say Aristotle or Thomas, and carries on a game of logical argumentations and refutations. In the epochē neither logic nor any a priori nor any philosophical demonstration in the venerable old style can provide us with artillery. Rather, like all objective-scientific discipline, they are naïve and are themselves to be subjected to the epochē. On the other hand, what is peculiarly proper to the essence of the incipient philosophy of this phenomenological-transcendental radicalism is that, as we have said before, rather than having a ground of things taken for granted and ready in advance, as does objective philosophy, it excludes in principle a ground of this or any other sort. Thus it must begin without any underlying ground. But immediately it achieves the possibility of creating a ground for itself through its own powers, namely, in mastering, through original self-reflection, the naïve world as transformed into a phenomenon or rather a universe of phenomena. Its beginning course, like that carried out above in rough outlines, is necessarily one of experiencing and thinking in naïve self-evidence. It possesses no formed logic and methodology in advance and can achieve its method and even the genuine sense of its accomplishments only through ever renewed self-reflections. Its fate (understood subsequently, to be sure, as an essentially necessary one) is to become involved again and again in paradoxes, which, arising out of uninvestigated and even unnoticed horizons, remain functional and announce themselves as incomprehensibilities.

§ 54. *The resolution of the paradox:*

a. We as human beings, and we as ultimately functioning-accomplishing subjects.

WHAT IS THE STATUS, now, of the paradox presently under discussion—that of humanity as world-constituting subjectivity and yet as incorporated in the world itself? In the naïveté of our first approach we were interested in the horizons of remarkable discoveries which opened up again and again; and in the direction of our gaze which naturally came first, we held fast to the correlation belonging to the first level of reflection: i.e., object-pole *vs.* manner of givenness (manner of appearance in the broadest sense). The ego was mentioned as the subject matter of the highest level of reflection; but in the careful analytic-descriptive procedure, which naturally favors the more detailed interconnections, it did not receive its full due. For the depths of its functioning being make themselves felt only belatedly. In connection with this, what was lacking was the phenomenon of the change of signification of [the form] "I"—just as I am saying "I" right now—into "other I's," into "all of us," we who are many "I's," and among whom I am but *one* "I." What was lacking, then, was the problem of the constitution of intersubjectivity—this "all of us"—from my point of view, indeed "in" me. These are problems which did not announce themselves on the pathway we allowed ourselves to be drawn into, along which we allowed ourselves to be propelled. Now they will compel our attention. For the necessity of stopping here and entering into self-reflection makes itself felt most sharply through the question which at last and unavoidably arises: who are *we,* as subjects performing the meaning- and validity-accomplishment of universal constitution—as those who, in community, constitute the world as a system of poles, as the intentional structure of community life? Can "we" mean "we human beings," human beings in the natural-objective sense, i.e., as real entities in the world? But are these real entities not themselves "phenomena" and as such themselves object-poles and subject matter for inquiry back into the correlative intentionalities of which they are the poles, through whose function they have, and have attained, their ontic meaning?

Naturally this question must be answered in the affirmative. Indeed, as in the case of all regional categories of the world, of all essential ontic types, we can actually exhibit the constitutive formation of meaning provided we have proceeded far enough in the method to ask the appropriate questions. Here it is a case of inquiries proceeding from real human beings back to their "manners of givenness," their manners of "appearing," first of all in perceptual appearance, i.e., in the mode of original self-givenness, of manners of harmonious verification and correction, of identification through rerecognition as the same human person: as the person previously known "personally" to us, the same one of whom others speak, with whom they also have become acquainted, etc. In other words, the obviousness of: "There stands a man, in this social group of persons well known to one another," must be resolved into its transcendental questions.

But are the transcendental subjects, i.e., those *functioning* in the constitution of the world, human beings? After all, the epochē has made them into "phenomena," so that the philosopher within the epochē has neither himself nor the others naïvely and straightforwardly valid as *human beings* but precisely only as "phenomena," as poles for transcendental regressive inquiries. Clearly here, in the radical consistency of the epochē, each "I" is considered purely as the ego-pole of his acts, habitualities, and capacities and thence as being directed at what appears in ontic certainty "through" the appearances, the manners of givenness of the latter—i.e., as directed toward the particular object-pole and its pole-horizon, the world. To all this, then, belong further regressive inquiries in all these directions of reflection. Concretely, each "I" is not merely an ego-pole but an "I" with all its accomplishments and accomplished acquisitions, including the world as existing and being-such. But in the epochē and in the pure focus upon the functioning ego-pole, and thence upon the concrete whole of life and of its intentional intermediary and final structures, it follows *eo ipso* that nothing human is to be found, neither soul nor psychic life nor real psychophysical human beings; all this belongs to the "phenomenon," to the world as constituted pole.

b. As primal ego, I constitute my horizon of transcendental others as cosubjects within the transcendental intersubjectivity which constitutes the world.

Nevertheless, we cannot be content; we are still caught in the paradox. Indeed, our naïve procedure was not quite correct, and this is because we have forgotten ourselves, the philosophizers; or, to put it more distinctly: *I* am the one who performs the epochē, and, even if there are others, and even if they practice the epochē in direct community with me, [they and] all other human beings with their entire act-life are included, for me, within my epochē, in the world-phenomenon which, in my epochē, is exclusively mine. The epochē creates a unique sort of philosophical solitude which is the fundamental methodical requirement for a truly radical philosophy. In this solitude I am not a single individual who has somehow willfully cut himself off from the society of mankind, perhaps even for theoretical reasons, or who is cut off by accident, as in a shipwreck, but who nevertheless knows that he still belongs to that society. I am not *an* ego, who still has his *you*, his *we*, his total community of cosubjects in natural validity. All of mankind, and the whole distinction and ordering of the personal pronouns, has become a phenomenon within my epochē; and so has the privilege of I-the-man among other men. The "I" that I attain in the epochē, which would be the same as the "ego" within a critical reinterpretation and correction of the Cartesian conception, is actually called "I" only by equivocation—though it is an essential equivocation since, when I name it in reflection, I can say nothing other than: it is I who practice the epochē, I who interrogate, as phenomenon, the world which is now valid for me according to its being and being-such, with all its human beings, of whom I am so fully conscious; it is I who stand above all natural existence that has meaning for me, who am the ego-pole of this transcendental life, in which, at first, the world has meaning for me purely as world; it is I who, taken in full concreteness, encompass all that. This does not mean that our earlier insights, already expressed as transcendental ones, were illusions and that it is not justifiable to speak, in spite of the above, of a transcendental intersubjectivity constituting the world as "world for all," in which I again appear, this time as "one" transcendental "I" among others, whereby "we all" are taken as functioning transcendentally.

But it was wrong, methodically, to jump immediately into transcendental intersubjectivity and to leap over the primal "I," the ego of my epochē, which can never lose its uniqueness and personal indeclinability. It is only an apparent contradiction to this that the ego—through a particular constitutive accomplishment of its own—makes itself declinable, for itself, transcendentally; that, starting from itself and in itself, it constitutes transcendental intersubjectivity, to which it then adds itself as a merely privileged member, namely, as "I" among the transcendental others. This is what philosophical self-exposition in the epochē actually teaches us. It can show how the always singular "I," in the original constituting life proceeding within it, constitutes a first sphere of objects, the "primordial" sphere; how it then, starting from this, in a motivated fashion, performs a constitutive accomplishment through which an intentional modification of itself and its primordiality achieves ontic validity under the title of "alien-perception," perception of others, of another "I" who is for himself an "I" as I am. This becomes understandable by analogy if we already understand, through the transcendental exposition of recollection, that to what is recollected, what is past (which has the ontic meaning of a present having passed) there belongs also a past "I" of that present, whereas the actual, original "I" is that of immediate presence; to this presence, recollection belongs as a present experience, in addition to what appears as the present sphere of facts. Thus the immediate "I" performs an accomplishment through which it constitutes a variational mode of itself as existing (in the mode of having passed). Starting from this we can trace how the immediate "I," flowingly-statically present, constitutes itself in self-temporalization as enduring through "its" pasts. In the same way, the immediate "I," already enduring in the enduring primordial sphere, constitutes in itself another as other. Self-temporalization through depresentation [*Ent-Gegenwärtigung*], so to speak (through recollection), has its analogue in my self-alienation [*Ent-Fremdung*] (empathy as a depresentation of a higher level—depresentation of my primal presence [*Urpräsenz*] into a merely presentified [*vergegenwärtigte*] primal presence). Thus, in me, "another I" achieves ontic validity as copresent [*kompräsent*] with his own ways of being self-evidently verified, which are obviously quite different from those of a "sense"-perception.

Only by starting from the ego and the system of its transcendental functions and accomplishments can we methodically exhibit transcendental intersubjectivity and its transcendental communalization, through which, in the functioning system of ego-poles, the "world for all," and for each subject *as* world for all, is constituted. Only in this way, in an essential system of forward steps, can we gain an ultimate comprehension of the fact that each transcendental "I" within intersubjectivity (as coconstituting the world in the way indicated) must necessarily be constituted in the world as a human being; in other words, that each human being "bears within himself a transcendental 'I' "—not as a real part or a stratum of his soul (which would be absurd) but rather insofar as he is the self-objectification, as exhibited through phenomenological self-reflection, of the corresponding transcendental "I." Nevertheless, every human being who carried out the epochē could certainly recognize his ultimate "I," which functions in all his human activity. The naïveté of the first epochē had the result, as we immediately saw, that I, the philosophizing "ego," in taking myself as functioning "I," as ego-pole of transcendental acts and accomplishments, proceeded in one leap and without grounding, that is, illegitimately, to attribute to the mankind in which I find myself the same transformation into functioning transcendental subjectivity which I had carried out alone in myself. In spite of the methodical illegitimacy, this contained a truth. At all events, however, we must—for the most profound philosophical reasons, which we cannot go into further, and which are not only methodical in character—do justice to the absolute singularity of the ego and its central position in all constitution.

§ 55.   *The correction in principle of our first application of the epochē by reducing it to the absolutely unique, ultimately functioning ego.*

ACCORDINGLY, AS AGAINST the first application of the epochē, a second is required, or rather a conscious reshaping of the epochē through a reduction to the absolute ego as the ultimately unique center of function in all constitution. This determines henceforth the whole method of transcendental phenomenology. In advance there is the world, ever pregiven and undoubted in ontic certainty and self-verification. Even though I have not [explicitly] "presupposed" it as a ground, it still has validity for me, the "I" of the *cogito*, through constant self-verification, together with everything that it is for me, in particular details sometimes objectively and legitimately so, sometimes not, and together with all sciences and arts, together with all social and personal configurations and institutions, insofar as it is just the world that is actual for me. There can be no stronger realism than this, if by this word nothing more is meant than: "I am certain of being a human being who lives in this world, etc., and I doubt it not in the least." But the great problem is precisely to understand what is here so "obvious." The method now requires that the ego, beginning with its concrete world-phenomenon, systematically inquire back, and thereby become acquainted with itself, the transcendental ego, in its concreteness, in the system of its constitutive levels and its incredibly intricate [patterns of] validity-founding.[1] At the onset of the epochē the ego is given apodictically, but as a "mute concreteness." It must be brought to exposition, to expression, through systematic intentional "analysis" which inquires back from the world-phenomenon. In this systematic procedure one at first attains the correlation between the world and transcendental subjectivity as objectified in mankind.

But then new questions impose themselves in regard to this mankind: are the insane also objectifications of the subjects being discussed in connection with the accomplishment of world-constitution? And what about children, even those who already have a certain amount of world-consciousness? After all, it is only from the mature and normal human beings who bring them up that they first become acquainted with the world in the full sense of the world-for-all, that is, the world of culture. And what about animals? There arise problems of intentional modifications through which we can and must attribute to all these conscious subjects—those that do not cofunction in respect to the world understood in the hitherto accepted (and always fundamental) sense, that is, the world which has truth through "reason"—their manner of transcendentality, precisely as "analogues" of ourselves. The meaning of this analogy will then itself represent a transcendental problem. This naturally extends into the realm of the transcendental problems which finally encom-

1. *Geltungsfundierungen*, i.e., the manner in which some validities are founded upon or presuppose others. For the notion of *Fundierung* see *Ideen*, Vol. I, §§ 116, 117.

pass all living beings insofar as they have, even indirectly but still verifiably, something like "life," and even communal life in the spiritual [geistige] sense. Also appearing thereby, in different steps, first in respect to human beings and then universally, are the problems of genesis [Generativität], the problems of transcendental historicity [Geschichtlichkeit], the problems of the transcendental inquiry which starts from the essential forms of human existence in society, in personalities of a higher order,[2] and proceeds back to their transcendental and thus absolute signification; further, there are the problems of birth and death and of the transcendental constitution of their meaning as world occurrences, and there is the problem of the sexes. And finally, concerning the problem of the "unconscious" that is so much discussed today—dreamless sleep, loss of consciousness, and whatever else of the same or similar nature may be included under this title—this is in any case a matter of occurrences in the pregiven world, and they naturally come under the transcendental problem of constitution, as do birth and death. As something existing in the world common to all, this sort of thing has its manners of ontic verification, of "self-giving," which are quite particular but which originally create the ontic meaning for beings of such particularity. Accordingly, within the absolutely universal epochē, in respect to beings having this or any other kind of meaning, the appropriate constitutional questions have to be posed.

In accord with all this it is clear that there is no conceivable meaningful problem in previous philosophy, and no conceivable problem of being at all, that could not be arrived at by transcendental phenomenology at some point along its way. This includes the problems that phenomenology itself poses, at a higher level of reflection, to the phenomenologist: that is, not only problems corresponding to the language, truth, science, and reason, in all their forms, which are constituted within the natural world, but problems of phenomenological language, truth, reason.

From this one also understands the sense of the demand for apodicticity in regard to the ego and all transcendental knowledge gained upon this transcendental basis. Having arrived at the ego, one becomes aware of standing within a sphere of self-evidence of such a nature that any attempt to inquire behind it would be absurd. By contrast, every ordinary appeal to self-evidence, insofar as it was supposed to cut off further regressive

2. I.e., communities, states, etc.

inquiry, was theoretically no better than an appeal to an oracle through which a god reveals himself. All natural self-evidences, those of all objective sciences (not excluding those of formal logic and mathematics), belong to the realm of what is "obvious," what in truth has a background of incomprehensibility. Every [kind of] self-evidence is the title of a problem, with the sole exception of phenomenological self-evidence, after it has reflectively clarified itself and shown itself to be ultimate self-evidence. It is naturally a ludicrous, though unfortunately common misunderstanding, to seek to attack transcendental phenomenology as "Cartesianism," as if its *ego cogito* were a premise or set of premises from which the rest of knowledge (whereby one naïvely speaks only of objective knowledge) was to be deduced, absolutely "secured." The point is not to secure objectivity but to understand it. One must finally achieve the insight that no objective science, no matter how exact, explains or ever can explain anything in a serious sense. To deduce is not to explain. To predict, or to recognize the objective forms of the composition of physical or chemical bodies and to predict accordingly—all this explains nothing but is in need of explanation. The only true way to explain is to make transcendentally understandable. Everything objective demands to be understood. Natural-scientific knowing about nature thus gives us no truly explanatory, no ultimate knowledge of nature because it does not investigate nature at all in the absolute framework through which its actual and genuine being reveals its ontic meaning; thus natural science never reaches this being thematically. This does not detract in the least from the greatness of its creative geniuses or their accomplishments, just as the being of the objective world in the natural attitude, and this attitude itself, have lost nothing through the fact that they are, so to speak, "understood back into" [*zurückverstanden*] the absolute sphere of being in which they ultimately and truly are. To be sure, the knowledge [attained through] the constitutive "internal" method, through which all objective-scientific method acquires its meaning and possibility, cannot be without significance for the scientist of nature or any other objective scientist. It is, after all, a matter of the most radical and most profound self-reflection of accomplishing subjectivity; how could it not be of service in protecting the naïve, ordinary accomplishment from misunderstandings such as are to be observed in abundance, for example, in the influence of naturalistic epistemology and in the idolization of a logic that does not understand itself?

B.

The Way into Phenomenological Transcendental Philosophy from Psychology

§ 56. *Characterization of the philosophical development after Kant from the perspective of the struggle between physicalistic objectivism and the constantly reemerging "transcendental motif."*

In the course of its development philosophy encounters theoretical situations in which momentous decisions have to be made, situations in which philosophers must reconsider, must place in question, and possibly redefine the whole sense of the purpose of their project and must accordingly resolve to undertake a radical change of method. The authors of the theoretical ideas that create these situations occupy, in the history of philosophy, a quite distinguished place. They are the representatives of developments which have a unified meaning because of their work, because of the new universal objectives outlined in their developed theories. Every great philosopher continues to have his effect in all subsequent historical periods; he exerts an influence. But not every one contributes a motif which gives unity to a historical sequence and possibly concludes one line of development, a motif which works as a driving force and sets a task that must be fulfilled, such that its fulfillment brings to an end [this particular] historical period of development. Those who have become significant for us as representatives of the philosophy of the modern period are Descartes, who marks a turning point in respect to all previous philosophy; Hume (in all justice Berkeley should actually also be mentioned); and—aroused by Hume—Kant, who in turn determines the line of development of the German transcendental philosophies. (We see, by the way, that the creators of the greatest, most intellectually massive systems do not as such belong in this series; no one would equate Hume and Berkeley in this respect with Kant or, among later philosophers, with Hegel.)

In the first series of lectures [1] we carried out a deeper analysis of the motifs of Cartesian philosophizing which continue to determine the whole modern development: on the one hand, those motifs which announce themselves in his first *Meditations* and, on the other hand, those which stand in internal contrast with these, i.e., the physicalistic (or mathematizing) idea of philosophy according to which the world in its full concreteness bears within itself an objectively true being in the form of the *ordo geometricus* and according to which, as interwoven with this (and this must be especially emphasized here), the metaphysical "in-itself" ascribed to the world involves a dualistic world of bodies and spirits. This was characteristic of the philosophy of objectivistic rationalism in the Enlightenment. Then we attempted the analysis of the Hume-Kant situation, and in the end we could elucidate it only by penetrating into its presuppositions and by proceeding from there to pose questions of our own, alien to the period itself, and by making clear to ourselves in a preliminary sketch, through a systematic process of thinking, the style of a truly scientific transcendental philosophy—"truly scientific" in the sense that it works up from the bottom in self-evident single steps and is thus in truth ultimately grounded and ultimately grounding. We attempted thereby to awaken the full insight that only such a philosophy, through such a regressive inquiry back to the last conceivable ground [*Grund*] in the transcendental ego, can fulfill the meaning which is inborn in philosophy from its primal establishment. Thus transcendental

---

1. I.e., Part II. It may seem strange that Husserl should continue to refer to the *Crisis* as a series of lectures. Comparison with the original lecture shows that this is not a matter of fragments inadvertently left over from Prague. But recall that the *Cartesian Meditations,* which even in the published French edition was expanded far beyond the scope of the original lectures, retained the references to the talks at the Sorbonne.

philosophy in its first immature forms in the English and in Kant, even though these philosophers hardly accomplished a serious scientific grounding, and even though Hume withdrew into an unhealthy academic skepticism, does not, on the whole, represent a wrong path, nor "one" among other possible paths at all, but the one path of the future which the development of philosophy absolutely had to take in order to penetrate to the fulfilled methodical form through which alone it could be truly scientific, a philosophy working in the actual self-understanding of the sense of its task, in the spirit of finality, working with an apodictic self-evidence of its ground, its goals, its methods. This fulfilled form could enter into historical actuality only as the result of the most radical self-reflections, in the form of a first beginning, a first attainment of the clarified task, of the apodictic ground and the method of access to it, a first beginning of an actual setting-to-work, the work of inquiring into the things themselves. As phenomenological transcendental philosophy (but exclusively in the sense prescribed here), this has become a truly living beginning. I may go so far as to say that from now on not only modern physicalistic naturalism but every objectivistic philosophy, whether of earlier or of future times, must be characterized as "transcendental naïveté."

Still, with this our task is not [yet] fulfilled. We ourselves, and the ideas we necessarily had to construct in order to evoke a genuine resonance from the ideas of the past, i.e., so that their directedness, as seminal forms toward a final form, would become evident—we ourselves, I say, also belong to the same unity of history. Thus we also have the task of meaningfully explicating the developments of philosophy up to our time and in our present situation. Precisely this is indicated, as we shall soon understand, by the mention of psychology in the title of these lectures.[2] The completion of our task does not require a detailed investigation of the many philosophies and particular currents of the subsequent period. Only a general characterization is needed, and this will proceed from the understanding we have attained of the history which has preceded us.

Philosophical objectivism of the modern sort, with its physicalistic tendency and its psychophysical dualism, does not die out; that is, many feel quite comfortable here in their "dogmatic slumbers." On the other side, those who have been aroused from

2. Again, a reference to the original title of the Prague lecture series: "The Crisis of European Sciences and Psychology."

them have been first aroused primarily by Kant. Here, then, originates the current of German transcendental idealisms, proceeding from Kant's transcendental philosophy. The great momentum which earlier, from Descartes on, had animated objectivistic philosophy sustains itself in them and is even renewed with a special force in the new form of the transcendental approach to the world. To be sure, even German Idealism was not fated to endure, in spite of the overwhelming impression temporarily made by the Hegelian system, which seemed to promise its total dominance for all time. The swelling reaction which rapidly took effect soon assumed the sense of a reaction against any sort of transcendental philosophy in this style; and although the style did not completely die out, the subsequent attempts at such philosophizing lost their original force and the vitality of their development.

As for the momentum of objectivistic philosophy, in a certain way it sustained itself as the momentum in the development of the positive sciences. But examined more closely, this is anything but a philosophical momentum. Recall the transformation of meaning these sciences, along with their development as special disciplines, had undergone, through which they finally completely lost the important sense which was alive in them earlier of being branches of philosophy. We have already spoken of this, but for the clarification of the situation which arose in the nineteenth century it is very important to go into it here in somewhat more detail. What had been sciences in that other sense, the only genuine one, had turned unnoticed into remarkable new arts, to be entered in the list of the other arts of higher and lower dignity on the scale, such as the fine arts, architecture, and also the arts at lower levels. They could be taught and learned in their institutes, their seminars, in collections of models, in museums. One could display skill, talent, even genius in them—for example, in the art of inventing new formulae, new exact theories, in order to predict the course of natural phenomena, in order to make inductions of a scope which would have been unthinkable in earlier times; or, also, in the art of interpreting historical documents, grammatically analyzing languages, constructing historical interconnections, etc. On all sides we find great trail-blazing geniuses who gain the highest admiration of their fellow men and abundantly deserve it. But art is not science, whose origin and intention, which can never be sacrificed, is to attain, through a clarification of the ultimate sources of meaning, a knowledge of what actually is and thus to understand it in its ultimate sense. Radically presuppositionless and ultimately grounded science, or philosophy—this is simply another expression for the same thing. Of course, this art of theory [3] has the peculiar property that, since it has developed out of philosophy (though out of an imperfect one), it has a meaning belonging to all its artful products, a meaning which comes from that philosophy but is concealed, such that it cannot be elicited by inquiring into mere methodical technique and its history but can be aroused only by the true philosopher and can be unfolded in its genuine depths only by the transcendental philosopher. Thus there is actually scientific knowledge concealed within the art of theory, but access to it is difficult.

We have already spoken of this in our systematic discussions; we have shown what is necessary in order to attain knowledge ultimately grounded and have shown that the like can be attained only in the universal framework, never as a naïve "special science" and certainly not with the prejudice of modern objectivism. The much lamented specialization [in the sciences] is not in itself a lack, since it is a necessity within universal philosophy, just as the development of an artlike method is necessary in every special discipline. What certainly is portentous, however, is the separation of the art of theory from philosophy. However, though the specialized scholars dropped out, there remained among them and alongside them philosophers who continued to treat the positive sciences as branches of philosophy; thus the statement is still valid that objectivistic philosophy did not die out after Hume and Kant. Alongside this runs the line of development of transcendental philosophies, and not only those derived from Kant. For there must be added to this a series of transcendental philosophers who owe their motivation to a continuation, or in the case of Germany a revival, of the influence of Hume. In England J. S. Mill is especially to be mentioned, who in the period of great reaction against the system-philosophies of German Idealism exercised a strong influence in Germany itself. But in Germany there arose much more seriously intended attempts at a transcendental philosophy basically determined by English empiricism (Schuppe, Avenarius), though their supposed radicalism falls far short of the genuine kind which alone can help. The renewal of positivistic empiricism is closely allied, though this is unnoticed, with the revivals of earlier and especially transcendental philosophies due to the

3. *die theoretische Kunst,* the art of making theories, as above.

growing urgency of transcendental motifs. By going back to these philosophies and critically overhauling them along lines prescribed by positivistic motifs, some hoped to arrive again at a philosophy of their own. Like Hume and Berkeley, Kant too is revived—a multicolored Kant, through the multiplicity of attempted interpretations and the reconstructions of neo-Kantianism. Kant is reinterpreted even in empiricist fashion, as the historical traditions are mixed and interwoven, creating for all scientists a quasiphilosophical atmosphere involving a widely discussed but by no means deeply or autonomously conceived "theory of knowledge." Alongside Kant, particularly, all the other idealists have had their renaissance; even a neo-Friesianism has been able to appear as a school. Everywhere, when we also take into account the rapid growth of bourgeois education, erudition, and literature in the nineteenth century, we observe that the confusion was becoming unbearable. More and more a skeptical mood spread which crippled from the inside the philosophical energy even of those who held fast to the idea of a scientific philosophy. The history of philosophy is substituted for philosophy, or philosophy becomes a personal world-view, and finally some even try to make out of a necessity a virtue: philosophy can exercise no other function at all for humanity than that of outlining a world-picture appropriate to one's individuality, as the summation of one's personal education.

Although the genuine though never radically clarified idea of philosophy has by no means been completely sacrificed, the multiplicity of philosophies, which can hardly be comprehended any more, nevertheless has the result that it is no longer divided into scientific directions, such that they could still seriously work together, carry on a scientific dialogue through criticism and countercriticism, and still guide the common idea of one science toward the path of realization, in the manner of the directions within modern biology or mathematics and physics; rather, they are contrasted as societies of aesthetic style, so to speak, analogous to the "directions" and "currents" in the fine arts. Indeed, in the splintering of philosophies and their literature, is it still possible at all to study them seriously as works of one science, to make use of them critically and to uphold the unity of the work done? The philosophies have their effects. But must one not honestly say that they have their effects as impressions, that they "inspire," that they move the feelings like poems, that they arouse vague "intimations"? But is this not done in a similar fashion (sometimes in a nobler style but even here, unfortunately, all too often in one of a rather different kind) by the many literary products of the day? We may credit the philosophers with the noblest intentions, we may even be firmly convinced of the teleological sense of history and accord even to their constructs a significance—but is it the significance that was historically entrusted to philosophy, given to it as a task? When one withdraws into this kind of philosophizing, has not something else, something of the highest value and necessity, been sacrificed? Even what we have already dealt with by way of criticism and the exhibiting of self-evidence gives us the right to ask this question, not as a question of romantic moods—since our aim is to turn all romanticism into responsible work—but as a question of the scientific conscience that calls to us in universal and radical reflection, which, when carried out with the greatest self-responsibility, must itself become the actual and highest truth.

After what was set forth in the first series of lectures, we hardly need to say what the [above] factual situation had to mean for the existential plight of European humanity, which sought—as the result of the Renaissance, determining the whole meaning of the modern period—to create the universal science as the instrument for giving itself a new rootedness and for transforming itself into a humanity based on pure reason. But our duty here is to make understandable the obvious failure of the great intention to realize gradually the idea of a *philosophia perennis*, a true and genuine universal science ultimately grounded. At the same time we have to justify our boldness in still daring to give a favorable prognosis (now and for our time) —as can be foreseen in our systematic-critical presentations— for the future development of a philosophy conceived as a science. The rationalism of the Age of Enlightenment is now out of the question; we can no longer follow its great philosophers or any other philosophers of the past. But their intention, seen in its most general sense, must never die out in us. For, as I emphasize once again, true and genuine philosophy or science and true and genuine rationalism are one. Realizing this rationalism, rather than the rationalism of the Enlightenment, which is laden with hidden absurdity, remains our own task if we are not to let specialized science, science lowered to the status of art or τέχνη or the fashionable degenerations of philosophy into irrationalistic busy-work be substituted for the inextinguishable idea of philosophy as the ultimately grounding and universal science.

§ 57. *The fateful separation of transcendental philosophy and psychology.*

LET US GO BACK to the times in which modern man and the modern philosopher still believed in themselves and in a philosophy, when, in the context of the transcendental motivation, they struggled for a new philosophy with the responsible seriousness of an inner, absolute calling that one senses in every word of the genuine philosopher. Even after the so-called collapse of the Hegelian philosophy, in which the line of development determined by Kant culminated, this seriousness remained intact for a time in the philosophies reacting against Hegel (even though its original force was weakened). But why did transcendental philosophy not achieve the unity of a development running through all its interruptions? Why did self-criticism and reciprocal criticism among those still animated by the old spirit not lead to the integration of compelling cognitive accomplishments into the unity of an edifice of knowledge which grew from generation to generation, which merely needed perfecting through constantly renewed criticism, correction, and methodical refinement? In this regard the following general remark must first be made: an absolutely novel procedure like that of transcendental science, which was lacking any sort of guidance by analogy, could be before the mind at first only as a sort of instinctive anticipation. An obscure dissatisfaction with the previous way of grounding in all science leads to the setting of new problems and to theories which exhibit a certain self-evidence of success in solving them in spite of many difficulties that are unnoticed or, so to speak, drowned out. This first self-evidence can still conceal within itself more than enough obscurities which lie deeper, especially in the form of unquestioned, supposedly quite obvious presuppositions. Yet such first theories continue to be helpful historically; the obscurities become more troublesome, what is supposedly obvious is questioned, the theories are criticized for this, and this creates the stimulus for new attempts. Furthermore, transcendental philosophy, for essential reasons (which are perfectly clear from our systematic presentations), can never undergo the unnoticed transformation into a

mere τέχνη and thus into a process of depletion whereby what
has become a technique retains only a hidden meaning—one
whose full depths, indeed, can be revealed only transcendentally.
We can understand, accordingly, that the history of transcendental philosophy first had to be a history of renewed attempts
just to bring transcendental philosophy to its starting point and,
above all, to a clear and proper self-understanding of what it
actually could and must undertake. Its origin is a "Copernican
turn," that is, a turning-away in principle from the manner of
grounding in naïve-objective science. As we know, transcendental philosophy appears in its primal form, as a seed, in the first
Cartesian *Meditations* as an attempt at an absolutely subjectivis-
tic grounding of philosophy through the apodictic ego; but here
it is unclear and ambiguous, and it immediately subverts its
genuine sense. Neither the new stage, the reaction of Berkeley
and Hume against the philosophical naïveté of mathematical,
natural-scientific exactness, nor even Kant's new beginning led
to the genuine sense of the required Copernican turn—the
sense, that is, of grounding once and for all a systematic transcendental philosophy in the rigorous scientific spirit. A true
beginning, achieved by means of a radical liberation from all
scientific and prescientific traditions, was not attained by Kant.
He does not penetrate to the absolute subjectivity which constitutes everything that is, in its meaning and validity, nor to the
method of attaining it in its apodicticity, of interrogating it and
of explicating it apodictically. From then on, the history of this
philosophy was necessarily a continued struggle precisely for the
clear and genuine sense of the transcendental turn to be carried
out and of its method of work; to put it in another way, it was a
struggle for the genuine "transcendental reduction." Our critical
reflections on Kant have already made clear to us the danger of
impressive and yet still unclear insights or, if you will, the
illumination of pure insights in the form of vague anticipations
while one is still working with questions posed on an unclarified
ground (that of what is "obvious"); and this also made comprehensible how he was forced into a mythical concept-construction
and into a metaphysics in the dangerous sense inimical to all
genuine science. All the transcendental concepts of Kant—those
of the "I" of transcendental apperception, of the different transcendental faculties, that of the "thing in itself" (which underlies souls as well as bodies)—are constructive concepts which
resist in principle an ultimate clarification. This is even more
true in the later idealistic systems. This is the reason for the

reactions, which were in fact necessary, against those systems, against their whole manner of philosophizing. To be sure, if one became willingly engrossed in such a system, one could not deny the force and moment of its thought-constructions. Yet their ultimate incomprehensibility gave rise to profound dissatisfaction among all those who had educated themselves in the great new sciences. Even though these sciences, according to our clarification and manner of speaking, furnish a merely "technical" self-evidence, and even though transcendental philosophy can never become such a τέχνη, this τέχνη is still an intellectual accomplishment which must be clear and understandable at every step, must possess the self-evidence of the step made and of the ground upon which it rests; and to this extent (taken thus formally) the same thing holds for it that holds for every technically self-evident science practiced artfully, such as mathematics, for example. It helps not at all to try to explain the incomprehensibility of the transcendental constructions by outlining, in the same spirit, a constructive theory of the necessity of such incomprehensible things; nor does it help to try to suggest that the overwhelming profundity of the transcendental theories implies corresponding difficulties of understanding and that people are too lazy to overcome them. So much is correct, that any transcendental philosophy must, and with essential necessity, create extraordinary difficulties for the natural man's understanding—for "common sense"[1]—and thus for all of us, since we cannot avoid having to rise from the natural ground to the transcendental region. The complete inversion of the natural stance of life, thus into an "unnatural" one, places the greatest conceivable demands upon philosophical resolve and consistency. Natural human understanding and the objectivism rooted in it will view every transcendental philosophy as a flighty eccentricity, its wisdom as useless foolishness; or it will interpret it as a psychology which seeks to convince itself that it is not psychology. No one who is truly receptive to philosophy is ever frightened off by difficulties. But modern man, as man shaped by science, demands insight; and thus, as the image of *sight* correctly suggest, he demands the self-evidence of "seeing" the goals and the ways to them and every step along the way. The way may be long, and many years of toilsome study may be necessary; this is true in mathematics, but it does not frighten him whose life-interest is mathematics. The great transcendental

1. Husserl uses the English term.

philosophies did not satisfy the scientific need for such self-evidence, and for this reason their ways of thinking were abandoned.

Turning back to our subject, we shall now be able to say, without being misunderstood: just as the emerging incomprehensibility of the rationalistic philosophy of the Enlightenment, understood as "objective" science, called forth the reaction of transcendental philosophy, so the reaction against the incomprehensibility of the attempted transcendental philosophies had to lead beyond them.

But now we are faced with the question: How is it to be understood that such an [unscientific] style could be developed and propagated at all, in great philosophers and their philosophies, when the development of modern philosophy was so animated by the will to science? These philosophers were by no means mere poets of ideas. They were not at all lacking in the serious will to create philosophy as an ultimately grounding science, however one may wish to transform the sense of ultimate grounding. (Consider, for example, the emphatic declarations of Fichte in the drafts of his *Wissenschaftslehre* or those of Hegel in the "Preface" to his *Phänomenologie des Geistes*.) How is it that they remained bound to their style of mythical concept-constructions and of world-interpretations based on obscure metaphysical anticipations and were not able to penetrate to a scientifically rigorous type of concepts and method and that every successor in the Kantian series conceived one more philosophy in the same style? Part of transcendental philosophy's own meaning was that it arose out of reflections on conscious subjectivity through which the world, the scientific as well as the everyday intuitive world, comes to be known or achieves its ontic validity for us; thus transcendental philosophy recognized the necessity of developing a purely mental [*geistige*] approach to the world. But if it had to deal with the mental, why did it not turn to the psychology that had been practiced so diligently for centuries? Or, if this no longer sufficed, why did it not work out a better psychology? One will naturally answer that the empirical man, the psychophysical being, himself belongs, in soul as well as body, to the constituted world. Thus human subjectivity is not transcendental subjectivity, and the psychological theories of knowledge of Locke and his successors serve as continued admonitions against "psychologism," against any use of psychology for transcendental purposes. But in exchange, transcendental philosophy always had to bear its cross of incomprehensibility.

The difference between empirical and transcendental subjectivity remained unavoidable; yet just as unavoidable, but also incomprehensible, was their identity. I myself, as transcendental ego, "constitute" the world, and at the same time, as soul, I am a human ego in the world. The understanding which prescribes its law to the world is my transcendental understanding, and it forms me, too, according to these laws; yet it is my—the philosopher's—psychic faculty. Can the ego which posits itself, of which Fichte speaks, be anything other than Fichte's own? If this is supposed to be not an actual absurdity but a paradox that can be resolved, what other method could help us achieve clarity than the interrogation of our inner experience and an analysis carried out within its framework? If one is to speak of a transcendental "consciousness in general," if I, this singular, individual ego, cannot be the bearer of the nature-constituting understanding, must I not ask how I can have, beyond my individual self-consciousness, a general, a transcendental-intersubjective consciousness? The consciousness of intersubjectivity, then, must become a transcendental problem; but again, it is not apparent how it can become that except through an interrogation of myself, [one that appeals to] inner experience, i.e., in order to discover the manners of consciousness through which I attain and have others and a fellow mankind in general, and in order to understand the fact that I can distinguish, in myself, between myself and others and can confer upon them the sense of being "of my kind." Can psychology be indifferent here? Must it not deal with all this? The same or similar questions address themselves, as they do to Kant, to all his successors who became so lost in obscure metaphysics or "mythology." One would think, after all, that we could attain a scientific concept even of an absolute reason and its accomplishments only after working out a scientific concept of our human reason and of human, or of humanity's, accomplishments—that is, only through a genuine psychology.

The first answer to this question is that transcendental philosophy (and also philosophy of any other attempted style), quite apart from concern about psychologism, had reason enough not to hope for any counsel from psychology. This was due to psychology itself and to the fateful, erroneous path forced upon it by the peculiarity of the modern idea of an objectivistic universal science *more geometrico,* with its psychophysical dualism. In the following I shall try to show (paradoxical as this thesis must appear here) that it is precisely this restriction placed upon psychology, which falsifies its meaning and to the present day has kept it from grasping its peculiar task, that bears the primary responsibility for the fact that transcendental philosophy found no way out of its uncomfortable situation and was thus caught in the concepts and construction it used to interpret its—in themselves valuable—empirical observations, concepts, and constructions, which are completely devoid of any legitimation from original self-evidence. If psychology had not failed, it would have performed a necessary mediating work for a concrete, working transcendental philosophy, freed from all paradoxes. Psychology failed, however, because, even in its primal establishment as a new kind of [science] alongside the new natural science, it failed to inquire after what was essentially the only genuine sense of its task as the universal science of psychic being. Rather, it let its task and method be set according to the model of natural science or according to the guiding idea of modern philosophy as objective and thus concrete universal science—a task which, of course, considering the given historical motivation, appeared to be quite obvious. So remote was any sort of doubt in this matter that it was not until the end of the nineteenth century that it became a philosophical motif of thought at all. Thus the history of psychology is actually only a history of crises. And for this reason psychology could also not aid in the development of a genuine transcendental philosophy, since this was possible only after a radical reform through which psychology's essentially proper task and method were clarified through the deepest sort of reflection upon itself. The reason for this is that the consistent and pure execution of this task had to lead, of itself and of necessity, to a science of transcendental subjectivity and thus to its transformation into a universal transcendental philosophy.

§ 58.   *The alliance and the difference between psychology and transcendental philosophy. Psychology as the decisive field.*

ALL THIS WILL BECOME understandable if, in order to elucidate the difficult, even paradoxical, relation between psychology and transcendental philosophy, we make use of the

systematic considerations through which we made clear to ourselves the sense and the method of a radical and genuine transcendental philosophy. By now we are without doubt that a
scientific psychology of the modern style—no matter which of the
many attempts since Hobbes and Locke we may consider—can
never take part in the theoretical accomplishments, can never
provide any premises for those accomplishments, which are the
task of transcendental philosophy. The task set for modern psychology, and taken over by it, was to be a science of psychophysical realities, of men and animals as unitary beings, though
divided into two real strata. Here all theoretical thinking moves
on the ground of the taken-for-granted, pregiven world of experience, the world of natural life; and theoretical interest is simply
directed as a special case to one of the real aspects of it, the
souls, while the other aspect is supposed to be already known, or
is yet to be known, by the exact natural sciences according to its
objective, true being-in-itself. For the transcendental philosopher, however, the totality of real objectivity—not only the scientific objectivity of all actual and possible sciences but also the
prescientific objectivity of the life-world, with its "situational
truths" and the relativity of its existing objects—has become a
problem, the enigma of all enigmas. The enigma is precisely the
taken-for-grantedness in virtue of which the "world" constantly
and prescientifically exists for us, "world" being a title for an
infinity of what is taken for granted, what is indispensable for
all objective sciences. As I, philosophizing, reflect in pure consistency upon myself as the constantly functioning ego throughout the alteration of experiences and the opinions arising out of
them, as the ego having consciousness of the world and dealing
with the world consciously through these experiences, as I inquire consistently on all sides into the *what* and the *how* of the
manners of givenness and the modes of validity, and the manner
of ego-centeredness, I become aware that this conscious life is
through and through an intentionally accomplishing life
through which the life-world, with all its changing representa-
tional contents [*Vorstellungsgehalten*], in part attains anew and
in part has already attained its meaning and validity. All real
mundane objectivity is constituted accomplishment in this
sense, including that of men and animals and thus also that of
the "souls." Psychic being, accordingly, and objective spirit of
every sort (such as human societies, cultures), and in the same
manner psychology itself, are among the transcendental problems. It would be absurdly circular to want to deal with such

problems on a naïve, objective basis through the method of the objective sciences.

Nevertheless, psychology and transcendental philosophy are allied with each other in a peculiar and inseparable way, namely, in virtue of the alliance of difference and identity—which is no longer an enigma for us, but has been clarified—between the psychological ego (the human ego, that is, made worldly in the spatiotemporal world) and the transcendental ego, its ego-life, and its accomplishment. According to our clarifications, the ultimate self-understanding here allows us to say: in my naïve self-consciousness as a human being knowing himself to be living in the world, for whom the world is the totality of what for him is valid as existing, I am blind to the immense transcendental dimension of problems. This dimension is in a hidden [realm of] anonymity. In truth, of course, I am a transcendental ego, but I am not conscious of this; being in a particular attitude, the natural attitude, I am completely given over to the object-poles, completely bound by interests and tasks which are exclusively directed toward them. I can, however, carry out the transcendental reorientation—in which transcendental universality opens itself up—and then I understand the one-sided, closed, natural attitude as a particular transcendental attitude, as one of a certain habitual one-sidedness of the whole life of interest. I now have, as a new horizon of interest, the whole of constituting life and accomplishment with all its correlations—a new, infinite scientific realm—if I engage in the appropriate systematic work. In this reorientation our tasks are exclusively transcendental; all natural data and accomplishments acquire a transcendental meaning, and within the transcendental horizon they impose completely new sorts of transcendental tasks. Thus, as a human being and a human soul, I first become a theme for psychophysics and psychology; but then in a new and higher dimension I become a transcendental theme. Indeed, I soon become aware that all the opinions I have about myself arise out of self-apperceptions, out of experiences and judgments which I —reflexively directed toward myself—have arrived at and have synthetically combined with other apperceptions of my being taken over from other subjects through my contact with them. My ever new self-apperceptions are thus continuing acquisitions of my accomplishments in the unity of my self-objectification; proceeding on in this unity, they have become habitual acquisitions, or they become such ever anew. I can investigate transcendentally this total accomplishment of which I myself, as the "ego," am the ultimate ego-pole, and I can pursue its intentional structure of meaning and validity.

By contrast, as a psychologist I set myself the task of knowing myself as the ego already made part of the world, objectified with a particular real meaning, mundanized, so to speak—concretely speaking, the soul—the task of knowing myself precisely in the manner of objective, naturally mundane knowledge (in the broadest sense), myself as a human being among things, among other human beings, animals, etc. Thus we understand that in fact an indissoluble inner alliance obtains between psychology and transcendental philosophy. But from this perspective we can also foresee that there must be a way whereby a concretely executed psychology could lead to a transcendental philosophy. By anticipation, one can say: If I myself effect the transcendental attitude as a way of lifting myself above all world-apperceptions and my human self-apperception, purely for the purpose of studying the transcendental accomplishment in and through which I "have" the world, then I must also find this accomplishment again, later, in a psychological internal analysis —though in this case it would have passed again into an apperception, i.e., it would be apperceived as something belonging to the real soul [als Realseelisches] as related in reality to the real living body.*

And, conversely: a radical, psychological unfolding of my apperceptive life and of the particular world appearing in it, in respect to the how of the particular appearances (thus of the human "world-picture")—this, in the transition to the transcendental attitude, would immediately have to take on transcendental significance as soon as I now, at the higher level, constantly take into account the meaning-conferring accomplishment [1] which is responsible for the objective apperception, i.e., the accomplishment through which the world-representation has the sense of something really existing, something

---

* If I learn to clarify, to understand from my own point of view as an ego, how other human beings are simply human beings for themselves, how the world is constantly valid for them as existing, the world in which they live together with others and with me, and how they, too, are ultimately transcendental subjects through their accomplishments of world- and self-objectification, then once again I must say to myself: I must take the results of my transcendental clarification in respect to the transcendental self-objectification of others and apply them to their human existence, which is to be judged psychologically.

1. Reading stets auch die für die for stets auch für die.

human and psychic, the sense of being my psychic life and that of other human beings—the life in which everyone has his world-representations, finds himself as existing, representing, acting according to purposes in the world.

This to us rather obvious consideration, which is nevertheless still in need of a deeper grounding, could of course not be accessible prior to the transcendental reduction; but was not the alliance between psychology and transcendental philosophy always strongly noticeable, in spite of all obscurity? Indeed, this alliance was, in fact, a motif which constantly codetermined the [historical] development. Thus it must at first appear curious that transcendental philosophy since Kant found no real usefulness at all in the psychology which, since the time of Locke, after all, wanted to be psychology grounded in inner experience. On the contrary, every transcendental philosophy which was not erring in the direction of empiricism and skepticism saw the slightest admixture of psychology as a betrayal of its true undertaking, and waged a constant battle against psychologism—a battle that was meant to have, and did have, the effect that the philosopher was not permitted to concern himself at all with objective psychology.

To be sure, even after Hume and Kant it remained a great temptation, for all those who were not to be aroused from their dogmatic slumbers, to want to deal psychologically with epistemological problems. In spite of Kant, Hume was still not understood; the very fundamental systematic work of his skepticism, the *Treatise,* was little studied; English empiricism, i.e., the psychological theory of knowledge in the Lockean style, continued to spread, even flourished. Thus it is true that transcendental philosophy, posing completely new kinds of questions, naturally had to struggle against this psychologism. But our present question is no longer concerned with this, for it is directed not at the philosophical naturalists but at the true transcendental philosophers, including the creators of the great systems themselves. Why did they not concern themselves at all with psychology, not even with analytic psychology based on inner experience? The answer already indicated, which still demands further exposition and grounding, is: psychology since Locke in all its forms, even when it sought to be analytic psychology based on "inner experience," mistook its peculiar task.

All of modern philosophy, in the original sense of a universal ultimately grounding science, is, according to our presentation, at least since Kant and Hume, a single struggle between two ideas of science: the idea of an objectivistic philosophy on the ground of the pregiven world and the idea of a philosophy on the ground of absolute, transcendental subjectivity—the latter being something completely new and strange historically, breaking through in Berkeley, Hume, and Kant.

Psychology is constantly involved in this great process of development, involved, as we have seen, in different ways; indeed, psychology is the *truly decisive field*.[2] It is this precisely because, though it has a different attitude and is under the guidance of a different task, its subject matter is universal subjectivity, which in its actualities and possibilities is *one*.

§ 59. *Analysis of the reorientation from the psychological attitude into the transcendental attitude. Psychology "before" and "after" the phenomenological reduction. (The problem of "flowing in.")*

HERE WE AGAIN take up the notion which we previously anticipated from the transcendental-philosophical point of view, the notion which already suggested to us the idea of a possible way from psychology into transcendental philosophy. In psychology the natural, naïve attitude has the result that the human self-objectifications of transcendental intersubjectivity, which belong with essential necessity to the makeup of the constituted world pregiven to me and to us, inevitably have a horizon of transcendentally functioning intentionalities which are not accessible to reflection, not even psychological-scientific reflection. "I, this man," and likewise "other men"—these signify, respectively, a self-apperception and an apperception of others which are transcendental acquisitions involving everything psychic that belongs to them, acquisitions which flowingly change in their particularity through transcendental functions which are

2. I.e., decisive for the struggle between subjectivism and objectivism. For by beginning as objective science and then becoming transcendental, it bridges the gap.

hidden from the naïve attitude. We can inquire back into the transcendental historical dimension, from which the meaning- and validity-accomplishment of these apperceptions ultimately stems, only by breaking with naïveté through the method of transcendental reduction. In the unbroken naïveté in which all psychology, all humanistic disciplines, all human history persists, I, the psychologist, like everyone else, am constantly involved in the performance of self-apperceptions and apperceptions of others. I can, of course, in the process thematically reflect upon myself, upon my psychic life and that of others, upon my and others' changing apperceptions; I can also carry out recollections; [1] observingly, with theoretical interest, I can carry out self-perceptions and self-recollections, and through the medium of empathy I can make use of the self-apperceptions of others. I can inquire into my development and that of others; I can thematically pursue history, society's memory, so to speak —but all *such reflection* remains within transcendental naïveté; it is the performance of the transcendental world-apperception which is, so to speak, ready-made, while the transcendental correlate—i.e., the (immediately active or sedimented) functioning intentionality, which is the universal apperception, constitutive of all particular apperceptions, giving them the ontic sense of "psychic experiences [*Erlebnisse*] of this and that human being"—remains completely hidden. In the naïve attitude of world-life, everything is precisely worldly: that is, [there is nothing but] the constituted object-poles—though they are not understood *as* that. Psychology, like every objective science, is bound to the realm of what is prescientifically pregiven, i.e., bound to what can be named, asserted, described in common language—in this case, bound to the psychic, as it can be expressed in the language of our linguistic community (construed most broadly, the European community). For the life-world— the "world for us all"—is identical with the world that can be commonly talked about. Every new apperception leads essentially, through apperceptive transference, to a new typification of the surrounding world and in social intercourse to a naming which immediately flows into the common language. Thus the

1. After consulting the MS I have deleted the following clause occurring at this point in Biemel's edition: "kann als Geisteswissenschaftler Geschichte sozusagen als Gemeinschafteserinnerung in thematischen Gang bringen." This clause is repeated almost exactly in the next sentence. The MS makes it clear that the first occurrence was to be deleted.

world is always such that it can be empirically, generally (inter-subjectively) explicated and, at the same time, linguistically explicated.

But with the break with naïveté brought about by the tran-scendental-phenomenological reorientation there occurs a signif-icant transformation, significant for psychology itself. As a phenomenologist I can, of course, at any time go back into the natural attitude, back to the straightforward pursuit of my theo-retical or other life-interests; I can, as before, be active as a father, a citizen, an official, as a "good European," etc., that is, as a human being in my human community, in my world. As before —and yet not quite as before. For I can never again achieve the old naïveté; I can only understand it. My transcendental insights and purposes have become merely inactive, but they continue to be my own. More than this: my earlier naïve self-objectification as the empirical human ego of my psychic life has become involved in a new movement. All the new sorts of apperceptions which are exclusively tied to the phenomenological reduction, together with the new sort of language (new even if I use ordinary language, as is unavoidable, though its meanings are also unavoidably transformed)—all this, which before was com-pletely hidden and inexpressible, now flows into the self-objecti-fication, into my psychic life, and becomes apperceived as its newly revealed intentional background of constitutive accom-plishments. I know through my phenomenological studies that I, the previously naïve ego, was none other than the transcendental ego in the mode of naïve hiddenness; I know that to me, as the ego again straightforwardly perceived as a human being, there belongs inseparably a reverse side which constitutes and thus really first produces my full concreteness; I know of this whole dimension of transcendental functions, interwoven with one an-other throughout and extending into the infinite. As was the case previously with the psychic, everything that has newly flowed in is now concretely localized in the world through the living body, which is essentially always constituted along with it. I-the-man, together with the transcendental dimension now ascribed to me, am somewhere in space at some time in the world's time. Thus every new transcendental discovery, by going back into the natu-ral attitude, enriches my psychic life and (apperceptively as a matter of course) that of every other.

§ 60. *The reason for the failure of psychology:*
dualistic and physicalistic presuppositions.

THIS IMPORTANT SUPPLEMENT to our systematic expositions clarifies the essential difference between the essentially
limited thematic horizon, beyond which a psychology on the
basis of the naïve having of the world [*Welthabe*] (i.e., any
psychology of the past prior to transcendental phenomenology)
cannot think in principle—it would have not the least conception of a *plus ultra*—and, on the other hand, the new thematic
horizon which a psychology receives only when the transcendental, coming from transcendental phenomenology, flows into
psychic being and life, i.e., only when naïveté is overcome.

With this the alliance between psychology and transcendental philosophy is illuminated and understood in a new way;
and at the same time we are provided with a new guideline for
understanding the failure of psychology throughout its whole
modern history, over and above everything we have attained in
our earlier systematic considerations by way of motives for evaluating it.

Psychology had to fail because it could fulfill its task, the
investigation of concrete, full subjectivity, only through a radical, completely unprejudiced reflection, which would then necessarily open up the transcendental-subjective dimension. For this
it would obviously have required considerations and analyses in
the pregiven world similar to those we carried out in an earlier
lecture in connection with Kant [§§ 28 ff., above]. There our gaze
was guided at first by bodies, in their manners of pregivenness in
the life-world; whereas, in the analyses required here, we would
have to take our point of departure from the manners in which
souls are pregiven in the life-world. An original reflective question is now directed toward what and how souls—first of all
human souls—are in the world, the life-world, i.e., how they
"animate" physical living bodies, how they are localized in
space-time, how each one "lives" psychically in having "consciousness" of the world in which it lives and is conscious of
living; how each one experiences "its" physical body, not merely
in general, as a particular physical body, but in a quite peculiar

way as "living body," as a system of its "organs" which it moves
as an ego (in holding sway over them); how it thus "takes a
hand" in its consciously given surrounding world as "I strike," "I
push," "I lift" this and that, etc. The soul "is," of course, "in" the
world. But does this mean that it is in the world in the way that
the physical body is and that, when men with living bodies and
souls are experienced in the world as real, their reality, as well as
that of their living bodies and souls, could have the same or even
a similar sense to that of the mere physical bodies? Even though
the human living body is counted among the physical bodies, it
is still "living"—"my physical body," which I "move," in and
through which I "hold sway," which I "animate." If one fails to
consider these matters—which soon become quite extensive—
thoroughly, and actually without prejudice, one has not grasped
at all what is of a soul's *own essence* as such (the word "soul"
being understood here not at all metaphysically but rather in the
sense of the original givenness of the psychic in the life-world);
and thus one has also failed to grasp the genuine ultimate
substrate for a science of "souls." Rather than beginning with
the latter, psychology began with a concept of soul which was
not at all formulated in an original way but which stemmed
from Cartesian dualism, a concept furnished by a prior constructive idea of a corporeal nature and of a mathematical natural
science. Thus psychology was burdened in advance with the task
of being a science parallel [to physics] and with the conception
that the soul—its subject matter—was something real in a sense
similar to corporeal nature, the subject matter of natural science. As long as the absurdity of this century-old prejudice is not
revealed, there can be no psychology which is the science of the
truly psychic, i.e., of what has its meaning originally from the
life-world; for it is to such a meaning that psychology, like any
objective science, is inevitably bound. It is no wonder, then, that
psychology was denied that constant, advancing development
displayed by its admired model, natural science, and that no
inventive spirit and no methodical art could prevent its repeated
involvement in crisis. Thus we have just witnessed a crisis in the
psychology which only a few years ago, as an international
institute-psychology, was filled with the inspiring certainty that
it could finally be placed on a level with natural science. Not that
its work has been completely fruitless. Through scientific objectivity many remarkable facts relating to the life of the human
soul have been discovered. But did this make it seriously a

psychology, a science in which one learned something about the mind's [*Geist*] own essence? (I emphasize once again that this refers not to a mystical "metaphysical" essence but to one's own being-in-oneself and for-oneself which, after all, is accessible to the inquiring, reflecting ego through so-called "inner" or "self-perception.")

§ 61. *Psychology in the tension between the (objectivistic-philosophical) idea of science and empirical procedure: the incompatibility of the two directions of psychological inquiry (the psycho-physical and that of "psychology based on inner experience").*

ALL SCIENTIFIC empirical inquiry [*Empirie*] has its original legitimacy and also its dignity. But considered by itself, not all such inquiry is science in that most original and indispensable sense whose first name was philosophy, and thus also in the sense of the new establishment of a philosophy or science since the Renaissance. Not all scientific empirical inquiry grew up as a partial function within such a science. Yet only when it does justice to this sense can it truly be called scientific. But we can speak of science as such only where, within the indestructible whole of universal philosophy, a branch of the universal task causes a particular science, unitary in itself, to grow up, in whose particular task, as a branch, the universal task works itself out in an originally vital grounding of the system. Not every empirical inquiry that can be pursued freely by itself is in this sense already a science, no matter how much practical utility it may have, no matter how much confirmed, methodical technique may reign in it. Now this applies to psychology insofar as, historically, in the constant drive to fulfill its determination as a philosophical, i.e., a genuine, science, it remains entangled in obscurities about its legitimate sense, finally succumbs to temptations to develop a rigorously methodical psychophysical

—or better, a psychophysicist's [1]—empirical inquiry, and then thinks that it has fulfilled its sense as a science because of the confirmed reliability of its methods. By contrast to the specialists' psychology of the present, our concern—the philosopher's concern—is to move this "sense as a science" to the central point of interest—especially in relation to psychology as the "place of decisions" for a proper development of a philosophy in general —and to clarify its whole motivation and scope.

In this direction of the original aim toward—as we say— "philosophical" scientific discipline, motifs of dissatisfaction arose again and again, setting in soon after the Cartesian beginnings. There were troublesome tensions between the [different] tasks which descended historically from Descartes: on the one hand, that of methodically treating souls in exactly the same way as bodies and as being connected with bodies as spatiotemporal realities, i.e., the task of investigating in a physicalistic way the whole life-world as "nature" in a broadened sense; and, on the other hand, the task of investigating souls in their being in-themselves and for-themselves by way of "inner experience" —the psychologist's primordial inner experience of the subjectivity of his own self—or else by way of the intentional mediation of likewise internally directed empathy (i.e., directed toward what is internal to other persons taken thematically). The two tasks seemed obviously connected in respect to both method and subject matter, and yet they refused to harmonize. Modern philosophy had prescribed to itself from the very beginning the dualism of substances and the parallelism of the methods of *mos geometricus*—or, one can also say, the methodical ideal of physicalism. Even though this became vague and faded as it was transmitted, and failed to attain even the serious beginnings of an explicit execution, it was still decisive for the basic conception of man as a psychophysical reality and for all the ways of putting psychology to work in order to bring about methodical knowledge of the psychic. From the start, then, the world was seen "naturalistically" as a world with two strata of real facts regulated by causal laws. Accordingly, souls too were seen as real annexes of their physical living bodies (these being conceived in terms of exact natural science); the souls, of course, have a different structure from the bodies; they are not *res*

---

1. *psychophysikalisch* as opposed to *psychophysisch*. The former perhaps refers to the "physical" treated in the strict sense of physics proper.

extensae, but they are still real in a sense similar to bodies, and because of this relatedness they must also be investigated in a similar sense in terms of "causal laws," i.e., through theories which are of the same sort in principle as those of physics, which is taken as a model and at the same time as an underlying foundation.

§ 62. *Preliminary discussion of the absurdity of giving equal status in principle to souls and bodies as realities; indication of the difference in principle between the temporality, the causality, and the individuation of natural things and those of souls.*

THIS EQUALIZATION in principle of bodies and souls in the naturalistic method obviously presupposes their more original equalization in principle in respect to their prescientific, experiential givenness in the life-world. Body and soul thus signified two real strata in this experiential world which are integrally and really [1] connected similarly to, and in the same sense as, two pieces of a body. Thus, concretely, one is external to the other, is distinct from it, and is merely related to it in a regulated way. But even this formal equalization is absurd; it is contrary to what is essentially proper to bodies and souls as actually given in life-world experience, which is what determines the genuine sense of all scientific concepts. Let us first of all pick out several concepts which are common to natural science and psychology and which supposedly have the same sense in both instances, and let us test this sameness of sense against what actual experience, as determining sense quite originally, shows, prior to the theoretical superstructures which are the concern of procuring exact science; that is, let us test it against what is given as physical and as psychic in straightforward life-world experience.

1. *reell und real. Reell* refers to the part-whole relation, *real* to the ontological status. Cf. *Ideen,* Vol. I, § 88.

What we must do now is something that has never been done seriously on either side and has never been done radically and consistently: we must go from the scientific fundamental concepts back to the contents of "pure experience," we must radically set aside all presumptions of exact science, all its peculiar conceptual superstructures—in other words, we must consider the world as if these sciences did not yet exist, the world precisely as life-world, just as it maintains its coherent existence in life throughout all its relativity, as it is constantly outlined in life in terms of validity.

Let us first reduce *spatiotemporality* (temporality as simultaneity and successivity) to the spatiotemporality of this pure life-world, the real world in the prescientific sense. Taken in this way it is the universal form of the real world in and through which everything real in the life-world is formally determined. But do souls have spatiotemporality in the true sense, inexistence [2] in this form, as do bodies? It has always been noted that psychic being in and for itself has no spatial extension and no location. This denial of the spatiality of the psychic was obviously oriented around the actual content of experience, [though] without a radical distinction between life-world and scientifically thought world.[3] But can world-time (the form of successivity) be separated from spatiality? Is it not, as full space-time, the proper essential form of mere bodies, in which form the souls take part only indirectly? All objects in the world are in essence "embodied," and for that very reason all "take part" in the space-time of bodies—"indirectly," then, in respect to what is not bodily about them. This applies to spiritual objects of every sort, primarily to souls, but also to spiritual objects of every other sort (such as art works, technical constructions, etc.). According to what gives them spiritual signification, they are "em-bodied" through the way in which they "have" bodily character. In an inauthentic [*uneigentliche*] way they are here or there and are coextended with their bodies. Equally indirectly they have past being and future being in the space-time of

2. *Inexistenz*, simply meaning "existence (essentially) in." The term harks back to Brentano's concept of the "intentionale Inexistenz" of objects in consciousness, the forerunner of Husserl's own concept of intentionality. Here the term is used in a strange context.

3. A stenographic marginal note, without a clear indication of where it should be inserted. In Biemel's version it is inserted after the sentence below, ending "take part only indirectly." But clearly it belongs in this position.

bodies. Everyone experiences the embodiment of souls in original fashion only in his own case. What properly and essentially makes up the character of a living body I experience only in my own living body, namely, in my constant and immediate holding-sway [over my surroundings] through this physical body alone. Only it is given to me originally and meaningfully as "organ" and as articulated into particular organs; each of its bodily members has its own features, such that I can hold sway immediately through it in a particular way—seeing with the eyes, touching with the fingers, etc.—that is, such that I can hold sway in a particular perception in just the ways peculiar to these functions. Obviously it is only in this way that I have perceptions and, beyond this, other experiences of objects in the world. All other types of holding-sway, and in general all relatedness of the ego to the world, are mediated through this. Through bodily "holding-sway" in the form of striking, lifting, resisting, and the like, I act as ego across distances, primarily on the corporeal aspects of objects in the world. It is only *my* being-as-ego, as holding sway, that I actually experience as itself, in its own essence; and each person experiences only his own. All such holding-sway occurs in modes of "movement," but the "I move" in holding-sway (I move my hands, touching or pushing something) is not in itself [merely] the spatial movement of a physical body, which as such could be perceived by everyone. My body —in particular, say, the bodily part "hand"—moves in space; [but] the activity of holding sway, "kinesthesis," which is embodied together with the body's movement, is not itself in space as a spatial movement but is only indirectly colocalized in that movement. Only through my own originally experienced holding-sway, which is the sole original experience of living-bodiliness as such, can I understand another physical body as a living body in which another "I" is embodied and holds sway; this again, then, is a mediation, but one of a quite different sort from the mediation of inauthentic localization upon which it is founded.[4] Only in this way do other ego-subjects firmly belong to "their" bodies for me and are localized here or there in space-time; that is, they are inauthentically inexistent in this form of bodies, whereas they themselves, and thus souls in general, considered purely in

4. A difficult stenographic insert. My recognition of another is mediated in two ways: (1) through my recognition of the localized *Körper* and (2) through my "analogizing apperception" from my own case. The second is "founded upon" the first, because I must first perceive a body (*Körper*) in order to make the analogy.

terms of their own essence, have no existence at all in this form.

Furthermore, causality too—if we remain within the life-world, which originally grounds ontic meaning—has in principle quite a different meaning depending on whether we are speaking of natural causality or of "causality" among psychic events or between the corporeal and the psychic. A body is what it is as this determined body, as a substrate of "causal" properties which is, in its own essence, spatiotemporally localized.* Thus if one takes away causality, the body loses its ontic meaning as body, its identifiability and distinguishability as a physical individual. The ego, however, is "this one" and has individuality in and through itself; it does not have individuality through causality. To be sure, because of the character of the physical living body, the ego can become distinguishable by any other ego and thus by everyone in respect to its position in the space of physical bodies, a position which is inauthentic and which it owes to its physical, living body. But its distinguishability and identifiability in space for everyone, with all the psychophysically conditioned factors that enter in here, make not the slightest contribution to its being as *ens per se*. As such it already has, in itself, its uniqueness. For the ego, space and time are not principles of individuation; it knows no natural causality, the latter being, in accord with its meaning, inseparable from spatiotemporality. Its effectiveness is its holding-sway-as-ego; this occurs immediately

* In terms of the life-world, this means nothing other than that a body, which as such can already be explicated with its experiential meaning through its own essential properties, is always at the same time a body, in its being-such, under particular "circumstances." First of all, it belongs to the most general structure of the life-world that the body has, so to speak, its habits of being in its being-such, that it belongs within a type which is either known or, if it is "new" to us, is still to be discovered, a type within which the explicable properties belong together in typical ways. But it is also part of the life-world's formal typology that bodies have typical ways of being together, in coexistence (above all in a given perceptual field) and in succession —i.e., a constant universal spatiotemporal set of types. It is due to the latter that each particular experienced body is not only necessarily there together with other bodies in general but is there *as* being of this type, among other bodies typically belonging to it, in a typical form of belonging together which runs its course within a typical pattern of succession. Accordingly each body "is," in the way that it is, under "circumstances"; a change of properties in one body indicates changes of properties in another—though this must be understood roughly and relatively, just as it is, essentially, in the life-world; there can be no question of "exact" causality, which pertains to the idealizing substructions of science.

through its kinestheses, as holding-sway in its living body, and only mediately (since the latter is also a physical body) extends to other physical bodies.

§ 63. *The questionable character of the concepts of "outer" and "inner" experience. Why has the experience of the bodily thing in the life-world, as the experience of something "merely subjective," not previously been included in the subject matter of psychology?*

THE FUNDAMENTAL MISTAKE of wanting to view men and animals seriously as double realities, as combinations of two different sorts of realities which are to be equated in the sense of their reality, and accordingly the desire to investigate souls also through the method of the science of bodies, i.e., souls as existing within natural causality, in space-time, like bodies—this gave rise to the supposed obviousness of a method to be formed as an analogue to natural science. The understandable result of both [natural-scientific method and the new psychological method] was the false parallelism of "inner" and "outer" experience. Both concepts remained unclear in respect to sense and function (their scientific function for physics, psychology, psychophysics).

On both sides, experiences are conceived as being performed in theoretical function; natural science is supposed to be based on outer, psychology on inner, experience. In the former, physical nature is given; and in the latter, psychic being, that of the soul. In accord with this, "psychological experience" becomes an equivalent expression for "inner experience." To put it more precisely: what is actually experienced is the world as simply existing, prior to all philosophy and theory—existing things, stones, animals, men. In natural, direct life, this is experienced as simply, perceptually "there" (as simply existing, ontically certain presence) or, just as simply, in terms of memory, as "having been there," etc. Even to this natural life, possible and occasionally necessary straightforward reflection belongs. Then relativity comes into view, and what is valid as simply being there, in the particularity of its manners of givenness in life itself, is transformed into a "merely subjective appearance"; and specifically it is called an appearance in relation to the one thing, the "entity itself," which emerges—though again only relatively —through corrections when the gaze is directed upon the alteration of such "appearances." And the same thing is true in respect to the other modalities of experience or their correlative temporal modalities.

This has already been carefully thought through in another connection, and if we bring it to mind here with renewed, lively clarity, there results the question: Why does the whole flowing life-world not figure at the very beginning of a psychology as something "psychic," indeed as the psychic realm which is primarily accessible, the first field in which immediately given psychic phenomena can be explicated according to types? And correlatively: why is the experience which actually, as experience, brings this life-world to givenness and, within it, especially in the primal mode of perception, presents mere bodily things— why is this experience not called psychological experience rather than "outer experience," supposedly by contrast to psychological experience? Naturally there are differences in the manner of life-world experience, depending on whether one experiences stones, rivers, mountains or, on the other hand, reflectively experiences one's experiencing of them or other ego-activity, one's own or that of others, such as holding sway through the living body. This may be a significant difference for psychology and may lead to difficult problems. But does this change the fact that everything about the life-world is obviously "subjective"? Can psychology, as a universal science, have any other theme than the totality of the subjective? Is it not the lesson of a deeper and not naturalistically blinded reflection that everything subjective is part of an indivisible totality?

§ 64. *Cartesian dualism as the reason for the parallelization. Only the formal and most general features of the schema "descriptive vs. explanatory science" are justified.*

FOR GALILEAN natural science, mathematical-physical nature is objective-true nature; it is this nature that is supposed to manifest itself in the merely subjective appearances. It is thus clear—and we have already pointed this out—that nature, in exact natural science, is not the actually experienced nature, that of the life-world. It is an idea that has arisen out of idealization and has been hypothetically substituted for actually intuited nature. [Cf. § 36.] The conceptual method of idealization is the fundament of the whole method of natural science (i.e., of the pure science of bodies), the latter being the method of inventing "exact" theories and formulae and also of reapplying them within the praxis which takes place in the world of actual experience.

Here, then, lies the answer—sufficient for our present train of thought—to the question posed, as to how it happens that nature, as given in the life-world, this merely subjective aspect of "outer experience," is not included under psychological experience in traditional psychology and that psychological experience is instead opposed to outer experience. Cartesian dualism requires the parallelization of *mens* and *corpus*, together with the naturalization of psychic being implied in this parallelization, and hence also requires the parallelization of the required methods. To be sure, because of the way in which the ready-made geometry of the ancients was taken over, the idealization which thoroughly determines its sense was almost forgotten; and on the psychic side [1] [such an] idealization, as an actually executed and original accomplishment in a manner appropriate to the nature of the psychic, was not required, or rather not missed. Of course it should have been evident that idealization in fact has

1. Better: the psychological side.

no place on this side, since there could be no question here of anything like perspectivization and kinestheses, of measurement or of anything analogous to measurement.

The prejudice of the [appropriateness of the] same method produced the expectation that, by practicing this method in its appropriate version, one could arrive, without any deeper subjective-methodical considerations, at stable theorizing and a methodical technique. But it was a vain hope. Psychology never became exact; the parallelization could not actually be carried out, and—as we understand—for essential reasons. This much we can say even here, though much still needs to be done for the sake of the much needed ultimate clarity on all sides, so that we can also understand the survival of those various forms in which modern dualistic and psychophysiological (or psychophysical) psychology for long periods could have the appearance of a properly aimed methodical execution and the conviction of continued success as truly a fundamental science of the psychic; also, so that we can understand why psychophysical empirical inquiry, which is thoroughly legitimate and quite indispensable, could not count as the pathway to or the execution of a genuine psychology which would do justice to the proper essence of the psychic itself. In any case, we can already say in advance, on the basis of insight, that the psychic, considered purely in terms of its own essence, has no [physical] nature, has no conceivable in-itself in the natural sense, no spatiotemporally causal, no idealizable and mathematizable in-itself, no laws after the fashion of natural laws; here there are no theories with the same relatedness back to the intuitive life-world, no observations or experiments with a function for theorizing similar to natural science—in spite of all the self-misunderstandings of empirical, experimental psychology. But because the fundamental insight has been lacking, the historical inheritance of dualism, with its naturalization of the psychic, retains its force; but it is so vague and unclear that the need is not even felt for a genuine execution of the dualism of the exact sciences on both sides, such as is required by the sense of this dualism.

Thus the schema of *descriptive* vs. *theoretically explanatory* science, too, was kept in readiness as being obvious; we find it sharply emphasized in respect to psychology in Brentano and Dilthey, and in general in the nineteenth century—the time of passionate efforts finally to bring about a rigorously scientific psychology which could show its face alongside natural science. By no means do we wish to imply by this that the concept of a pure description and of a descriptive science, or beyond that even the difference between descriptive and explanatory method, can find no application at all in psychology, any more than we deny that the pure experience of bodies must be distinguished from the experience of the psychic or the spiritual. Our task is critically to make transparent, down to its ultimate roots, the naturalistic—or, more exactly, the physicalistic—prejudice of the whole of modern psychology, on the one hand in respect to the never clarified concepts of experience which guide the descriptions and on the other hand in respect to the way in which the contrast between descriptive and explanatory disciplines is interpreted as parallel and similar [to the same contrast in natural science].[2]

It has already become clear to us that an "exact" psychology, as an analogue to physics (i.e., the dualistic parallelism of realities, of methods, and of sciences), is an absurdity. Accordingly there can no longer be a descriptive psychology which is the analogue of a descriptive natural science. In no way, not even in the schema of description *vs.* explanation, can a science of souls be modeled on natural science or seek methodical counsel from it. It can only model itself on its own subject matter, as soon as it has achieved clarity on this subject matter's own essence. There remains only the formal and most general notion that one must not operate with empty word-concepts, must not move in the sphere of vagueness, but must derive everything from clarity, from actually self-giving intuition, or, what is the same thing, from self-evidence—in this case from the original life-world experience of, or from what is essentially proper to, the psychic and nothing else. This results, as it does everywhere, in an applicable and indispensable sense of description and of descriptive science and also, at a higher level, of "explanation" and explanatory science. Explanation, as a higher-level accomplishment, signifies in this case nothing but a method which surpasses the descriptive realm, a realm which is realizable through actually experiencing intuition. This surpassing occurs on the basis of the "descriptive" knowledge, and, as a scientific method, it occurs through a procedure of insight which ultimately verifies itself by means of the descriptive data. In this formal and general sense there is in *all* sciences the necessary fundamental level of description and the elevated level of explanation. But

2. Literally: "in respect to the manner of the parallelizing and similar interpretation of the contrast between descriptive and explanatory disciplines."

this must be taken only as a formal parallel and must find its meaning-fulfillment in each science through its own essential sources; and the concept of ultimate verification must not be falsified in advance by assuming, as in physics,[3] that certain propositions in the specifically physical (that is, the mathematically idealized) sphere are the ultimately verifying propositions.

§ 65. *Testing the legitimacy of an empirically grounded dualism by familiarizing oneself with the factual procedure of the psychologist and the physiologist.*

WHEN DESCRIPTION is understood in this way, then, it must characterize the beginning of the only psychology which is true to its origins, the only possible psychology. But it soon becomes manifest that clarity, genuine self-evidence, in general but especially here, is not to be bought cheaply. Above all, as we have already indicated, the arguments of principle against dualism, against the double stratification which already falsifies the sense of experience purely within the life-world, against the supposed likeness of the reality (in the life-world) of physical and psychic being in respect to the innermost sense of reality, against the likeness of temporality and individuality [in the two cases]—these arguments are too philosophically oriented, too oriented toward principle, to be able to make any sort of lasting impression on the psychologists and scientists of our time or even on the "philosophers." One is tired of arguments of principle, which, after all, lead to no agreement; from the start one listens with only half an ear, prefers to trust in the power of the indubitable accomplishments performed in the great experiential sciences, to trust in their actual methods, their actual work of experiencing—experiencing which is, naturally, in each case peculiar to the area in question: experience of the physical for the physicists, of the biological for the biologists, of the human [1] for the humanists. Certainly it is quite proper that they are

3. Literally: "must not, as in physics, be falsified."
1. *die geisteswissenschaftliche Erfahrung.*

called experiential sciences. If we pay attention not to the reflections in which scientists speak about their method and their work, i.e., philosophize (as in the usual academic orations for special occasions), but rather to the actual method and work itself, it is certain that the scientists here constantly have recourse in the end to experience. But [2] if we place ourselves within this experience, the experience itself shows—it will be argued against us—that, in respect to the corporeal and the spiritual, the mistaken dualistic interpretation is taken up into the supposed experiential meaning and gives researchers the right to do justice to dualism, which is actually purely empirically grounded, and to operate just as they do with inner and outer experience, with temporality, reality, and causality. The philosopher can speak as insistently as he wants about absurdity in principle, but he cannot prevail against the power of tradition. Now we too, of course, are by no means ready to sacrifice our objections, precisely because they are radically different from argumentations using concepts which are historically inherited and not newly interrogated in respect to their original sense, and because our objections themselves where derived from precisely the most original sources, as anyone can convince himself who tests our presentation.[3] This does not mean, however, that the procedure of the working experiential sciences, the sense and the limitation of their legitimacy, is explicitly made clear; and as for psychology in particular, our present subject, its procedure, always psychophysiological, is not made clear—neither its legitimacy nor the temptations it offers. This is true not only of all the primitive methodical forms of former times but also of the most highly developed forms [that have appeared] since the second half of the nineteenth century. The necessity of separating the experience of bodies from the experience of the spirit has not been clearly established; nor has the legitimacy, claimed in advance, of taking the experience of bodies, with the constant signification it has for the psychologist as for everyone else, and including it in the psychic, thus making its universality an all-encompassing one. This, of course, involves [us] in paradoxical difficulties. But difficulties that can be pushed to one side by good, successfully functioning work cannot be pushed to one side by a universal philosophy; rather, they must be overcome,

2. Various marginal notes indicate Husserl's extreme dissatisfaction with the text from here to the end of this section.
3. From "can speak as insistently" to this point crossed out, but not replaced by anything.

since philosophy exists precisely in order to remove all the blinders of praxis, especially scientific praxis, and to reawaken, indeed to rescue, the true and actual, the full purpose, that science (here psychology) should fulfill as its inborn meaning. Thus we cannot be spared from inquiring back into the most general ground from which the possible tasks of psychology, as of every objective science, arise, namely, the ground of the common experience within which the experiential sciences work, to which, then, they appeal, if—denying all "metaphysics"—they claim to satisfy the inviolable demands of experience.

§ 66. *The world of common experience: its set of regional types and the possible universal abstractions within it: "nature" as correlate of a universal abstraction; the problem of "complementary abstractions."*

We shall begin with a general consideration in which we simply repeat what has been said earlier, though deepening it, in order to be able to say something decisive, with original and vital clarity, about the questions raised. We already know that all theoretical accomplishment in objective science has its place on the ground of the pregiven world, the life-world—that it presupposes prescientific knowing and the purposive reshaping of the latter. Straightforward experience, in which the life-world is given, is the ultimate foundation of all objective knowledge. Correlatively, this world itself, as existing prescientifically for us (originally) purely through experience, furnishes us in advance, through its invariant set of essential types, with all possible scientific topics.

First we consider what is most general here: that the universe is pregiven as a universe of "things." In this broadest sense "thing" is an expression for what ultimately exists and what "has" ultimate properties, relations, interconnections (through which its being is explicated); the thing itself is not what is "had" in this manner but precisely what ultimately "has"—in short (but understood quite unmetaphysically), it is the ultimate substrate. Things have their concrete set of types, finding their expression in the "substantives" of a given language. But all particular sets of types come under the most general of all, the set of "regional" types. In life it is the latter that determines praxis, in constant factual generality; and it first becomes explicit with essential necessity through a method of inquiry into essences. Here I mention distinctions such as living *vs.* lifeless things [and,] within the sphere of living things, the animals, i.e., those living not merely according to drives but also constantly through ego-acts, as opposed to those living only according to drives (such as plants). Among animals, human beings stand out, so much so, in fact, that mere animals have ontic meaning [as such] only by comparison to them [*erst von ihnen her*], as variations of them. Among lifeless things, humanized things are distinguished, things that have signification (e.g., cultural meaning) through human beings. Further, as a variation on this, there are things which refer meaningfully in a similar way to animal existence, as opposed to things that are without signification in this sense. It is clear that these very general separations and groupings derived from the life-world, or the world of original experience, determine the separation of scientific areas, just as they also determine the internal interconnections between the sciences in virtue of the internal interconnection and overlapping of the regions. On the other hand, universal abstractions, which encompass all concretions,[1] at the same time also determine subjects for possible sciences. It is only in the modern period that this latter path has been followed; and it is precisely this path that is relevant for us here. The natural science of the modern period, establishing itself as physics, has its roots in the consistent abstraction through which it *wants* to see, in the life-world, only corporeity. Each "thing" "*has*" corporeity even though, if it is (say) a human being or a work of art, it is not merely bodily but is only "embodied," like everything real. Through such an abstraction, carried out with universal consistency, the world is reduced to abstract-universal nature, the subject matter of pure natural science. It is here alone that geometrical idealization, first of all, and then all further mathematizing theorization, has found its possible meaning. It is based on the self-evidence of "outer experience," which is thus in fact an abstracting type of experience. But within the abstraction it has its essential forms of explication, it relativities, its ways of motivating idealizations, etc.

1. I.e., encompass the concrete members of all regions.

Now what about human souls? It is human beings that are concretely experienced. Only after their corporeity has been abstracted—within the universal abstraction which reduces the world to a world of abstract bodies—does the question arise, presenting itself now as so obvious, as to the "other side," that is, the complementary abstraction. Once the bodily "side" has become part of the general task of natural science and has found its theoretically idealizing treatment there, the task of psychology is characterized as the "complementary" task, i.e., that of subjecting the psychic side to a corresponding theoretical treatment with a corresponding universality. Does this ground the dualistic science of man and assign to psychology its original sense, as it almost seems to do, in an unassailable manner, i.e., truly purely on the basis of life-world experience, without any metaphysical admixture? Thus it applies first to the realm of human beings and then, obviously in the same manner, to the realm of animals. This would also, then—or so it seems—give order in advance to the procedure of the sciences of social and objectified spirit [versachlichte Geistigkeit] (the humanistic disciplines). As the correlative abstraction teaches us, man (and everything else that is real in animal form) is, after all, something real having two strata and is given as such in pure experience, purely in the life-world; what is required for the regional science of man, then, is obviously first of all what is sometimes called (by contrast to social psychology) individual psychology. Human beings, concretely, in the space-time of the world, have their abstractly distinguished souls distributed among bodies, which make up, when we adopt the purely naturalistic consideration of bodies, a universe to be considered in itself as a totality. The souls themselves are external to one another [ein Ausserein-ander] [only] in virtue of their embodiment; that is, in their own abstract stratum they do not make up a parallel total universe. Thus psychology can be the science of the general features of individual souls only; this follows from the way in which they are determined in their own essence by the psychophysical framework, by their being integrated into nature as a whole. This individual psychology must, then, be the foundation for a sociology and likewise for a science of objectified spirit (of cultural things), which after all refers, in its own way, to the human being as person, i.e., to the life of the soul. And all this can be applied by analogy—just as far as the analogy reaches—to animals, to animal society, to the surrounding world with its specifically animal signification.

Do these considerations, which have led us back to the ground of life-world experience—that is, to the source of self-evidence, to which we must ultimately appeal here—not justify the traditional dualism of body and psychic spirit or the dualistic interrelation between physiology, as the science of the human (and also animal) body, on the one hand, and psychology, as the science of the psychic side of man, on the other? Even more than this: is this not indeed an improvement upon dualism as compared with the rationalistic tradition instituted by Descartes, who also influenced empiricism? Namely, is dualism not freed from all metaphysical substruction by the fact that it wants to be nothing more than a faithful expression of what experience itself teaches? To be sure, this is not quite the case,[2] according to the way in which psychologists, physiologists, and physicists understand "experience"; and we have indicated the sense of experience which is decisive for [the scientists'] work, correcting their usual self-interpretation.[3] A metaphysical residuum is to be found in the fact that natural scientists consider nature to be concrete and overlook the abstraction through which their nature has been shaped into a subject matter for science. Because of this, the souls, too, retain something of a substantiality of their own, though it is not a self-sufficient substantiality, since, as experience teaches us,[4] the psychic can be found in the world only in connection with bodies. But before we could pose further and now important questions, we had to take this step.[5] We had first to help empirical inquiry toward an understanding of itself; we had to make visible, through reflection, its anonymous accomplishment, namely, the "abstraction" we described. In doing this, we are thus more faithful to empirical inquiry than the psychologists and the natural scientists; the last residuum of the Cartesian theory of two substances is defeated simply because *abstracta* are not "substances."

2. I.e., not quite the case that it is a faithful expression, etc.
3. Literally: "and we have corrected its decisive sense for work, as opposed to a very usual self-interpretation."
4. According to this view.
5. I.e., the step of presenting this still inadequate view.

§ 67. *The dualism of the abstractions grounded in experience. The continuing historical influence of the empiricist approach (from Hobbes to Wundt). Critique of data-empiricism*

BUT NOW WE MUST ASK what there is in dualism and in the "stratification" of man and of the sciences, after the new legitimacy of the latter has been shown through [the above theory of] abstraction, that is and remains truly meaningful. We have deliberately made no use of our first critique of this dualism, of our indication of the way in which the spatiotemporal localization and individuation of psychic being are secondary in principle; our intention was to familiarize ourselves completely with the psychophysical dualistic empiricism of the scientists in order to arrive at our decisions within the universal framework of the total world of experience as the primal ground. In addition to new insights, which are fundamentally essential, as we shall see, for the understanding of the genuine task of psychology, we shall also find again those earlier insights mentioned above.

Let us take up the abstraction we discussed; it will reveal its hidden difficulties all too soon. Let us take it quite straightforwardly and naturally as a differentiated direction of gaze and interest on the basis of the concrete experience of man. Obviously we can pay attention to his mere corporeity and be one-sidedly and consistently interested [only] in it; and likewise we can pay attention to the other side, being interested purely in what is psychic about him. In this way the distinction between "outer" and "inner" experience (and first of all perception) also seems to be automatically clear, to have an inviolable legitimacy, together with the division of man himself into two real sides or strata. To the question of what belongs to the psychic side and what of this is given purely in inner perception, one answers in the familiar way: it is a person, substrate of personal properties, of original or acquired psychic dispositions (faculties, habits). This, however, [supposedly] refers back to a flowing "life of consciousness," a temporal process in which the first and especially noticeable feature is that of the ego-acts, though these are on a background of passive states [*Zuständlichkeiten*]. It is [supposedly] this current of "psychic experiences" [*Erlebnisse*] that is experienced [*erfahren*] in that abstractive attitude of focus upon the psychic. What is directly and actually perceived (and it is even thought to be perceived with a particular sort of apodictic self-evidence) is the presence-sphere of the psychic experiences of one man, and only by that man himself, as his "inner perception"; the experiences of others are given only through the mediated type of experience called "empathy"—unless this latter type of experience is reinterpreted as an inference, as it generally used to be.

However, all this is by no means so simple and so obvious as it was taken to be, without any closer consideration, for centuries. A psychology derived from an abstraction which is parallel [to the physicist's abstraction], on the basis of an "inner perception" and other types of psychological experience which are parallel to outer perception, must be seriously questioned; indeed, taken in this way, it is impossible in principle. This obviously applies to every dualism of the two real sides or strata of man, and every dualism of the sciences of man, which appeals purely to experiencing intuition.

From the historical point of view we must consider the empiricist psychology and the sensationalism that have become dominant since the time of Hobbes and Locke and have corrupted psychology up to our own day. In this first form of naturalism, supposedly on the basis of experience, the soul is set off by itself in the closed unity of a space of consciousness as its own real sphere of psychic data. The naïve equation of these data of psychological data-experience with those of the experience of bodies leads to a reification [*Verdinglichung*] of the former; the constant view to the exemplary character of natural science misleads one into taking these data as psychic atoms or atom-complexes and into considering the tasks of the two sides to be parallel. Psychic faculties—or, as they later come to be called, psychic dispositions—become analogues of physical forces, titles for merely causal properties of the soul, either belonging to its own essence or arising from its causal relationship with the living body, but in any case in such a way that reality and causality are understood in the same way on both sides. Of course, right away, in Berkeley and Hume, the enigmatic difficulties of such an interpretation of the soul announce themselves and press toward an immanent idealism which swallows up one of the two "parallels." Yet up through the nineteenth century this changes nothing about the way in which psychology and physiology, which supposedly follow experience, in fact do their work. It was easy to carry the "idealistic" naturalism of the immanent philosophy of those successors of Locke over into the dualistic psychology. The epistemological difficulties made so noticeable by Hume's fictionalism were overcome—precisely through "epistemology." Reflections which were appealing, but which unfortunately evaded genuine radicalism, were undertaken in order to justify *ex post facto* what one does in any case in the natural striving to follow the evidence of experience. Thus the growing acquisition of obviously valuable empirical facts took on the appearance of having a meaning which could be understood philosophically. We have a perfect example of the sort of epistemological-metaphysical interpretations which follow in the footsteps of science in the reflections of Wundt and his school, in the doctrine of the "two points of view," of the theoretical utilization of the one common experience through a twofold "abstraction." This doctrine appears to be on the way toward overcoming all traditional metaphysics and to lead to a self-understanding of psychology and natural science; but in fact it merely changes empirical dualistic naturalism into a monistic naturalism with two parallel faces—i.e., a variation of Spinozistic parallelism. In addition, this Wundtian way, as well as the other ways of justifying the psychology which is bound to empirical dualism, retains the naturalistic data-interpretation of consciousness in accord with the Lockean tradition; though this does not keep them from speaking of representation and will, of value and the setting of goals as data in consciousness, without radically posing the question of how, through such data and their psychic causality, one is supposed to understand the rational activity presupposed by all psychological theories, which are reason's accomplishments—whereas here, in the theories themselves, this activity is supposed to appear as one result among the others.

§ 68. *The task of a pure explication of consciousness as such: the universal problem of intentionality. (Brentano's attempt at a reform of psychology.)*

THE FIRST THING we must do here is overcome the naïveté which makes the conscious life, in and through which the world is what it is for us—as the universe of actual and possible experience—into a real property of man, real in the same sense as his corporeity, i.e., according to the [following] schema. In the world we have things with different peculiarities, and among these there are also some that experience, rationally know, etc., what is outside them. Or, what is the same thing: The first thing we must do, and first of all in immediate reflective self-experience, is to take the conscious life, completely without prejudice, just as what it quite immediately gives itself, as itself, to be.[1] Here, in immediate givenness, one finds anything but color data, tone data, other "sense" data or data of feeling, will, etc.; that is, one finds none of those things which appear in traditional psychology, taken for granted to be immediately given from the start. Instead, one finds, as even Descartes did (naturally we ignore his other purposes), the *cogito, intentionality,* in those familiar forms which, like everything actual in the surrounding world, find their expression in language: "I see a tree which is green; I hear the rustling of its leaves, I smell its blossoms," etc.; or, "I remember my schooldays," "I am saddened by the sickness of a friend," etc. Here we find nothing other than "consciousness of . . ."—consciousness in the broadest sense, which is still to be investigated in its whole scope and its modes.

This is the place to recall the extraordinary debt we owe to Brentano for the fact that he began his attempt to reform psychology with an investigation of the peculiar characteristics of the psychic (in contrast to the physical) and showed intentionality to be one of these characteristics; the science of "psychic

---

1. *als was es sich da als es selbst ganz unmittelbar gibt.*

phenomena," then, has to do everywhere with conscious experiences [*Bewusstseinserlebnisse*]. Unfortunately, in the most essential matters he remained bound to the prejudices of the naturalistic tradition; these prejudices have not yet been overcome if the data of the soul, rather than being understood as sensible (whether of outer or inner "sense"), are [simply] understood as data having the remarkable character of intentionality; in other words, if dualism, psychophysical causality, is still accepted as valid. This also applies to his idea of a descriptive natural science, as is shown by [his conception of their] parallel procedure—setting the task of classifying and descriptively analyzing psychic phenomena completely in the spirit of the old traditional interpretation of the relation between descriptive and explanatory natural sciences. None of this would have been possible if Brentano had penetrated to the true sense of the task of investigating conscious life as intentional—and investigating it first of all on the basis of the pregiven world, since it was a question of grounding psychology as an objective science. Thus Brentano set up a psychology of intentionality as a task only formally, but had no way of attacking it. The same is true of his whole school, which also, like Brentano himself, consistently refused to accept what was decisively new in my *Logical Investigations* (even though his demand for a psychology of intentional phenomena was put into effect here). What is new in the *Logical Investigations* is found not at all in the merely ontological investigations, which had a one-sided influence contrary to the innermost sense of the work, but rather in the subjectively directed investigations (above all the fifth and sixth, in the second volume of 1901) in which, for the first time, the *cogitata qua cogitata*, as essential moments of each conscious experience as it is given in genuine inner experience, come into their own and immediately come to dominate the whole method of intentional analysis. Thus "self-evidence" (that petrified logical idol) is made a problem there for the first time, freed from the privilege given to scientific evidence and broadened to mean original self-giving in general. The genuine intentional synthesis is discovered in the synthesis of several acts into one act, such that, in a unique manner of binding one meaning to another, there emerges not merely a whole, an amalgam whose parts are meanings, but rather a single meaning in which these meanings themselves are contained, but in a meaningful way. With this the problems of correlation, too, already announce themselves;

and thus, in fact, this work contains the first, though of course
very imperfect, beginnings of "phenomenology."

§ 69.   *The basic psychological method of
"phenomenological-psychological reduction"
(first characterization: [1] intentional
relatedness and the epochē; [2] levels of
descriptive psychology; [3] establishing
the "disinterested spectator").*

YET THIS CRITIQUE of data-psychology, and also of the
psychology which, in the manner of Brentano, takes intentionality into account, now needs systematic justification. Let us
consider somewhat more closely what is taken for granted, as
presented earlier, as the supposed straightforward experiential
grounding of dualism, of the parallel abstractions, of the separation of outer and inner experience, these being understood as the
types of abstractive experience pertaining to natural science and
psychology, respectively. If we direct our attention in particular
to "inner" or psychic experience, it is not as if we immediately
obtained, in the straightforward experience of a human being,
by abstracting from everything belonging to [physical] nature,
his pure psychic life as a stratum of intentional experiences
[*Erlebnisse*] belonging to him as an integral part [*ihm reell
eigen*]; that is, this is not simply the reverse side of the abstraction which gives us his pure corporeity as subject matter. In
straightforward world-experience we find human beings intentionally related to certain things—animals, houses, fields, etc.
—that is, as consciously affected by these things, actively attending to them or in general perceiving them, actively remembering
them, thinking about them, planning and acting in respect to
them.
    If, as psychologists, we abstract from a man's physical living
body (as belonging to the subject matter of natural science),
this changes nothing about these intentional relations to what is
real in the world. The man who effects these relations is thereby

certain of the actuality of the real things he deals with; and even the psychologist who has some man as his subject and who empathetically understands [*nachversteht*] what this man perceives, what he thinks, deals with, etc., also has his own certainties about those things. Here it must be noted that the straightforwardly, naturally experienced and expressed intentionalities of a person (the person being understood already under the abstraction from the living body) have the sense of *real relations* between the person and other realities. These realities are naturally not component parts of the psychic essence of the person who relates himself to these realities; whereas we must ascribe to his own essence his perceiving, his thinking, his valuing, etc. Thus, in order to attain the pure and actual subject matter of the required "descriptive psychology," a fully consciously practiced method is required which I call the *phenomenological-psychological reduction*—taken in this context as a method for psychology. (We shall leave open the question of how this reduction stands in relation to the transcendental reduction.)

As a psychologist I stand naïvely on the ground of the intuitively pregiven world. Distributed throughout it are things, and men and animals with their souls. Now I wish to explicate, through an example and then in generality, what is concretely and essentially proper to a man purely in his spiritual or psychic being. What is essentially proper to the soul includes all intentionalities, the experiences of the type called "perception," for example, considered precisely as those performed by the person serving as an example and exactly in the way he accomplishes them; and always [one must take care] that nothing is brought in which goes beyond the person's or the "soul's" own essence. In perceiving, the person is conscious of the perceived. But whether the perception has the mode of an observing and explicating act or the mode of passively being conscious of the unnoticed background of what is directly observed, one thing is clear: whether the perceived [object] exists or not, whether the perceiving person is mistaken about this or not, and also whether I, the psychologist, who in my empathetic understanding of the person unhesitatingly concur in the belief in the perceived [object], am mistaken about it or not—this must remain irrelevant for me as a psychologist. None of this may enter into the psychological description of the perception. Whether it is a case of being or of illusion, it does not affect at all the fact that the subject in question does, in fact, carry out a perception (for example), that he does in fact have the consciousness: "This tree here," that he thereby effects the straightforward certainty that belongs to the essence of perceiving, i.e., the certainty of straightforward existence. Thus all actually, immediately descriptive statements about persons, about ego-subjects, as they are straightforwardly given in experience, necessarily go beyond what is purely essentially proper to these subjects. The latter can be attained purely only through the peculiar method of the epochē. This is an epochē of validity: we abstain, in the case of perception, from the coperformance of the validity that the perceiving person performs. This is within our freedom. One cannot arbitrarily and unhesitatingly modalize a validity: one cannot transform certainty into doubt or negation, or pleasure into displeasure, love into hate, desire into abhorrence. But one can unhesitatingly abstain from any validity, that is, one can put its performance out of play for certain particular purposes. But we must reflect further on this. Every act is, for the acting person, a being certain or a modality of being certain ([considering something as] being doubtful, being presumable, being null and void) with a particular content. But at the same time this being certain— or, as we also say, having-in-validity—involves essential differentiations, for example, certainty of being is different from certainty of value, both are different from practical certainty (for example, that of a project), and each has its modalities. In addition, we have differences among act-validities through their *implication* of other acts and their own implied validities, for example, through the horizon-consciousness surrounding every act.

Let us not consider the fact that even the concept of "horizon"-consciousness [or of] horizon-intentionality contains very diverse modes of an intentionality which is "unconscious" in the usual narrower sense of the word but which can be shown to be vitally involved and cofunctioning in different ways; these modes of intentionality have their own modalities of validity and their own ways of changing them. Yet there are still, over and above these, "unconscious" intentionalities, as can be shown by a more detailed analysis. This would be the place for those repressed emotions of love, of humiliation, of *ressentiments*, and the kinds of behavior unconsciously motivated by them which have been disclosed by recent "depth psychology" (although this does not mean that we identify ourselves with their theories). These too have their modes of validity (certainties of being, certainties of value, volitional certainties and their modal variations). And thus what we made clear to ourselves in connection with the example of perception applies to them all in advance. In pursuit of a pure psychology the psychologist must never allow the validities, no matter how diverse, of the persons who make up his subject matter to be valid for himself; during his research he must have and take up no position of his own in regard to them; and this must hold universally and in advance in regard to all the intentionalities of these persons which are as yet unknown, which lie in the depths of their lives and are still hidden from the psychologist, regardless, of course, of whether they are conscious or unconscious intentionalities in the special sense for the person himself. This encompasses all habitualities, all interests, those which endure for a short time and those which govern a whole life. In advance, once and for all, the psychologist in his vocational life, and in the periods of the exercise of his vocation, denies himself every manner of being "cointerested" in the interests of the persons who make up his subject matter. If he repudiated this precept, he would immediately depart from his subject. Immediately, the intentionalities through which persons (purely psychically) are what they are in themselves and for themselves, their own immanent "relating of themselves" and being related, would become real relations between these persons and some objects in the world which are external to them and in whose real relations they are involved.

But the specific subject matter of descriptive psychology is what is purely, essentially proper to persons as such, as subjects of a life which is in itself exclusively intentional and which, in particular, as individual soul, is to be regarded as a purely intentional nexus of its own. But each soul also stands in community with others which are intentionally interrelated, that is, in a purely intentional, internally and essentially closed nexus, that of intersubjectivity. This will concern us later. But what confronts us here as extremely remarkable is this twofold manner in which subjects can become thematic, in which they can, through two different attitudes toward them, display [sets of] properties which, though they are very different, yet essentially correspond to each other: on the one hand, a purely internal relating of the persons to things of which they are conscious, which are intentionally valid for them within the world which is intentionally valid for them; and, on the other hand, persons' real being-in-relation, as realities in the real world, to the things of this world. Purely descriptive psychology thematizes persons in the pure internal attitude of the epochē, and this gives it its subject matter, the soul.

Here we construe the concept of a descriptive psychology just as broadly as that of the other descriptive sciences, which after all are not bound to the mere data of direct intuition but make their inferences to those things which cannot be made present as actually existing through any actually experiencing intuition but which must be representable through analogous variations of intuition. Thus geology and paleontology are "descriptive sciences" even though they reach into climatic periods of the earth in which the analogous intuitions of inductively inferred living beings cannot in principle represent possible experience. Something similar is naturally true of a descriptive psychology. It too has its realm of manifold psychic phenomena which can be disclosed only in a very mediate way. What is immediately experienceable, however, takes precedence. But psychology attains its subject matter in general, as we said, only thanks to a universal epochē of validity. Its first points of attack are probably those real intentionalities which are distinguishable within the natural attitude, i.e., human beings' ways of behaving in what they do and refrain from doing. In these first of all, then, it grasps something "internal" by declining to take part in their validity. But this does not yet make it a truly descriptive psychology; it has not yet arrived at its pure and self-enclosed field of work, has not yet arrived at a "pure soul" or the self-enclosed universe of pure souls in its own essential and thoroughly intentional exclusiveness. For this a psychologist's universal epochē is required, and that in advance. "With one blow" he must put out of effect the totality of his participation in the validities explicitly or implicitly effected by the persons who are his subjects; and this means all persons. For psychology is, after all, supposed to be the universal science of souls, the parallel to the universal science of bodies; and just as the latter is from the start a science through a universal "epochē," through a habitual vocational attitude established in advance in order to investigate abstractively only the corporeal in its own essential interrelations, so also for psychology. Accordingly, it, too, requires its habitual "abstractive" attitude. Its epochē applies to all souls and thus also to the psychologist's own: this involves refraining— *qua* psychologist—from the concurrent performance of his own validities as exercised in the manner of natural everyday life in relation to real things in the objective world. The psychologist establishes in himself the "disinterested spectator" and investigator of himself as well as of all others, and that once and for all, i.e., for all "vocational periods" of his psychological work. But the epochē must be actually universally carried out, and in a radical way. It must not be meant, for example, as a critical epochē, serving the purposes of self-criticism or criticism of others, of a theoretical or a practical criticism. Also, it must not be meant, in the sense of a generally philosophical undertaking, as a universal critique of experience, of the possibility of knowledge of truths-in-themselves for an objectively existing world; and naturally it must also not be meant as a skeptical, agnostic epochē. All these involve the taking-up of positions. But the psychologist as such in his inquiry must, we repeat, take and have no position: he must neither concur nor refuse, nor remain in problematic suspense, as if he had some say in the validities of the persons who are his subjects. So long as he has not acquired this posture as a serious and consciously established one, he has not arrived at his true subject matter; and as soon as he violates it, he has lost his subject matter. Only through this posture does he have the essentially unitary, absolutely self-enclosed "internal" world of the [conscious] subjects; only in this way does he have the universal, total unity of the intentional life as his horizon of work: his own life, in primal originality, but also, proceeding from his own life, those others who also live, and their life, whereby each life with its own intentionality reaches intentionally into the life of every other, and all are interwoven in different, closer, or more distant ways in an association of life. To the psychologist, in the midst of this, but with his attitude of "disinterested observer," every intentional life as it is lived by each subject and each particular community of subjects, the performance of acts, the perceptual and other sorts of experiencing activity, the changing acts of meaning in respect to being, will, etc.—to the psychologist, all this is accessible thematically. Thus in general, as his first and most fundamental subject matter, he has the pure act-life of the persons, i.e., primarily the conscious life in the narrower sense. This is, so to speak, the outer surface of the spiritual world, which first becomes visible to him, and only gradually do the intentional depths open themselves up; also, only through groping experiential work do the method and the systematic interconnection of things reveal themselves. To be sure, the whole long history of philosophy and its sciences was needed before the consciousness of the necessity for this radical reorientation, and the resolve to observe it with conscious consistency, could be motivated, together with the insight that only through such a descriptive psychology could a psychology in general fulfill its peculiar sense as a science and do justice to the legitimate sense of psychophysical thematics through an appropriate limitation of its own [i.e. psychology's] legitimate sense.

§ 70. *The difficulties of psychological "abstraction." (The paradox of the "intentional object"; the intentional primal phenomenon of "sense.")*

IT IS NOT SO SIMPLE for psychology, as it is for natural science through its straightforwardly performed universal abstraction of everything mental, to arrive at *its* subject matter through a straightforwardly performed complementary abstraction of everything that is merely bodily. Even after the phenomenological epochē is recognized as necessary, the pathway to psychology's self-understanding is obstructed by extraordinary difficulties, indeed by puzzling paradoxes, which must be clarified and overcome in their proper order. This will concern us now. In first place stands the paradoxical difficulty of the *intentional objects as such.* Let us take up the question: What has become of all those objects which, in the "consciousness" of the subjects, were objects of consciousness in various modes of validity, objects which, prior to the epochē, were posited as really existing (or possibly existing, or even as not existing) objects? What has become of them if now, in the psychologist's epochē, the taking of a position on any such positing is to be excluded? We answer: The very epochē itself frees our gaze not only for the intentions running their course within the purely intentional life (i.e., the "intentional experiences" [*Erlebnisse*]) but also for that which these intentions in themselves, with their own "what"-content, posit as valid in each case as their object; and it also frees our gaze for the way in which they do this, i.e., in what modalities of validity or of being, in what subjective modalities of time, such as perceptually present, past in memory (i.e., having been present, etc.), with what meaning-content, or as what type of object, etc. The intention and the intentional object [*Gegenständlichkeit*] as such, and then the latter in the "how of its manners of givenness," provide at first an overabundant theme in the sphere of acts. Soon enough, one is driven to a careful broadening of the concepts and problems of correlation.

Thus the sentence in my *Ideas toward a Pure Phenomenology and Phenomenological Philosophy* [§ 89], which was able to give rise to objections when it was torn from the context of the presentation there of the phenomenological epochē, was completely correct: one can say of a simple tree that it burns up, but a perceived tree "as such" cannot burn up; that is, it is absurd to say this of it, for one is expecting a component of a pure perception, thinkable only as a moment belonging to an ego-subject's own essence, to do something which can have meaning only for a wooden body: to burn up. For the psychologist, as long as he limits himself to pure description, the only simple objects are ego-subjects and what can be experienced "in" these ego-subjects themselves (and then only through the epochē) as what is immanently their own, in order to make this the subject matter of further scientific work. But everywhere he finds not only intentions but also, contained in them as correlates, the "intentional objects"—in an essential and completely peculiar way of "being contained." They are not integral [*reelle*] parts of the intention but are something meant in it, its particular meaning, and this in modalities which only have meaning precisely for something like "meaning." One must not merely talk about acts of meaning and what is meant, about conscious experiences and what they are conscious of, about intentions and what is intended—words which, in a phenomenological psychology, must unavoidably be used with an extremely broadened signification; rather, all this must methodically become a subject for psychological work. The other [i.e., merely talking about it] is the manner of data-psychology. Even Hume says (and how could he avoid it?): impressions *of*, perceptions *of*, trees, stones, etc.; and so does psychology to the present day. But precisely through its blindness for intentional being-in [*Darinnensein*] or "having something in mind" [*etwas-im-Sinne-haben*], as it is called, in language, by contrast, psychology denied itself the possibility of truly intentional analysis and, in the other direction, of the thematics of intentional synthesis—and that means nothing less than the whole subject matter of research which has to do with the psychic in its own essence, that is, descriptive-psychological research. In extrapsychological life it is not unusual to pay attention sometimes to personal deeds and sufferings, sometimes to their "sense" (to what one "has in mind"); and even in the sphere of the sciences we sometimes have, within certain limitations of interest, the thematics of explicating sense, as, for example, in philology, with its constant reflection and inquiry back into what the person who used the words had in view in his speech, what his experiential, conceptual, practical meaning was, what he had in mind. But only when one with universal consistency wants to see nothing else, wants to pursue nothing other [than this meaning] in all its subjective modes and in the universal concreteness of the meaning-bestowing and meaning-having life and its all-encompassing synthesis of all meaning-bestowals and meanings— only then does one have purely psychological problems; one never has them in isolation. In other words, only he who lives within the universal epochē and through it has before him the universal horizon of the pure "internal life," the intentional life as accomplishing meaning and validity, only he has also before him the actual, genuine, and—I emphasize once again—absolutely self-enclosed problematics of intentionality, i.e., the problematics of pure psychology, which belong, then, to all sciences dealing with the psychic (the psychophysical, the biological sciences).

The psychologist has the problematics of intentionality through his own original sphere,[1] but this is never isolable for him. Through the empathy of his original sphere of consciousness, through what arises out of it, as a component which is never lacking, he also already has a universal intersubjective horizon, even though he may not notice it at first.

Of course, the epochē, as an explicit methodical basic requirement, could be a matter of the subsequent reflection only of one who, with a certain naïveté and through a historical situation, was already pulled into the epochē, so to speak, who had already taken possession of a piece of this new "internal world," in a certain sense a proximal field within it, with an obscurely prefigured distant horizon. Thus it was not until four years after concluding the *Logical Investigations* that he arrived at an explicit but even then imperfect self-consciousness of its method. But along with this also arose the extraordinarily difficult problems connected with the method itself, with the epochē and the reduction and their own phenomenological understanding and their extraordinary philosophical significance.

Before proceeding to the treatment of these difficulties and thus to the full unfolding of the sense of the psychological epochē and reduction, let us deal explicitly with the differentiation in the use of these two words which is obvious according to the whole presentation up to this point. In pure psychology, that

1. *Originalsphäre,* i.e., the sphere of his own subjective life.

is, in the true sense, descriptive psychology, the epochē is the means for making experienceable and thematizable, in their own essential purity, the [conscious] subjects which in natural world-life are experienced and experience themselves as standing in intentional-real relations to objects that are [also] real in the mundane sense. Thus, for the absolutely disinterested psychological observer, the subjects become "phenomena" in a peculiarly new sense—and this reorientation is called, here, the phenomenological-psychological reduction.

§ 71. *The danger of misunderstanding the "universality" of the phenomenological-psychological epochē. The decisive signifiance of the correct understanding.*

WE SHALL NOW UNDERTAKE to discuss several fundamentally essential points in order to bring to light from different sides the deeper sense of the epochē and reduction, and then of psychology itself. And indeed it does have depths, and it does force paradoxes upon us, which a psychologist who has no other interest than an objective science of souls could not anticipate. But our presentation will perhaps cause him to put the naturalistic sensationalism of his psychology of consciousness to the test and to recognize that a true psychology requires a universal epochē. At first he will probably think that without proclaiming it expressly as a method he has already been quietly practicing the epochē and, focusing upon what is immanent and proper to persons, has excluded realities external to these persons in respect to their true being or nonbeing, under the rubric of descriptions through inner perception, inner experience, or else through empathy. But he will perhaps admit that this natural and naïve manner of being directed toward the "inwardness" of men, which is by no means unknown even to prescientific life, does not suffice and that the pure being-in-himself and for-himself of a subject in his full concreteness can become a thematic field only through the conscious method of the universal epochē. He must see, and say to himself: Only after I have excluded everything that is extrapsychic, the world which is valid in psychic life, so that the purely psychic universe has become a closed world for me—only then does it become self-evident to me, or only then docs the self-evidence become compelling, that the proper essence of the psychic itself includes the fact that it has the character of meaning objects, etc.

Universally, then, I have before me a flowing manifold intentionality and within it a flowingly valid world as such, but not in such a way that thereby something nonpsychic is actually posited as world. Perhaps the psychologist will also be in agreement when we add, here, that it is the psychophysiological attitude, the prevalent orientation toward discoveries of psychophysical causations or conditionings, which for so long has caused the psychologist to give privileged status to sense-data and has kept him from inquiring into the descriptive place of those data in the intentional framework, and into their meaning, which can only be determined in this context. This, he may finally admit, is indeed something of importance: the thematics of intentionality, understood as a title for correlations [*als ein korrelativer Titel*]. And indeed this is, in accord with our whole presentation, the main point, about which one must be perfectly certain before one can even begin. It is only through the universal epochē that one sees, as a thematic field of its own, what pure ego-life actually is: as an intentional life, as being affected in this intentionality by intentional objects which are valid as appearing in this intentional life, as being directed toward them in many different ways, as dealing with them. Everything "with which" one deals in this way itself belongs to pure immanence and must be descriptively grasped in its purely subjective modes, in its implications, together with all the intentional mediations contained in these implications.

But the habits of thought of a centuries-old tradition are not so easy to overcome, and they make themselves felt even when one expressly renounces them. Inwardly, the psychologist will persist in regarding this whole descriptive psychology as a discipline which is not self-sufficient, which presupposes natural science as the science of bodies, and which is at the same time a preliminary step toward a psychophysiologically or possibly psychophysically explanatory natural science. And even if it were accorded an autonomous existence as a purely descriptive psychology, it would still require an "explanatory" psychology alongside it (this was still the standpoint of Brentano and Dilthey at the end of the past century). The beginner (and every institute-psychologist is, in terms of his education, a beginner here) will think at first that [what we have described as] pure psychology is simply a matter of a limited set of tasks, a useful but secondary, auxiliary discipline. This opinion is based in part on the necessity of beginning with the ways in which human beings behave and on the consideration that these ways of behaving, as real relations, are in need of the reduction to what in them is internal to the soul. Thus it appears obvious that a necessary universal reduction has in advance the significance of a resolve henceforth to reduce all of men's ways of behaving, one by one, so as to describe scientifically, perhaps with the help of experimentation, the psychic as it already finds its expression in common language, i.e., human activity and suffering or, to put it crudely, the psychic sphere of acts according to its empirical types—and these always involve, in their meaning, psychophysical causality. But all this is done for the purpose of enabling oneself subsequently, quite in the manner of natural science, to draw inductive conclusions and thus to penetrate into the obscure realm of the unconscious, forging new concepts which are expressions for analogues and modifications of actually experienceable acts. This on the psychic side. With respect to the complementary side, that of the *physis,* the psychophysical problems arise, interwoven with the purely psychological. Is there anything to object to in this? Will anyone become somehow dubious if we remark, here, that the notion of "ways of behavior" must finally include not only all representations, perceptions, memories, expectations, but also all acts of empathy and, further, all associations and also the variations of acts, which can indeed be followed descriptively in their obscured forms, sedimentations—and also all instincts and drives, not to mention the "horizons"?

In any case, universal reduction, in spite of the resolve to carry out immanent description, will be understood [in the above view] as universality of individual reduction.[1] And here something else very important must be noted. The path of the psychologist goes from external observation to internal observation, that is, from the mutual externality of men and animals to the consideration of their inner being and life.[2] The first thing one must do, then—precisely in order to give to psychological universality a sense parallel to the natural-scientific world-universality —is to conceive of performing the universal reduction in such a

1. That is (as Husserl's marginal note here indicates), reduction applied "to each [individual] act—and then to each [other] person and to each of his acts."
2. Husserl's marginal note on the first three sentences of this paragraph: "everything unclear."

way that it is exercised individually upon all individual subjects accessible through experience and induction and in each case, then, in regard to individual experiences. How could it be possible otherwise? Human beings are external to one another, they are separated realities, and so their psychic interiors are also separated. Internal psychology can thus be only individual psychology of individual souls, and everything else is a matter for psychophysical research; the same thing is true for the animal kingdom and finally for the whole series of organic beings, if there are grounds for saying that every organic being has its psychic side. All this appears to be perfectly obvious. Thus one will take it in part as a gross exaggeration, in part as an absurdity, if I say in advance that the properly understood epochē, with its properly understood universality, totally changes all the notions that one could ever have of the task of psychology, and it reveals everything that was just put forward as obvious to be a naïveté which necessarily and forever becomes impossible as soon as the epochē and the reduction are actually, and in their full sense, understood and carried out.

Phenomenological psychology reveals itself, in accord with its sense, in various steps, because the phenomenological reduction itself—and this is part of its essence—could reveal its sense, its inner, necessary requirements, and its scope only in steps. Each step required new reflections, new considerations, which in turn were possible only through the self-understanding and the practiced accomplishment of the other steps. Or, as I also used to put it: In order to attain its total horizon, the phenomenological reduction would require a "phenomenology of the phenomenological reduction." [3] But even at the first step, where one focuses upon individual subjects and must leave the accomplishment of psychophysical or biological science an open question, one must still painstakingly extract for oneself the meaning of these subjects; one does not obtain this meaning simply by carrying out the behavioristic [4] reductions with which one necessarily began.*

* Naturally I am ignoring here the exaggerations of the behaviorists, who operate only with the external side of modes of behavior, as if behavior would not then lose its sense, i.e., the sense given to it by empathy, the understanding of the "expression."

3. Cf. p. 188, above.

4. The term "behavioristic" (*behavioristisch*) is crossed out in the MS but is not replaced by anything. Husserl seems to refer to reducing concrete persons to their "ways of behaving" in the *psychic*

With this first reduction, one has not yet arrived at what is essentially proper to the soul. Thus one can say: the genuine phenomenological-psychological epochē is an attitude which is completely strange and artificial not only to the whole of natural life but also to the psychologist of the past. Hence, in regard to what is essentially proper to the ego-subjects, in regard to their psychic aspect in general, the experiential field which is necessary for scientific description, as well as the familiar set of types that can arise only out of repetition, was lacking. "Inner perception" in the sense of genuine psychology, and psychological experience in general, understood as the experience of souls according to their own pure being, is so far from being an immediate and everyday affair, something gained through a simple "epochē" at the very beginnings, that it was not possible at all prior to the introduction of the peculiar method of the phenomenological epochē. Accordingly, anyone taking the phenomenological attitude first had to learn to see, gain practice, and then in practice acquire at first a rough and shaky, then a more and more precise, conception of what is essentially proper to himself and others. In this way, a true infinity of descriptive phenomena gradually becomes visible, and does so with the strongest and most unconditioned of all self-evidence, the self-evidence of this sole genuine "inner experience."

To be sure, this looks like a bad exaggeration, but only to the beginner who is bound to the tradition, who, starting with the experiences of the external attitude (the natural, anthropological subject-object attitude, the psychomundane attitude), at first thinks that this is a matter of an obvious, simple "purification" of oneself from one's load of realistic [realen] presuppositions, whereas the psychic experiential content is essentially already known and even expressible in ordinary language. But this is a fundamental error. If this were correct, one would need only to explicate analytically the experiential concept, derived from common experience, of man as a thinking, feeling, acting subject, a subject experiencing pleasure and pain and the like; but that is only the outside, so to speak, the surface of the psychic, that part of it which has objectified itself in the external world. It is similar to the case of the child, who certainly has experiences of things but has no idea yet of inner structures, which are still quite lacking in his apperceptions of things. Likewise, for the

sense (cf. above, p. 246), then distinguishes this in the footnote from "behaviorism," which he thinks is quite different. This consideration probably led him to strike out "behavioristic" as a misleading term.

psychologist who has not learned, in the phenomenological sense which makes the true epochē possible, to understand the superficial as such and to inquire into its immense depth-dimensions, all the genuinely psychological apperceptions are lacking and thus also all possibilities of asking genuinely psychological questions, i.e., working questions, which must already have a prefigured horizon of meaning.

Thus the alleged "purification" or, as it is often called, "clarification of psychological concepts," makes the psychic accessible for the first time, brings its own being and everything "involved" in it into view for the first time, *only* if one penetrates from the externalized intentionalities into the internal ones which constitute the others intentionally. Only in this way does one come to understand what psychological analysis actually means, and conversely what psychological synthesis actually means, and to understand the gulf of meaning which separates these from what one was able to understand by analysis and synthesis through the sciences of the external attitude.

The first epochē is, to be sure, the necessary beginning for a purely psychic experience. But now it is necessary to spend some time surveying and penetrating the purely psychic and seizing upon its own essence with stubborn consistency. If empiricism had done more honor to its name by being thus [tied to pure experience] [5] it could never have missed the phenomenological reduction, its descriptions would never have led it to data and complexes of data, and the spiritual world, in its own specificity and infinite totality, would not have remained closed. Is it not paradoxical that no traditional psychology up to the present day has been able to give even a true exposition of perception, or even of the special type, the perception of bodies, or of memory, of expectation, of "empathy," or of any other manner of presentification; or an intentional, essential description of judgment, or of any other class-type of acts, or an intentional clarification of the syntheses of agreement and discrepancy (in their different modalizations)? Is it not paradoxical that no one had any idea of the diverse and difficult working problems contained under each of these headings? One did not have the experiential field, had not carved out the special psychological sphere of facts, the field of the descriptions to be accomplished; one was not at all situated within actually psychological experience, which offers the

5. Biemel's interpolation. There is simply a blank space in the MS.

psychic, first of all as unanalyzed, and predelineates in an indistinct way, through the inner and outer experiential horizons of the psychic, what is to be exhibited intentionally. What good, then, was the demand for a descriptive psychology, made so frequently and so emphatically, as long as one had not recognized the necessity of the universal epochē and reduction, through which alone one first becomes capable of arriving at substrates of descriptions and intentional analyses and thus at a field of work? I cannot do otherwise than deny that hitherto existing psychology has actually set foot on the soil of a genuine psychology. Only when such a psychology exists will it be possible to make use, according to their actual psychological content, of the doubtless very valuable facts [collected by] psychophysics and the psychology which relies on it; only then will one be able to be clear on what, on both sides [i.e., the psychic and the physiological sides] the related terms are which are involved in the empirical regularities.

So great is the power of prejudices that, although for decades now the transcendental epochē and reduction have been presented in various stages of their development, nothing more has been achieved than sense-distorting applications of the first results of the genuine intentional description to the old psychology. Our subsequent considerations will show how seriously this remark about the sense-distorting character of such applications must be taken. These considerations, arising as they do out of the most mature self-reflection, will make possible—or so I hope —a correspondingly deeper transparency and clarity. In addition, the difficulty will be cleared away which attaches to a *discours de la méthode* such as the one sketched out here, namely, that the concrete investigations which are behind it, carried out for decades, cannot concurrently serve as supports, especially since even the published writings can have their proper effect only through an actual and of course always very difficult understanding of the reduction. It will become clear very soon in the sequel why this is stated here, even though the reduction in those writings is introduced as a transcendental philosophical reduction.

Our next task, one which is very pressing for the clarification of the genuine sense of the epochē, is to make evident the fact that what was taken for granted in the first interpretation of the universality in which the epochē must be accomplished was in fact a self-misunderstanding. It is basically wrong, in taking one's point of departure from men's ways of behaving toward the real surrounding world and from the reduction of them one by one to the psychic, to think that universal reduction consists in the attitude of universally purifying reductively all occurring individual intentionalities and then dealing with these individuals. To be sure, reflecting upon myself in my self-consciousness, I find myself to be living in the world in such a way that I am affected by and deal with individual things; and so the reduction continually yields individual representations, individual feelings, individual acts. But I must not overlook, as does the psychology of "data on a tablet of consciousness," that this "tablet" has consciousness of itself as a tablet, is in the world, and has consciousness of the world: I am continually conscious of individual things in the world, as things that interest me, move me, disturb me, etc., but in doing this I always have consciousness of the world itself, as that in which I myself am, although it is not there as is a thing, does not affect me as things do, is not, in a sense similar to things, an object of my dealings. If I were not conscious of the world as world, without its being capable of becoming objective in the manner of an [individual] object, how could I survey the world reflectively and put knowledge of the world into play, thus lifting myself above the simple, straightforwardly directed life that always has to do with things? How is it that I, or all of us, constantly have world-consciousness? Each thing that we experience, that we have to do with in any way whatever—and this includes ourselves when we reflect upon ourselves—gives itself, whether we notice it or not, *as* a thing in the world, as a thing in the given field of perception, the latter being merely a perceptual sector of the world. We can take notice of this and inquire into this constant world-horizon; indeed we do this continually.

The psychological reduction thus has to reduce at once the consciousness of the individual thing and also its world-horizon; thus all reduction is world-universal.[6]

This is an a priori for psychology: It is unthinkable that a psychologist, in inquiring into psychological matters, should not have his world-consciousness or should not be dealing in a wakeful manner with objects which necessarily bear their world-horizon with them or that, in representing others, he could represent

6. *Welt-universal:* i.e., it takes in not only the totality ("universe") of consciousness but also the totality of the world.

them in any other way than as being like himself—as men with world-consciousness, which is at the same time self-consciousness: consciousness of oneself as being in the world.

This, then, and perhaps much more of a similar nature, belongs to the beginning, to the first establishment, of a psychology; [7] and it would be just as absurd to overlook it as if the physicist, in beginning a theory of bodies, were to overlook the fact that extension belongs to the essence of a body. To be sure, what went off smoothly in the founding of a method in physics—taking note of the a priori structures, letting oneself be guided by them, even making them into a methodical fundament as a scientific system of norms in its own right, as mathematics —all this involved extraordinary and strange difficulties in the development of psychology, in spite of all the apparent analogies with physics. What is relatively easy in the method of physics, i.e., carrying out the universal abstraction of nature and mathematically mastering nature through idealization, for the most profound reasons entangles us here, where the complementary abstraction is supposed to be undertaken, where world- and self-consciousness are to become a universal subject matter, in difficult preliminary reflections on method. [8]

Psychology, the universal science of pure souls in general— therein consists its abstraction—requires the epochē, and it must in advance reduce the world-consciousness of all souls, each in its particularity, in its particular contents and modalities. To this belongs the self-apperception of each one, together with the sense of the validities, the habitualities, the interests, the ways of thinking that each attributes to himself, the particular experiences, judgments that he performs, etc., each in the manner in which he appears to himself, is meant [by himself], but at the same time is meant as being in the world; [all this] [9] is to be reduced.

But we must not omit the question: How, more precisely, does each [subject] have world-consciousness while he has self-

7. Marginal note: "This concerns the life-world! That must be said!" Other notes express considerable dissatisfaction with the paragraphs leading up to this point, perhaps because they repeat much of the discussion of the life-world in Part IIIA (as one note explicitly points out) but do not show the connection.

8. Marginal note on the last sentence: "The life-world typology is a priori. But it does not thereby have to be formulated or to guide [the scientist] in a formulated way."

9. Biemel's interpolation.

apperception [of himself] as this human being? Here we soon see, as another a priori, that self-consciousness and consciousness of others are inseparable; it is unthinkable, and not merely [contrary to] fact,[10] that I be man in a world without being *a* man. There need be no one in my perceptual field, but fellow men are necessary as actual, as known, and as an open horizon of those I might possibly meet. Factually I am within an interhuman present and within an open horizon of mankind; I know myself to be factually within a generative framework, in the unitary flow of a historical development in which this present is mankind's present and the world of which it is conscious is a historical present with a historical past and a historical future. Of course I am free here to transform fictively [the factual details];[11] but this form of generativity and historicity is unbreakable, as is the form, belonging to me as an individual ego, of my original perceptual present as a present with a remembered past and an expectable future. To be sure, it is a large and open question as to how far this a priori reaches in terms of content and how it is to be formulated in rigorous and stable laws, so to speak as an ontology of world- and self-consciousness; but in any case it is a question which concerns the sense of the universal epochē and applies to what can be attained within it as the reduced phenomenon of internal psychology, i.e., what one is to have in view from the start as the subject matter of psychology. But we must be more precise here. The psychologist will naturally have to carry out the epochē and reduction from his own vantage point and first of all upon himself; he must begin with his original self-experience and his own original world-consciousness, i.e., the self-apperception of himself as the man to whom he accords whatever he does accord—being this good man or this sinner, along with everything else he supposedly is; when the psychologist becomes a disinterested observer of himself, all this loses all its cofunctioning validity, whereas such validity itself, together with the act of according validity and that which has validity as such, becomes a phenomenon, in such a way that nothing at all can be lost. But he has original consciousness of all this, consciousness which, as reduced, is

10. Literally: "it is unthinkable, and not just a mere fact."
11. Here it is necessary to differ with Biemel, who interpolates "Weltbewusstsein." His version is: "Of course I am free to transform [world-consciousness] fictively." But world-consciousness, as the general structure or form of experience, is precisely what *cannot* be transformed.

primary; and it includes his world-consciousness in its flowing particularity and its historicity, with everything that he attributes to the world by way of spatiotemporality and content through his acts of meaning. Through the reduction, this world —and he has no other one which is valid for him (another one would have no meaning at all for him)—becomes a mere phenomenon for him.

But he has to have performed the epoché in his experience of others as he has in his self-experience, and this must apply in advance to every possible experience of others; all human beings become pure souls, ego-subjects of self- and world-apperceptions, which can become thematic purely in respect to the correlation between according validity and that-which-has-validity. But now let us consider the fact that everyone, in his commerce with others within his world-consciousness, at the same time has consciousness of others in the form of particular others; that in an amazing fashion his intentionality reaches into that of the other and vice versa; that thereby one's own and others' ontic validities combine in modes of agreement and discrepancy; and that always and necessarily, through reciprocal correction, agreeing consciousness of the same common world with the same things finally achieves validity [12]—the same things that are viewed in one way by one and another way by the other. The world-consciousness of any individual is always in advance— and indeed in the mode of ontic certainty—the consciousness of one and the same world for all, all those who are known and not known, all subjects that could ever possibly be met, who all, in advance, must themselves be subjects in the world. I from my vantage point and every other from his vantage point has his oriented world, a world which presupposes others who from their respective vantage points have others, who in turn have others; and thus these others are presupposed, through mediations of the intentional complex, as subjects for a common world-apperception, while each individual has his own world-apperception in his self-apperception. And [all] this is a process of unceasingly flowing change, which is also always a process of reciprocal correction. In other words, each of us has his life-world, meant as the world for all. Each has it with the sense of a polar unity of subjectively, relatively meant worlds which, in the course of

12. *zur Geltung kommt*, here used in a strange sense, since in Husserl's usual terminology it is the *world*, not consciousness, that "achieves validity."

correction, are transformed into mere appearances of *the* world, the life-world for all, the intentional unity which always persists, which in turn is itself a universe of particulars, of things. This is the world; another world would have no meaning at all for us. And in the epochē it becomes a phenomenon. What remains, now, is not a multiplicity of separated souls, each reduced to its pure interiority, but rather: just as there is a sole universal nature as a self-enclosed framework of unity, so there is a sole psychic framework, a total framework of all souls, which are united not externally but internally, namely, through the intentional interpenetration [*Ineinander*] which is the communalization of their lives. Each soul, reduced to its pure interiority, has its being-for-itself and its being-in-itself, has its life which is originally its own. And yet it belongs to each soul that it have its particular world-consciousness in a way which is originally its own, namely, through the fact that it has empathy experiences, experiencing consciousness of others as [also] having a world, the same world, that is, each apperceiving it in his own apperceptions.

Just as every ego-subject has an original perceptual field within a horizon that can be opened up through free activity, which leads to ever new perceptual fields, repeatedly preindicated through a combination of the determinate and the indeterminate: so every ego-subject has his horizon of empathy, that of his cosubjects, which can be opened up through direct and indirect commerce with the chain of others, who are all others for one another, for whom there can be still others, etc. But this means that each has an oriented world in such a way that he has a nucleus of relatively original data; and this is the nucleus of a horizon, "horizon" being here a title for a complicated intentionality which, in spite of its indeterminacy, is covalid and anticipated. But this means at the same time that within the vitally flowing intentionality in which the life of an ego-subject consists, every other ego is already intentionally implied in advance by way of empathy and the empathy-horizon. Within the universal epochē which actually understands itself, it becomes evident that there is no separation of mutual externality at all for souls in their own essential nature. What is a mutual externality for the natural-mundane attitude of world-life prior to the epochē, because of the localization of souls in living bodies, is transformed in the epochē into a pure, intentional, mutual internality. With this the world—the straightforwardly existing world and, within it, existing nature—is transformed into the all-communal phenomenon "world," "world for all actual and possible subjects," none of whom can escape the intentional implication according to which he belongs in advance within the horizon of every other subject.

Thus we see with surprise, I think, that in the pure development of the idea of a descriptive psychology, which seeks to bring to expression what is essentially proper to souls, there necessarily occurs a transformation of the phenomenological-psychological epochē and reduction into the *transcendental;* and we see that we have done and could do nothing else here but repeat in basic outlines the considerations that we had to carry out earlier in quite another interest, i.e., in the interest not of a psychology as a positive science but of a universal and then transcendental philosophy.

But with this there also returns the necessity of thinking through to the end this correction of that first and most obvious [i.e., psychological] type of epochē and reduction. Striving for objective scientific discipline in psychology as elsewhere, we consider human beings just as we do other things in the world; for psychology, too, objectivity signifies the exclusion of everything that is merely subjective and thus also ourselves as the functioning subjectivity in whose function the ontic meaning "world" arises. As a psychologist I put up with the fact that even in such considerations, directed at the intentional construction of the world, I have others through the experiential mode of empathy as existing actualities with whom I know myself to be merely in community. But when I practice the reducing epochē on myself and *my* world-consciousness, the other human beings, like the world itself, fall before the epochē; that is, they are merely intentional phenomena for me. Thus the radical and perfect reduction leads to the *absolutely single ego* of the pure psychologist, who thus at first absolutely isolates himself and as such no longer has validity for himself as a human being or as really existing in the world but is instead the pure subject of his intentionality, which through the radical reduction is universal and pure, with all its intentional implications. This is the apodictic ego, existing apodictically in its intentionalities, which are apodictically contained within itself and can be opened up. And if the coexistence of other subjects, but as implied other egos, and thus the primal division between "I" and "other," can be established [as being] in these intentionalities—and essentially so—then one of the main tasks of pure intentional psychology is to make understandable, by way of the progressive reduction of world-validity, the subjective and pure function through which the world as the "world for us all" is a world for all from my—the ego's—vantage point, with whatever particular content it may have. The empty generality of the epoché does not of itself clarify anything; it is only the gate of entry through which one must pass in order to be able to discover the new world of pure subjectivity. The actual discovery is a matter of concrete, extremely subtle and differentiated work.

One main result must still be emphasized with a remark. Our considerations show that the epoché would be mistaken, not only [if conceived] as an individual reduction within the individual soul, but also [if conceived] as [such] an individual reduction proceeding from soul to soul.[13] All souls make up a single unity of intentionality with the reciprocal implication of the life-fluxes of the individual subjects, a unity that can be unfolded systematically through phenomenology; what is a mutual externality from the point of view of naïve positivity or objectivity is, when seen from the inside, an intentional mutual internality.

§ 72. *The relation of transcendental psychology to transcendental phenomenology as the proper access to pure self-knowledge. Definitive removal of the objectivistic ideal from the science of the soul.*

THE SURPRISING RESULT of our investigation can also, it seems, be expressed as follows: a pure psychology as positive science, a psychology which would investigate universally the human beings living in the world as real facts in the world, similarly to other positive sciences (both sciences of nature and humanistic disciplines), does not exist. There is only a transcendental psychology, which is identical with transcendental philosophy. We must now consider in what sense this needs to be corrected. It would naturally be wrong to say that there can be no psychology as a science on the ground of the pregiven world,

13. This sentence as it stands in the text, involving two corrections by Fink, is counter to Husserl's meaning. The problem is solved by removing the second *nicht*.

i.e., a science dealing straightforwardly with human beings (and also animals) in the world. It is certain that no psychology in this sense is possible without an inquiry into what is purely essentially proper to psychic being; and it is equally certain that the latter is not something to be had gratis, so to speak, as something one need only look at, something that is already there but simply unnoticed. Everything that is "there" in this way belongs to the world as what is apperceived by him who sees it in this way [1] and falls along with everything else within the domain of what is to be reduced. But if the universal epochē, which encompasses all having-consciousness-of-the-world, is necessary, then the psychologist loses, during this epochē, the ground of the objective world. Thus pure psychology in itself is identical with transcendental philosophy as the science of transcendental subjectivity. This is unassailable. But now let us remember what we learned before about the phenomenological reduction as a reorientation of the natural mundane attitude. We can return from the reorientation into the natural attitude; as we said in advance, psychology, like every other science and every life-vocation, has its vocational times and the epochē belonging to these vocational times. During the time in which I am a transcendental or pure phenomenologist, I am exclusively within transcendental self-consciousness, and I am my own subject matter exclusively as transcendental ego in terms of everything intentionally implied therein. Here there is no objectivity as such at all; here there are objectivity, things, world, and world-science (including, then, all positive sciences and philosophies), only as my—the transcendental ego's—phenomena. All the ontic validities that I may perform and wish to perform as a transcendental investigator are related to myself; but this also includes the actual and possible "empathies," perceptions of others, that appear among my original intentions. Through the reduction [others] [2] are transformed from human beings existing for me into alter egos existing for me, having the ontic meaning of *implicata* of my original intentional life. And the reverse also holds: I, with my whole original life, am implied in them; and they are all likewise implied in one another. What I say here scientifically, I say about myself and to myself; but at the same time, paradoxically, I say it to all the others as being transcendentally implied in me and in one another.

1. Reading *als dessen, der es* for *als dem, der es.*
2. Biemel's interpolation.

Pure psychology simply knows nothing other than the subjective; to admit into it something objective as existing is already to abandon pure psychology. Infinite psychological inquiry, as transcendentally pure inquiry, applies to this intentional mutual internality of subjects and their transcendental life and is necessarily carried out in the form of being oriented around me. But this is done in such a way that, in egological self-reflection, I delimit my original sphere (the sphere of "primordiality") and reveal within its network intentional syntheses and implications in their strata of intentional modification; withholding validity from all my empathies in a methodical way, through a sort of epochē within the epochē, and maintaining them only as my experiences [*Erlebnisse*], I attain the essential structures of an original life. If I accord validity to empathy (together with its intentional validity-correlates [revealed through my] "coperformance"),[3] these essential structures become those of any alter ego I can conceive of; and then there arise the problems of the universal community produced through empathy and of its essential particular forms, the very same forms that turn up in objectivized manner in the natural world-view, namely, as family, people, community of peoples, and then as essential structures of human historicity; here, however, in reduced form, they give rise to the essential structures of absolute historicity, namely, those of a transcendental community of subjects as one which, living in community through intentionality in these most general and also in particularized a priori forms, has in itself and continues ever to create the world as intentional validity-correlate, in ever new forms and strata of a cultural world. This, systematically developed through the most rigorous of all conceivable methods—that is, the method of transcendental subjectivity reflecting apodictically upon itself and apodictically explicating itself—is precisely transcendental philosophy; thus pure psychology is and can be nothing other than what was sought earlier from the philosophical point of view as absolutely grounded philosophy, which can fulfill itself only as phenomenological transcendental philosophy. But I as a pure psychologist or transcendental philosopher have not thereby ceased being a human being; no more has the actual being of the world and of all men and other beings in the world

3. I.e., I am aware, through empathy, not only of the acts of others, but also, by "coaccomplishing" these acts, of their correlates, valid objects.

changed in the least. And I have also not ceased having this particular worldly interest which bears the title: universal science of human beings in respect to their psychic being, both individual-psychic and social; I thus return to the natural attitude, changing my vocation: I take up my work as a psychologist on the ground of the world. It was precisely as a psychologist that I was compelled to decide upon developing a pure psychology. This is obviously similar, then, to the way in which the interest of the natural scientist demands the development of a pure mathematics and would have demanded it even if mathematics had not grown up earlier as the result of a theoretical interest of its own. In fact, for a genuine psychology, and for the exactness which belongs essentially to it, transcendental philosophy plays the role of the a priori science to which it must have recourse in all its actually psychological knowledge, the science whose a priori structural concepts it must utilize in its mundane inquiry. Of course, in this exhibition of the genuine parallel between psychology and natural science,[4] indeed between psychology and every other positive science, an enormous difference becomes evident. The psychologist, in search of the purely psychic, in the absolutely unavoidable necessity of placing out of action all real covalidities,[5] effects the epochē; then, carrying it out methodically, and again unavoidably, through difficult reflection, he frees himself from the naïveté which is unconsciously inherent in all world-life and all objective world-sciences. In the subscientific everydayness of natural life everyone believes that he has knowledge of himself and of human beings; he may be ever so humble in judging the perfection of this knowledge, certain that he often errs, but he knows that this knowledge can be improved; and everyone believes in a similar fashion that he has knowledge of the world, or at least of his proximate surroundings. Positive science says that this is naïve and that it, positive science, achieves true knowledge of the world through its scientific methods. The psychologist wants only the same thing that the other positive sciences want whose efforts have been successful; he is in search of nothing other than a method of positive scientific character for passing beyond everyday self-knowledge and knowledge of human beings. But

4. I.e., that each has a pure and an empirical part. Husserl often says that phenomenology stands in the same relation to psychology as mathematics to physics.

5. *reale Mitgeltungen*, i.e., the validity of anything real which would count outside his psychological interest.

in finding himself compelled to develop the method of phenomenological reduction, he makes the discovery that in fact no
one actually arrives in his [ordinary] self-knowledge at his true
and actual self, the being which is his own as ego-subject and as
the subject of all his world-knowledge and mundane accomplishments, that all this shows itself only through the reduction, and
that pure psychology is nothing other than the infinitely toilsome
way of genuine and pure self-knowledge; but the latter also
includes knowledge of human beings, as knowledge of their true
being and life as egos or as souls; and then [it includes also the
knowledge of] the true being of the world, which in principle no
positive science, no matter how successful, can ever attain.
What positive science calls knowledge of the world is knowledge
of the things of the world, their genera and species, their interconnections and separations, their changes and lack of change,
their laws of persistent being throughout the course of change,
their all-encompassing structure, forms, and the lawfulness of
these forms to which all being of things is bound. But all the
knowledge belonging to positive science, all its questions and
answers, all its hypotheses and confirmations, stand or move
upon the ground of the pregiven world; the world is the constant
presupposition; the question concerns only what the world is,
what is found to belong to it in the movement of induction from
the known into the unknown. The world is not a hypothesis in
that sole sense in which hypotheses have meaning for positive
science—for example, hypotheses about the structure of the
galaxies of the Milky Way; all hypotheses in the positive sphere
are hypotheses upon the ground of the "hypothesis" of the world,
and to seek a grounding for *this* "hypothesis" in the same sense,
in the positive scientific way, would be absurd. Indeed, it is only
from the vantage point of transcendental psychology or philosophy that we can see and understand what is lacking here by way
of a questioning of the "hypothesis" of the world, what it is and
what is required to put it in question. As the functioning subjects
in and through whose function the world *is* for us, we are all
completely extrathematic [in the natural attitude], forgotten, as
it were, apart from the validity [we have,] with particular content which attains and bestows meaning within us. One cannot
say that functioning subjectivity has long since been discovered
through the empiricist theory of knowledge since Locke. For
either this was psychology in the positive sphere and spoke of
human beings as the functioning subjects, in which case it presupposed the ground of the world and moved in a circle; or it

actually put this ground in question, as did Hume—who in this respect was much more radical than Kant—in which case it plunges us into a paradoxical solipsism and skepticism and, in any case, into a horrid situation where the being of the world is incomprehensible. The reason for this has become evident to us. The problem of the world's validity-as-ground [*Bodengeltung*], as the world that is what it is through actual and possible knowledge, or in general through actual and possible functioning subjectivity, had announced itself. But great difficulties had to be overcome in order not only to begin the method of epochē and reduction but also to bring it to its full understanding of itself and thus for the first time to discover the absolutely functioning subjectivity, not as human subjectivity, but as the subjectivity which objectifies itself, [at least] at first, in human subjectivity.

With this we recognize that it is naïve to stop at the subject-object correlation conceived in the anthropological, mundane manner and to misinterpret what was shown phenomenologically in my first writings as belonging to this correlation. To do this is to be blind precisely to the great problems of this paradox, namely, that man, and in communalization mankind, is subjectivity for the world and at the same time is supposed to be in it in an objective and worldly manner. The world which is for us is the world which has meaning in our human life and gains ever new meaning for us—meaning and also validity. This is true, and it is also true that in respect to knowledge, for us men, our own being goes before that of the world; but this does not mean that this same thing holds in respect to the actuality of being.[6] But the transcendental correlation between the world in the transcendental life of constituting subjectivity and the world itself, as it constantly outlines and confirms itself in the life-community of transcendental intersubjectivity as a pole-idea, is not the puzzling correlation which occurs in the world itself. In the concreteness of transcendental intersubjectivity, in the universal interconnection of life, the pole, or rather the system of individual poles which is called the world, is contained as intentional object in exactly the same way that any intention contains its intentional object, [the latter being] strictly inseparable from its relative concreteness.[7] All previous discussions of idealism

6. *der Wirklichkeit des Seins nach*, i.e., man's objective being (as subject *in* the world) comes first in the order of knowing but not in the order of being.

7. I.e., the relativity of its concrete givenness (in perspective, etc.).

and realism have failed to penetrate to the consciousness of the genuine problem which lies, sought for but undiscovered, behind all theories of knowledge; much less have they grasped the transcendental reduction in its difficult sense as the gate of entry to genuine knowledge of self and of the world.

Yet the question will still be put to us now as to how pure psychology, which with transcendental subjectivity has taken leave of the ground of the world, can serve the psychologist in his positive work upon this very ground. What interests him is not transcendental interiority but the interiority which exists in the world—human beings and human communities found in the world; and when he speaks of the life of the soul and of the properties of a person, and poses or would pose similar questions in regard to communities, he refers merely to what really occurs in the world; he refers to what takes place in real human beings, what is experienceable in their human self-consciousness through unprejudiced self-experience or, in the case of others, through experience of others. For this the first stage of the epochē and reduction suffices, the stage that we did not yet acknowledge as being genuinely transcendental or as being primary within a higher self-reflection. In their human commissions and omissions, human beings are related to realities which are valid for them; the psychologist must not allow what they take to be real to be valid for himself, etc. And is it not the case, after all, that psychophysical or psychophysiological dualism has its experiential legitimacy for the world, whatever the world may signify transcendentally, and that it sets a task for the psychology of human beings and animals which is analogous to the task of natural science?

The old temptations return; and what must be said here above all, apart from the objections of principle that we have already begun to make in respect to localization and causality [cf. § 62, above], is that it is only absolute freedom from prejudice, [freedom] gained through the unsurpassable radicalism of the full transcendental epochē, that makes possible a true liberation from the traditional temptations; and this is to say that it is only by being in possession of the totality of the subjective sphere, in which man, the communities of men intentionally and internally bound together, and the world in which they live, are themselves included as intentional objects—it is only by being in possession of this totality that one becomes capable of seeing and systematically investigating what we characterized as the "*how* of manners of givenness." It was in just this way that one could first discover that every worldly datum is a datum within the *how* of a horizon, that, in horizons, further horizons are implied, and, finally, that anything at all that is given in a worldly manner brings the world-horizon with it and becomes an object of world-consciousness in this way alone. W. James was alone, as far as I know, in becoming aware of the phenomena of horizon—under the title of "fringes" [8]—but how could he inquire into it without the phenomenologically acquired understanding of intentional objectivity and of implication? But if this happens, if world-consciousness is freed from its anonymity, then the breakthrough into the transcendental is accomplished. Once this has happened, however, and the transcendental field of work, as that of total and universal subjectivity, has been reached, then the return to the natural—though now no longer naïve—attitude has the remarkable result that the souls of men have entered, with the advance of phenomenological inquiry, into a remarkable movement of their own psychic content. For every new piece of transcendental knowledge is transformed, by essential necessity, into an enrichment of the content of the human soul. As transcendental ego, after all, I am the same ego that in the worldly sphere is a human ego. What was concealed from me in the human sphere I reveal through transcendental inquiry. Transcendental inquiry is itself a world-historical process insofar as it enlarges the history of the constitution of the world, not only by adding a new science to it but also by enlarging the content of the world in every respect; everything mundane has its transcendental correlates, and every new revelation of the latter adds, for the investigator of man, the psychologist, new determinations to man in the world. No positive psychology that does not have a transcendental psychology already at work at its disposal is ever able to discover such determinations of man and of the world. All this is self-evident and yet paradoxical for all of us who have been raised in centuries-old—and in part millennia-old—habits of thought. This exhibits in a new way the profound difference between mathematics, between every a priori science of the world, and phenomenology as a priori psychology, that is, as the theory of the essence of transcendental subjectivity. The a priori of nature "precedes the being of the world" but not in such a way that advances in the knowledge of the mathematical a priori could influence the being of nature itself. Nature is in itself what it is, and is in itself mathematical,

8. Husserl uses the English term.

no matter how much we know or do not know of mathematics; everything is decided in advance as pure mathematics and as nature itself. Such is the dominant hypothesis which has guided natural science through the centuries. But for the world as a world which also contains spiritual beings, this "being-in-advance" is an absurdity; here a Laplacean spirit is unthinkable. The idea of an ontology of the world, the idea of an objective, universal science of the world, having behind it a universal a priori according to which every possible factual world is knowable *more geometrico*—this idea which led even Leibniz astray— is a *nonsens*. For the realm of souls there is in principle no such ontology, no science corresponding to the physicalistic-mathematical ideal, although psychic being is investigatable in transcendental universality, in a fully systematic way, and in principle in essential generality in the form of an a priori science. Phenomenology frees us from the old objectivistic ideal of the scientific system, the theoretical form of mathematical natural science, and frees us accordingly from the idea of an ontology of the soul which could be analogous to physics. Only blindness to the transcendental, as it is experienceable and knowable only through phenomenological reduction, makes the revival of physicalism in our time possible—in the modified form of a logicist mathematicism which abandons the task, put to us by history, of a philosophy based on ultimate insight and on an absolute universality within which there must be no unasked questions, nothing taken for granted that is not understood. To call physicalism philosophy is only to pass off an equivocation as a realization of the perplexities concerning our knowledge in which we have found ourselves since Hume. Nature can be thought as a definite manifold, and we can take this idea as a basis hypothetically. But insofar as the world is a world of knowledge, a world of consciousness, a world with human beings, such an idea is absurd for it to unsurpassable degree.[9]

9. The text of the *Crisis* breaks off here. For the manuscript appended to the text at this point in the German edition see Appendix IV, pp. 335–41.

Appendixes

A.

The Vienna Lecture

Appendix I:
Philosophy and the Crisis
of European Humanity[1]

I

In this lecture I shall venture the attempt to find new interest in the frequently treated theme of the European crisis by developing the philosophical-historical idea (or the teleological sense) of European humanity. As I exhibit, in the process, the essential function that philosophy and its branches, our sciences, have to exercise within that sense, the European crisis will also receive a new elucidation.

Let us begin with something that is familiar to all, the difference between scientific medicine and the lore of the so-called nature cure. While the latter arises in the common life of the people out of native experience and tradition, scientific medicine arises from the application of the insights of purely theoretical sciences, those of the human body, primarily anatomy and physiology. But these, in turn, are themselves based on the universally explanatory, fundamental sciences of nature as such, physics and chemistry.

1. A lecture presented before the Vienna Cultural Society on May 7 and May 10, 1935 (i.e., six months before the Prague lecture, on which the *Crisis* is based) with the original title "Philosophy in the Crisis of European Mankind." It appears in the German edition as the third "Abhandlung," pp. 314–48.

[269]

Let us now turn our attention from the human body to the human spirit, the subject matter of the so-called humanist disciplines. Here theoretical interest is directed at human beings exclusively as persons, at their personal life and accomplishments, and correlatively at the products of such accomplishments. Personal life means living communalized as "I" and "we" within a community-horizon, and this in communities of various simple or stratified forms such as family, nation, supranational community. The word *life* here does not have a physiological sense; it signifies purposeful life accomplishing spiritual products: in the broadest sense, creating culture in the unity of a historical development.[2] All this is the subject matter of numerous humanistic disciplines. Now clearly there exists the distinction between energetic thriving and atrophy, that is, one can also say, between health and sickness, even in communities, peoples, states. Accordingly the question is not far removed: How does it happen that no scientific medicine has ever developed in this sphere, a medicine for nations and supranational communities? The European nations are sick; Europe itself, it is said, is in crisis. We are by no means lacking something like nature doctors. Indeed, we are practically inundated by a flood of naïve and excessive suggestions for reform. But why do the so richly developed humanistic disciplines fail to perform the service here that is so admirably performed by the natural sciences in their sphere?

Those familiar with the spirit of the modern sciences will not be at a loss for an answer. The greatness of the natural sciences consists in the fact that they are not content with an intuitive, empirical procedure, since for them all description of nature is meant to be only a methodical passage to exact—ultimately physical-chemical—explanation. They say: "merely descriptive" sciences confine us to the finitudes of our earthly surrounding world. But mathematical-exact natural science, through its method, encompasses the infinities in their actualities and real possibilities. It understands what is intuitively given as merely subjectively relative appearance and teaches us how to investigate suprasubjective ("objective") nature itself, by systematic approximations, in terms of its unconditionally universal elements and laws. At the same time it teaches us to explain all intuitively pregiven concrete entities, whether men, animals, or

2. *Geschichtlichkeit.* Here, as is often the case, Husserl uses this term to mean, not "historicity," but a particular historical process or development. Cf. above, § 6, note 2.

heavenly bodies, in terms of what ultimately is; namely, beginning with particular, factually given appearances, to induce future possibilities and probabilities with a scope and an exactness which surpasses all intuitively limited empirical procedure. The result of the consistent development of the exact sciences in the modern period was a true revolution in the technical control of nature.

Quite different, unfortunately (in the sense of the point of view we have already come to understand well) is the methodical situation in the humanistic disciplines, and this for internal reasons. The human spirit, after all, is grounded on the human *physis;* each individual human psychic life is founded upon corporeity, and thus each community upon the bodies of the individual human beings who are members of it. So if a truly exact explanation of the phenomena of the humanistic disciplines is to be possible, and accordingly a far-reaching scientific praxis similar to that in the natural sphere, the humanists must not only consider the spirit as spirit but must also go back to the corporeal basis and carry out their explanations by means of exact physics and chemistry. But this fails (and this cannot change in the foreseeable future) because of the complexity of the required exact psychophysical research even in the case of the individual human being, not to mention that of the great historical communities. If the world were built up of two spheres of realities with equal rights, so to speak, nature and spirit, neither of which was prior methodically or materially, then the situation would be different. But only nature can be treated by itself as a closed world; only natural science can abstract with unbroken consistency from everything spiritual and investigate nature purely as nature. On the other hand, vice versa, such a consistent abstraction from nature does not lead the humanist, interested solely in what is spiritual, to a self-enclosed, purely spiritually coherent "world" which could become the subject matter of a pure and universal humanistic science as a parallel to pure natural science. For animal spirituality, that of human and animal "souls," to which all other spirituality must be traced back, is individually, causally founded in corporeity. Thus it is understandable that the humanist, interested solely in the spiritual as such, does not get beyond the descriptive level, beyond a spiritual history,[3] and thus remains limited to intuitive finitudes.

3. *Geisteshistorie.* Husserl is thinking of something parallel to "natural history."

Every example shows this. A historian, for example, cannot treat of ancient Greek history without bringing in the physical geography of ancient Greece, or of its architecture without bringing in the corporeity of its buildings, etc., etc. That seems quite obvious.

But what if the whole way of thinking that manifests itself in the foregoing presentation rested on portentous prejudices and, in its effects, itself shared in the responsibility for the European sickness? This is, indeed, my conviction; and I hope also to make it understandable that this is also a fundamental source of the unhesitating way in which the modern scientist holds the possibility of grounding a purely self-enclosed and general science of the spirit to be not even worth considering and thus flatly denies it.

It is in the interest of our Europe-problem to go into this a bit further and to uproot the above argument, which seemed so obvious at first glance. The historian, the investigator of the spirit or of culture in every sphere, certainly has physical nature constantly among his phenomena—nature in ancient Greece, in our example above. But this nature is not nature in the sense of natural science but rather that which for the ancient Greeks counted as nature, that which confronted them as natural reality in their surrounding world. To express it more fully: the historical surrounding world of the Greeks is not the objective world in our sense but rather their "world-representation," i.e., their own subjective validity with all the actualities which are valid for them within it, including, for example, gods, demons, etc.

"Surrounding world" is a concept that has its place exclusively in the spiritual sphere. That we live in our particular surrounding world, which is the locus of all our cares and endeavors—this refers to a fact that occurs purely within the spiritual realm. Our surrounding world is a spiritual structure in us and in our historical life. Thus there is no reason for him who makes spirit as spirit his subject matter to demand anything other than a purely spiritual explanation for it. And so generally: to look upon the nature of the surrounding world as something alien to the spirit, and consequently to want to buttress humanistic science with natural science so as to make it supposedly exact, is absurd.

What is obviously also completely forgotten is that natural science (like all science generally) is a title for spiritual accomplishments, namely, those of the natural scientists working together; as such they belong, after all, like all spiritual occurrences, to the region of what is to be explained by humanistic disciplines. Now is it not absurd and circular to want to explain the historical event "natural science" in a natural-scientific way, to explain it by bringing in natural science and its natural laws, which, as spiritual accomplishment, themselves belong to the problem?

Blinded by naturalism (no matter how much they attack it verbally), the humanists have totally failed even to pose the problem of a universal and pure humanistic science and to inquire after a theory of the essence of spirit purely as spirit which would pursue what is unconditionally universal, by way of elements and laws, in the spiritual sphere, with the purpose of proceeding from there to scientific explanations in an absolutely final sense.

The foregoing considerations on the philosophy of the spirit provide us with the proper attitude for grasping and dealing with our subject of spiritual Europe as a problem purely within the humanistic disciplines, and first of all in the manner of spiritual history. As already indicated in our introductory statements, a remarkable teleology, inborn, as it were, only in our Europe, will become visible in this way, one which is quite intimately involved with the outbreak or irruption of philosophy and its branches, the sciences, in the ancient Greek spirit. We can foresee that this will involve a clarification of the deepest reasons for the origin of the portentous naturalism, or, what will prove to be equivalent, of modern dualism in the interpretation of the world. Finally this will bring to light the actual sense of the crisis of European humanity.

We pose the question: How is the spiritual shape of Europe to be characterized? Thus we refer to Europe not as it is understood geographically, as on a map, as if thereby the group of people who live together in this territory would define European humanity. In the spiritual sense the English Dominions, the United States, etc., clearly belong to Europe, whereas the Eskimos or Indians presented as curiosities at fairs, or the Gypsies, who constantly wander about Europe, do not. Here the title "Europe" clearly refers to the unity of a spiritual life, activity, creation, with all its ends, interests, cares, and endeavors, with its products of purposeful activity, institutions, organizations. Here individual men act in many societies of different levels: in families, in tribes, in nations, all being internally, spiritually bound together, and, as I said, in the unity of a spiritual shape. In this way a character is given to the persons, associations of persons, and all their cultural accomplishments which binds them all together.

"The spiritual shape of Europe"—what is it? [We must] exhibit the philosophical idea which is immanent in the history of Europe (spiritual Europe) or, what is the same, the teleology which is immanent in it, which makes itself known, from the standpoint of universal mankind as such, as the breakthrough and the developmental beginning of a new human epoch—the epoch of mankind which now seeks to live, and only can live, in the free shaping of its existence, its historical life, through ideas of reason, through infinite tasks.

Every spiritual shape exists essentially within a universal historical space or in a particular unity of historical time in terms of coexistence and succession; it has its history. So if we pursue the historical interconnections, beginning, as is necessary, with ourselves and our nation, the historical continuity leads us further and further from our nation to neighboring nations, and thus from nation to nation, from one time to the next. In antiquity ultimately, we are led from the Romans to the Greeks, the Egyptians, the Persians, etc.; clearly, there is no end. We move back into prehistoric time, and we cannot avoid turning to that significant and conceptually rich work of Menghin, the *World History of the Stone Age*.[4] Through such a procedure mankind appears as a single life of men and peoples bound together by only spiritual relations, with a plenitude of human and cultural types which nevertheless flowingly interpenetrate one another. It is like a sea, in which men and peoples are the fleetingly formed, changing, and then disappearing waves, some with richer, more complicated ripples, others with more primitive.

However, upon more consistent and internally directed observation we notice new, peculiar interrelations and differences. No matter how hostile they may be toward one another, the European nations nevertheless have a particular inner kinship of spirit which runs through them all, transcending national differences. There is something like a sibling relationship which gives all of us in this sphere the consciousness of homeland. This comes immediately to the fore as soon as we think ourselves into the Indian historical sphere [*die indische Geschichtlichkeit*], for

4. Oswald Menghin, *Weltgeschichte der Steinzeit* (Vienna: A. Schroll & Co., 1931).

example, with its many peoples and cultural products. In this sphere, too, there exists the unity of a family-like kinship, but one which is alien to us. Indian people, on the other hand, experience us as aliens and only one another as confreres. Yet this essential difference between familiarity and strangeness, a fundamental category of all historicity which relativizes itself in many strata, cannot suffice. Historical mankind does not always divide itself up in the same way in accord with this category. We feel this precisely in our own Europe. There is something unique here that is recognized in us by all other human groups, too, something that, quite apart from all considerations of utility, becomes a motive for them to Europeanize themselves even in their unbroken will to spiritual self-preservation; whereas we, if we understand ourselves properly, would never Indianize ourselves, for example. I mean that we feel (and in spite of all obscurity this feeling is probably legitimate) that an entelechy is inborn in our European civilization which holds sway throughout all the changing shapes of Europe and accords to them the sense of a development toward an ideal shape of life and being as an eternal pole. Not that this is a case of one of those well-known types of purposeful striving which give the organic beings their character in the physical realm; thus it is not something like a biological development from a seminal form through stages to maturity with succeeding ages and dying-out. There is, for essential reasons, no zoology of peoples. They are spiritual unities; they do not have, and in particular the supranational unity of Europe does not have, a mature shape that has ever been reached or could be reached as a shape that is regularly repeated. Psychic humanity has never been complete and never will be, and can never repeat itself. The spiritual *telos* of European humanity, in which the particular telos of particular nations and of individual men is contained, lies in the infinite, is an infinite idea toward which, in concealment, the whole spiritual becoming aims, so to speak. As soon as it becomes consciously recognized in the development as telos, it necessarily also becomes practical as a goal of the will; and thereby a new, higher stage of development is introduced which is under the guidance of norms, normative ideas.

Now all this is not intended as a speculative interpretation of our historical development but as the expression of a vital presentiment which arises through unprejudiced reflection. But this presentiment gives us an intentional guide for seeing in

European history highly significant interconnections in the pursuit of which the presentiment becomes a confirmed certainty for us. Presentiment is the felt signpost for all discoveries.

Let us proceed to the exposition. Spiritual Europe has a birthplace. By this I mean not a geographical birthplace, in one land, though this is also true, but rather a spiritual birthplace in a nation or in individual men and human groups of this nation. It is the ancient Greek nation in the seventh and sixth centuries B.C. Here there arises a *new sort of attitude* of individuals toward their surrounding world. And its consequence is the breakthrough of a completely new sort of spiritual structure, rapidly growing into a systematically self-enclosed cultural form; the Greeks called it *philosophy*. Correctly translated, in the original sense, that means nothing other than universal science, science of the universe, of the all-encompassing unity of all that is. Soon the interest in the All, and thus the question of the all-encompassing becoming and being in becoming, begins to particularize itself according to the general forms and regions of being, and thus philosophy, the one science, branches out into many particular sciences.

In the breakthrough of philosophy in this sense, in which all sciences are thus contained, I see, paradoxical as it may sound, the primal phenomenon of spiritual Europe. Through more detailed considerations, short as they may be, the apparent paradox will soon disappear.

Philosophy, science, is the title for a special class of cultural structures. The historical movement that has been taken on by the style-form of European supranationality aims at an infinitely distant normative shape, but not one that could simply be read off the changing succession of shapes by a morphological observation from the outside. The constant directedness toward a norm inhabits the intentional life of individual persons, and thence the nations with their particular social units, and finally the organism of the nations bound together as Europe. Of course it does not inhabit all persons, it is not fully developed in the personalities of a higher level that are constituted by intersubjective acts; nevertheless, it inhabits them in the form of a necessary course of development and spreading of the spirit of norms that are valid for all. But this has at the same time the significance of an advancing transformation of all humanity through the formations of ideas that become effective in the smallest of circles. Ideas, meaning-structures that are produced in individual persons and have the miraculous new way of containing intentional infinities within themselves, are not like real things in space; the latter, though they enter into the field of human experience, do not yet thereby have any significance for human beings as persons. With the first conception of ideas, man gradually becomes a new man. His spiritual being enters into the movement of an advancing reconstruction. This movement proceeds from the beginning in a communicative way, awakens a new style of personal existence in one's sphere of life, a correspondingly new becoming through communicative understanding. Within this movement at first (and then later even beyond it) there grows a new sort of humanity, one which, living in finitude, lives toward poles of infinity. Precisely in this way there arises a new type of communalization and a new form of enduring community whose spiritual life, communalized through the love of ideas, the production of ideas, and through ideal life-norms, bears within itself the future-horizon of infinity: that of an infinity of generations being renewed in the spirit of ideas. This, then, is accomplished at first within the spiritual space of a single nation, the Greek nation, as the development of philosophy and of philosophical communities. Together with this there arises, first in this nation, a common cultural spirit [which,] drawing all of humanity under its spell, is thus an advancing transformation in the form of a new [type of] historical development.[5]

This rough sketch will be filled in and better understood if we pursue the historical origin of philosophical and scientific humanity and, proceeding from there, clarify the sense of Europe and its new sort of historicity which distinguishes itself through [the above-mentioned] type of development from history in general.

Let us illuminate first of all the remarkable, peculiar character of philosophy, unfolding in ever new special sciences. Let us contrast it with other cultural forms already present in prescientific mankind: artifacts, agriculture, domestic arts, etc. All these signify classes of cultural products with their own methods for assuring successful production. Otherwise [6] they have a passing existence in the surrounding world. Scientific acquisitions, on the other hand, after their method of assured successful production has been attained, have quite another manner of being,

5. *Historizität*, used in the same sense as *Geschichtlichkeit*, above.
6. I.e., apart from the methods, which persist through time.

quite another temporality. They are not used up; they are imperishable; repeated production creates not something similar, at best equally useful; it produces in any number of acts of production by one person or any number of persons something identically the same, identical in sense and validity. Persons bound together in direct mutual understanding cannot help experiencing what has been produced by their fellows in similar acts of production as being identically the same as what they themselves produce. In a word, what is acquired through scientific activity is not something real but something ideal.

But what is more, that which is so acquired as valid, as truth, is serviceable as material for the possible production of idealities on a higher level, and so on again and again. For the developed theoretical interest each goal acquires in advance the sense of a merely relative goal; it becomes the pathway to ever newer, ever higher goals within an infinity marked off as a universal field of work, as the "domain" of the science. Science, then, signifies the idea of an infinity of tasks, of which at any time a finite number have been disposed of and are retained as persisting validities. These make up at the same time the fund of premises for an infinite horizon of tasks as the unity of one all-encompassing task.

But something important must be added here to fill out our remarks. In science the ideality of the individual products of work, the truths, does not merely denote repeatability, such that sense is identified [with what was produced before] and confirmed: the idea of truth in the sense of science is set apart (and of this we shall say more later) from the truth of the prescientific life. It wants to be unconditioned truth. This involves an infinity which gives to each factual confirmation and truth the character of being merely relative, of being a mere approach in relation precisely to that infinite horizon in which the truth-in-itself counts, so to speak, as an infinitely distant point. Correlatively, this infinity lies also in what "actually is" in the scientific sense, as well as, again, in "universal" validity, validity for "everyone," the latter being understood as the subject of all groundings ever to be accomplished; and this "everyone" is no longer everyone in the finite sense of prescientific life.

After this characterization of science's own peculiar sort of ideality, with the ideal infinities variously implied in its sense, we are confronted from a historical perspective with the contrast which can be expressed as follows: no other cultural shape on the historical horizon prior to philosophy is in the same sense a culture of ideas knowing infinite tasks, knowing such universes of idealities which as a whole and in all their details, and in their methods of production, bear infinity within themselves in keeping with their sense.

Extrascientific culture, culture not yet touched by science, consists in tasks and accomplishments of man in finitude. The openly endless horizon in which he lives is not disclosed; his ends, his activity, his trade and traffic, his personal, social, national, and mythical motivation—all this moves within the sphere of his finitely surveyable surrounding world. Here there are no infinite tasks, no ideal acquisitions whose infinity is itself the field of work, and specifically in such a way that it consciously has, for those who work in it, the manner of being of such an infinite field of tasks.

But with the appearance of Greek philosophy and its first formulation, through consistent idealization, of the new sense of infinity, there is accomplished in this respect a thoroughgoing transformation which finally draws all finite ideas and with them all spiritual culture and its [concept of] mankind into its sphere. Hence there are, for us Europeans, many infinite ideas (if we may use this expression) which lie outside the philosophical-scientific sphere (infinite tasks, goals, confirmations, truths, "true values," "genuine goods," "absolutely" valid norms), but they owe their analogous character of infinity to the transformation of mankind through philosophy and its idealities. Scientific culture under the guidance of ideas of infinity means, then, a revolutionization [*Revolutionierung*] of the whole culture, a revolutionization of the whole manner in which mankind creates culture. It also means a revolutionization of [its] historicity, which is now the history of the cutting-off of finite mankind's development [7] as it becomes mankind with infinite tasks.

Here we encounter an obvious objection: philosophy, the science of the Greeks, is not something peculiar to them which came into the world for the first time with them. After all, they themselves tell of the wise Egyptians, Babylonians, etc., and did in fact learn much from them. Today we have a plethora of works about Indian philosophy, Chinese philosophy, etc., in which these are placed on a plane with Greek philosophy and are taken as merely different historical forms under one and the same idea of culture. Naturally, common features are not lacking. Nevertheless, one must not allow the merely morphologi-

7. *Geschichte des Entwerdens des endlichen Menschentums.*

cally general features to hide the intentional depths so that one becomes blind to the most essential differences of principle.

Before everything else the very attitudes of the two sorts of "philosophers," their universal directions of interest, are fundamentally different. In both cases one may notice a world-encompassing interest that leads on both sides—thus also in Indian, Chinese, and similar "philosophies"—to universal knowledge of the world, everywhere working itself out as a vocation-like life-interest, leading through understandable motivations to vocational communities in which the general results are propagated or develop from generation to generation. But only in the Greeks do we have a universal ("cosmological") life-interest in the essentially new form of a purely "theoretical" attitude, and this as a communal form in which this interest works itself out for internal reasons, being the corresponding, essentially new [community] of philosophers, of scientists (mathematicians, astronomers, etc.). These are the men who, not in isolation but with one another and for one another, i.e., in interpersonally bound communal work, strive for and bring about *theōria* and nothing but *theōria*, whose growth and constant perfection, with the broadening of the circle of coworkers and the succession of the generations of inquirers, is finally taken up into the will with the sense of an infinite and common task. The theoretical attitude has its historical origin in the Greeks.

Attitude, generally speaking, means a habitually fixed style of willing life comprising directions of the will or interests that are prescribed by this style, comprising the ultimate ends, the cultural accomplishments whose total style is thereby determined. The individual life determined by it runs its course with this persisting style as its norm. The concrete contents of culture change [8] according to a relatively closed historical process. Humanity (or a closed community such as a nation, tribe, etc.), in its historical situation, always lives under some attitude or other. Its life always has its norm-style and, in reference to this, a constant historicity or development.

Thus the theoretical attitude, in its newness, refers back to a previous attitude, one which was earlier the norm; [with reference to this] it is characterized as a reorientation. [9] Universally considering the historicity of human existence in all its communal forms and in its historical stages, we now see that a

8. Reading *es wechseln* for *es wechselt*.
9. I.e., an *Umstellung* of the original *Einstellung*.

certain attitude is essentially and in itself the first, i.e., that a certain norm-style of human existence (speaking in formal generality) signifies a first [type of] historicity within which particular factual norm-styles of culture-creating existence remain formally the same in spite of all rising, falling, or stagnating. We speak in this connection of the natural primordial attitude, of the attitude of original natural life, of the first originally natural form of cultures, whether higher or lower, whether developing uninhibitedly or stagnating. All other attitudes are accordingly related back to this natural attitude as reorientations [of it]. To put it more concretely: in one of the historically factual civilizations of the natural attitude, motives must arise out of its concrete internal and external situation at a particular time which motivate, first, individual men and groups within it to make [such] a reorientation.

How is the essentially original attitude, the fundamental historical mode of human existence, to be characterized? We answer: men obviously always live, for generative reasons, in communities, in family, tribe, nation, which are themselves in turn divided, in varying degrees of complexity, into particular social groups. Now natural life can be characterized as a life naïvely, straightforwardly directed at the world, the world being always in a certain sense consciously present as a universal horizon, without, however, being thematic as such. What is thematic is whatever one is directed toward. Waking life is always a directedness toward this or that, being directed toward it as an end or as means, as relevant or irrelevant, toward the interesting or the indifferent, toward the private or public, toward what is daily required or intrusively new. All this lies within the world-horizon; but special motives are required when one who is gripped in this world-life reorients himself and somehow comes to make the world itself thematic, to take up a lasting interest in it.

But here a more detailed exposition is required. The individual men who reorient themselves, as men within their universal life-community (their nation), continue to have their natural interests, each his individual interests; through no reorientation can they simply lose them; this would mean that each would cease to be what he has become from birth onward. In any circumstances, then, the reorientation can only be a periodical one; it can have habitually enduring validity for one's whole remaining life only in the form of an unconditional resolve of the will to take up, at periodic but internally unified points of time, the same attitude and, through this continuity that intentionally bridges the gaps, to sustain its new sort of interests as valid and as ongoing projects and to realize them through corresponding cultural structures.

We are familiar with something similar to this in the vocations that arise even in naturally original cultural life with their periodical vocational times that run through the rest of life and its concrete temporality (the working hours of the official, etc.).

Now there are two possibilities. One is that the interests of the new attitude are meant to serve the natural interests of life or, what is in essence the same thing, natural praxis. In this case the new attitude is itself a practical one. This can have a sense similar to that of the practical attitude of the politician, who, as a natural functionary, is directed toward the general welfare, i.e., who in his praxis would serve the praxis of all (and thus mediately also his own). This, of course, still belongs to the sphere of the natural attitude, which is essentially differentiated according to the different types of community members and is in fact one thing for those who govern the community and another for the "citizens"—these terms being understood, of course, in the broadest possible sense. But in any case the analogy makes it understandable that the universality of a practical attitude, now related to the whole world, by no means need imply an interest and a concern with all the details or all the particular totalities within the world, which would of course be unthinkable.

But in addition to the higher-level practical attitude (which we shall soon meet [again] in the religious-mythical attitude)[10] there exists yet another essential possibility for altering the general natural attitude, namely, the *theoretical attitude*. To be sure, it is so named only by anticipation because out of it, according to a necessary development, philosophical *theōria* grows and becomes an end in itself or a field of interest. The theoretical attitude, though it is again a vocational attitude, is totally unpractical. In the sphere of its own vocational life, then, it is based on a voluntary epochē of all natural praxis, including the higher-level praxis that serves the natural sphere.

Yet it must be said immediately that this is still not a matter of a definitive "severing" of the theoretical from the practical life or of a division of the theoretician's concrete life into two life-continuities that sustain themselves without any interrelation;

10. I have changed the position of this parenthetical phrase. In the original its position makes no sense.

socially speaking, this would signify the emergence of two spirit-ually unrelated cultural spheres. For yet a third form of univer-sal attitude is possible (as opposed to both the religious-mythical attitude, which is founded in the natural attitude, and the theo-retical attitude), namely, the synthesis of the two interests ac-complished in the transition from the theoretical to the practical attitude, such that the *theōria* (universal science), arising within a closed unity and under the epochē of all praxis, is called (and in theoretical insight itself exhibits its calling) to serve mankind in a new way, mankind which, in its concrete exist-ence, lives first and always in the natural sphere. This occurs in the form of a new sort of praxis, that of the universal critique of all life and all life-goals, all cultural products and systems that have already arisen out of the life of man; and thus it also becomes a critique of mankind itself and of the values which guide it explicitly or implicitly. Further, it is a praxis whose aim is to elevate mankind through universal scientific reason, accord-ing to norms of truth of all forms, to transform it from the bottom up into a new humanity made capable of an absolute self-responsibility on the basis of absolute theoretical insights. Yet prior to this synthesis of theoretical universality and univer-sally interested praxis there is obviously another synthesis of theory and praxis, that of the use of the limited results of theory, of limited sciences which allow the universality of the theoretical interest to fall into specialization. Here, then, the original natu-ral attitude and the theoretical are bound together through a process of finitization.

For a deeper understanding of Greek-European science (uni-versally speaking: philosophy) in its fundamental difference from the oriental "philosophies" judged equal to it, it is now necessary to consider more closely the practical-universal atti-tude which created these philosophies prior to European science and to clarify it as the religious-mythical attitude. It is a known fact, but also a necessity essentially available to insight, that religious-mythical motifs and a religious-mythical praxis belong to every civilization living in the natural sphere—i.e., prior to the outbreak and the effects of Greek philosophy and thus of a scientific world-view. The mythical-religious attitude exists when the world as a totality becomes thematic, but in a practical way; by "world" we mean here, of course, the world which is con-cretely, traditionally valid for the civilization in question (a nation for example), i.e., the world as apperceived mythically. Here not only men and animals and other subhuman and suban-

imal beings but also superhuman beings belong to the mythical-
natural [world].[11] The gaze which encompasses it as a totality is
practical—not that [the individual] man, who in natural
straightforward living is immediately interested only in particular realities, could ever come to a state in which everything
together would suddenly become practically relevant for him in
the same way. But insofar as the whole world is seen as thoroughly dominated by mythical powers, so that man's fate depends mediately or immediately upon the way in which they
hold sway, a universal-mythical world-view is possibly incited by
praxis and then itself becomes a practically interested world-
view. Those motivated to adopt this religious-mythical attitude
are understandably priests belonging to a priestly caste which
manages the religious-mythical interests and their tradition in a
unified way. In this priesthood the linguistically structured
"knowledge" of the mythical powers (understood as persons, in
the broadest sense) arises and spreads. Of itself, it takes on the
form of mystical speculation which, appearing as naïvely convincing interpretation, reconstructs the myth itself. The view is
here always directed also, of course, upon the rest of the world
which is governed by the mythical powers and upon the human
and subhuman beings that belong to it (and which also, incidentally, since they are not firmly fixed in their own essential being,
stand open to the influx of mythical elements), upon the ways in
which mythical powers govern the events of this world, the ways
in which they themselves come together in a unified supreme
order of power, the ways in which they exercise various individual functions, as functionaries, intervening [in the world] by
creating, fulfilling tasks, decreeing fate. But all this speculative
knowledge is meant to serve man in his human purposes so that
he may order his worldly life in the happiest possible way and
shield it from disease, from every sort of evil fate, from disaster
and death. It is understandable that this mythical-practical
world-view and world-knowledge can give rise to much knowledge of the factual world, the world as known through scientific
experience, that can later be used scientifically. But within their
own framework of meaning this world-view and world-knowledge are and remain mythical and practical, and it is a mistake,
a falsification of their sense, for those raised in the scientific
ways of thinking created in Greece and developed in the modern
period to speak of Indian and Chinese philosophy and science

11. Substituting *Welt* for *Einstellung*.

(astronomy, mathematics), i.e., to interpret India, Babylonia, China, in a European way.

Sharply distinguished from this universal but mythical-practical attitude is the "theoretical" attitude, which is not practical in any sense used so far, the attitude of θαυμάζειν, to which the great figures of the first culminating period of Greek philosophy, Plato and Aristotle, traced the origin of philosophy. Man becomes gripped by the passion of a world-view and world-knowledge that turns away from all practical interests and, within the closed sphere of its cognitive activity, in the times devoted to it, strives for and achieves nothing but pure *theōria*. In other words, man becomes a nonparticipating spectator, surveyor of the world; he becomes a philosopher; or rather, from this point on his life becomes receptive to motivations which are possible only in this attitude, motivations for new sorts of goals for thought and methods through which, finally, philosophy comes to be and he becomes a philosopher.

Naturally the outbreak of the theoretical attitude, like everything that develops historically, has its factual motivation in the concrete framework of historical occurrence. In this respect one must clarify, then, how θαυμάζειν could arise and become habitual, at first in individuals, out of the manner and the life-horizon of Greek humanity in the seventh century, with its contact with the great and already highly cultivated nations of its surrounding world. We shall not go into this in detail; what is more important for us is to understand the path of motivation, the path of the bestowal and creation of meaning which leads from the mere reorientation, from mere θαυμάζειν, to *theōria*—a historical fact that must nevertheless have something essential about it. We must clarify the transformation from original *theōria*, the fully disinterested seeing of the world (following from the epochē of all practical interests, world-knowledge through pure, universal seeing) to the *theōria* of genuine science, the two being mediated through the contrast of δόξα and ἐπιστήμη. Incipient theoretical interest, as θαυμάζειν, is obviously a variant of curiosity, which has its original place in natural life as an intrusion into the course of "serious living," either as a result of originally developed life-interests or as a playful looking-about when one's quite immediate vital needs are satisfied or when working hours are over. Curiosity (here understood not as a habitual "vice") is also a variant, an interest which has separated itself off from life-interests, has let them fall.

In this attitude, man views first of all the multiplicity of nations, his own and others, each with its own surrounding world which is valid for it, is taken for granted, with its traditions, its gods, its demons, its mythical powers, simply as the actual world. Through this astonishing contrast there appears the distinction between world-representation and actual world, and the new question of truth arises: not tradition-bound, everyday truth, but an identical truth which is valid for all who are no longer blinded by traditions, a truth-in-itself. Part of the theoretical attitude of the philosopher, then, is his constant and prior resolve to dedicate his future life always, and in the sense of a universal life, to the task of *theōria*, to build theoretical knowledge upon theoretical knowledge *in infinitum*.

Through isolated personalities like Thales, etc., there arises thus a new humanity: men who [live] the philosophical life, who create philosophy in the manner of a vocation as a new sort of cultural configuration. Understandably a correspondingly new sort of communalization arises. These ideal structures of *theōria* are concurrently lived through and taken over without any difficulty by others who reproduce the process of understanding and production. Without any difficulty they lead to cooperative work, mutual help through mutual critique. Even the outsiders, the nonphilosophers, become aware of this peculiar sort of activity. Through sympathetic understanding they either become philosophers themselves, or, if they are otherwise vocationally too occupied, they learn from philosophers. Thus philosophy spreads in a twofold manner, as the broadening vocational community of philosophers and as a concurrently broadening community movement of education [*Bildung*]. But this is also the source of the subsequently so fateful internal division of the folk-unity into the educated and the uneducated. Clearly, on the other hand, this tendency to spread is not limited to the home nation. Unlike all other cultural works, philosophy is not a movement of interest which is bound to the soil of the national tradition. Aliens, too, learn to understand it and generally take part in the immense cultural transformation which radiates out from philosophy. But precisely this needs to be further characterized.

Philosophy, spreading in the form of inquiry and education, has a twofold spiritual effect. On the one hand, what is most essential to the theoretical attitude of philosophical man is the peculiar universality of his critical stance, his resolve not to accept unquestioningly any pregiven opinion or tradition so that he can inquire, in respect to the whole traditionally pregiven universe, after what is true in itself, an ideality. But this is not only a new cognitive stance. Because of the requirement to subject all empirical matters to ideal norms, i.e., those of unconditioned truth, there soon results a far-reaching transformation of the whole praxis of human existence, i.e., the whole of cultural life: henceforth it must receive its norms not from the naïve experience and tradition of everyday life but from objective truth. Thus ideal truth becomes an absolute value which, through the movement of education and its constant effects in the training of children, brings with it a universally transformed praxis. If we reflect a little more closely on the manner of this transformation, we immediately understand the unavoidable result: if the general idea of truth-in-itself becomes the universal norm of all the relative truths that arise in human life, the actual and supposed situational truths, then this will also affect all traditional norms, those of right, of beauty, of usefulness, dominant personal values, values connected with personal characteristics, etc.

There arises, then, a particular humanity and a particular life-vocation correlative to the accomplishment of a new culture. Philosophical knowledge of the world creates not only those particular sorts of results but also a human posture which immediately intervenes in the whole remainder of practical life with all its demands and ends, the ends of the historical tradition in which one is brought up and which receive their validity from this source. A new and intimate community—we could call it a community of purely ideal interests—develops among men, men who live for philosophy, bound together in their devotion to ideas, which not only are useful to all but belong to all identically. Necessarily there develops a communal activity of a particular sort, that of working with one another and for one another, offering one another helpful criticism, through which there arises a pure and unconditioned truth-validity as common property. In addition, this interest has a natural tendency to propagate itself through the sympathetic understanding [by others] of what is sought and accomplished in it; there is a tendency, then, for more and more still nonphilosophical persons to be drawn into the community of philosophers. This occurs first within the home nation. The spread cannot occur exclusively as one of vocational scientific inquiry; it occurs [rather] [12] as a movement of education, [reaching] [12] far beyond the vocational sphere.

Now if the movement of education extends over larger and

12. Biemel's interpolations.

larger groups of people, and naturally over the higher or dominant groups, those less exhausted by the cares of life, what are
the results? Clearly this leads not simply to a homogeneous
transformation of the generally satisfactory life of the national
state but probably to great internal schisms in which this life
and the whole national culture suffer an upheaval. Those con-
servatives who are satisfied with the tradition and the philosophical men will fight each other, and the struggle will surely occur
in the sphere of political power. The persecution begins at the
very beginnings of philosophy. Men who live for these ideas
become objects of contempt. And yet, ideas are stronger than
any empirical powers.

Here we must further take into account the fact that philosophy, which has grown up out of the universal critical attitude
toward anything and everything pregiven in the tradition, is not
inhibited in its spread by any national boundaries. Only the
capacity for a universal critical attitude, which, to be sure, presupposes a certain level of prescientific culture, must be present.
So the upheaval of national culture can proliferate, first of all
when the advancing universal science becomes the common
property of nations that were formerly alien to one another and
the unity of a scientific community and the community of the
educated spreads throughout the multiplicity of nations.

One more important thing must be mentioned concerning the
comportment of philosophy toward the traditions. For there are
two possibilities to be considered here. What is traditionally
valid is either completely discarded, or its content is taken over
philosophically and thereby formed anew in the spirit of philosophical ideality. An outstanding case of this is religion. From
this I would exclude the "polytheistic religions." Gods in the
plural, mythical powers of every sort, are objects of the surrounding world having the same reality as animals and men. In
the concept of God the singular is essential. Proper to it, from
the human standpoint, is the fact that God's ontic validity and
his value-validity are experienced as an absolute internal bond.
The next step here is the coalescence of this absoluteness with
that of philosophical ideality. In the general process of idealization, which proceeds from philosophy, God is logicized, so to
speak; indeed he becomes the bearer of the absolute *logos*. I
would cite as something logical, incidentally, the fact that religion appeals theologically to the evidence of belief as a peculiar
manner, and the deepest manner, of grounding true being. National gods, on the other hand, are [simply] there without ques-

tion, as real facts in the surrounding world. Prior to philosophy no one poses questions critical of knowledge, questions of evidence.

In essence, though somewhat schematically, we have now sketched the historical motivation which makes understandable how, beginning with a few Greek eccentrics, a transformation of human existence and its whole cultural life could be initiated, at first in their own and then in neighboring nations. But we can also see how, starting from this, a supranationality of a completely new sort could arise. I am referring, of course, to the spiritual shape of Europe. Now it is no longer a conglomeration of different nations influencing one another only through commerce and power struggles. Rather, a new spirit, stemming from philosophy and its particular sciences, a spirit of free critique and norm-giving aimed at infinite tasks, dominates humanity through and through, creating new, infinite ideals. They are such for the individual men in their nations, such for the nations themselves. But ultimately they are also infinite ideals for the spreading synthesis of nations in which each nation, precisely by pursuing its own ideal task in the spirit of infinity, gives its best to the nations united with it. Through this giving and receiving the supranational whole, with all its social levels, ascends, filled with the exuberant spirit of an infinite task, a task which is divided into various infinite spheres but is still one. Within this ideally directed total society philosophy retains its guiding function and its particular infinite task: the function of free and universal theoretical reflection, which encompasses all ideals and the total ideal, i.e., the universe of all norms. Within European civilization, philosophy has constantly to exercise its function as one which is archontic for the civilization as a whole.

II

BUT NOW WE MUST LISTEN to those certainly very pressing misunderstandings and objections which, it seems to me, derive their suggestive force from fashionable prejudices and their phraseologies.

Is it not the case that what we have presented here is something rather inappropriate to our time, an attempt to rescue the honor of rationalism, of "enlightenment," of an intellectualism which loses itself in theories alienated from the world, with its necessary evil consequences of a superficial lust for erudition and an intellectualistic snobbism? Does this not mean that we are being led again into the fateful error of believing that science makes man wise, that it is destined to create a genuine and contented humanity that is master of its fate? Who would still take such notions seriously today?

This objection certainly has its relative merit in relation to the state of the European development from the seventeenth to the end of the nineteenth centuries. But it does not apply to the proper sense of my presentation. I would like to think that I, the supposed reactionary, am far more radical and far more revolutionary than those who in their words proclaim themselves so radical today.

I too am certain that the European crisis has its roots in a misguided rationalism. But we must not take this to mean that rationality as such is evil or that it is of only subordinate significance for mankind's existence as a whole. Rationality, in that high and genuine sense of which alone we are speaking, the primordial Greek sense which in the classical period of Greek philosophy had become an ideal, still requires, to be sure, much clarification through self-reflection; but it is called in its mature form to guide [our] development. On the other hand we readily admit (and German Idealism preceded us long ago in this insight) that the stage of development of *ratio* represented by the rationalism of the Age of Enlightenment was a mistake, though certainly an understandable one.

Reason is a broad title. According to the old familiar definition, man is the rational animal, and in this broad sense even the Papuan is a man and not a beast. He has his ends and he acts reflectively, considering the practical possibilities. The works and methods that grow [out of this] go to make up a tradition, being understandable again [by others] in virtue of their rationality. But just as man and even the Papuan represent a new stage of animal nature, i.e., as opposed to the beast, so philosophical reason represents a new stage of human nature and its reason. But the stage of human existence [under] [13] ideal norms for infinite tasks, the stage of existence *sub specie aeterni*, is possible only through absolute universality, precisely the universality contained from the start in the idea of philosophy. True— universal philosophy, together with all the special sciences, makes up only a partial manifestation of European culture. Inherent in the sense of my whole presentation, however, is that this part is the functioning brain, so to speak, on whose normal

13. Reading *unter* for *und der*.

function the genuine, healthy European spiritual life depends. The humanity of higher human nature or reason requires, then, a genuine philosophy.

But now this is the danger point: "philosophy"; here we must certainly distinguish between philosophy as a historical fact at a given time and philosophy as idea, as the idea of an infinite task. Any philosophy that exists at a given historical time is a more or less successful attempt to realize the guiding idea of the infinity and at the same time even the totality of truths. Practical ideals —namely, ideals discerned as eternal poles of which one cannot lose sight throughout one's whole life without compunction, without being untrue to oneself and thus becoming unhappy— are by no means always clearly and determinately discerned; they are anticipated in ambiguous generality. Determinateness results only when one concretely sets to work and succeeds, at least in a relative way. There is the constant threat of succumbing to one-sidedness and to premature satisfaction, which take their revenge in subsequent contradictions. Hence the contrast between the great [common] claims of the philosophical systems [and the fact that] they are nevertheless incompatible with one another. Also, there is the necessity—and at the same time the danger—of specialization.

In this way, a one-sided rationality can certainly become an evil. One can also say: it belongs to the essence of reason that the philosophers at first understand and labor at their task in an absolutely necessary one-sided way. Actually there is nothing perverse in this; it is not an error; rather, as we said, the straight and necessary path they must take allows them to see only one side of the task, at first without noticing that the whole infinite task of theoretically knowing the totality of what is has other sides as well. If inadequacy announces itself through obscurities and contradictions, this motivates the beginning of a universal reflection. Thus the philosopher must always devote himself to mastering the true and full sense of philosophy, the totality of its horizons of infinity. No line of knowledge, no single truth may be absolutized and isolated. Only through this highest form of self-consciousness, which itself becomes one of the branches of the infinite task, can philosophy fulfill its function of putting itself, and thereby a genuine humanity, on the road [to realization]. [The awareness] that this is the case itself belongs to the domain of philosophical knowledge at the level of highest self-reflection. Only through this constant reflexivity is a philosophy universal knowledge.

I said that the way of philosophy passes through naïveté. This is the place for the criticism offered by the irrationalism that is so highly esteemed [today], or rather the place to unmask the naïveté of that rationalism which is taken for philosophical rationality as such, which is admittedly characteristic of the philosophy of the whole modern period since the Renaissance and which takes itself to be the true, i.e., universal, rationalism. In this naïveté, then, unavoidable as a beginning stage, are caught all the sciences whose beginnings were already developed in antiquity. To put it more precisely, the most general title for this naïveté is *objectivism*, taking the form of the various types of naturalism, of the naturalization of the spirit. Old and new philosophies were and remain naïvely objectivist. In fairness we must add, though, that the German Idealism proceeding from Kant was passionately concerned with overcoming this naïveté, which had already become very troublesome, though it was unable to attain the higher stage of reflexivity which is decisive for the new form of philosophy and of European humanity.

I can make what has been said understandable only in rough outlines. Natural man (let us consider him as man in the prephilosophical period) is directed toward the world in all his concerns and activities. The field of his life and his work is the surrounding world spread out spatiotemporally around him, of which he counts himself a part. This remains the case [even] in the theoretical attitude, which at first can be nothing other than that of the nonparticipating spectator of the world, whereby the world loses its mythical character. Philosophy sees in the world the universe of what is, and the world becomes the objective world as opposed to representations of the world, those which vary according to nation or individual subject; thus truth becomes objective truth. In this way philosophy begins as cosmology; it is first—as it were, obviously—directed in its theoretical interest toward corporeal nature, since, after all, everything given in space-time has in any case, at least at its basis, the existential formula of corporeity. Men and animals are not merely bodies, but in the orientation toward the surrounding world they appear as something with bodily existence and thus as realities ordered within universal space-time. In this sense all psychic occurrences, those of the particular ego, such as experiencing, thinking, willing, have a certain objectivity. The life of the community, that of families, peoples, etc., then seems to be resolved into that of particular individuals as psychophysical objects; the spiritual interrelation of psychophysical causality lacks a purely spiritual continuity; physical nature is everywhere involved.

The historical course of development is prefigured in a determined way by this attitude toward the surrounding world. Even the most fleeting glance at the corporeity to be found in the surrounding world shows that nature is a homogeneous, totally interrelated whole, a world by itself, so to speak, encompassed by homogeneous space-time, divided into particular things, all being alike as *res extensae* and determining one another causally. Quite rapidly, a first and great step of discovery is taken, namely, the overcoming of the finitude of nature already conceived as an objective in-itself, a finitude in spite of its open endlessness. Infinity is discovered, first in the form of the idealization of magnitudes, of measures, of numbers, figures, straight lines, poles, surfaces, etc. Nature, space, time, become extendable *idealiter* to infinity and divisible *idealiter* to infinity. From the art of surveying comes geometry, from the art of numbers arithmetic, from everyday mechanics mathematical mechanics, etc. Now without its being advanced explicitly as a hypothesis, intuitively given nature and world are transformed into a mathematical world, the world of the mathematical natural sciences. Antiquity led the way: in its mathematics was accomplished the first discovery of both infinite ideals and infinite tasks. This becomes for all later times the guiding star of the sciences.

What effect did the intoxicating success of this discovery of physical infinity have on the scientific mastery of the spiritual sphere? In the attitude directed toward the surrounding world, the constantly objectivistic attitude, everything spiritual appeared as if it were [simply] spread over [the surface of] physical bodies.[14] Thus the application [to it] of the natural-scientific way of thinking seemed the obvious thing to do. Hence we find at the very beginnings [of philosophy] the materialism and determinism of Democritus. But the greatest spirits have recoiled from this and also from any sort of psychophysics in the more modern style. Since Socrates, man has become a theme in his specifically human qualities, as a person, man within the spiritual life of the community. Man still has a place within the order of the objective world; but for Plato and Aristotle this world becomes a great theme [in its own right]. Here a remarkable split makes itself felt; the human belongs to the sphere of objective facts, but as persons, as egos, men have goals, ends, norms given by the

14. *wie der physischen Körperlichkeit auferlegt.*

tradition, norms of truth—eternal norms. Though the development weakened in antiquity, it was nevertheless not lost. Let us make the leap to the so-called modern period. With a burning enthusiasm the infinite task of a mathematical knowledge of nature and of knowledge of the world in general is taken up. The immense successes in the knowledge of nature are now supposed to be shared by the knowledge of the spirit. Reason has demonstrated its force in relation to nature. "Just as the sun is the one all-illuminating and warming sun, so reason is also the one reason" (Descartes). The method of natural science must also disclose the secrets of the spirit. The spirit is real, objectively in the world, and is founded as such on the living body. Thus the world-view immediately and dominantly assumes the form of a dualistic, and specifically a psychophysical, world-view. One causality, simply split into two sectors, encompasses the one world; the sense of rational explanation is everywhere the same, yet in such a way that all explanation of the spirit, if it is to be the sole and thus universal philosophical explanation, leads back to the physical. There can be no pure and self-enclosed explanatory inquiry into the spirit, a psychology or theory of spirit turned inward, extending from the ego, the psychic sphere of self-experience, to the alien psyche; the external path, the path of physics and chemistry, must be taken. All the beloved expressions about the community spirit, the will of the people, the ideal and political goals of nations, etc., are so much romanticism and mythology, arising out of a transposition by analogy of concepts that have a genuine meaning only in the sphere of individual persons. Spiritual being is fragmentary. To the question concerning the source of all our difficulties we must now reply: this objectivism, or this psychophysical world-view, in spite of its apparent obviousness, is naïvely one-sided and has constantly failed to be understood as such. The reality of the spirit as a supposed real annex to bodies, its supposed spatiotemporal being within nature, is an absurdity.

What we must do, however, in connection with our problem of the crisis, is to show how it happens that the "modern age," which has been so proud for centuries of its theoretical and practical successes, finally becomes involved in a growing dissatisfaction, indeed must view its situation as one of distress. In all the sciences distress is felt, ultimately as a distress concerning method. But our European distress, though it is not understood, concerns very many people.

These are, throughout, problems which arise from the naïveté through which objectivist science takes what it calls the objective world for the universe of all that is, without noticing that no objective science can do justice to the [very] subjectivity which accomplishes science. Someone who is raised on natural science takes it for granted that everything merely subjective must be excluded and that the natural-scientific method, exhibiting itself in subjective manners of representation, determines objectively. Thus he seeks what is objectively true even for the psychic. Here it is immediately assumed that the subjective that has been excluded by the physicist is to be investigated as the psychic in psychology, and then naturally in psychophysical psychology. But the researcher of nature does not make clear to himself that the constant fundament of his—after all subjective —work of thought is the surrounding life-world; it is always presupposed as the ground, as the field of work upon which alone his questions, his methods of thought, make sense. Where is that huge piece of method subjected to critique and clarification [—that method] that leads from the intuitively given surrounding world to the idealization of mathematics and to the interpretation of these idealizations as objective being? Einstein's revolutionary innovations concern the formulae through which the idealized and naïvely objectified *physis* is dealt with. But how formulae in general, how mathematical objectification in general, receive meaning on the foundation of life and the intuitively given surrounding world—of this we learn nothing; and thus Einstein does not reform the space and time in which our vital life runs its course.

Mathematical natural science is a wonderful technique for making inductions with an efficiency, a degree of probability, a precision, and a computability that were simply unimaginable in earlier times. As an accomplishment it is a triumph of the human spirit. As for the rationality of its methods and theories, however, it is a thoroughly relative one. It even presupposes a fundamental approach that is itself totally lacking in rationality. Since the intuitively given surrounding world, this merely subjective realm, is forgotten in scientific investigation, the working subject is himself forgotten; the scientist does not become a subject of investigation. (Accordingly, from this standpoint, the rationality of the exact sciences is of a piece with the rationality of the Egyptian pyramids.)

To be sure, since Kant we have an epistemology in its own right, and on the other hand there is psychology, which, with its claims to natural-scientific exactness, seeks to be the universal fundamental science of the spirit. But our hope for true rationality, i.e., for true insight, is disappointed here as elsewhere. The psychologists do not notice at all that even they do not approach, in their subject matter, themselves as accomplishing scientists and their surrounding life-world. They do not notice that they necessarily presuppose themselves in advance as communalized men in their surrounding world and their historical time, even by the very fact that they seek to attain truth-in-itself, as truth valid for anyone at all. Because of its objectivism psychology is completely unable to obtain as its subject matter the soul in its own essential sense, which is, after all, the ego that acts and suffers. It may objectify and deal inductively with valuative experience, willing experience, as connected with bodily life. But can it do this with ends, values, norms? Can it take reason as its subject matter, perhaps as a "disposition"? What is completely overlooked is the fact that objectivism, as the genuine accomplishment of an investigator oriented toward true norms, presupposes precisely those norms and that objectivism thus is not meant to be based on facts, since facts are thereby already meant as truths rather than mere opinion. Of course, some sense the difficulties involved here; and so the battle over psychologism breaks out. But the repudiation of a psychological grounding of norms, especially of norms for truth-in-itself, accomplishes nothing. The need for a reform of the whole of modern psychology is felt more and more on all sides, but it is not yet understood that it has failed because of its objectivism, that it does not at all attain the proper essence of the spirit, that its isolation of the objectively conceived soul and its psychophysical reinterpretation of being-in-community are a mistake. To be sure, it has not been without results, and it has revealed many, even practically valuable, empirical rules. But it is not a true psychology, any more than statistics about morals, with their no less valuable knowledge, constitute a moral science.

But everywhere, in our time, the burning need for an understanding of the spirit announces itself; and lack of clarity about the methodical and material relation between the natural sciences and the humanistic disciplines has become almost unbearable. Dilthey, one of the greatest humanists, devoted the energies of his whole life to a clarification of the relation between nature and spirit, to a clarification of the accomplishment of psychophysical psychology, which, as he thought, needed to be complemented by a new descriptive, classifying psychology. Efforts by Windelband and Rickert have unfortunately not produced the desired insights. Like all the others, they remain caught up in objectivism; and this is especially true of the new reformers in psychology, who think that the fault lies entirely in the long-dominant prejudice of atomism and that a new era has dawned with holistic psychology.[15] But the situation can never improve so long as the objectivism arising out of a natural attitude toward the surrounding world is not seen through in its naïveté and so long as the recognition has not emerged that the dualistic view of the world, in which nature and spirit are to count as realities in a similar sense, though one is built on the other causally, is a mistake. In all seriousness, I think that an objective science of the spirit, an objective theory of the soul— objective in the sense that it attributes to souls, to personal communities, inexistence in the forms of space-time—has never existed and will never exist.

The spirit, and indeed only the spirit, exists in itself and for itself, is self-sufficient; and in its self-sufficiency, and only in this way, it can be treated truly rationally, truly and from the ground up scientifically. As for nature, however, in its natural-scientific truth, it is only apparently self-sufficient and can only apparently be brought by itself to rational knowledge in the natural sciences. For true nature in the sense of natural science is a product of the spirit that investigates nature and thus presupposes the science of the spirit. The spirit is by its essence capable of practicing self-knowledge, and as scientific spirit it is capable of practicing scientific self-knowledge, and this in an iterative way. Only in the knowledge belonging purely to the science of the spirit is the scientist not open to the objection that his own accomplishment conceals itself. Accordingly, it is a mistake for the humanistic disciplines to struggle with the natural sciences for equal rights. As soon as they concede to the latter their objectivity as self-sufficiency, they themselves fall prey to objectivism. But as they are now developed in their manifold disciplines, they lack the ultimate, true rationality made possible by the spiritual world-view. Precisely this lack of a genuine rationality on all sides is the source of man's now unbearable lack of clarity about his own existence and his infinite tasks. These are inseparably united in one task: *Only when the spirit returns from its naïve external orientation to itself, and remains with itself and purely with itself, can it be sufficient unto itself.*

But how did a beginning of such self-reflection occur? A

15. *Ganzheitspsychologie,* i.e., Gestalt psychology.

beginning was not possible so long as sensationalism, or better, data-psychologism, the psychology of the *tabula rasa,* commanded the field. Only when Brentano made the demand for psychology as a science of intentional experiences was an impulse given that could lead further, although Brentano himself had not yet overcome objectivism and psychological naturalism. The development of an actual method for grasping the fundamental essence of the spirit in its intentionalities, and for constructing from there an analysis of the spirit that is consistent *in infinitum,* led to transcendental phenomenology. It overcomes naturalistic objectivism and every sort of objectivism in the only possible way, namely, through the fact that he who philosophizes proceeds from his own ego, and this purely as the performer of all his validities, of which he becomes the purely theoretical spectator. In this attitude it is possible to construct an absolutely self-sufficient science of the spirit in the form of consistently coming to terms with oneself and with the world as spiritual accomplishment. Here the spirit is not in or alongside nature; rather, nature is itself drawn into the spiritual sphere. Also, the ego is then no longer an isolated thing alongside other such things in a pregiven world; in general, the serious mutual exteriority of ego-persons, their being alongside one another, ceases in favor of an inward being-for-one-another and mutual interpenetration.

But of all this we cannot speak here; no lecture could exhaust it. I hope to have shown, however, that the old rationalism, which was an absurd naturalism incapable of grasping at all the spiritual problems that immediately concern us, is not being revived here. The *ratio* presently under discussion is nothing other than the spirit's truly universal and truly radical coming to terms with itself in the form of universal, responsible science, in which a completely new mode of scientific discipline is set in motion where all conceivable questions—questions of being and questions of norm, questions of what is called "existence" [*Existenz*]—find their place. It is my conviction that intentional phenomenology has made of the spirit *qua* spirit for the first time a field of systematic experience and science and has thus brought about the total reorientation of the task of knowledge. The universality of the absolute spirit surrounds everything that exists with an absolute historicity, to which nature is subordinated as a spiritual structure. Intentional phenomenology, and specifically transcendental phenomenology, was first to see the light through its point of departure and its methods. Only through it do we understand, and from the most profound reasons, what naturalistic objectivism is and understand in particular that psychology, because of its naturalism, had to miss entirely the accomplishment, the radical and genuine problem, of the life of the spirit.

III

LET US CONDENSE the fundamental notions presented here. The "crisis of European existence," talked about so much today and documented in innumerable symptoms of the breakdown of life, is not an obscure fate, an impenetrable destiny; rather, it becomes understandable and transparent against the background of the *teleology of European history* that can be discovered philosophically. The condition for this understanding, however, is that the phenomenon "Europe" be grasped in its central, essential nucleus. In order to be able to comprehend the disarray of the present "crisis," we had to work out the *concept of Europe as the historical teleology of the infinite goals of reason;* we had to show how the European "world" was born out of ideas of reason, i.e., out of the spirit of philosophy. The "crisis" could then become distinguishable as the *apparent failure of rationalism*. The reason for the failure of a rational culture, however, as we said, lies not in the essence of rationalism itself but solely in its being rendered superficial, in its entanglement in "naturalism" and "objectivism."

There are only two escapes from the crisis of European existence: the downfall of Europe in its estrangement from its own rational sense of life, its fall into hostility toward the spirit and into barbarity; or the rebirth of Europe from the spirit of philosophy through a heroism of reason that overcomes naturalism once and for all. Europe's greatest danger is weariness. If we struggle against this greatest of all dangers as "good Europeans" with the sort of courage that does not fear even an infinite struggle, then out of the destructive blaze of lack of faith, the smoldering fire of despair over the West's mission for humanity, the ashes of great weariness, will rise up the phoenix of a new life-inwardness and spiritualization as the pledge of a great and distant future for man: for the spirit alone is immortal.

B.

Appendix II:
Idealization and the Science of Reality—
The Mathematization of Nature[1]

SCIENCE HAS ITS ORIGIN in Greek philosophy with the discovery of the idea and of the exact science which determines by means of ideas. It leads to the development of pure mathematics as pure science of ideas, science of possible objects in general as objects determined by ideas. Science is confronted with the problem of that which is, as the real which exists in itself, existing in itself over against the multiplicity of subjective manners of givenness belonging to the particular knowing subject; [it is confronted with] the question concerning the flux of being in becoming and concerning the conditions of the possibility of the identity of being in becoming, of the identical determinability of an existing real [entity] as the determinability of intuitively given continuity through the mathematization of continua. But this must be independent of accidental subjectivity, and this means, first of all, independent of the accidental character of the particular sensibility [which apprehends it].

Confronted with the task of resolving these questions, the

1. Biemel's note: "Before 1928." This text is found in the German edition as the first "Abhandlung," pp. 279–93 (see Translator's Introduction, pp. xx f.). Its date marks it as an early attempt to work out some of the ideas found in the the *Crisis*. Also, it represents a link between that work and themes in *Formal und transzendentale Logik*.

process leads to the *development of the logic of being as the logic of reality,* and first of all of natural reality, and to the development of apophantic logic as the formal logic of predicative determination.

As for the latter, it deals with entities in general as identical substrates of identical determinations; furthermore, it has to do with the multiplicity of forms of judgment, with the forms of substrates as determined, with the forms of determining predicates, and with the possibilities of hypothetical, disjunctive manners of determination, the modal variations, etc., which belong to determination. Something identical is the correlate of [the act of] identifying; to determine is to judge, and something determined is as such the correlate of [the act of] judging.

To this belong also the norms for possible judgments which are capable of being truths, as norms for possible ways of inferential derivation, of the deduction of truths out of truths (the mediate production of truths), or the attainment of hypothetical truths from hypothetical stipulations (stipulated truths, hypotheses); further, there is the consideration of the forms of thought, the forms of possible productions in thought, of the possible forms of the ways of production, or of the thoughts derived from deductive productions, and the critique of thoughts according to the possible forms of true thoughts; also, there is the problem of the identity of the "object," the "meant" [*das Vermeinte*], being carried over into self-evidence. And through self-evidence, the necessities belonging to the possible maintenance of identity become generally known; while that which is identical undergoes only those variations which maintain its identity. Here one is led to an identity of the forms of thought which run through all determinations and which do not break the identity of the determined objects.

Against the first seeds of the development of science there arose the skeptical critique of science and of all practical norms which lay claim to objective validity. The Socratic return to self-evidence represents a reaction; and specifically this is making clear to oneself, by means of example, the fields of pure possibilities, the free variation which upholds the identity of meaning, identity of the object as substrate of determination, and makes it possible to discern this identity. Over against these alterations are others which break the identity. The variations are accomplished in the transition to the pure "in general," to the general forms of possibilities and the essential possibilities and essential impossibilities belonging to them. There arise norm-concepts of the good, the beautiful, the truly good statesman, the genuine judge, true honor, true courage and justice, and the fundamental concepts of criticism itself: just, unjust, true, false, etc.

Thus skepticism forces the critique of the skeptical critique, and since this critique concerns the possibility of truth and of knowable being in general, it forces a radical consideration of the conditions of possible truth and possible being; and it forces the recognition that not vague thinking and talking but only radical thinking, aimed at the ultimate showing of possible being, carried out in self-evidence, [indeed] only self-evidence itself, can help in assuring ourselves of truth and being. I must not talk vaguely on, must not follow vague traditional concepts or the sediments of passively accumulated experiential residues, analogies, etc.; rather, I must create my concepts anew in autonomous thinking through pure intuition; then I shall attain truths which are destined to be norms. Every truth derived from pure self-evidence is a genuine truth and is a norm. On the other hand, it does not need to contain any normative concepts within itself, i.e., none of the variational forms of "genuine," "correct"; these themselves, when grasped conceptually, result in concepts and predications about genuineness, truth; such predications must themselves be derived from self-evidence—they must [be shown to] be true, and they can be false.[2]

Science is not naïve knowledge in the theoretical interest; rather, to its essence there belongs from now on a certain critique—a critique based on principle, a critique which justifies every step of the knowing activity through "principles," which at every step involves the consciousness that any step of such a form is necessarily a correct one, that in this way the path of cognitive grounding, of the progress of that which grounds and that which is grounded upon it, is a correct path aimed at the goal, so that [the resulting] knowledge is a genuine knowledge and that the being known is not merely supposed [*vermeintes*] but known in the pregnant sense, true being itself, exhibiting its legitimacy in the knowledge itself. Now this is true first of all of present [*aktuelle*] knowledge in its progress through thoroughgoing self-evidence. But science makes use of the cognitive results of earlier knowledge. The norm-consciousness involved in such

---

2. This harks back to the *Logische Untersuchungen* (Vol. I: *Prolegomena zu reinen Logik,* Chapter II), in which the dependence of normative disciplines on theoretical disciplines is demonstrated.

knowledge implies [a present] consciousness referring back to [such] earlier groundings [and having] the real capacity to reestablish the [earlier] grounding, to trace the [present] conviction of its legitimacy back to its origin, and to justify it anew.

What has antiquity offered us here? What path has it thus opened up? [It has offered] in part seminal beginnings and impulses, in part fragments of science actually set upon its way.

The path that it indicates is that of the development of the principle of self-evidence which is general and based on principle:

Singular experience, experience of individual existence, results in no assertion that can be justified objectively. But then how can singular judgments of fact be valid at all? How can the *experienced* world even be in truth? Being reveals itself to be an ideal pole for "infinities" of presumptive self-evidences with self-evidently given sense-adumbrations ("sides," appearances) through which the same being is adumbrated in self-evident manner but is [merely] presumptive in every finite series [of adumbrations]—though this is a legitimate presumption.* Real truth is the correlate of real being, and just as real being is an infinitely distant idea, the idea of a pole for systematic infinities of appearances, of "experiences" in constantly legitimate presumption, so real truth is an infinitely distant idea, [that of] what is identical in the agreement of experiential judgments, in each of which truth "appears," achieves legitimate subjective givenness. The infinitely distant idea is determinable a priori in the pure form of generality which contains all possibilities, and in accord with this form one can construct, out of the finitely closed total experience (that is, out of its relatively "closed-off appearance," out of the realm of determined sensible things, out of the sensible experiential predicates) an anticipation of an appropriate idea required by this experience and implied in it.

Included in the form of the idea of something real are one-sided, partial ideas, just as, in the full truth which determines the entity (the totality of the predicates belonging to it which determine it as itself), there is a multiplicity of individual predicable determinations, of individual truths which leave the being still undetermined in other directions. Insofar as every

* But here it is always merely nature which is in view, and an idea of reality is thereby presupposed for the world, whose correlate is the idea of a truth-in-itself, the idea of a mathematically constructible truth, even though it is [given only] in any number of approximations.

experience can a priori contain elements of discrepancy which will be separated out in further experience and its synthesis, the idea-determination which is to be gained from it is capable of being not only one-sided but also in part false, though required, for the sake of truth, by this experience up to now.[3] To the idea of the real [entity] itself, and to the idea as a pure form, there belongs correlatively an infinite system of experiences which set up a system of pure harmony (through the continued exclusion of what is experienced as discrepant and the adoption of what agrees) and which characterize themselves *as* [possible] experiences.[4] And then there belongs a priori to every experience, or every appropriately delimited experience, an idea which is proper to it but which is never the last idea but rather a starting point, in a certain way a representation of the infinitely distant and unattainable idea, of which only the form, as an absolute norm for the construction of all starting points, is given.

To make all these things clear and to outline a priori the form of a possible determination of what is in itself true of nature, a determination which is relatively true and relatively necessary for every stage of experience—this is the theory of natural science; as method: the theory of natural-scientific method. Yet a twofold distinction must be made:

1. Ontology of nature "in itself": what is necessary for a nature in general, the necessary form, the ideal essence, of a nature and the necessary forms of determinations of every individual which *idealiter* and "in itself" can belong to nature. Such considerations of the *pure idea* are accomplished by the sciences of the pure mathematics of nature.

2. A priori methodology of a possible knowledge of nature in itself, through truths in themselves: if, instead of pure nature as an idea (as a mathematical, supersensible idea), we think of a *nature as experienced* by experiencing beings, or, if we take a mathematical nature as an ideal in-itself belonging to nature-experiences (ontically: sensibly intuited natures),[5] then we have *another pure idea.* We attain then a science of the possibility of knowledge of a nature in itself through nature-experience, and this is the a priori science of the possibility of a mathematical

3. I.e., a given experience (e.g., illusory experience) may now require a certain determination of the object which is later excluded.
4. Reading *Erfahrungen* for *Erfahrenes.* Husserl crossed out *-renes* from the latter; and if we assume he meant to write *Erfahrungen,* the clause makes more sense.
5. I.e., views of nature as given in sense-intuition.

natural science, or the science of the method of natural-scientific determination of nature through the data of experience.

In a more limited sense: we allow only "normal experience" to count as experience, normal sensibility in relation to normal "understanding." How can mathematical, true nature be determined through normal appearances? This occurs through the methods of rendering the continua exact, through the transformation of sensible causalities into mathematical causalities, etc. Only then must one take the psychophysically abnormal into account.[6]

But can one really distinguish in this way between an a priori *ontology of nature* and an a priori *methodology* of a possible determination of a nature in itself through the experiences of it? How do I, the knower, attain the a priori ontological knowledge of nature? I live then in possible experiences, in possible perceptions and possible perceptual judgments. What belongs to the identical itself, throughout all the alteration of the sensible manners of appearance, when it is precisely the latter which, whatever else they may do, are supposed to be able to go together into identity-agreement and to make identical determinations possible?

Not every *change* in the sensible stock of characteristics disturbs identity, and not every one maintains it under the title of a "change in the object." Anomalous changes of appearance are not apperceived or need not be apperceived as "changes [in the object]." If they are so apperceived, they are later suspended under the title of "illusions." If I am living in experience (in its apperceptions, through which I have experience as [being that of] sensibly intuited reality), and if I hold the lines of agreement secure, all anomalies are separated out, and every intuitively given change is a real change [7] *for me* in the framework of the synthesis of my own experiences. If I now enter into relation with *another*, I may find that he (in his normality—but he is color-blind) differs from me in his judgments about samenesses, differences, etc., while we are experiencing the same thing. (He can also have a finer sense than I—he has good eyes, I bad, etc. —and the relation changes with each different human being.) Here, in terms of possibility, very many and, ideally, infinitely many differences—and also contradictions—are open. What can help us here?

6. I.e., illusions, etc., caused by psychophysical occurrences involving the perceiver.

7. *reale Veränderung*, i.e., a change in the object.

If we look to developed natural science, the answer is: Every sensible difference experienced by the single subject is an index of a true difference, and what is true is determined by measurement in the sphere of the κοινά. Hand in hand with the qualitative differences, in a certain rough way, go quantitative differences. In the quantitative sphere, in the realm of extension, everything true expresses itself.

On the other hand, not everything that can be established quantitatively, by way of magnitudes and dependencies of magnitudes, is "noticeable" to me or to anyone in the same way. Through measuring methods, I can convince myself that certain quantitative relations and laws are valid, relations and laws that I know about as persistently obtaining and as valid only through the method, whereas before using the method I am dependent upon sensibility and "perceptual judgments."

Could natural science arrive at such a view any other way than through general reflections about a method—reflections about how, in the face of the relativity of the appearances, something true which appears in them is to be determined, and first of all through reflections about how, in the alteration of the appearances, true being is able to announce itself, manifest itself? But clearly such reflections, carried out purely eidetically, lead to an ontology of nature.

Thus we can also say: *How could I arrive at an a priori ontology* other than by rendering self-evident [the following]:

1. If I have nature as harmoniously experienced, and if I remain within the framework of this harmony and specifically within the framework of certain harmoniously experienced things or processes; and if in any number of other cases I have experienced the same things, etc., or if another has experienced them (as I become convinced through understanding [8] him): the possibility of the knowledge of the same [thing or process] through the experiences on the two sides necessarily presupposes the *res extensa*, the spatiotemporal *skeleton* of the qualities perceived on the two sides, the identity of the shape-distribution through communal time, identity of the temporal sequences and thus also of the causal dependency of the corresponding configurations. By contrast, the alteration of the qualities perceived and of the judgments about these qualities is "accidental." In this sense, that is, even if contradictions arise from them, they do not damage the identity. (Even in solitary experience, the identity of

8. *Einverständnis,* here, rather than the usual term, *Einfühlung.*

what is experienced in different modalities of sense is necessarily the identity of the "spatiotemporal" skeleton. It is the latter that is necessarily identical, a necessarily identical content of determination throughout all differences of sensible "manner of appearance.") The first separating-out of what essentially—i.e., of necessity—belongs to the identical [object] leads to geometry, phoronomy, and could also have led to a priori mechanics, to disciplines of the possible forms of functional dependences among changes or to a discipline of the forms of possible quantitative causality and its possible causal laws. The real is in itself determined if it is lawfully fixed not only in respect to its geometrical form but also in respect to its possible changes in form. Something real has real properties, its empirically causal properties. In order to be identical in itself, it must have empirically knowable quantitative-causal properties.

Thus, the new natural science is distinguished by the fact that it first of all elevated to the central point of concern what is in a determined sense necessary by contrast to the alteration of (legitimate) sensible appearance, and [it] recognized that quantitative causal laws belong to this necessary element.

A *second* element [in the development of an a priori ontology] was made up of such observations as: I hear a tone and see a vibrating motion [of a string], and the tone is qualitatively the same, independently of color, of the sensibly qualitative, but it is dependent on the strength of tension, the thickness [of the string]—and the latter are all measurable factors. The quantitative is not merely [what is found] in the appearing extensional processes [as such]; the quantitative is also something indicated by what is merely qualitative. And it is possible that the quantitative [in the latter sense] be subsequently exhibited sensibly through sensible manners of appearance (somehow "clothed" qualitatively).

Conversely: every qualitative change, every qualitative being-such [*Sosein*], should, if the quality belongs to a normal appearance, be a property of the real itself. But quality (secondary quality) cannot belong to the object in itself; possibly it is a subjectively altering quality, [differing among] subjects, each of whom, for himself, experiences harmoniously the reality in question. If every experienced quality shall have its right to objectivity, this is possible only if it is an index for something mathematical and indicates the mathematical for one person as well as another only in differing degrees of perfection: methodically, everyone must be able to attain the quantitative on the basis of the indications, perhaps with the help of another; whereas he can determine the qualitative himself. Thus every "in-itself" is a mathematical in-itself, and all causal laws must be mathematical laws. Real properties are causal properties which are determined on the basis of causal laws.

Yet we would have to make a twofold distinction here:

1. The recognition, discussed in detail above, that in harmonious experience (as sensible manner of appearance) one must distinguish between the accidental and the necessary, i.e., between primary characteristics, which necessarily run through all sensible experience, and the specifically sensible, the secondary characteristics; the recognition, that is, that the "common" sense-characteristics are not accidentally but necessarily common.

2. The perceived, the experienced as such, is thoroughly "vague"; it always stands, taken in harmonious experience, under the essential law of a certain gradation of perfection which always exists as an ideal possibility. Accordingly I can have the same characteristic given more or less "clearly"; and, no matter how clear it is, yet another gradation is still thinkable. It is always thinkable that what I clearly find to be undifferentiated will, given greater clarity, exhibit differentiations, both for me and intersubjectively. Belonging correlatively to the differentiations of perfection are free "can"-possibilities of approximation to the absolutely perfect, the true self [of the object]—though, to be sure, the latter is forever receding. Our talk of the "manners of appearance" of the same thing also applies thus in respect to the graduality of clarity. But behind this lies the idea of an identical self, the in-itself. The true characteristics are the limit-points of possible gradation. But since only mathematical characteristics are "true" ones, the true mathematical characteristics are mathematical limits.

Explicated more distinctly: in the continuing synthesis of experience the primary as well as the secondary characteristics have their differentiations of perfection. Corresponding to this in the case of the primary characteristics is the graduality of the perfection of measurement and of approximation through measurement, and what proceeds from this, or is carried out in connection with it, namely, quantification through geometrical and similar concepts. This leads to the limit-idealization of the exact mathematics of nature with its determinations of thought. Whereas the primary characteristics are intersubjective as long as harmonious identification can take place at all, and have only [the above-mentioned] relativity of perfection and approximation (and also the relativity of interreal causality),[9] the secondary characteristics are relative in another way, namely, relative to the normality and abnormality of experience and thus "accidentally" to the subjects, and can change with the subjects.* In addition, the perfection-limit of the secondary qualities is not measurable; it is only "intuitable." But it is intersubjectively determined and determinable through relation to the mathematical limits of the primary characteristics.

3. To determine is to predicate; to determine originally and self-evidently is to form perceptual judgments, and to determine mediately is to form empirically general judgments (inductive, experiential judgments) and empirically causal judgments, etc. Determininative thinking, judging, inferring, generalizing, particularizing, which are accomplished in the actual sphere of experience, take the appearing things, characteristics, regularities as the true ones; but this truth is a relative and "subjectively conditioned" truth. A *new sort of thinking,* or a peculiar *method,* is required in order to relate what results here (which suffices for lower-level practical ends) to its "objectivity," † to extract from it, by technique, truth in itself and true reality in itself. The consideration of the conditions in principle of the possibility of something identical that gives itself (harmoniously) in flowing and subjectively changing manners of appearance ‡ leads to the mathematization of the appearances as a necessity which is immanent in them, or to the necessity of a constructive method, in order to construct out of the appearances the identical and its identical determinations. §

But can appearances of different senses contain something identical? And in what sense can they? Manifolds of appearances which harmoniously belong together and which constitute something identical must correspond to the conditions of the possibility of the identical (true) object [*Gegenständlichkeit*], and all the laws of mathematics as applied to the real [*reale Mathematik*] must be particularizations of the laws of formal

* We have two kinds of normality: (1) The presupposition of comunication, [i.e., that there is a] communal nature, and the necessary here is the quantitative; (2) as opposed to this, the accidental— that is, agreement on secondary qualities is "accidental."

† This objectivity is the idea of a "nonrelative" truth in itself.

‡ But also which in principle gives itself only in this way.

§ This identical is necessarily a substruction.

9. I.e., they are "relative" to (dependent on) their real causal circumstances.

ontology, of formal mathematics (theory of manifolds). They are particularizations because formal mathematics teaches us how to construct and constructively determine the infinitely many forms, indeed all possible forms of objects and infinities of objects; and every given system of appearances, every unity of experiences, outlines an objective totality or nature: in respect to its form.

In ancient philosophy the focus of interest is first of all upon the compelling necessity of reason, whose denial is absurdity. This necessity first entered the scene purely in the mathematical sphere as geometrical and arithmetical necessity. In this sphere of magnitudes, and initially of spatial magnitudes—first of all in classes of privileged cases (straight lines, limited plane figures, and the corresponding cases of spatial magnitudes), first of all in the empirical intuition that magnitudes divide into equal parts and are composed again of equal parts—or of aggregates [*Mengen*] of like elements which decompose into partial aggregates and can be expanded into new aggregates through the addition of elements or of aggregates of such elements—in this sphere, there arose the "exact" comparisons of magnitudes which led back to the comparison of numbers. Upon the vague "greater," "smaller," "more," "less," and the vague "equal" one could determinately superimpose the exact "so much" greater or less, or "how many times" greater or less, and the exact "equal." Every such exact consideration presupposed the possibility of stipulating an equality which excluded the greater and the smaller and of stipulating units of magnitude which were strictly substitutable for one another, were identical as magnitudes, i.e., which stood under an identical concept or essence of magnitude. Belonging to [the essence of] the spatial magnitudes, as objects of empirical intuition, is the fact that one can come nearer to them, can look at them with more "exactness." In practical life the "exact" is determined by the [particular] end in view; the "equal" is that which counts equally for this end, for which there can also be irrelevant differences which do not count. Here, with the exclusion of all practical limitation, the idea of the absolutely equal, the mathematically exactly equal, could be developed.

Here, then, first began the thought process of the idealizing development of concepts, that logicization which makes possible "rigorous" truths, logical truths, and makes it possible, in this logical sphere, to think with the rigorous necessity and universal validity which was able to mark every negation, and insightfully

so, with the sign of absurdity. The naturally developing significations of words are vague and flowing, such that it is not
determinately fixed what comes under the "concept," the general
sense. Logical signification is exact. The logically general, the
concept, is absolutely identical with itself, and subsumption is
absolutely unambiguous. But logical concepts are not concepts
taken from what is simply intuitive; they arise through a rational activity proper to them, the development of ideas, *exact*
development of concepts, e.g., through that sort of idealization
which produces, out of the empirically straight and curved, the
geometrical straight line and circle.

The practical needs of field-measurement force one at first
only vaguely, i.e., in the realm of the sensibly typical, to distinguish what typically counts as equal (for the particular practical
needs) from what typically counts as not equal. What counted
as being equal for certain sorts of practical ends was posited as
being equal, and differences of characteristics within the equality were "indifferent" differences, i.e., they were regarded as not
disturbing the equal validity and could be ignored. Thus it was
possible to establish measurement and calculation, to express
and even prove "geometrical" propositions—with certain reser-
vations, to be sure. For when a thousand "equal" lengths were
laid in a row, each of which differed from the following only by a
finger's breadth (an indifferent difference), the measurement
could give the result that 1000 yards = 1001. That is, different
measurements with the same standard could give different results, i.e., not indifferently different. It was only the conception
of pure mathematical "ideas" as ideal norms and the development of approximative methods of application that led to a pure
material mathematics[10] and a mathematical technique. It was of
the nature of spatial experience that one had to recognize, in
comparing things in experience, possible differences of perfection in equality: for example, what was seen from a certain
distance to be fully "equal" could be seen, when approached
more closely, to be different after all; what remained equal could
be looked at even more closely, etc.

Thus it was possible to conceive of processes converging
idealiter through which an absolute equal could be constructed
ideally as the limit of the constant approach to equality, provided
that one member [of the system] was thought of as absolutely
fixed, as absolutely identical with itself in magnitude. In this

10. *eine reine sachhaltige Mathematik.*

exact thinking with ideas one operated with ideal concepts of the unchanging, of rest, of lack of qualitative change, with ideal concepts of equality and of the general (magnitude, shape) that gives absolute equalities in any number of ideally unchanged and thus qualitatively identical instances; every change was constructed out of phases which were looked upon as momentary, exact, and unchanging, having exact magnitudes, etc.

Platonic idealism, through the fully conscious discovery of the "idea" and of approximation, opened up the path of logical thinking, "logical" science, rational science. Ideas were taken as archetypes, in which everything singular participates more or less "ideally," which everything approaches, which everything realizes more or less fully; the ideal truths belonging to the ideas were taken as the absolute norms for all empirical truths. If we designate as rationalism the conviction that all reasonable knowing must be rational [11]—whether purely rationally, in the thinking that investigates the essential relations between the purely rational concepts (or rather, the thinking that investigates, in terms of laws, everything that is possible, insofar as it stands under purely rational ideas, or is thought in an exactly determinate way) or else in such a way that it measures the empirical against the pure ideals through methods of approximation and other norms for judging the empirical according to corresponding pure ideas—then the whole modern conviction is rationalistic.

A true object in the sense of logic is an object which is absolutely identical "with itself," that is, which is, absolutely identically, what it is; or, to express it in another way: an object *is* through its determinations, its quiddities [*Washeiten*], its predicates, and it is identical if these quiddities are identical as belonging to it or when their belonging absolutely excludes their not belonging. But only ideals have a rigorous identity; the consequence would be that an individual is truly something identical—i.e., an entity—if it is the ideally identical substrate for general absolute ideas. But how can something individual participate in the general, not only approximately but exactly? How can the subsumption-relation be exact?

Purely mathematical thinking is related to possible objects which are thought determinately through ideal-"exact" mathematical (limit-) concepts, e.g., spatial shapes of natural objects which, as experienced, stand in a vague way under shape-con-

11. *dass alles vernünftige Erkennen rational sein muss.*

cepts and [thus] have their shape-determinations; but it is of the nature of these experiential data that one can and by rights must posit, beneath the identical object which exhibits itself in harmonious experience as existing, an ideally identical object which is ideal in all its determinations; all [its] determinations are exact —that is, whatever [instances] fall under their generality are equal—and this equality excludes inequality; or, what is the same thing, an exact determination, in belonging to an object, excludes the possibility that this determination not belong to the same object. And for every particular [kind of] determination, as delimited by the "general nature" of the object—within the [particular] domain, that is; e.g., spatial shape in the case of natural objects—one [such determination] belongs [to the object], and every other [such determination] does not belong. (Principle of the excluded middle.)

An object has spatial shape generally. Empirically experienced spatial shapes have their different empirical types. But it can happen that an object has a (lowest) type—that is, I experience that it has this particular shape—and that it does not have it—that is, I see upon further experience that it does not have it (without [its] having changed). (In the empirical sphere the principle of the excluded middle does not hold.) I can take no empirical determination as actually belonging to the object; I can only say that it is experienced under this determination. Even in thought I cannot hold fast to the determination in an absolutely identical way; I can never, in approaching the experienced object, say that the determination I experience now is absolutely the same as the one I have experienced.

But I can posit, beneath every spatial shape I experience, the idea of a pure spatial shape in which the seen shape "participates"; and spatial shape in general becomes an empirical genus which has behind it a pure genus of purely exact spatial shapes. Every empirical object is empirically shaped (is necessarily experienceable and is equipped in experience with an intuited shape), but it also has a true shape, the exact shape. Exact ideas of shapes are absolutely distinguished; if an object has a particularization of one [such shape], then every other, different one is excluded. Of two exact shapes (lowest differences of spatial shapes), to any object there belongs one and not the other. (Principle of the excluded middle.)

Appendix III:
The Attitude of Natural Science and the Attitude
of Humanistic Science. Naturalism, Dualism,
and Psychophysical Psychology[1]

NATURALISTIC ATTITUDE.* The world as the universe of realities in the form of mutual exteriority. Nature as the realm of the pure *res extensae*. Everything real is a body or has a body, but only the body has actual and true *coextensio*, understood at once temporally and spatially. Unity of an unchanging (but changeable) or a changing shape in the unity of a duration, the shape-extensional form, filled out with qualitative determinations. Every body [stands][2] under rules of general causality, universal nature under an a priori of causality so as to be determinable, constructible through truths in themselves according to determined causal laws which can be discovered inductively.

Corporeal being is thus extensional-coexisting being, and in its circumstances—i.e., the bodies existing together, coexisting in the unity of nature—it is unambiguously determined being— if nature is a self-sufficient nature. Naturalism looks at man as filled-out extension and thus considers the world in general only as nature in a broader sense. The duration of a man's spirit is taken as an objective duration, and the soul is taken at every phase of the duration as being, though not actually spatially

* The "naturalistic attitude" is not a constitutively prescribed universal direction of the gaze, belonging to the natural world-view, but is the naturalistic prejudice.

1. Biemel's note: "Before 1930." This text is found in the German edition as the second "Abhandlung," pp. 294–313 (see Translator's Introduction, pp. xx f.). Another early attempt at subjects dealt with in the *Crisis*. The theme is also treated in *Ideen*, Vol. II.

2. Biemel's interpolation.

shaped in a way parallel to the shape of the body, nevertheless a coexistence of psychic data, a being-simultaneously which can somehow be coordinated to simultaneity in the form of what coexists in spatial extension and what coexists spatially in general.

Now it is, to be sure, naturally correct that human psychic life proceeds in the form of an immanent time and that we find every momentary present to be a unity of coexistence of manifold "data." But fundamentally essential insights must first be attained here about the structure of this immanent time and, on the other hand, about how "objective time" receives constitutive meaning as the form of transcendent natural being, in which form the immanent times of souls are made objectively temporal and with them the souls [themselves].

Naturalism simply assumes that essentially the whole world can be thought on the analogy of its [concept of] nature and, accordingly, that the being-in-itself of the world can be thought as the correlate of truths-in-themselves, indeed constructible truths-in-themselves, exactly as in the case of (self-sufficient) nature.* The world [is the] subject matter of a universal inductive world-science, empirical induction being the ground for an idealizing, mathematical method of finding exact world-laws (including natural laws) or of arriving at laws for human beings and animals as psychophysical beings, for their souls, their personal being and activity, as well as for their bodies. Thus, expressed in an extreme way, God has a universal mathematics of the world, God knows the world-laws that are valid for everything in the world in all its determinations; thus [these are] exact laws of the coexistence of whatever is, and is such spatio-temporally; these are causal laws but are simply more complicated, more manifold, being extended to the spiritual sphere.

The problem of psychophysics, with its indubitable empirical discoveries, is: What can be subsumed under a psychophysical order?

The scientific attitude which aims at objective knowledge (as practiced by natural science), and this universally, as objective knowledge of the world, the universe of realities existing in

---

* Nature, as idealized, is constructible, and thereby it is factual actuality in ontological, indeed mathematical, unconditioned generality; also it is idealization of the empirical coordination of empirical qualities with empirical quantities. But if the concrete factual world, that of experience, is to be idealizable and constructible, this requires that it have its world-encompassing mathematics.

themselves, would be the attitude with the intent of knowing being-in-itself through truths in themselves. But is this not the task of science in general? What does the in-itself mean in the case of nature, of an animal, of a human being, of a human community, of cultural objects and the universal culture of a human civilization?

And can one distinguish between the thematic attitude directed at the "objective" world (as scientific theme) and the thematic attitude directed toward universal subjectivity, understood as subjectivity and everything subjective through which the world is experienced, appears, is judged about, valued, etc.? But is that not the personal attitude?

What is that, the personal attitude? Human beings, like animals, are in space; the world of realities is always pregiven with human beings in it. Interest is directed toward human beings as persons who, in personal actions and passions, are related to "the" world, who, in the community of life, of personal interrelations, of activities and other ways of being determined by and comporting oneself toward worldly things, have one and the same surrounding world, a world of which they are conscious [that it is] one and the same.

The world toward which they comport themselves, which motivates them, with which they constantly have to deal, is of course precisely *the* world, the one existing world; but, in the personal attitude, interest is directed toward the persons and their comportment toward the world, toward the ways in which the thematic persons have consciousness of whatever they are conscious of as existing for them, and also toward the particular objective sense the latter has in their consciousness of it. In this sense what is in question is not the world as it actually is but the particular world which is valid for the persons, the world appearing to them with the particular properties it has in appearing to them; the question is how they, as persons, comport themselves in action and passion—how they are motivated to their specifically personal acts of perception, of remembering, of thinking, of valuing, of making plans, of being frightened and automatically starting, of defending themselves, of attacking, etc. Persons are motivated only by what they are conscious of and in virtue of the way in which this [object of consciousness] exists for them in their consciousness of it, in virtue of its sense—how it is valid or not valid for them, etc.

Interest in persons is naturally not the mere interest in their modes of behavior and their motives, but [also] interest in what makes them identical persons. One will say: interest in personal habitualities and characters. But these point first of all to the modes of behavior in which they manifest themselves (first of all immediately as the same ego-subjects) and from which they spring.*

How are the thematics of the humanistic sciences—and those of a general humanistic science which might someday be grounded—related to anthropology, zoology (in the sense of the science of human beings and animals as "objective" realities, as nature), and psychology, as the science of those objective, real component elements of real human beings and animals which are otherwise called soul, psychic life, psychic characteristics?

Humanistic science is the science of human subjectivity in its conscious relation to the world as appearing to it and motivating it in action and passion; and, conversely, [it is] the science of the world as the surrounding world of persons, or as the world appearing to them, having validity for them. In the alteration of the manners of appearance, in the alteration of the apperceptions that human beings go through in their "inner life," both individually and in common through mutual understanding, they are conscious of "the" things, the relations, likewise the persons and groups of persons that motivate them and are thematic for them in the surrounding world; and they are conscious of them as the same but as appearing now one way, now another, to them and different persons, as being valid for them, possibly being valid once as existing in certainty, etc.

But in general, in personal life, these same things are not objects of thematic, scientific interest; personal life is generally not theoretical, things are not generally scientifically thematic for persons in terms of how they are "in objective truth," "in themselves"; rather, [they are present] just as they happen to be valid for them, just as the things which otherwise motivate them, determine them in their extrascientific action and passion. If we make into a scientific theme the things, nature, the animal and human worlds, living bodies and souls as they are in and for "themselves" (objectively), then we are natural scientists, zoologists, anthropologists, and, specifically, psychologists (here in the sense of the parallel to natural-scientific zoology).

* But what is scientific in the personal sciences applies also, correlatively, to the surrounding world which motivates the persons, i.e., of which they are conscious, the surrounding world which is actually present, actually experienced and experienceable for them in its style of manners of appearance.

Here we do, of course, have the realities in question given to us again and again as appearing realities; but our objective interest in them, as the theoretical reality-interest understood ultimately in full universality, is directed toward their [determinations] which appear through the appearances, through the subjective manners of givenness, and can be determined in their exact, objectively true being through absolutely, universally valid scientific judgments—in the true being which is the being of these realities themselves and not just their being for us or for this or that group of persons which they motivate in various ways.*

Here a particular kind of motivation is privileged, which is designated by the expression "theoretical interest in objectively real being." Objective nature, or its objectively true being-in-it-self, as a subject matter for science, is of course also a personal accomplishment—or rather the idea of such an accomplishment, the accomplishment of a method which bears within itself the infinite idea, the idea of an infinite process of perfection—namely, as the real in-itself of nature which is *idealiter* continually determined, or more and more perfectly determined, through the natural-scientific method. But it is [also] the correlate of an infinite accomplishment, a particular accomplishment-correlate of that personal community which is called the community of scientists. Insofar as humanistic science, as the all-encompassing science of the spiritual world, has as its subject matter all persons, all sorts of persons and personal accomplishments, personal structures that are called cultural structures, it also encompasses natural science and natural-scientific nature in itself, nature as reality. [Now] ³ the experience of nature, with its thoroughgoing, consciously produced identity of what is experienced, runs constantly through each personal life. But the interest which determines personal life (which is only in exceptional cases the life of a natural scientist) does not concern nature "existing in itself" and separated out (or to be separated out) by natural science but concerns nature free from all theory, as it appears and is meant in this way or that, just as it enters into the personal life of mankind and determines this life in particular forms of praxis. For all human beings, the nature about which they talk, the world in which they live and know

* This is the general sense of science—though of course beginning naïvely, it does not attain the full world but at first remains caught, unbeknown to itself, in the bonds of tradition.

3. Striking *aber*.

themselves to be living together, is the nature or world which determines them, the one world which is identified and corrected in social interaction; and it is identified as the same world that the objective scientist, in his particular style of personal activity, has as his subject matter. In this sense the personal world is not other than the "objective" world. But the world pregiven in every person, valid for every human culture at every time and for every individual human being in his particular praxis, the world posited as actual, is a world through a particular "manner of appearance," a particular apperception, open for further reshaping variations which may transform being into nonbeing (illusion); yet through these variations, though with certain corrections, there is established the unity of a world having enduring validity as existing, always open to further determinations—including the determination of reality for scientific theory. It persists in this openness. And humanistic science, which has as its subject matter factual persons, peoples, and [historical] times, and the things supposed by them to exist in their supposed worlds, which appear to them concretely, intuitively, in such and such a way, which are apperceived as such mythologically or in some other way, the natures experienced by them, the cultures which exist for them and motivate them—[this humanistic science] has its thematic focus necessarily and exclusively upon the world in the "subjective" *how* of [its appearance to] the persons which make up its subject matter. This world cannot be broken down into merely individual-subjective and temporally constantly changing aspects. Through such aspects a communal surrounding world is constituted for the historical community. In the community of its life, the community, or the life of its persons, is related to the surrounding world which is communal for them (the personal "world"), and this surrounding world has relative actuality for them—and a changing actuality for different personal communities and their personal times; but this [fact] does not exclude the possibility that personal communities, each of which has its personal surrounding world, can, by entering into or already being in relation with one another, have or attain an overlapping, common surrounding world or that they know themselves in their interrelations to be related to the same "real" world, only finding that each community views the world in quite a different way, accords it a completely different kind of actuality. But this common "reality," which necessarily extends as far as any possible kind of communalization, while it is an object of consciousness in its identity, is such only as an interpersonally emerging unity of identification, of verification to be constated in communal life. Only through science does it become determined as reality in terms of "objective" (i.e., scientific) truth, as it is in itself, when the science of reality determines it through its particular personal actions and lasting accomplishments.*

For the attitude of the humanistic sciences the point of departure is the "natural attitude," in which everyone, and thus also the beginning humanist, is situated in waking life prior to all scientific intent and activity and through which he can find himself to be such. He finds himself in a world which surrounds him, which appears now in one way, now in another, motivates him now in one way, now in another, into which he gazes and listens; generally speaking, he is practically determined in different ways by this world, and through his praxis he is always giving it a new face. And he himself belongs to this world, as do his fellow men; depending on the circumstances, they are either objects of praxis for him or cosubjects of it, acting together with him and at the same time seeing with him, hearing with him, the *same* things in the surrounding world, especially those involved in praxis which are "in question" for them in their communal practical direction [of interest]. In the natural attitude, the world, as being the same throughout the alteration of actual and possible, subjective and intersubjectively interrelated appearances, opinions, interests, is generally speaking not a scientific subject matter; rather, the human being's subject matter, in a broader sense, is everything that momentarily affects him or that concerns him enduringly, possibly becoming a fixed habituality (as in a vocation): in "seriousness" or in play, in effecting or creating things of value or things without value, temporary or lasting things, accomplishing things in egoistic or in the communal interest, as an individual or as a functionary of the community in communal work; his own and the generative memory leads him to the communal life of the past.

What has just been said is itself a universal reflection with which the humanistic scientist can and must begin; he can do it

---

* The goal of "objectivity," i.e., [that of] science, is: that which is, not as experienced and verified by *particular* persons and civilizations, as it is experienced and can be validated through experience by them, but rather: that which is—for *all conceivable* civilizations (including Papuans), [for all] experiences, [all] surrounding worlds, which are assumed to be experiencing the same things.

because, as a European, he is already acquainted with science, already knows the universal theoretical attitude, has been raised in it, and can now arrive at his subject matter through this survey. Man, then, men in community, the communities themselves in their life and undertakings, are the scientific subject matter of humanistic science, in correlation with the [human] accomplishments themselves in accomplishing activity and the accomplished structures; but also passive man in the periods of his indolence, the temporarily sleeping and then awakening man, the whole man in the unity of his life as a personal life, as "I," as "we" in action and passion.

What the person does and suffers, what happens within him, how he stands in relation to his surrounding world, what angers him, what depresses him, what makes him cheerful or upset—these are questions relating to persons; and so are questions of a similar sort relating to communities of every level: marriages, friendships, clubs, civic communities, communities of peoples, etc.—first in historical factualness and then in generality.* Is it then not the case that the general science that must arise here is psychophysical psychology—"individual psychology" and social psychology?

Is the human being, as person, not the psychophysical human being? Indeed, he is, after all, the human being who knows himself to be in the world with living body and soul, who moves in space and works with his hands, as a manual worker, or in some other way with his living body, who, in battle, also fights with his living body, is naturally always coconscious of his living body, acting through it upon his external world or experiencing through it a touch, a push, a wound. The human being is naturally the same in the science of persons as in natural-scientific biological anthropology. In the transition from the one to the other science, the identification is accomplished as a matter of course. And yet the thematic direction is fundamentally and

* There is some question as to how generality is meant here—in terms of "natural history," morphology, or as unconditioned generality analogous to that of exact natural science. The only objectivity that belongs to exact natural science is based upon "geometrization," an idealization which is able to encompass theoretically, by idealizing them, all the possibilities of experience as experience of what is identical *in infinitum;* it does this by means of ideal concepts—concepts of what is in itself and of ideal truths as truths in themselves. Is there a method for encompassing the realm of the "spirit," of history, in all its essential possibilities, so that one can arrive at "exact" truths through exact concepts for this realm?

essentially a different one. Man, in humanistic science, is not the subject matter as an identical reality whose being-in-itself can be determined objectively; rather it is historical man insofar as he acts and holds sway subjectively in his surrounding world.

The opposition between "natural-scientific"-psychological and humanistic inquiry, as I said earlier, consists in the fact that natural science and humanistic science take the spiritual, as soul, as their subject matter from different points of view, namely, in natural science as localized subject, as an annex * to the body existing "there," as existing with it and unified with it inductively—psychophysically (in the sense of Cartesian dualism); whereas the humanistic attitude is the personal attitude, directed purely at the person; it is pure in a sense similar to that in which natural science is pure—apparently through "abstraction." For the person, the living body is the privileged object in the surrounding world, over which it holds sway immediately, etc. But this is apperceived inductively, and the apperception is an objective one.

Naturally the person is localized, and this through his physical living body in natural space and in natural time. If one stands within exact space, this is concrete localization. Obviously one can direct one's thematic interest purely toward nature, and within it the physical living bodies, and then find the subjects, the souls, to be in nature (empirical or exact nature) with them, or rather at the corresponding spatiotemporal positions. But there is first some question as to what one can expect from this "being-together-with," as to what makes up the unified sense of this real unity "man" or "animal," as to the extent to which one can and may speak of the "combination" of living body and soul and even look upon this combination as a causal one of a sort similar to that of natural causality. Belonging from

---

* One should not say "annex." The annex-view is already a falsification. Subjectively, in experience, the experienced living body of another points, through the experienced complexes of bodily data (i.e., this experienced thing as such), to the psychic and to the ego; here there is "association," then, but just as there is in every apperception.

In the pregiven world, nature is, in terms of constitution, a "causal" unity of mutual exteriority. [When we speak of] "the spirit in nature," "localization" is easily misconstrued as a spatial being-together and actually as a spatiotemporal coexistence, i.e., in the same sense in which things, real elements of things, coexist. But in what way is the spirit together with the body? We must ask this question. As holding sway—this enters in only with the apperception.

the start to the constitution of the world, as the pure world of experience, i.e., as my and our surrounding world, is the fact that, within it, here mere things, there men, here animals, works of art, tools, there manual workers, soldiers, etc., are experienced, pregiven in this way, apperceived; and this in a changing manner which nevertheless has a most general set of structural types, to which set the appearing of human beings (including myself as a human being) necessarily belongs. Everywhere, one can put inductive questions to this world: wherever there is coexistence with regularity, there is also a set of inductive problems. In every simple apperception, coexistence with regularity is involved and can be uncovered; that is, such coexistence belongs to every apperceptive type, but also to the universal apperception, that of the world, and to the apperception of a near world or domestic world and [that of] a distant world as well as to the apperception of a single near thing or distant thing. One can and will, then, find implicitly indicated inductive regularities which relate "data" concerning the physical living body to psychic "data"; but this is far from implying anything about a natural causality or about a combination into a whole analogous to [such a combination in] nature. To be sure, this distinction characterizes a type of psychophysics which traditionally counts as anthropology, grounded in traditional sensationalism.

The spirit (the soul, concrete personal being) is there in space-time where his living body is; and from there he lives into and acts upon the world, the universe of what exists in space-time. He is spirit, person, ego *of* his surrounding world (and thus of a world [as such]) in having consciousness of it; the possibility of his acting [on the world] is based on the fact that, in a definite, ordered way, he has experience of the world, or can be with the world in an experiencing way, can be nearer and farther [from things], etc. And to this belongs the fact that he constantly has a privileged experiential consciousness of "his" living body, that is, he has the consciousness of being with this object in a quite immediate way and of always "living" and "being able to do" things through it as the affected ego and the ego holding sway. This relation, and any manner in which personal experience occurs, through which the surrounding world is intuitively "there," etc., is, as relating to persons, a fact for humanistic science.

Humanistic science has to do with the spirit; and here first of all natural science in the narrower sense is separated from humanistic science: on the one hand science of physical things and on the other hand science of human beings as persons, as having their living bodies in wielding them, being related to all other realities through the living body as perceptual body, etc.*

But now we must note that nature is also in the surrounding world—our surrounding world of today, the hypothetical surrounding world of the Indians, of the Stone Age, etc.—as long as humanistic science is our subject and not "objective" natural science, as long as our subject matter is precisely not objective nature, as long as nature remains tied to the surrounding world as it is in natural history in the old sense (even if this subject-relatedness is not explicitly expressed or is even unnoticed by the scientist and remains extrathematic). Only when our aim is objectivity, nature's being-in-itself in the ontological and then mathematical sense, rather than its being as it exhibits itself to us empirically, etc., do we have natural-scientific biology † rather than natural history (which belongs together with the general history of mankind as [dealing with] a historical surrounding world).

But if this is the case, then the question arises whether one ought not to make the same distinction in regard to the psychic, in regard to the spirit, the person, or rather whether an objective humanistic science ought not to be distinguished from a historical one. More precisely, in the attitude focused upon the world as an empirical universe of realities [there are two possibilities]: (1) exact nature, through ontological-mathematical construction, and then an exact psychophysics as opposed to the empirical togetherness of physical body and soul (dealing with persons); (2) the spiritual attitude from the start—the historical attitude.

Everything becomes perfectly clear when we say to ourselves, or each of us says to himself: the world of which I speak, the world of which the Chinese speaks, of which the Greek of Solon's time, the Papuan speaks, is always a world having subjective validity, even the world of the scientist, who as such is a Greek-European man.

---

* Then humanistic science must be understood as twofold: (1) spirit as spatiotemporally existing together with bodies, together in space, in space-time, as the subject matter of a universal inductive world-science—with the large question of whether this prescribes the scientific goal of an exact natural science in a broadened sense, a dualistic, exact psychophysics, as meaningful, as possible. [2] Otherwise, humanistic science as purely personal science.

† This contains the hypothesis of idealization.

In practical life I have the world as a traditional world, no matter where the tradition comes from; it may even come from second-hand scientific acquisitions, even false ones, which I get from the newspaper or from school and which I may transform in one way or another in my own motivations or [through] those of my fellows who accidentally influence me. I can now look around and take up a theoretical interest in the world which is valid for me precisely through tradition, or I can put myself in the place of the ancient Greeks prior to science, etc. The first universal theoretical interest, at the very beginning, was of this sort—to wish to know the objective world is to wish to know the world as such. It is a world through tradition, but the fact that it is this is hidden and in any case can be completely left aside. For now let us not understand objective science in the sense of the naturalistic ways of thinking, etc. Objective science means straightforwardly taking the world as one's subject matter; humanistic science means taking the world as one's subject matter *as* the world of the subjectivity which functions for it, the world insofar as it is subject-related. (Only the subjects are thematic and, within them, the "represented" world with its spatiotemporality.) It is possible to make not only nature but also human beings, human civilizations, peoples, etc., one's subject matter "straightforwardly," objectively; and, on the other hand, one can make human beings, human civilizations, and nature one's subject matter in a subjectively relative manner. The correlation is iterated. Everything that exists exists in subjective manners of givenness, everything can be a subject matter either straightforwardly or subjectively-relatively. Here "subjectively" means: taking the subjects straightforwardly as one's subject matter, without inquiring into objective nature; one will say: making them one's subject matter by abstraction. From the beginning, in the theoretical attitude, the world is the universe of what is; and everything that is, including what belongs to humanistic science at one level of reflection, takes its place again in the order of the world, and so *in infinitum*. But now I turn around, through the transcendental reduction, and there now arises a humanistic science which does not have the world in advance and does not constantly hold onto the world.

When we seek natural-historical truth for living beings, it is already presupposed that the latter are observed through harmonious experience (according to their bodily and their psychic being, both of which are given in unified experience) and are described, in accord with this experience, through adequately suited experiential (descriptive) concepts. Thus I may make mistakes about others and perhaps even about myself; but as long as experience verifies itself and as long as I follow its harmoniousness, I attain empirical truth, I get to know the person. As it is for the physical living bodies as natural objects, so it is (and to this extent we have an analogy) with souls: that experience in relation to them has no end. But do they have an essential structure (which can be established purely) which prescribes to the souls an objective (exact-ontological) in-itself similar in meaning to that of natural things? Now it is clear from the start that an essential form of a spirit can be extracted and known, although it is just as clear that there is an immense difference between the essence of psychic subjectivity and the essence of a thing. From the start one must strictly avoid all the false analogizing which does violence [to this difference]. On the other hand, is it not obviously a good and necessary guiding notion that one seek to ground an investigation of factual spirits in their historicity upon an essential knowledge of the spirit (and of the community in which spirits live) and that one proceed from these to create "exact concepts" and exact, unconditionally valid truths as ideal poles for all spiritual factuality? *

Attitude toward nature, which is not naturalistic: [4] If we now speak of different experiential attitudes on the ground of the natural world, we must distinguish: (1) the attitude focused upon nature, in this case experienced nature, upon mere things, or abstractly upon animals' bodies or cultural objects as mere things; (2) personalistic attitude: attitude focused upon persons or upon human beings as persons.

What belongs to this? What persons are as persisting unities, what characters they have, what makes up their "life," what they do and suffer as persons, how they "behave" in different life-situations in respect to their surrounding world, how they are personally affected by this world and how they react to it in a personal way; and finally their "surrounding world" itself, which exists for them, is valid for them, determines them. Here the question will also be: how their surrounding world is transformed, what types of objects belong to it; thus, in generality: what essential structure does a personal surrounding world have, and, in particular, what general structure does it have

* But what does essential knowledge of historical knowledge look like?

4. *Naturale Einstellung, die nicht naturalistisch ist.* This is a marginal note inserted by Biemel into the text.

specifically as a surrounding world which has taken shape, and continues to take on new shapes, through the personal world-life itself? What types of cultural objects does it have?

The structure of the personal surrounding world stands in essential relation to the structure of personal life (with personal habituality) which, as world-life, is a comporting of oneself toward objects appearing in the surrounding world and their properties belonging to the surrounding world.

A particularly privileged position in the surrounding world is occupied by its persons. An important role, however, is played by the following distinction, which is a thematic one: [on the one hand] persons (not only other persons but also possibly I myself) are thematic as objects—as objects belonging to the surrounding world which is already pregiven to the practical ego, practical in the broadest sense, i.e., concrete, living wakefully into the world—and are thus thematic as being of the surrounding world in the full sense, as objects to which something happens, objects which one finds existing in the surrounding world, which one sees but has nothing to do with, nothing in common with: they are here and over there like mere things; perhaps what is especially in question here is the external seeing and understanding of the other without becoming intimately familiar with him, living with him. On the other hand, [there are] the other subjects as cosubjects, with whom one forms a community in experiencing, in thinking, in acting, with whom one has common praxis in the surrounding world even though each one still also has his own. We already have a certain "community" in being mutually "there" for one another in the surrounding world (the other in my surrounding world)—and this always means being physically, bodily "there." We experience one another as seeing the same objects—or in part the same—in the same world, which is a world for us. For the most part, as regards this common seeing, this is inauthentic experience, the empty understanding of the others and their experiential situation. But the community of persons, as a community of personal life and possibly as a lasting personal interrelation, is something special. A first step is explicitly to be vitally at one with the other person in the intuitive understanding of his experiencing, his life-situation, his activity, etc. From there one proceeds to communication through expression and language, which is already an interrelation of egos. Every sort of communication naturally presupposes the commonality of the surrounding world, which is established as soon as we are persons for one another at all—though this can be completely empty, inactive. But it is something else to have them as fellows in communal life, to talk with them, to share their concerns and strivings, to be bound to them in friendship and enmity, love and hate. It is only here that we enter the sphere of the "social-historical" world.

When we live in the natural—the nontranscendental—attitude, different thematic directions, and thus different directions of theoretical interest, open themselves to us in accord with the structure of the pregiven world—the latter being given to us as our communal surrounding world and, through this, as objective world. "Through this" means that the surrounding world is something changeable, that we progress, in life, from one surrounding world to another, whereas throughout this alteration the same world is yet continuously experienced, the surrounding world becoming a manner of appearance of this world. In [5] the attitude oriented toward essences we can, beginning with the factual, common world, investigate the essential form of a human surrounding world and [investigate] the essential form of a surrounding world which, in the alteration of surrounding worlds through penetration into alien human civilizations, is ever constituting itself anew; and, assuming the possibility that this process could go on infinitely, we can sketch out the structure of an existing world as world of possible experience, i.e., as emerging through an ongoing process of correction throughout possible transitional surrounding worlds. This could be the idea of an ontology of the experiential world purely as such. The theoretical attitude can be directed toward nature alone, in which case we have a "natural" attitude which is nevertheless not "naturalistic." On the other hand, we can orient our attitude toward persons and personal communities; we can orient our attitude toward possible concrete surrounding worlds and the "true" world which is outlined within them.

The attitude oriented toward nature can have a different sense. In general, in the natural attitude it is *we* who are the persons carrying out the investigation; and thus, already in advance, it is we who live alongside one another and with one another. But here, as subjects for the world, we and our life are anonymous—as long as we have not made ourselves thematic for ourselves. Thus the attitude oriented toward nature is pre-

5. The passage beginning here and ending "ontology of the experiential world purely as such" is a later insert and refers to a much higher level of reflection than what is described in the rest of the paragraph.

cisely: making nature thematic and nothing else; to make thematic is thus in a certain sense at the same time to "abstract," although this must [not] [6] at first (and thus not necessarily) be understood as an active abstracting-from-something but rather, as is usual, only [as] [6] an exclusive looking-at-something which consequently notices nothing else. Of course, underlying a scientific attitude oriented toward nature is ultimately a willful making of nature into one's subject matter—in fact, pure nature, with the conscious exclusion, or will to exclude, everything that is merely subjective.

Now the nature that becomes thematic thereby can be the nature of the surrounding world, just as it is pregiven, just as it gives itself in actual and possible experiential perception and establishes itself as actually existing in the course of our experiential life through the harmony of experiences (though with occasional corrections). [Nature's] being thematic means experiential knowledge, the fixing [7] [of nature] through consistent experience—one's own and that of others, supplemented by the experiential anticipations of mediate inductions—and through description, striving toward descriptive science, the universal descriptive science of nature, encompassing the universe of possible experiences of nature—sense-perception, memory, the induction which is actually verifiable through these—for all time. Underlying this, though not actually developed, is the ontology of the "world of possible experience." From this [8] one can already distinguish the inductive broadening [of experience] through making what is too distant to be experienced homogeneous with what is near, and this leads to the idealization of infinities.

The goal of "exact" natural science is a different one, i.e., that of going beyond the relativity of intuited nature, nature relative to the surrounding world, to determine nature "in itself," as the in-itself which is identical throughout all relativities, through "truths in themselves." Descriptive nature is relative in the personal, human sense, namely, relative to us, to our nation, to our European civilization, to us earthly men in our historical time; but we ourselves are not thematic here, nor is this relation; the latter needs no thematization insofar as we are, after all, the same earthly human civilization from generation to generation in this unitary historical time or sphere of time; thus, scientific

6. Biemel's interpolations.
7. Reading *das* (*das Festlegen*) for *die*.
8. Reading *davon* for *da*.

conclusions understandably continue to have validity for us from generation to generation.*

We need only direct our thematic gaze toward this relativity in order to recognize that this natural science belongs to the broader content of the personal science of earthly humanity in general, the latter being understood as "we men," i.e., humanity acquiring its temporal horizon and its relative and (in a broad sense) historical temporality from us who are the investigators. Penetrating more deeply here, we see that European man, arising out of the philosophizing Greeks, was the first to take up the theoretical attitude oriented toward the outermost attainable surrounding world—and that only he could do this. The surrounding world is relative to a subjectivity which functions for it —the typology of functioning subjectivities is itself historical: human beings are necessarily members of generative communities and thus necessarily live in every communal surrounding world as their own surrounding world, in which, in this respect, a universal historicity holds sway. This is not to say, however, that there belongs to every such community a possible theoretical attitude; for this too, and first of all the "descriptive" scientific attitude, is essentially historical. If this attitude has established itself, however, then the development is prescribed, for the further progress of history, from the pure description of nature to psychophysical description.

Thus the attitude which is oriented toward men and animals is a ncw one—toward men and animals not as bodies to be investigated consistently and descriptively in the attitude oriented toward nature but as men (or animals) who have their bodies as living bodies, who have their personal surrounding world, oriented around their living bodies as the near-far world and, at the same time, in the manners of appearing of right-left, up-down—all these manners of appearing standing in a successive relation of dependence to subjective manners of "I move my living body" in a system of kinestheses which can be realized

* Descriptive universal science, as the science of the pregiven world in its universality, remains within the realm of actual and possible, direct and indirect, experience; thus it necessarily advances, starting from the world pregiven in the manner of a horizon as present, through opening up the copresent, developing itself as descriptive science of the open, universal present, but then also as the science of the past (paleontology), through continual opening-up of past times and then also of future times. It is naturally directed toward typical generalities, typical ways in which the types change, and then [toward] the explanation of individual facts according to such rules.

even voluntarily. The thematics of the human being includes what is valid for him as surrounding world, what is valid for him within this surrounding world, both his individual and also the communal surrounding world; the "how" of the appearance of this surrounding world which can be grasped reflectively, not only for him but also for the community; how the manners of appearance belonging to the communicating individuals correspond to one another; how each individual gives his being-human a position in the space of the surrounding world as the zero-point object of the oriented surrounding world in experiential apperception; how, when persons change position, e.g., when two persons exchange positions, the orientations, the same objects, must change or, rather, the manners of appearance must be exchanged.

Whereas descriptive nature belongs to the personal surrounding world of all men, or to the surrounding world of all "European" men—and thus belongs within anthropology—exact scientific nature obviously does not belong to this but only to the surrounding world of those men who are exact natural scientists (or who understand natural science). Of course, scientific natural history also does not belong to the surrounding world of every man, insofar as it has taken his general surrounding world under investigation and brought to light what a possible surrounding world might have been like but was not present and is not present, except again for scientists. Natural science is a culture, [and] it belongs only within the cultural world of that human civilization which has developed this culture and within which, for the individual, possible ways of understanding this culture are present.

What can become thematic in addition is the universal unity of a "civilization," extending as far as communal life, both immediate and mediate, extends; and correlative to this is the community of the surrounding world (in the "how" of its manners of appearing and being conceived), in particular the community of culture. It can become thematic in the unity of its temporal life, in the unity of that temporality which is the form of this life itself—not the temporality of exact, natural-scientific nature, which, according to its meaning, is the identical time of an absolutely identical nature beyond all the natures making up the surrounding worlds of whatever particular civilizations there may be; natural-scientific time is not a relative time, essentially belonging to a particular communally living and existing civilization, with all its past periods and open future which, from the point of view of the man of the present, has meaning as his future, that of his civilization.

Also, civilizations that have only loose contacts with one another can become thematic, as can the ways in which civilizations enter into community with one another and historically become or have become one civilization; a major part of this would be the history of one's own civilization, as well as its historical becoming out of earlier civilizations and cultures, etc. Here we have left natural-scientific descriptive inquiry behind and have entered into problems of the humanistic sciences; or rather, we have placed descriptive nature within the humanistic science of history.

All this is still superficial; no account has yet been taken of the normative ideas of civilizations and their culture or rather of those ideas which, as the "oughts" functioning in life-decisions, [determine] [9] the life of man, both as individual and as variously organized into communities; but these also occasionally function in universal decisions and already-made resolves of the will which regulate once and for all one's own life and the communal life. *This leads, then, to the "meaning" which is immanent in history*, to the problems of developmental teleology, to the problems of the development of universal ideas which give direction to a new sort of civilization: thus, for example, the ideas of the infinite and true world as correlate of the idea of world-science; ideas of the true and genuine individual personal life and of a genuine community; and finally those of a genuine civilization and the "ethical" ideas belonging to it, ideas of a universal science not merely of the world but of everything that is at all, be it an idea, an ideal norm, etc.*

In the end, the universal personal science itself seems to transform itself into the all-encompassing science, to resolve itself into a universal philosophy, and eidetically into a universal ontology. For everything proceeds from us, the living human beings who pose theoretical questions; and we ourselves are persons and have, in our common world, the subject matter of all possible subject matters, for all possible posings of questions, and thus also for the highest and most ultimate questions of man.

The regression from this universal, personally oriented view of the world, which is historical in its fashion, which moves

* But this is the consistent execution of humanistic science—in the natural attitude.
9. Biemel's interpolation.

upon the ground of the pregiven world, back to the absolute ground, that of transcendental subjectivity.

Here the point of departure is: we, who carry out the universal consideration of persons, drawing into it the universal consideration of the surrounding world, etc., are ourselves men, European men; we ourselves have developed historically; as historians we ourselves create world history and world science in every sense, a historical cultural structure within the motivation of the European history in which we are situated. The world which is for us is itself a historical structure belonging to us, who are ourselves in our being a historical structure. What does all this relativity itself presuppose as being nonrelative? Subjectivity as transcendental subjectivity. Another point of departure: eidetically general personal science—psychology. Universal psychology, fallback into transcendental philosophy.

Appendix IV:
Philosophy as Mankind's Self-Reflection; the Self-Realization of Reason[1]

THE TASK WHICH the philosopher puts to himself, his life-goal as a philosopher: universal science of the world, universal, definitive knowledge, the universe of truths in themselves about the world, the world in itself. What about this goal and its attainability? Can I begin with a truth, a definitive truth? A definitive truth, a truth through which I can assert something about something that is in itself and be indubitably certain of its definitiveness? If I already had such "immediately self-evident" truths, then I could perhaps mediately derive new ones from them. But where do I have them? Is any entity in itself so indubitably certain to me through immediate experience that I could, in accord with this experience, with descriptive concepts which immediately fit this experience or the content of this experience, express immediate truths in themselves? But what about any and every experience of what is in the world, experience of what I am immediately certain of as existing spatiotemporally? It is certain; but this certainty can modalize itself, it can become doubtful, it can dissolve in the course of experience into illusion: no immediate experiential assertion gives me an entity as what it is in itself but only something meant with certainty that must verify itself in the course of my experiencing life. But the verification which lies merely in the harmonious character of actual experience does not prevent the possibility of illusion.

Experiencing—in general, living as an ego (thinking, valuing, acting)—I am necessarily an "I" that has its "thou," its "we,"

1. This is the manuscript that Biemel places at the end of the *Crisis* text as "§ 73—Schlusswort," pp. 269–76. My reasons for placing it among the supplementary texts are given in the Translator's Introduction, p. xx.

its "you"—the "I" of the personal pronouns. And equally necessarily, I am and we are, in the community of egos, correlates of
everything to which we address ourselves as existing in the
world, which we always presuppose as being commonly experienceable in addressing ourselves to it, naming it, speaking about
it, grounding our knowledge, and which as such is there for us, is
actual, is valid for us in the community of conscious life as a life
which is not individually isolable but is internally communalized. But this is always such that the world is our common world,
necessarily having ontic validity; yet in particular matters I can
enter into contradiction with others, into doubt and negation of
being, similarly to the way I do this with myself. Now where and
how do I have something that exists definitively in itself?
[Corrected] experience—either as communal experience and reciprocal correction or as one's own personal experience and
self-correction—does not change the relativity of experience;
even as communal experience it is relative, and thus all descriptive assertions are necessarily relative, and all conceivable inferences, deductive or inductive, are relative. How can thinking
achieve anything but relative truths? The man of everyday life is
after all not without reason; he is a thinking being, he has the
καθόλου, unlike the animal, hence he has language, description,
he makes inferences, he asks questions of truth, he verifies,
argues, and decides in a rational way—but does the whole idea
of "truth in itself" have a meaning for him? Is this [idea],
together with its correlate, what exists in itself, not a philosophical invention? But it is not a fiction, not a dispensable invention
without significance, but one which raises—or is called to raise
—man to a new level in a new historical development
[*Historizität*] of human life, a historical development whose entelechy is this new idea and the philosophical or scientific praxis
belonging to it, the method of a new sort of scientific thinking.

"In-itself" means as much as "objective," at least in the way
that the objective is opposed in the exact sciences to the merely
subjective, the latter being understood as that which merely
indicates something objective or that in which something objective is supposed merely to appear. It is merely a phenomenon of
something objective; to come to know the objective by recognizing it within the phenomena and to determine it through objective concepts and truths, this is the task.

But the sense of the task thus posed and of its presuppositions, that is, the presuppositions of all method, has never been
seriously considered and itself investigated in a scientific man-

ner, in an ultimately responsible manner, so that one has not even become clear on the fact that the sense of natural-scientific objectivity, or of the task and method of natural science, is fundamentally and essentially different from the sense of objectivity, task, and method in the humanistic disciplines. This is as true of psychology as it is of the so-called concrete humanistic disciplines. One has expected the same objectivity from psychology as from physics, and because of this a psychology in the full and actual sense has been quite impossible; for an objectivity after the fashion of natural science is downright absurd when applied to the soul, to subjectivity, whether as individual subjectivity, individual person, and individual life or as communally historical subjectivity, as social subjectivity in the broadest sense.

This is the ultimate sense of the objection that one must make to the philosophies of all times—with the exception of the philosophy of idealism, which of course failed in its method: that it was not able to overcome the naturalistic objectivism which was from the beginning and always remained a very natural temptation. As I said, only idealism, in all its forms, attempts to lay hold of subjectivity as subjectivity and to do justice to the fact that the world is never given to the subject and the communities of subjects in any other way than as the subjectively relative valid world with particular experiential content and as a world which, in and through subjectivity, takes on ever new transformations of meaning; and that even the apodictically persisting conviction of one and the same world, exhibiting itself subjectively in changing ways, is a conviction motivated purely within subjectivity, a conviction whose sense—the world itself, the actually existing world—never surpasses the subjectivity that brings it about. But idealism was always too quick with its theories and for the most part could not free itself from hidden objectivistic presuppositions; or else, as speculative idealism, it passed over the task of interrogating, concretely and analytically, actual subjectivity, i.e., subjectivity as having the actual phenomenal world in intuitive validity—which, properly understood, is nothing other than carrying out the phenomenological reduction and putting transcendental phenomenology into action. This explains, by the way, why I call the phenomenology I have developed transcendental and why I speak in it of transcendental subjectivity. For when Kant gives the old word a new meaning through his critique of reason, one can easily convince oneself that the quite different idealism of Berkeley and Hume, indeed any idealism, looked at more closely, has the same thematic field and poses questions within this field which are only differently formulated.

Reason is the specific characteristic of man, as a being living in personal activities and habitualities. This life, as personal life, is a constant becoming through a constant intentionality of development. What becomes, in this life, is the person himself. His being is forever becoming; and in the correlation of individual-personal and communal-personal being this is true of both, i.e., of the [individual] man and of unified human civilizations.

Human personal life proceeds in stages of self-reflection and self-responsibility from isolated occasional acts of this form to the stage of universal self-reflection and self-responsibility, up to the point of seizing in consciousness the idea of autonomy, the idea of a resolve of the will to shape one's whole personal life into the synthetic unity of a life of universal self-responsibility and, correlatively, to shape oneself into the true "I," the free, autonomous "I" which seeks to realize his innate reason, the striving to be true to himself, to be able to remain identical with himself as a reasonable "I"; but there is an inseparable correlation here between individual persons and communities by virtue of their inner immediate and mediate interrelatedness in all their interests—interrelated in both harmony and conflict—and also in the necessity of allowing individual-personal reason to come to ever more perfect realization only as communal-personal reason and vice versa.

The universally, apodictically grounded and grounding science arises now as the necessarily highest function of mankind, as I said, namely, as making possible mankind's development into a personal autonomy and into an all-encompassing autonomy for mankind—the idea which represents the driving force of life for the highest stage of mankind.

Thus philosophy is nothing other than [rationalism],[2] through and through, but it is rationalism differentiated within itself according to the different stages of the movement of intention and fulfillment; it is *ratio in the constant movement of self-elucidation,* begun with the first breakthrough of philosophy into mankind, whose innate reason was previously in a state of concealment, of nocturnal obscurity.

The image of the dawn characterizes Greek philosophy in its beginning stage, the first elucidation through the first cognitive

2. Biemel's interpolation.

conception of "what is" as universe, as world of what is; following soon after this, in a subjective direction of gaze, is the correlative discovery of long-familiar man as the subject of the world, this subject being conceived, however, as man within mankind, who is related through his reason to the totality of being and to himself. From the viewpoint of merely external historical scholarship, with its focus upon men existing in the world and upon the philosophies as theoretical constructs (systems of propositions), the history of philosophy is [merely] one cultural configuration among others and, in its external, faded sequence (which the historical point of view—*lucus a non lucendo*—calls a development), a causal process occurring in the world, in the world's space-time.

Seen from the inside, however, it is a struggle of the generations of philosophers, who are the bearers of this spiritual development, living and surviving in spiritual community, in the constant struggle of "awakened" reason to come to itself, to an understanding of itself, to a reason which concretely understands itself in understanding the existing world, existing in its whole universal truth. [To say that] philosophy, science in all its forms, is rational—that is a tautology. But in all its forms it is on its way to a higher rationality; it is rationality which, discovering again and again its unsatisfying relativity, is driven on in its toils, in its will to attain the true and full rationality. But finally it discovers that this rationality is an idea residing in the infinite and is *de facto* necessarily [only] on the way; but [it discovers] also that there is a final form here which is at the same time the beginning form of a new sort of infinity and relativity—this, however, in a double sense of discovery which signifies, historically, two epochs of beginning and advance.

The first is the epoch in which the demand of apodicticity is discovered and for the first time lucidly taken up into the will by a historically individualized philosophical personality: that is, Descartes, as the initiator of the historical epoch of the modern period. The discovery is submerged for a time, lapsing into misinterpretation; [but] it is relatively fruitful even under this misinterpretation, taking effect in the sciences of rationalism, its a priori and empirical sciences. The consciousness of the inadequacy of this philosophy arouses reaction: apart from the sensationalistic and finally skeptical philosophy (Hume) there is the Kantian and subsequent transcendental philosophy—in which the transcendental primal motive, however, the motive which arises out of the demand for apodicticity, is still not aroused.

The up-and-down of the historical movements—newly strengthened empiricist sensationalism and skepticism, newly strengthened rationalism in the older scientific style, German Idealism and the reaction against it—all this together characterizes the first epoch, that of the whole "modern period." The second period is the renewed beginning, as the reappropriation of the Cartesian discovery, the fundamental demand of apodicticity; and in this beginning, through the changed historical situation (to which all the fateful developments and philosophies of the first epoch belong), there arise forces of motivation, a radical thinking-through of the genuine and imperishable sense of apodicticity (apodicticity as a fundamental problem), the exhibiting of the true method of an apodictically grounded and apodictically progressing philosophy; and included within this is the discovery of the radical contrast between what is usually called apodictic knowledge and what, in the transcendental understanding, outlines the primal ground and the primal method of all philosophy. It is precisely with this that there begins a philosophy with the deepest and most universal self-understanding of the philosophizing ego as the bearer of absolute reason coming to itself, of the same ego as implicating, in his apodictic being-for-himself, his fellow subjects and all possible fellow philosophers; [this is] the discovery of absolute intersubjectivity (objectified in the world as the whole of mankind), as that in which reason, in obscurity, in elucidation, in the movement of lucid self-understanding, is in infinite progress; the discovery of the necessary concrete manner of being of absolute (in the ultimate sense, transcendental) subjectivity in a transcendental life of constant "world-constitution"; the new discovery, correlative to this, of the "existing world," whose ontic meaning, as transcendentally constituted, results in a new meaning for what, in the earlier stages, was called world, world-truth, world-knowledge; but within this a new meaning is also given to human existence: [man's] existence in the spatiotemporally pregiven world as the self-objectification of transcendental subjectivity and its being, its constituting life; what follows this is the ultimate self-understanding of man as being responsible for his own human being: his *self-understanding as being in being called to a life of apodicticity*, not only in abstractly practicing apodictic science in the usual sense but [as being mankind] which realizes its whole concrete being in apodictic freedom by becoming apodictic mankind in the whole active life of its reason —through which it is human; as I said, mankind understanding itself as rational, understanding that it is rational in seeking to be rational; that this signifies an infinity of living and striving toward reason; that reason is precisely that which man *qua* man, in his innermost being, is aiming for, that which alone can satisfy him, make him "blessed"; that reason allows for no differentiation into "theoretical," "practical," "aesthetic," or whatever; that being human is teleological being and an ought-to-be, and that this teleology holds sway in each and every activity and project of an ego; that through self-understanding in all this it can know the apodictic *telos;* and that this knowing, the ultimate self-understanding, has no other form than self-understanding according to a priori principles as self-understanding in the form of philosophy.

Appendix V:
[Objectivity and the World of Experience] [1]

IN PRESCIENTIFIC experiential life we stand within the Heraclitean flux of the changing data of sensible things; and throughout the alteration of these data we do have, with naïve experiential self-evidence, the certainty of coming to know, through seeing, touching, feeling, hearing, etc., the same thing through its properties and of confirming it, through "repetition" of the experiences, as something which objectively and actually is, and is such-and-such; yet clearly what we gain hereby as knowledge of the thing is, in all its identifiable determinations, something that remains unwaveringly approximate, suspended in vague differentiations of greater or less perfection. What becomes well known through repeated experience is always still only relatively known in regard to everything known about it, and it thus has in all respects a peculiar horizon of open unfamiliarity. There is, then, belonging modally to the experiencing itself, always something like coming nearer to the thing, getting to know it more exactly; and this involves, under the title of "more exact determination," a continually possible process of correction, for example, finding what was seen as smooth and even, as purely red, and the like, to be "in truth" a bit rough, uneven, spotted, etc. And this is especially so in the communalization of our experiential life with that of our fellow men. Each of us has his own experiential representations, but with the normal certainty that everyone present experiences the same things and in the possible course of his experiences can come to know the same things through similar properties. This applies, then, to the everyday common world in which the whole of our

1. Biemel: "From 1936 (?)" This text appears in the German edition as "Beilage II," pp. 357–64. Titles in brackets have been added by the translator to manuscripts which bear no title in the original.

normal practical life runs its course. Everything that is valid for us as actually existing there is always already understood as existing for all, precisely through common experience. And it is not only that every determination which is identifiably valid here stands within a horizon of open, possibly closer determination; every [object] stands within another open horizon extending beyond what is coperceived and already cofamiliar in the way of experiential objects, extending into the infinity of unknown things, things of possible experiential knowledge. To these also correspond, as belonging to the vague things, horizons of causalities which are also only vague; these, insofar as they have become known determinately through experience, are related to the circumstances and changes in circumstances which are experienced with approximate determinateness and have, in addition, their horizon of as yet fully undetermined causalities, related to the horizon of unfamiliar external things.

This style of the experiential world, a manner of being which is in suspension in regard to more or less perfect determination within open, undetermined horizons, does not disturb the course of normal practical life, the everyday world which is that of normal men; their life is related to a sphere of normal things which become known to them in common through a set of normal types of experience; all their life reckons with such things only in regard to what is identifiable in vague types. Whatever remains in suspension over and above this is practically irrelevant; hence there is here a practically perfect sort of exactness and a practically perfect acquaintance with the things as they really are and [as they] can be exhibited [to be] again and again in their true being—in the only truth which normal, practical life knows and needs.

But given this inalterable style of our experiential world— the world we constantly have in life as the world of actual experience, which gives to the word "world" its sole original sense—how is scientific knowledge of the world, "philosophy" in the language of the ancients, possible? Indeed, how can it even be motivated as a task, and specifically with that sense of scientific objectivity which has come to be taken completely for granted by us, a sense that had first to be formed in the development and transformation of the original world-concept? This sense has come to be taken so much for granted by us that we have difficulty even making clear to ourselves that we are confronted here with the product of a development into whose original motives and original self-evidence we must inquire.

With the first breakthrough of a universal theoretical interest, through which philosophy enters history with its universal subject matter of everything that is at all, a totality and an all-encompassing unity of what is, the most general and invariant characteristics of the world, as the world of original experience, are also noticed, and correlatively the invariant properties of the experience of them itself; thus in particular the universal causal style of this world, as well as the universal structure, on the other side, of the always vague and undetermined way of knowing the experienced things. A deeper inspection of this knowledge soon gives rise also to the recognition of its relativity to those who experience, individually and together, those who cognitively identify the same things throughout the alteration of wavering, subjective, sensible manners of givenness. But how, from this point, did the idea arise of an absolute, exact determinateness of things, and not only those actually experienced and actually experienceable but also the things of the universal, open, infinite world-horizon which can never be traversed by actual experience with its finite progress? How did the idea arise of an exact universal causality and, as opposed to all empirical induction in the realm of what is factually experienceable, the idea of an exact universal inducibility of everything that is undetermined and open *ad infinitum* in virtue of the experiential structure of the original world? Thus, as we can also say: how did the leap occur from δόξα to ἐπιστήμη and, under the latter heading, to the idea of a rationally knowable in-itself which exhibits itself merely subjectively and relatively as mere appearance in the things of sense-experience?

Exact objectivity is the accomplishment of method, practiced by men generally in the world of experience (the "sense-world") —practiced not as a commercial praxis, as a technique of shaping and reshaping things pregiven in experience, but as a praxis in which those imperfectly determining thing-representations make up the material; and it involves a general attitude of thought such that, taking an exemplary individual thing as an example of "any given thing at all," the open, endless multiplicity of its imperfect but perfectible subjective representations is thought of as having been run through, and this in the exercise of the capacity of proceeding from each [representation] [2] along the lines of its possible perfection. The capacity of carrying out the series of gradations is limited, not only in the case of experi-

2. Biemel's interpolation.

ences (of fact), but also in that of intuitive fiction; both, considered as actual intuitions of the exemplary thing that one would come to know experientially in a more and more perfect way, soon break off. True, an empty anticipation of something "more perfect" is necessarily given at the same time, but not in such a way that the practical intuition aimed at the *plus ultra* could ever be fulfilled, any more than the continuation of the perfection-series, now prefigured in an empty way, [could be fulfilled] as a series to be continued. Here the idealizing accomplishment begins: the conception of the "again and again"—in the direction of the empty prior design of the series, the empty thought of its fulfillment conceived of as possible, whereby a new series would attain a prior design, again conceived with a possible fulfillment, and so on again and again—*in infinitum*.

What arises first is the idea of continuation which is repeatable with unconditional generality, with its own self-evidence, as a freely thinkable and self-evident possible infinity, rather than the open endlessness [described above]: rather than finite iteration, this is iteration within the sphere of the unconditional "again-and-again," of what can be renewed with ideal freedom. With this the properties of the examplary thing as such are idealized, as an example for thought which becomes self-evident thereby of a thing as such in unconditional generality. There arises the ideal property, as the unity of the conceived infinity of thinkable and exact, relatively perfect exhibitings, through which, *idealiter*, harmonious identification would proceed. The thing itself is idealized as something existing through its properties—all its properties, and these in all their exhibitings, which, in running through the conceived, infinite totality, the all-encompassing unity, exhaust the identity of all the properties and of the thing itself—perfectly. In the ideal running-through of this infinite totality there would then arise an ideal knowledge of the thing itself, as a thing with its not merely actual but also ideally possible experiences. Accordingly, such an idealization overcomes even the limits of our finite capacity for coming to know the open world-horizon which continuously accompanies all actual, experiential knowing. Even externally, in the progress of experience from relatively known toward unknown things and spheres of things, idealizing thinking conquers the infinity of the experiential world, as a world-knowledge to be attained *idealiter* through the thought and conceivably thought continuation and infinite perfection of external experience, knowledge based on a conceivable renewal "again and again" of the enrichment of experience.

The idealized world, then, is an ideal infinity of things, each of which is itself an index for an ideal infinity of relative exhibitings whose harmonious unity of identity—*idealiter*—the thing is.

This idealization of the world—which, as can be seen, is very complicated—prescribes to each of the things of factual world-experience an ideal, the ideal of a knowledge [of it] which is thinkable *idealiter,* can be perfected *in infinitum,* and can come to absolute perfection in the traversing of the conceived infinity. But this is not yet the accomplishment which creates, for each pregiven thing, *its* individual ideal being and thus builds the bridge to the utilization of the attained ideal multiplicity of ideas in application to the particular pregiven world of actual experience. And indeed, seen from the standpoint of this accomplishment's already having occurred (insofar as it is actually to be found as exact science), exact objectivity is a cognitive accomplishment which (1) presupposes a method of systematic and determined idealization creating a world of ideals which can be produced determinately and constructed systematically *in infinitum* and (2) makes self-evident the applicability of these constructible idealities to the world of experience.

The problem which is thus formulated in general terms is the radical *problem of the historical possibility of "objective" science,* objectively scientific philosophy—the science which, after all, has long been present, in its way, as a historical fact, which developed through the appropriation of the above idea of its task, and which has attained, at least in one branch, a supremely fruitful realization, namely, as exact mathematics and mathematical natural science. It is a matter not merely of establishing science's historical, factual point of origin in terms of place, time, and actual circumstances, of tracing philosophy back to its founders, to the ancient physicists, to Ionia, etc.; rather, it must be understood through its original spiritual motives, i.e., in its most original *meaningfulness* [*Sinnhaftigkeit*] and in the original forward development of this meaningfulness. Belonging to this, constantly cofunctioning as meaning-fundament, is the world which gives itself, and just *as* it gives itself, in actual experience, the "world of sensibility." This world is historically changing in its particular styles but [is] invariant in its invariant structure of generality.

As to how the other problem of the possibility of knowledge —as the [problem of the] possibility of objective-scientific knowledge (here one would speak of the purely "epistemological" problem)—is related to that of the historical possibility [of such knowledge], this can find clarification only in the further course of our reflections. Also, because of the historical place in which we find ourselves, the first origin is not immediately accessible to the historical regressive inquiry. Our first concern is to look back to the origins of a successful rational objectification within a fundamental stratum of the world; and by this I naturally mean the objectification which has been accomplished as geometry, as pure mathematics.

Objectification is a matter of *method,* founded upon prescientific data of experience. Mathematical method "constructs," out of intuitive representation, ideal objects and teaches how to deal with them operatively and systematically.* It does not produce things out of other things in the manner of handwork; it produces ideas. Ideas arise through a peculiar sort of mental accomplishment: idealization.

First comes the idealizing accomplishment together with the exactly identifiable ideas it can produce, as mental structures based on the multiplicities of appearance which are suspended in relativity. Second, there is the operative construction of idea-structures out of pregiven ideas. The interconnection of both makes up the objective-scientific mind which [encompasses] [3] both infinities, that of the multiplicities of appearance, in which one and the same thing exhibits itself, and that of the things [themselves].

The idealizing mental accomplishment has its material in the "thing-appearances," the "thing-representations." In perceiving, with its flow of appearances having vital ontic validity, these appearances are found in the mode of performance and are not appearances as "material." I am there, performing ontic validity, performing its horizon. In the "synthetic" progression [of perception] I do not put the horizon together, "joining" something to

* It conceives an ideal of perfection on the basis of a conception of the infinity of imperfection, motivated by a graduality belonging to its own essence. It idealizes the properties of things. With this it idealizes, correlatively, their identifiability; and, on the other side, it also idealizes the imperfect experienceability according to which our direct experience proceeds from known to unknown things; thus, for a course of iterative perfectings a strict infinity of iteration is substructed—as an ideal.

3. Biemel's interpolation.

something else, dealing with it as material; in "act," in the course [of perceiving], I am directed toward the ontically valid unity, directed toward the mobile, continual overlapping of the horizons, which is concretely the whole intentionality of appearances and horizons of appearances; concrete intentionality is in the mobility of fulfillment by becoming intuitive through appearances. But in idealizing thinking the manner of performance is changed: first there is the process of continually making intuitive the undetermined, coming appearances; then there is the exemplary, then the conception of infinity, etc.

The two parts of exact objectification, which exhibits itself in the finished accomplishment as physics, are represented, on the one hand, by the accomplishment of pure mathematics, science through "pure thinking"—that is, the science which idealizes, in the sense more precisely given above, and which remains purely within the realm of the ideals. Its full accomplishment is in fact designated by its method of determined idealization and of a systematic operative construction of ideal objects out of pregiven objects, which ultimately makes it possible to master the totality. This world [the totality of such objects] is already objective insofar as the knowledge it affords, the ideals formed of it, are absolutely identical for anyone who practices the method, no matter how much his empirically intuitive representation may differ from what serves others in their intuition-based idealization.

The mathematical accomplishment was of course limited to the mere spatiotemporal shapes or to the structure of space-time belonging universally to the world. It can be seen that such an accomplishment was possible only through the essence of this structure and that, accordingly, exact objectification could have significance for the world, at least at first, only as a world of bodies, whereby everything about the things that was itself noncorporeal was abstracted.

Here a peculiar question arises. When we methodically and systematically bring to recognition the a priori of history, is this itself a facticity of history? Does it not then presuppose the a priori of history? The a priori is related to the being of mankind and the surrounding world that is valid for it in experience, thinking, and acting. But the a priori is something ideal and general, which on the one hand refers to men themselves as objects and on the other hand is a structure within men, in us who form it. And what of the objectivity of these ideal structures? What of the objectivity of this a priori? Here we come again to the presuppositions of the possibility of the uninterrupted tradition. What secures, then, the objectivity of this a priori as being precisely a priori the being of mankind and its cultural world, which always bears its a priori within itself, is always valid, is identifiable in all periods of time? Does this not presuppose ascending culture and, within it, men, motivated in such a way that they have an interest in essential history [*Wesenshistorie*], enter into scientific contact with one another, and continually attain and hand down a priori acquisitions? Would this not be an infinite fact?

But we come back again to the fact that historical facts (including the present fact that we are) are objective only on the basis of the a priori. Yet the a priori presupposes historical being?

What would be the status of the a priori of geometry and other a priori sciences if men were to become quite incapable in principle of carrying out the horizon-exposition through free variation and thus of discovering the invariant essential structure of the historical world? Could one then know whether a science is a priori? Or, if for accidental, factual reasons a science's access to its a priori sources were blocked, how could the kind of thinking we have attempted here ever begin, such that the blocked sources could again be opened up?

It must be shown, then, indeed as something belonging to the individual essence of man and thus to the world, that in mankind this capacity can never cease, can never be completely absent, even if it remains undeveloped for factual reasons. This leads to the most general and deepest problems of reason.

Let us now consider the fact that geometry and the other sciences related to it are ultimately all either actual or still to be accomplished branches of the one philosophy, which is supposed to be an accomplishment of theoretical mankind, philosophizing mankind, and that their goal is truth—not everyday finite truth, whose limitedness, whose finitude, whose relativity consists in the fact that it is historical but keeps the historical horizon in the dark. There is to be an unconditioned, absolute truth, encompassing the world, including man who lives in it, with his practical interests, his relative knowledge, and the valuations and projects based on it; and also philosophizing man, with his philosophical truth-structures.

Does this not then apply to all science, no matter how different its peculiar characteristics may be, and thus to all truth in the scientific sense, as science's guiding ideal? Does it not derive from an idealization which is itself in the historical sphere, and does it not presuppose the a priori of history, which itself derives from an idealization?

For the first time in this work, its historical path requires that we pose questions in this manner and that we undertake new investigations with their own direction. Out of these—not in these investigations themselves but in their interweaving with further ones, and resulting from further historical paths—there will gradually arise a style of philosophical questioning which is new in principle, and a new method of philosophical work.

Even the problem-analyses of this section offer troublesome difficulties; and because of pathways that diverge considerably from the old familiar ones in philosophy and science, pathways whose pinnacles cannot be discerned in advance, they probably first appeared to the reader as excursuses of little interest which interrupt the coherent style of the treatise. Here I must ask the reader for a little restraining patience. Later it will be understood that none of the expositions in this work are dispensable to it and its task of leading up to transcendental phenomenology. To this, its over-all meaning, belongs the interweaving of historical investigations and the systematic investigations they motivate, arranged from the start according to that peculiar sort of reflexivity through which alone the self-reflection of the philosopher can function—the philosopher, who is in the position of not being able to presuppose any pregiven philosophy, his own or another, since the possibility of a philosophy as such, as the sole philosophy, is to be his problem.

Appendix VI:
[*The Origin of Geometry*] [1]

THE INTEREST THAT propels us in this work makes it
necessary to engage first of all in reflections which surely never
occurred to Galileo. We must focus our gaze not merely upon the
ready-made, handed-down geometry and upon the manner of
being which its meaning had in his thinking; it was no different
in his thinking from what it was in that of all the late inheritors
of the older geometric wisdom, whenever they were at work,
either as pure geometers or as making practical applications of
geometry. Rather, indeed above all, we must also inquire back
into the original meaning of the handed-down geometry, which
continued to be valid with this very same meaning—continued
and at the same time was developed further, remaining simply
"geometry" in all its new forms. Our considerations will necessarily lead to the deepest problems of meaning, problems of
science and of the history of science in general, and indeed in
the end to problems of a universal history in general; so that our
problems and expositions concerning Galilean geometry take on
an exemplary significance.

Let it be noted in advance that, in the midst of our historical
meditations on modern philosophy, there appears here for the
first time with Galileo, through the disclosure of the depth-problems of the meaning-origin of geometry and, founded on this, of
the meaning-origin of his new physics, a clarifying light for our
whole undertaking: namely, [the idea of] seeking to carry out, in

1. This manuscript was written in 1936 and was edited and published (beginning with the third paragraph) by Eugen Fink in the
Revue internationale de philosophie, Vol. I, No. 2 (1939) under the
title "Der Ursprung der Geometrie als intentional-historisches Problem." It appears in Biemel's edition of the *Crisis* as "Beilage III," pp.
365–86. The first paragraphs suggest it was meant for inclusion in
the *Crisis*.

the form of historical meditations, self-reflections about our own present philosophical situation in the hope that in this way we can finally take possession of the meaning, method, and beginning of philosophy, the *one* philosophy to which our life seeks to be and ought to be devoted. For, as will become evident here, at first in connection with one example, our investigations are historical in an unusual sense, namely, in virtue of a thematic direction which opens up depth-problems quite unknown to ordinary history, problems which, [however,] in their own way, are undoubtedly historical problems. Where a consistent pursuit of these depth-problems leads can naturally not yet be seen at the beginning.

The question of the origin of geometry (under which title here, for the sake of brevity, we include all disciplines that deal with shapes existing mathematically in pure space-time) shall not be considered here as the philological-historical question, i.e., as the search for the first geometers who actually uttered pure geometrical propositions, proofs, theories, or for the particular propositions they discovered, or the like. Rather than this, our interest shall be the inquiry back into the most original sense in which geometry once arose, was present as the tradition of millennia, is still present for us, and is still being worked on in a lively forward development; * we inquire into that sense in which it appeared in history for the first time—in which it had to appear, even though we know nothing of the first creators and are not even asking after them. Starting from what we know, from our geometry, or rather from the older handed-down forms (such as Euclidean geometry), there is an inquiry back into the submerged original beginnings of geometry as they necessarily must have been in their "primally establishing" function. This regressive inquiry unavoidably remains within the sphere of generalities, but, as we shall soon see, these are generalities which can be richly explicated, with prescribed possibilities of arriving at particular questions and self-evident claims as answers. The geometry which is ready-made, so to speak, from which the regressive inquiry begins, is a tradition. Our human existence moves within innumerable traditions. The whole cultural world, in all its forms, exists through tradition. These forms have arisen as such not merely causally; we also know

---

* So also for Galileo and all the periods following the Renaissance, continually being worked on in a lively forward development, and yet at the same time a tradition.

already that tradition is precisely tradition, having arisen within our human space through human activity, i.e., spiritually, even though we generally know nothing, or as good as nothing, of the particular provenance and of the spiritual source that brought it about. And yet there lies in this lack of knowledge, everywhere and essentially, an implicit knowledge, which can thus also be made explicit, a knowledge of unassailable self-evidence. It begins with superficial commonplaces, such as: that everything traditional has arisen out of human activity, that accordingly past men and human civilizations existed, and among them their first inventors, who shaped the new out of materials at hand, whether raw or already spiritually shaped. From the superficial, however, one is led into the depths. Tradition is open in this general way to continued inquiry; and, if one consistently maintains the direction of inquiry, an infinity of questions opens up, questions which lead to definite answers in accord with their sense. Their form of generality—indeed, as one can see, of unconditioned general validity—naturally allows for application to individually determined particular cases, though it determines only that in the individual that can be grasped through subsumption.

Let us begin, then, in connection with geometry, with the most obvious commonplaces that we have already expressed above in order to indicate the sense of our regressive inquiry. We understand our geometry, available to us through tradition (we have learned it, and so have our teachers), to be a total acquisition of spiritual accomplishments which grows through the continued work of new spiritual acts into new acquisitions. We know of its handed-down, earlier forms, as those from which it has arisen; but with every form the reference to an earlier one is repeated. Clearly, then, geometry must have arisen out of a *first* acquisition, out of first creative activities. We understand its persisting manner of being: it is not only a mobile forward process from one set of acquisitions to another but a continuous synthesis in which all acquisitions maintain their validity, all make up a totality such that, at every present stage, the total acquisition is, so to speak, the total premise for the acquisitions of the new level. Geometry necessarily has this mobility and has a horizon of geometrical future in precisely this style; this is its meaning for every geometer who has the consciousness (the constant implicit knowledge) of existing within a forward development understood as the progress of knowledge being built into the horizon. The same thing is true of every science. Also, every science is related to an open chain of the generations of those who work for and with one another, researchers either known or unknown to one another who are the accomplishing subjectivity of the whole living science. Science, and in particular geometry, with this ontic meaning, must have had a historical beginning; this meaning itself must have an origin in an accomplishment: first as a project and then in successful execution.

Obviously it is the same here as with every other invention. Every spiritual accomplishment proceeding from its first project to its execution is present for the first time in the self-evidence of actual success. But when we note that mathematics has the manner of being of a lively forward movement from acquisitions as premises to new acquisitions, in whose ontic meaning that of the premises is included (the process continuing in this manner), then it is clear that the *total* meaning of geometry (as a developed science, as in the case of every science) could not have been present as a project and then as mobile fulfillment at the beginning. A more primitive formation of meaning necessarily went before it as a preliminary stage, undoubtedly in such a way that it appeared for the first time in the self-evidence of successful realization. But this way of expressing it is actually overblown. Self-evidence means nothing more than grasping an entity with the consciousness of its original being-itself-there [*Selbst-da*]. Successful realization of a project is, for the acting subject, self-evidence; in this self-evidence, what has been realized is there, *originaliter*, as itself.

But now questions arise. This process of projecting and successfully realizing occurs, after all, purely within the *subject* of the inventor, and thus the meaning, as present *originaliter* with its whole content, lies exclusively, so to speak, within his mental space. But geometrical existence is not psychic existence; it does not exist as something personal within the personal sphere of consciousness; it is the existence of what is objectively there for "everyone" (for actual and possible geometers, or those who understand geometry). Indeed, it has, from its primal establishment, an existence which is peculiarly supertemporal and which —of this we are certain—is accessible to all men, first of all to the actual and possible mathematicians of all peoples, all ages; and this is true of all its particular forms. And all forms newly produced by someone on the basis of pregiven forms immediately take on the same objectivity. This is, we note, an "ideal" objectivity. It is proper to a whole class of spiritual products of the cultural world, to which not only all scientific constructions and the sciences themselves belong but also, for example, the constructions of fine literature.* Works of this class do not, like tools (hammers, pliers) or like architectural and other such products, have a repeatability in many like exemplars. The Pythagorean theorem, [indeed] all of geometry, exists only once, no matter how often or even in what language it may be expressed. It is identically the same in the "original language" of Euclid and in all "translations"; and within each language it is again the same, no matter how many times it has been sensibly uttered, from the original expression and writing-down to the innumerable oral utterances or written and other documentations. The sensible utterances have spatiotemporal individuation in the world like all corporeal occurrences, like everything embodied in bodies as such; but this is not true of the spiritual form itself, which is called an "ideal object" [*ideale Gegenständlichkeit*]. In a certain way ideal objects do exist objectively in the world, but it is only in virtue of these two-leveled repetitions and ultimately in virtue of sensibly embodying repetitions. For language itself, in all its particularizations (words, sentences, speeches), is, as can easily be seen from the grammatical point of view, thoroughly made up of ideal objects; for example, the word *Löwe* occurs only once in the German language; it is identical throughout its innumerable utterances by any given persons. But the idealities of geometrical words, sentences, theories—considered purely as linguistic structures—are not the idealities that make up what is expressed and brought to validity as truth in geometry; the latter are ideal geometrical objects, states of affairs, etc. Wherever something is asserted, one can distinguish what is thematic, that about which it is said (its meaning), from the assertion, which itself, during the asserting, is never and can never be thematic. And what is thematic here is precisely ideal objects, and quite different ones from those coming under the concept of language. Our problem now concerns precisely the ideal objects which are thematic in geometry: how does geometrical ideality (just like that of all sciences) proceed from its primary intrapersonal

---

* But the broadest concept of literature encompasses them all; that is, it belongs to their objective being that they be linguistically expressed and can be expressed again and again; or, more precisely, they have their objectivity, their existence-for-everyone, only as signification, as the meaning of speech. This is true in a peculiar fashion in the case of the objective sciences: for them the difference between the original language of the work and its translation into other languages does not remove its identical accessibility or change it into an inauthentic, indirect accessibility.

origin, where it is a structure within the conscious space of the first inventor's soul, to its ideal objectivity? In advance we see that it occurs by means of language, through which it receives, so to speak, its linguistic living body [*Sprachleib*]. But how does linguistic embodiment make out of the merely intrasubjective structure the *objective* structure which, e.g., as geometrical concept or state of affairs, is in fact present as understandable by all and is valid, already in its linguistic expression as geometrical speech, as geometrical proposition, for all the future in its geometrical sense?

Naturally, we shall not go into the general problem which also arises here of the origin of language in its ideal existence and its existence in the real world grounded in utterance and documentation; but we must say a few words here about the relation between language, as a function of man within human civilization, and the world as the horizon of human existence.

Living wakefully in the world we are constantly conscious of the world, whether we pay attention to it or not, conscious of it as the horizon of our life, as a horizon of "things" (real objects), of our actual and possible interests and activities. Always standing out against the world-horizon is the horizon of our fellow men, whether there are any of them present or not. Before even taking notice of it at all, we are conscious of the open horizon of our fellow men with its limited nucleus of our neighbors, those known to us. We are thereby coconscious of the men on our external horizon in each case as "others"; in each case "I" am conscious of them as "my" others, as those with whom I can enter into actual and potential, immediate and mediate relations of empathy; [this involves] a reciprocal "getting along" with others; and on the basis of these relations I can deal with them, enter into particular modes of community with them, and then know, in a habitual way, of my being so related. Like me, every human being—and this is how he is understood by me and everyone else—has his fellow men and, always counting himself, civilization in general, in which he knows himself to be living.

It is precisely to this horizon of civilization that common language belongs. One is conscious of civilization from the start as an immediate and mediate linguistic community. Clearly it is only through language and its far-reaching documentations, as possible communications, that the horizon of civilization can be an open and endless one, as it always is for men. What is privileged in consciousness as the horizon of civilization and as the linguistic community is mature normal civilization (taking away the abnormal and the world of children). In this sense civilization is, for every man whose we-horizon it is, a community of those who can reciprocally express themselves, normally, in a fully understandable fashion; and within this community everyone can talk about what is within the surrounding world of his civilization as objectively existing. Everything has its name, or is namable in the broadest sense, i.e., linguistically expressible. The objective world is from the start the world for all, the world which "everyone" has as world-horizon. Its objective being presupposes men, understood as men with a common language. Language, for its part, as function and exercised capacity, is related correlatively to the world, the universe of objects which is linguistically expressible in its being and its being-such. Thus men as men, fellow men, world—the world of which men, of which we, always talk and can talk—and, on the other hand, language, are inseparably intertwined; and one is always certain of their inseparable relational unity, though usually only implicitly, in the manner of a horizon.

This being presupposed, the primally establishing geometer can obviously also express his internal structure. But the question arises again: How does the latter, in its "ideality," thereby become objective? To be sure, something psychic which can be understood by others [*nachverstehbar*] and is communicable, as something psychic belonging to this man, is *eó ipso* objective, just as he himself, as concrete man, is experienceable and namable by everyone as a real thing in the world of things in general. People can agree about such things, can make common verifiable assertions on the basis of common experience, etc. But how does the intrapsychically constituted structure arrive at an inter-subjective being of its own as an ideal object which, as "geometrical," is anything but a real psychic object, even though it has arisen psychically? Let us reflect. The original being-itself-there, in the immediacy [*Aktualität*] of its first production, i.e., in original "self-evidence," results in no persisting acquisition at all that could have objective existence. Vivid self-evidence passes— though in such a way that the activity immediately turns into the passivity of the flowingly fading consciousness of what-has-just-now-been. Finally this "retention" disappears, but the "disappeared" passing and being past has not become nothing for the subject in question: it can be reawakened. To the passivity of what is at first obscurely awakened and what perhaps emerges with greater and greater clarity there belongs the possible activity of a recollection in which the past experiencing [*Erleben*] is lived through in a quasi-new and quasi-active way. Now if the originally self-evident production, as the pure fulfillment of its intention, is what is renewed (recollected), there necessarily occurs, accompanying the active recollection of what is past, an activity of concurrent actual production, and there arises thereby, in original "coincidence," the self-evidence of identity: what has now been realized in original fashion is the same as what was previously self-evident. Also coestablished is the capacity for repetition at will with the self-evidence of the identity (coincidence of identity) of the structure throughout the chain of repetitions. Yet even with this, we have still not gone beyond the subject and his subjective, evident capacities; that is, we still have no "objectivity" given. It does arise, however—in a preliminary stage—in understandable fashion as soon as we take into consideration the function of empathy and fellow mankind as a community of empathy and of language. In the contact of reciprocal linguistic understanding, the original production and the product of one subject can be *actively* understood by the others. In this full understanding of what is produced by the other, as in the case of recollection, a present coaccomplishment on one's own part of the presentified activity necessarily takes place; but at the same time there is also the self-evident consciousness of the identity of the mental structure in the productions of both the receiver of the communication and the communicator; and this occurs reciprocally. The productions can reproduce their likenesses from person to person, and in the chain of the understanding of these repetitions what is self-evident turns up as the same in the consciousness of the other. In the unity of the community of communication among several persons the repeatedly produced structure becomes an object of consciousness, not as a likeness, but as the one structure common to all.

Now we must note that the objectivity of the ideal structure has not yet been fully constituted through such actual transferring of what has been originally produced in one to others who originally reproduce it. What is lacking is the *persisting existence* of the "ideal objects" even during periods in which the inventor and his fellows are no longer wakefully so related or even are no longer alive. What is lacking is their continuing-to-be even when no one has [consciously] realized them in self-evidence.

The important function of written, documenting linguistic expression is that it makes communications possible without immediate or mediate personal address; it is, so to speak, communication become virtual. Through this, the communalization of man is lifted to a new level. Written signs are, when considered from a purely corporeal point of view, straightforwardly, sensibly experienceable; and it is always possible that they be intersubjectively experienceable in common. But as linguistic signs they awaken, as do linguistic sounds, their familiar significations. The awakening is something passive; the awakened signification is thus given passively, similarly to the way in which any other activity which has sunk into obscurity, once associatively awakened, emerges at first *passively* as a more or less clear memory. In the passivity in question here, as in the case of memory, what is passively awakened can be transformed back,* so to speak, into the corresponding activity: this is the capacity for reactivation that belongs originally to every human being as a speaking being. Accordingly, then, the writing-down effects a transformation of the original mode of being of the meaning-structure, [e.g.,] within the geometrical sphere of self-evidence, of the geometrical structure which is put into words. It becomes sedimented, so to speak. But the reader can make it self-evident again, can reactivate the self-evidence.†

There is a distinction, then, between passively understanding the expression and making it self-evident by reactivating its meaning. But there also exist possibilities of a kind of activity, a thinking in terms of things that have been taken up merely receptively, passively, which deals with significations only passively understood and taken over, without any of the self-evidence of original activity. Passivity in general is the realm of things that are bound together and melt into one another associatively, where all meaning that arises is put together passively. What often happens here is that a meaning arises which is apparently possible as a unity—i.e., can apparently be made self-evidence through a possible reactivation—whereas the attempt at actual reactivation can reactivate only the individual members of the combination, while the intention to unify them into a whole, instead of being fulfilled, comes to nothing; that is,

* This is a transformation of which one is conscious as being in itself patterned after [what is passively awakened].

† But this is by no means necessary or even factually normal. Even without this he can understand; he can concur "as a matter of course" in the validity of what is understood without any activity of his own. In this case he comports himself purely passively and receptively.

the ontic validity is destroyed through the original consciousness of nullity.

It is easy to see that even in [ordinary] human life, and first of all in every individual life from childhood up to maturity, the originally intuitive life which creates its originally self-evident structures through activities on the basis of sense-experience very quickly and in increasing measure falls victim to the *seduction of language*. Greater and greater segments of this life lapse into a kind of talking and reading that is dominated purely by association; and often enough, in respect to the validities arrived at in this way, it is disappointed by subsequent experience.

Now one will say that in the sphere that interests us here— that of science, of thinking directed toward the attainment of truths and the avoidance of falsehood—one is obviously greatly concerned from the start to put a stop to the free play of associative constructions. In view of the unavoidable sedimentation of mental products in the form of persisting linguistic acquisitions, which can be taken up again at first merely passively and be taken over by anyone else, such constructions remain a constant danger. This danger is avoided if one not merely convinces oneself ex post facto that the particular construction can be reactivated but assures oneself from the start, after the self-evident primal establishment, of its capacity to be reactivated and enduringly maintained. This occurs when one has a view to the univocity of linguistic expression and to securing, by means of the most painstaking formation of the relevant words, propositions, and complexes of propositions, the results which are to be univocally expressed. This must be done by the individual scientist, and not only by the inventor but by every scientist as a member of the scientific community after he has taken over from the others what is to be taken over. This belongs, then, to the particulars of the scientific tradition within the corresponding community of scientists as a community of knowledge living in the unity of a common responsibility. In accord with the essence of science, then, its functionaries maintain the constant claim, the personal certainty, that everything they put into scientific assertions has been said "once and for all," that it "stands fast," forever identically repeatable with self-evidence and usable for further theoretical or practical ends—as indubitably reactivatable with the identity of its actual meaning.*

---

* At first, of course, it is a matter of a firm direction of the will, which the scientist establishes in himself, aimed at the certain capacity for reactivation. If the goal of reactivatability can be only

However, two more things are important here. First: we have not yet taken into account the fact that scientific thinking attains new results on the basis of those already attained, that the new ones serve as the foundation for still others, etc.—in the unity of a propagative process of transferred meaning.

In the finally immense proliferation of a science like geometry, what has become of the claim and the capacity for reactivation? When every researcher works on his part of the building, what of the vocational interruptions and time out for rest, which cannot be overlooked here? When he returns to the actual continuation of work, must he first run through the whole immense chain of groundings back to the original premises and actually reactivate the whole thing? If so, a science like our modern geometry would obviously not be possible at all. And yet it is of the essence of the results of each stage not only that their ideal ontic meaning in fact comes later [than that of earlier results] but that, since meaning is grounded upon meaning, the earlier meaning gives something of its validity to the later one, indeed becomes part of it to a certain extent. Thus no building block within the mental structure is self-sufficient; and none, then, can be immediately reactivated [by itself].

This is especially true of sciences which, like geometry, have their thematic sphere in ideal products, in idealities from which more and more idealities at higher levels are produced. It is quite different in the so-called descriptive sciences, where the theoretical interest, classifying and describing, remains within the sphere of sense-intuition, which for it represents self-evidence. Here, at least in general, every new proposition can by itself be "cashed in" for self-evidence.

How, by contrast, is a science like geometry possible? How, as a systematic, endlessly growing stratified structure of idealities, can it maintain its original meaningfulness through living reactivatability if its cognitive thinking is supposed to produce something new without being able to reactivate the previous levels of knowledge back to the first? Even if this could have succeeded at a more primitive stage of geometry, its energy would ultimately have been too much spent in the effort of procuring self-evidence and would not have been available for a higher productivity.

---

relatively fulfilled, then the claim which stems from the consciousness of being able to acquire something also has its relativity; and this relativity also makes itself noticeable and is driven out. Ultimately, objective, absolutely firm knowledge of truth is an infinite idea.

Here we must take into consideration the peculiar "logical" activity which is tied specifically to language, as well as to the ideal cognitive structures that arise specifically within it. To any sentence structures that emerge within a merely passive understanding there belongs essentially a peculiar sort of activity best described by the word "explication." [2] A passively emerging sentence (e.g., in memory), or one heard and passively understood, is at first merely received with a passive ego-participation, taken up as valid; and in this form it is already our meaning. From this we distinguish the peculiar and important activity of explicating our meaning. Whereas in its first form it was a straightforwardly valid meaning, taken up as unitary and undifferentiated—concretely speaking, a straightforwardly valid declarative sentence —now what in itself is vague and undifferentiated is actively explicated. Consider, for example, the way in which we understand, when superficially reading the newspaper, and simply receive the "news"; here there is a passive taking-over of ontic validity such that what is read straightway becomes our opinion.

But it is something special, as we have said, to have the intention to explicate, to engage in the activity which articulates what has been read (or an interesting sentence from it), extracting one by one, in separation from what has been vaguely, passively received as a unity, the elements of meaning, thus bringing the total validity to active performance in a new way on the basis of the individual validities. What was a passive meaning-pattern has now become one constructed through active production. This activity, then, is a peculiar sort of self-evidence; the structure arising out of it is in the mode of having been originally produced. And in connection with this self-evidence, too, there is communalization. The explicated judgment becomes an ideal object capable of being passed on. It is this object exclusively that is meant by logic when it speaks of sentences or judgments. And thus the *domain of logic* is universally designated; this is universally the sphere of being to which logic pertains insofar as it is the theory of the sentences [or propositions] in general.

Through this activity, now, further activities become possible —self-evident constructions of new judgments on the basis of those already valid for us. This is the peculiar feature of logical thinking and of its purely logical self-evidences. All this remains intact even when judgments are transformed into assumptions,

2. *Verdeutlichung*, i.e., making explicit.

where, instead of ourselves asserting or judging, we think ourselves into the position of asserting or judging.

Here we shall concentrate on the sentences of language as they come to us passively and are merely received. In this connection it must also be noted that sentences give themselves in consciousness as reproductive transformations of an original meaning produced out of an actual, original activity; that is, in themselves they refer to such a genesis. In the sphere of logical self-evidence, deduction, or inference in forms of consequence, plays a constant and essential role. On the other hand, one must also take note of the constructive activities that operate with geometrical idealities which have been explicated but not brought to original self-evidence. (Original self-evidence must not be confused with the self-evidence of "axioms"; for axioms are in principle already the results of original meaning-construction and always have this behind them.)

Now what about the possibility of complete and genuine reactivation in full originality, through going back to the primal self-evidences, in the case of geometry and the so-called "deductive" sciences (so called, although they by no means merely deduce)? Here the fundamental law, with unconditionally general self-evidence, is: if the premises can actually be reactivated back to the most original self-evidence, then their self-evident consequences can be also. Accordingly it appears that, beginning with the primal self-evidences, the original genuineness must propagate itself through the chain of logical inference, no matter how long it is. However, if we consider the obvious finitude of the individual and even the social capacity to transform the logical chains of centuries, truly in the unity of one accomplishment, into originally genuine chains of self-evidence, we notice that the [above] law contains within itself an idealization: namely, the removal of limits from our capacity, in a certain sense its infinitization. The peculiar sort of self-evidence belonging to such idealizations will concern us later.

These are, then, the general essential insights which elucidate the whole methodical development of the "deductive" sciences and with it the manner of being which is essential to them.

These sciences are not handed down ready-made in the form of documented sentences; they involve a lively, productively advancing formation of meaning, which always has the documented, as a sediment of earlier production, at its disposal in that it deals with it logically. But out of sentences with sedimented signification, logical "dealing" can produce only other

sentences of the same character. That all new acquisitions express an actual geometrical truth is certain a priori under the
presupposition that the foundations of the deductive structure
have truly been produced and objectified in original self-evidence, i.e., have become universally accessible acquisitions. A
continuity from one person to another, from one time to another, must have been capable of being carried out. It is clear
that the method of producing original idealities out of what is
prescientifically given in the cultural world must have been
written down and fixed in firm sentences prior to the existence
of geometry; furthermore, the capacity for translating these sentences from vague linguistic understanding into the clarity of
the reactivation of their self-evident meaning must have been, in
its own way, handed down and ever capable of being handed
down.

Only as long as this condition was satisfied, or only when the
possibility of its fulfillment was perfectly secured for all time,
could geometry preserve its genuine, original meaning as a deductive science throughout the progression of logical constructions. In other words, only in this case could every geometer be
capable of bringing to mediate self-evidence the meaning borne
by every sentence, not merely as its sedimented (logical) sen-
tence-meaning but as its actual meaning, its truth-meaning. And
so for all of geometry.

The progress of deduction follows formal-logical self-evidence;
but without the actually developed capacity for reactivating
the original activities contained within its fundamental concepts, i.e., without the "what" and the "how" of its prescientific
materials, geometry would be a tradition empty of meaning; and
if we ourselves did not have this capacity, we could never even
know whether geometry had or ever did have a genuine meaning, one that could really be "cashed in."

Unfortunately, however, this is our situation, and that of the
whole modern age.

The "presupposition" mentioned above has in fact never been
fulfilled. How the living tradition of the meaning-formation of
elementary concepts is actually carried on can be seen in elementary geometrical instruction and its textbooks; what we actually learn there is how to deal with *ready-made* concepts and
sentences in a rigorously methodical way. Rendering the concepts sensibly intuitable by means of drawn figures is substituted
for the actual production of the primal idealities. And the rest is
done by success—not the success of actual insight extending

beyond the logical method's own self-evidence, but the practical successes of applied geometry, its immense, though not understood, practical usefulness. To this we must add something that will become visible further on in the treatment of historical mathematics, namely, the dangers of a scientific life that is completely given over to logical activities. These dangers lie in certain progressive transformations of meaning * to which this sort of scientific treatment drives one.

By exhibiting the essential presuppositions upon which rests the historical possibility of a genuine tradition, true to its origins, of sciences like geometry, we can understand how such sciences can vitally develop throughout the centuries and still not be genuine. The inheritance of propositions and of the method of logically constructing new propositions and idealities can continue without interruption from one period to the next, while the capacity for reactivating the primal beginnings, i.e., the sources of meaning for everything that comes later, has not been handed down with it. What is lacking is thus precisely what had given and had to give meaning to all propositions and theories, a meaning arising from the primal sources which can be made self-evident again and again.

Of course, grammatically coherent propositions and concatenations of propositions, no matter how they have arisen and have achieved validity—even if it is through mere association— have in all circumstances their own logical meaning, i.e., their meaning that can be made self-evident through explication; this can then be identified again and again as the same proposition, which is either logically coherent or incoherent, where in the latter case it cannot be executed in the unity of an actual judgment. In propositions which belong together in one domain and in the deductive systems that can be made out of them we have a realm of ideal identities; and for these there exist easily understandable possibilities of lasting traditionalization. But propositions, like other cultural structures, appear on the scene in the form of tradition; they claim, so to speak, to be sedimentations of a truth-meaning that can be made originally self-evident; whereas it is by no means necessary that they [actually] have such a meaning, as in the case of associatively derived falsifications. Thus the whole pregiven deductive science, the total sys-

---

* These work to the benefit of logical method, but they remove one further and further from the origins and make one insensitive to the problem of origin and thus to the actual ontic and truth-meaning of all these sciences.

tem of propositions in the unity of their validities, is first only a claim which can be justified as an expression of the alleged truth-meaning only through the actual capacity for reactivation.

Through this state of affairs we can understand the deeper reason for the demand, which has spread throughout the modern period and has finally been generally accepted, for a so-called "epistemological grounding" of the sciences, though clarity has never been achieved about what the much-admired sciences are actually lacking.*

As for further details on the uprooting of an originally genuine tradition, i.e., one which involved original self-evidence at its actual first beginning, one can point to possible and easily understandable reasons. In the first oral cooperation of the beginning geometers, the need was understandably lacking for an exact fixing of descriptions of the prescientific primal material and of the ways in which, in relation to this material, geometrical idealities arose together with the first "axiomatic" propositions. Further, the logical superstructures did not yet rise so high that one could not return again and again to the original meaning. On the other hand, the possibility of the practical application of the derived laws, which was actually obvious in connection with the original developments, understandably led quickly, in the realm of praxis, to a habitually practiced method of using mathematics, if need be, to bring about useful things. This method could naturally be handed down even without the ability for original self-evidence. Thus mathematics, emptied of meaning, could generally propagate itself, constantly being added to logically, as could the methodics of technical application on the other side. The extraordinarily far-reaching practical usefulness became of itself a major motive for the advancement and appreciation of these sciences. Thus also it is understandable that the lost original truth-meaning made itself felt so little, indeed, that the need for the corresponding regressive inquiry had to be reawakened. More than this: the true sense of such an inquiry had to be discovered.

Our results based on principle are of a generality that extends over all the so-called deductive sciences and even indicates similar problems and investigations for all sciences. For all of them have the mobility of sedimented traditions that are worked upon, again and again, by an activity of producing new struc-

* What does Hume do but endeavor to inquire back into the primal impressions of developed ideas and, in general, scientific ideas?

tures of meaning and handing them down. Existing in this way, they extend enduringly through time, since all new acquisitions are in turn sedimented and become working materials. Everywhere the problems, the clarifying investigations, the insights of principle are *historical*. We stand within the horizon of human civilization, the one in which we ourselves now live. We are constantly, vitally conscious of this horizon, and specifically as a temporal horizon implied in our given present horizon. To the one human civilization there corresponds essentially the one cultural world as the surrounding life-world with its [peculiar] manner of being; this world, for every historical period and civilization, has its particular features and is precisely the tradition. We stand, then, within the historical horizon in which everything is historical, even though we may know very little about it in a definite way. But it has its essential structure that can be revealed through methodical inquiry. This inquiry prescribes all the possible specialized questions, thus including, for the sciences, the inquiries back into origin which are peculiar to them in virtue of their historical manner of being. Here we are led back to the primal materials of the first formation of meaning, the primal premises, so to speak, which lie in the prescientific cultural world. Of course, this cultural world has in turn its own questions of origin, which at first remain unasked.

Naturally, problems of this particular sort immediately awaken the total problem of the universal historicity of the correlative manners of being of humanity and the cultural world and the a priori structure contained in this historicity. Still, questions like that of the clarification of the origin of geometry have a closed character, such that one need not inquire beyond those prescientific materials.

Further clarifications will be made in connection with two objections which are familiar to our own philosophical-historical situation.

In the first place, what sort of strange obstinacy is this, seeking to take the question of the origin of geometry back to some undiscoverable Thales of geometry, someone not even known to legend? Geometry is available to us in its propositions, its theories. Of course we must and we can answer for this logical edifice to the last detail in terms of self-evidence. Here, to be sure, we arrive at first axioms, and from them we proceed to the original self-evidence which the fundamental concepts make possible. What is this, if not the "theory of knowledge," in this case specifically the theory of geometrical knowledge? No one would think of tracing the epistemological problem back to such a supposed Thales. This is quite superfluous. The presently available concepts and propositions themselves contain their own meaning, first as nonself-evident opinion, but nevertheless as true propositions with a meant but still hidden truth which we can obviously bring to light by rendering the propositions themselves self-evident.

Our answer is as follows. Certainly the historical backward reference has not occurred to anyone; certainly theory of knowledge has never been seen as a peculiarly historical task. But this is precisely what we object to in the past. The ruling dogma of the separation in principle between epistemological elucidation and historical, even humanistic-psychological explanation, between epistemological and genetic origin, is fundamentally mistaken, unless one inadmissibly limits, in the usual way, the concepts of "history," "historical explanation," and "genesis." Or rather, what is fundamentally mistaken is the limitation through which precisely the deepest and most genuine problems of history are concealed. If one thinks over our expositions (which are of course still rough and will later of necessity lead us into new depth-dimensions), what they make obvious is precisely that what we know—namely, that the presently vital cultural configuration "geometry" is a tradition and is still being handed down —is not knowledge concerning an external causality which effects the succession of historical configurations, as if it were knowledge based on induction, the presupposition of which would amount to an absurdity here; rather, to understand geometry or any given cultural fact is to be conscious of its historicity, albeit "implicitly." This, however, is not an empty claim; for quite generally it is true for every fact given under the heading of "culture," whether it is a matter of the lowliest culture of necessities or the highest culture (science, state, church, economic organization, etc.), that every straightforward understanding of it as an experiential fact involves the "coconsciousness" that it is something constructed through human activity. No matter how hidden, no matter how merely "implicitly" coimplied this meaning is, there belongs to it the self-evident possibility of explication, of "making it explicit" and clarifying it. Every explication and every transition from making explicit to making self-evident (even perhaps in cases where one stops much too soon) is nothing other than historical disclosure; in itself, essentially, it is something historical, and as such it bears, with essential necessity, the horizon of its history within itself. This is of course also to say that the whole of the cultural present, understood as a totality, "implies" the whole of the cultural past in an undetermined but structurally determined generality. To put it more precisely, it implies a continuity of pasts which imply one another, each in itself being a past cultural present. And this whole continuity is a *unity* of traditionalization up to the present, which is our present *as* [a process of] traditionalizing itself in flowing-static vitality. This is, as has been said, an undetermined generality, but it has in principle a structure which can be much more widely explicated by proceeding from these indications, a structure which also grounds, "implies," the possibilities for every search for and determination of concrete, factual states of affairs.

Making geometry self-evident, then, whether one is clear about this or not, is the disclosure of its historical tradition. But this knowledge, if it is not to remain empty talk or undifferentiated generality, requires the methodical production, proceeding from the present and carried out as research in the present, of differentiated self-evidences of the type discovered above (in several fragmentary investigations of what belongs to such knowledge superficially, as it were). Carried out systematically, such self-evidences result in nothing other and nothing less than the universal a priori of history with all its highly abundant component elements.

We can also say now that history is from the start nothing other than the vital movement of the coexistence and the interweaving of original formations and sedimentations of meaning.

Anything that is shown to be a historical fact, either in the present through experience or by a historian as a fact in the past, necessarily has its *inner structure of meaning;* but especially the motivational interconnections established about it in terms of everyday understanding have deep, further and further-reaching implications which must be interrogated, disclosed. All [merely] factual history remains incomprehensible because, always merely drawing its conclusions naïvely and straightforwardly from facts, it never makes thematic the general ground of meaning upon which all such conclusions rest, has never investigated the immense structural a priori which is proper to it. Only the disclosure of the essentially general structure * lying in our present and then in every past or future

* The superficial structure of the externally "ready-made" men within the social-historical, essential structure of humanity, but also

historical present as such, and, in totality, only the disclosure of the concrete, historical time in which we live, in which our total humanity lives in respect to its total, essentially general structure—only this disclosure can make possible historical inquiry [*Historie*] which is truly understanding, insightful, and in the genuine sense scientific. This is the concrete, historical a priori which encompasses everything that exists as historical becoming and having-become or exists in its essential being as tradition and handing-down. What has been said was related to the total form "historical present in general," historical time generally. But the particular configurations of culture, which find their place within its coherent historical being as tradition and as vitally handing themselves down, have within this totality only relatively self-sufficient being in traditionality, only the being of nonself-sufficient components. Correlatively, now, account would have to be taken of the subjects of historicity, the persons who create cultural formations, functioning in totality: creative personal civilization.*

In respect to geometry one recognizes, now that we have pointed out the hiddenness of its fundamental concepts, which have become inaccessible, and have made them understandable as such in first basic outlines, that only the consciously set task of [discovering] the historical origin of geometry (within the total problem of the a priori of historicity in general) can provide the method for a geometry which is true to its origins and at the same time is to be understood in a universal-historical way; and the same is true for all sciences, for philosophy. In principle, then, a history of philosophy, a history of the particular sciences in the style of the usual factual history, can actually render nothing of their subject matter comprehensible. For a genuine history of philosophy, a genuine history of the particular sciences, is nothing other than the tracing of the historical meaning-structures given in the present, or their self-evidences, along the documented chain of historical back-references into the hidden dimension of the primal self-evidences which underlie

---

the deeper [structures] which disclose the inner historicities of the persons taking part. ["Structures" is Biemel's interpolation.]

* The historical world is, to be sure, first pregiven as a social-historical world. But it is historical only through the inner historicity of the individuals, who are individuals in their inner historicity, together with that of other communalized persons. Recall what was said in a few meager beginning expositions about memories and the constant historicity to be found in them [pp. 359 f., above].

them.* Even the very problem here can be made understandable only through recourse to the historical a priori as the universal source of all conceivable problems of understanding. The problem of genuine historical explanation comes together, in the case of the sciences, with "epistemological" grounding or clarification.

We must expect yet a second and very weighty objection. From the historicism which prevails extensively in different forms [today] I expect little receptivity for a depth-inquiry which goes beyond the usual factual history, as does the one outlined in this work, especially since, as the expression "a priori" indicates, it lays claim to a strictly unconditioned and truly apodictic self-evidence extending beyond all historical facticities. One will object: what naïveté, to seek to display, and to claim to have displayed, a historical a priori, an absolute, supertemporal validity, after we have obtained such abundant testimony for the relativity of everything historical, of all historically developed world-apperceptions, right back to those of the "primitive" tribes. Every people, large or small, has its world in which, for that people, everything fits well together, whether in mythical-magical or in European-rational terms, and in which everything can be explained perfectly. Every people has its "logic" and, accordingly, if this logic is explicated in propositions, "its" a priori.

However, let us consider the methodology of establishing historical facts in general, thus including that of the facts supporting the objection; and let us do this in regard to what such methodology presupposes. Does not the undertaking of a humanistic science of "how it really was" contain a presupposition taken for granted, a validity-ground never observed, never made thematic, of a strictly unassailable [type of] self-evidence, without which historical inquiry would be a meaningless enterprise? All questioning and demonstrating which is in the usual sense historical presupposes history [*Geschichte*] as the universal horizon of questioning, not explicitly, but still as a horizon of implicit certainty, which, in spite of all vague background-indeterminacy, is the presupposition of all determinability, or of all intention to seek and to establish determined facts.

What is historically primary in itself is our present. We always already know of our present world and that we live in it,

* But what counts as primal self-evidence for the sciences is determined by an educated person or a sphere of such persons who pose new questions, new historical questions, questions concerning the inner depth-dimension as well as those concerning an external historicity in the social-historical world.

always surrounded by an openly endless horizon of unknown actualities. This knowing, as horizon-certainty, is not something learned, not knowledge which was once actual and has merely sunk back to become part of the background; the horizon-certainty had to be already there in order to be capable of being laid out thematically; it is already presupposed in order that we can seek to know what we do not know. All not-knowing concerns the unknown world, which yet exists in advance for us *as* world, as the horizon of all questions of the present and thus also all questions which are specifically historical. These are the questions which concern men, as those who act and create in their communalized coexistence in the world and transform the constant cultural face of the world. Do we not know further—we have already had occasion to speak of this—that this historical present has its historical pasts behind it, that it has developed out of them, that historical past is a continuity of pasts which proceed from one another, each, as a past present, being a tradition producing tradition out of itself? Do we not know that the present and the whole of historical time implied in it is that of a historically coherent and unified civilization, coherent through its generative bond and constant communalization in cultivating what has already been cultivated before, whether in cooperative work or in reciprocal interaction, etc.? Does all this not announce a universal "knowing" of the horizon, an implicit knowing that can be made explicit systematically in its essential structure? Is not the resulting great problem here the horizon toward which all questions tend, and thus the horizon which is presupposed in all of them? Accordingly, we need not first enter into some kind of critical discussion of the facts set out by historicism; it is enough that even the claim of their factualness presupposes the historical a priori if this claim is to have a meaning.

But a doubt arises all the same. The horizon-exposition to which we recurred must not bog down in vague, superficial talk; it must itself arrive at its own sort of scientific discipline. The sentences in which it is expressed must be fixed and capable of being made self-evident again and again. Through what method do we obtain a universal and also fixed a priori of the historical world which is always originally genuine? Whenever we consider it, we find ourselves with the self-evident capacity to reflect —to turn to the horizon and to penetrate it in an expository way. But we also have, and know that we have, the capacity of complete freedom to transform, in thought and phantasy, our human historical existence and what is there exposed as its life-world. And precisely in this activity of free variation, and in running through the conceivable possibilities for the life-world, there arises, with apodictic self-evidence, an essentially general set of elements going through all the variants; and of this we can convince ourselves with truly apodictic certainty. Thereby we have removed every bond to the factually valid historical world and have regarded this world itself [merely] as one of the conceptual possibilities. This freedom, and the direction of our gaze upon the apodictically invariant, results in the latter again and again—with the self-evidence of being able to repeat the invariant structure at will—as what is identical, what can be made self-evident *originaliter* at any time, can be fixed in univocal language as the essence constantly implied in the flowing, vital horizon.

Through this method, going beyond the formal generalities we exhibited earlier, we can also make thematic that apodictic [aspect] of the prescientific world that the original founder of geometry had at his disposal, that which must have served as the material for his idealizations.

Geometry and the sciences most closely related to it have to do with space-time and the shapes, figures, also shapes of motion, alterations of deformation, etc., that are possible within space-time, particularly as measurable magnitudes. It is now clear that even if we know almost nothing about the historical surrounding world of the first geometers, this much is certain as an invariant, essential structure: that it was a world of "things" (including the human beings themselves as subjects of this world); that all things necessarily had to have a bodily character —although not all things could be mere bodies, since the necessarily coexisting human beings are not thinkable as mere bodies and, like even the cultural objects which belong with them structurally, are not exhausted in corporeal being. What is also clear, and can be secured at least in its essential nucleus through careful a priori explication, is that these pure bodies had spatio-temporal shapes and "material" [*stoffliche*] qualities (color, warmth, weight, hardness, etc.) related to them. Further, it is clear that in the life of practical needs certain particularizations of shape stood out and that a technical praxis always [aimed at] [3] the production of particular preferred shapes and the improvement of them according to certain directions of gradualness.

3. Biemel's interpolation.

First to be singled out from the thing-shapes are surfaces—
more or less "smooth," more or less perfect surfaces; edges, more
or less rough or fairly "even"; in other words, more or less pure
lines, angles, more or less perfect points; then, again, among the
lines, for example, straight lines are especially preferred, and
among the surfaces the even surfaces; for example, for practical
purposes boards limited by even surfaces, straight lines, and
points are preferred, whereas totally or partially curved surfaces are undesirable for many kinds of practical interests.
Thus the production of even surfaces and their perfection (pol-
ishing) always plays its role in praxis. So also in cases where
just distribution is intended. Here the rough estimate of magnitudes is transformed into the measurement of magnitudes by
counting the equal parts. (Here, too, proceeding from the factual, an essential form becomes recognizable through a method
of variation.) Measuring belongs to every culture, varying only
according to stages from primitive to higher perfections. We can
always presuppose some measuring technique, whether of a
lower or higher type, in the essential forward development of
culture, [as well as] the growth of such a technique, thus also
including the art of design for buildings, of surveying fields,
pathways, etc.; [4] such a technique is always already there, already abundantly developed and pregiven to the philosopher who
did not yet know geometry but who should be conceivable as its
inventor. As a philosopher proceeding from the practical, finite
surrounding world (of the room, the city, the landscape, etc.,
and temporally the world of periodical occurrences: day, month,
etc.) to the theoretical world-view and world-knowledge, he has
the finitely known and unknown spaces and times as finite
elements within the horizon of an open infinity. But with this he
does not yet have geometrical space, mathematical time, and
whatever else is to become a novel spiritual product out of these
finite elements which serve as material; and with his manifold
finite shapes in their space-time he does not yet have geometrical
shapes, the phoronomic shapes; [his shapes, as] formations developed out of praxis and thought of in terms of [gradual] perfection, clearly serve only as bases for a new sort of praxis out of
which similarly named new constructions grow.

It is evident in advance that this new sort of construction

4. I have reverted to the original version of this sentence as given
in the critical apparatus; I can make no sense of the emended version
given in the text.

will be a product arising out of an idealizing, spiritual act, one of "pure" thinking, which has its materials in the designated general pregivens of this factual humanity and human surrounding world and creates "ideal objects" out of them.

Now the problem would be to discover, through recourse to what is essential to history [*Historie*], the historical original meaning which necessarily was able to give and did give to the whole becoming of geometry its persisting truth-meaning.

It is of particular importance now to bring into focus and establish the following insight: Only if the apodictically general content, invariant throughout all conceivable variation, of the spatiotemporal sphere of shapes is taken into account in the idealization can an ideal construction arise which can be understood for all future time and by all coming generations of men and thus be capable of being handed down and reproduced with the identical intersubjective meaning. This condition is valid far beyond geometry for all spiritual structures which are to be unconditionally and generally capable of being handed down. Were the thinking activity of a scientist to introduce something "time-bound" in his thinking, i.e., something bound to what is merely factual about his present or something valid for him as a merely factual tradition, his construction would likewise have a merely time-bound ontic meaning; this meaning would be understandable only by those men who shared the same merely factual presuppositions of understanding.

It is a general conviction that geometry, with all its truths, is valid with unconditioned generality for all men, all times, all peoples, and not merely for all historically factual ones but for all conceivable ones. The presuppositions of principle for this conviction have never been explored because they have never been seriously made a problem. But it has also become clear to us that every establishment of a historical fact which lays claim to unconditioned objectivity likewise presupposes this invariant or absolute a priori.

Only [through the disclosure of this a priori] [5] can there be an a priori science extending beyond all historical facticities, all historical surrounding worlds, peoples, times, civilizations; only in this way can a science as *aeterna veritas* appear. Only on this fundament is based the secured capacity of inquiring back from the temporarily depleted self-evidence of a science to the primal self-evidences.

5. Biemel's interpolation.

Do we not stand here before the great and profound prob-lem-horizon of reason, the same reason that functions in every man, the *animal rationale,* no matter how primitive he is?

This is not the place to penetrate into those depths them-selves.

In any case, we can now recognize from all this that histori-cism, which wishes to clarify the historical or epistemological essence of mathematics from the standpoint of the magical circumstances or other manners of apperception of a time-bound civilization, is mistaken in principle. For romantic spirits the mythical-magical elements of the historical and prehistorical aspects of mathematics may be particularly attractive; but to cling to this merely historically factual aspect of mathematics is precisely to lose oneself to a sort of romanticism and to overlook the genuine problem, the internal-historical problem, the episte-mological problem. Also, one's gaze obviously cannot then be-come free to recognize that facticities of every type, including those involved in the [historicist] objection, have a root in the essential structure of what is generally human, through which a teleological reason running throughout all historicity announces itself. With this is revealed a set of problems in its own right related to the totality of history and to the full meaning which ultimately gives it its unity.

If the usual factual study of history in general, and in partic-ular the history which in most recent times has achieved true universal extension over all humanity, is to have any meaning at all, such a meaning can only be grounded upon what we can here call internal history, and as such upon the foundations of the universal historical a priori. Such a meaning necessarily leads further to the indicated highest question of a universal teleology of reason.

If, after these expositions, which have illuminated very gen-eral and many-sided problem-horizons, we lay down the follow-ing as something completely secured, namely, that the human surrounding world is the same today and always, and thus also in respect to what is relevant to primal establishment and lasting tradition, then we can show in several steps, only in an explora-tory way, in connection with our own surrounding world, what should be considered in more detail for the problem of the idealizing primal establishment of the meaning-structure "geom-etry."

Appendix VII:
[*The Life-World and the World of Science*] [1]

CONSCIOUSLY WE ALWAYS live in the life-world; normally there is no reason for making it explicitly thematic for ourselves universally *as* world. Conscious of the world as a horizon, we live for our particular ends, whether as momentary and changing ones or as an enduring goal that guides us. [The latter] can be a goal that we have elected for ourselves as a life-vocation, to be the dominant one in our active life, or it can be one that we have somehow drifted into through our upbringing. In this case a self-enclosed "world"-horizon is constituted. Thus as men with a vocation we may permit ourselves to be indifferent to everything else, and we have an eye only for this horizon as our world and for its own actualities and possibilities —those that exist in this "world"—i.e., we have an eye only to what is "reality" here (what is correct, true in relation to this goal) or "unreality" (the incorrect, the mistaken, the false).

That this whole effective life and this whole work-world is held within the always obviously existing world in the most universal and full sense of the life-world, that the particular activity and works presuppose *its* "truth and falsity" in terms of what exists and does not exist, of what is right and wrong in the broader and broadest sphere of being—this lies outside our interest, although in the life of particular interests we make use according to our particular needs of what exists in the broader sphere. Thus when we are living thematically only in the particular world (under the rule of the highest end that "makes" it), the life-world is unthematic for us; and as long as it remains such, we have our particular world, the only world that is thematic as such, as our horizon of interest. It may be, here, that

1. Biemel's note: "winter 1936–37 (?)" This manuscript appears in the German edition as "Beilage XVII," pp. 459–62.

this ruling end is ultimately a communal end, i.e., a personal life-task which is a partial task (if one can speak of a "part" in such a case) within a communal task, so that the individual personal undertaking of work functions concurrently, and consciously so for each of the "participants," in a communal undertaking.

The goal-directed life which is that of the scientists' life-vocation clearly falls under the generality of the characterization just made, together with the "world" that is awakened therein in the communalization of scientists (running through the successive generations of researchers) as the horizon of scientific works. [But] scientific works have a typical peculiarity which does not necessarily belong to all such worlds and ends. All the works belonging to this scientific world, with their specific communal sense of being (actual and true being and, on the other hand, incorrect, false being for all persons of the community), do not merely make up a multiplicity belonging together according to their [mode of] being; rather, the particular works—the particular scientific results—become premises, building stones for works of a higher level, and this of necessity and *in infinitum* and, at the same time, in such a way that all the works of science [come together] [2] in a coherent total work, the theoretical system (the theory contained in an ideal textbook). The scientific world, the scientists' horizon of being, has the character of a single work or edifice growing *in infinitum,* upon which the generations of scientists, belonging to it correlatively, are unendingly at work. The theoretical system here, however, is a work of predicative truth in which there is awakened correlatively, as a thoroughgoing universal substrate, the [idea of its] theoretically being true in that "domain"—under the highest end-idea, the truly all-determining one, of working through to an unconditionally true being (an infinitely distant idea). In the theoretical system of assertions, this "being-in-truth" is the identical subject matter [of such assertions], contained in their theoretical sense as the ideal "concept" of the domain and its entities.

Now the scientific world—[the subject matter of] systematic theory—and what is contained in it as existing in scientific truth (in natural science, in the universal theory, [this is] its nature, nature which counts as the substrate of the propositions, the formal ones), like all other worlds [determined by particular] ends, itself "belongs" to the life-world, just as all men and all

2. Biemel's interpolation.

human communities generally, and their human ends both individual and communal, with all their corresponding working structures, belong to it. But this is also true of philosophy in the old sense, which we have particular reason to mention last, whose theoretical "universe" is the world in the fullest sense. Each of these "worlds" has its particular universality determined by the end of the vocation; each has the infinite horizon of a certain "totality." But all these totalities take their place within the world, which encompasses all that exists and all existing totalities, as well as all their ends and all purposeful men and civilizations. All these take their place within it, and all presuppose it. What does this mean? And what does it mean for the world of "philosophy"? *Does there not arise here a necessary and at the same time dangerous double meaning of "world," of the domain of philosophy*, which is after all supposed to have the full and complete world, together with all the particular worlds mentioned above, as its subject matter? And the universal theory sought by philosophy, after all, should also be the theory of mankind's existence and of its ends and works and should even encompass itself, since philosophy itself is a purposeful structure of men.

One must not allow oneself to be confused. One must *distinguish* [on the one hand] the "domain" that *precedes* all ends, [even] the unitary end-idea that guides at the highest level, [the latter being] that domain in terms of which this end is sought, the domain that it deals with, that it has in view in a coherent way in advance in order to act in a purposeful way and create structured works for it, in relation to it; and, *on the other hand, the domain of goals*, the domain of *what has already been purposefully attained and what is yet to be attained* in its own universality, the horizon of actualities conceived of earlier or later as awakened and to be awakened in particularity for the sciences. Pregiven nature—the domain of the life-world—corporeal nature, [is that] which is familiar to the ordinary man in everyday life and which he can get to know "in more detail" but which he simply has no reason to single out and consider in a coherent way in its abstract unitary character, as natural science proposes to do. For [the scientist] it is the pregiven sphere of being for which he wishes to accomplish something new: theory for nature, theoretically true being, predicative determination—under the idea of unconditionally, universally valid truth. This is the "domain" of the natural scientist oriented purely toward the ends of his vocation, and within this domain in turn are distinguished: [on the one hand] that which has already been theoretically established and in a certain sense the whole horizon of the science to which it belongs, but in such a way that this [in particular] has been established within it; and on the other hand what must be set in the way of new tasks for the science, since what has been taken care of is always at the same time, after all, a foundation on which more must be built theoretically; namely, new questions must be posed and answered.

Finally, in the case of "philosophy" (in the old sense), we must likewise distinguish [on the one hand] the world simply, the always taken-for-granted, known-unknown life-world, as the universal domain for which a universal goal—theory, science for this world—is set; and [on the other hand] the scientists' life that is appropriate to the setting of this goal, their horizon of interests and horizon of "actualities," of results, not only those under the title of "nature existing in scientific truth" but also that of "world in general." This truth is a theoretical, purposeful structure related to the world that exists in prescientific life without question, in ontic certainty and in taken-for-granted actuality; but it is not this world itself.

It is clear what makes for the radical distinction here. The life-world is the world that is constantly pregiven, valid constantly and in advance as existing, but not valid because of some purpose of investigation, according to some universal end. Every end presupposes it; even the universal end of knowing it in scientific truth presupposes it, and in advance; and in the course of [scientific] work it presupposes it ever anew, as a world existing, in its own way [to be sure], but existing nevertheless. The scientific world (nature in the sense of natural science, world in the sense of philosophy as universal positive science) is a purposeful structure extending to infinity—a structure [made by] men who are presupposed, for the presupposed life-world. Now though we must [further] make evident the fact that the life-world itself is a "structure," it is nevertheless not a "purposeful structure," even though to its being, which precedes all purpose, belong men, just as we encounter them and become acquainted with them as a matter of course with all their purposes and their works, which, as developed by men, henceforth also belong as a matter of course to the life-world.

Here is again something confusing: every practical world, every science, presupposes the life-world; as purposeful structures they are *contrasted* with the life-world, which was always and continues to be "of its own accord." Yet, on the other hand, everything developing and developed by mankind (individually and in community) is itself a piece of the life-world: thus the contrast is suspended. But this is only confusing because the scientists, like all who live communalized under a vocational end ("life-purpose"), have eyes for nothing but their ends and horizons of work. No matter how much the life-world is the world in which they live, to which even all their "theoretical works" belong, and no matter how much they make use of elements of the life-world, which is precisely the "foundation" of theoretical treatment as that which is treated, the life-world [itself] is just not their subject matter, not as it is pregiven to them in each case and as it afterwards takes over their work; and thus [their subject matter] is not, in a full survey, the universe of what is, which is ever in unceasing movement of relativity for us and is the ground for all particular projects, ends, [and] end- and work-horizons for ends of a higher level.

Whenever the scientist speaks as a scientist, he is in the scientific attitude, thinking within the horizon of his theoretical end, thinking into it, so to speak, and at the same time having it as horizon in a privileged universal validity as the immediate horizon of his vocational interest. The rest of the world, the world-totality which *eo ipso* takes all human purposeful structures up into itself as world-totality, lies outside his interest. The full universal being of the life-world—especially in its [function of making possible] [3] his theoretical world and what is pregiven as belonging to it in particular—is completely unconsidered.

But now the paradoxical question: Can one not [turn to] the life-world, the world of which we are all conscious in life as the world of us all, without in any way making it into a subject of universal investigation, being always given over, rather, to our everyday momentary individual or universal vocational ends and interests—can one not survey it universally in a changed attitude, and can one not seek to get to know it, as what it is and how it is in its own mobility and relativity, make it the subject matter of a universal science, but one which has by no means the goal of universal theory in the sense in which this was sought by historical philosophy and the sciences?

3. Biemel's interpolation.

Appendix VIII:
Fink's Appendix on the Problem of the "Unconscious"[1]

THE ORDERING PRINCIPLE which lies in the essence of intentionality or of intentional references (for example, the reference of the analysis of memory to a prior analysis of perception) also marks off the whole total sphere of "wakefulness" as the unavoidable field of first approach in the analytic explication of subjectivity. The genuine problem-character of the problems announcing themselves under the title of the "unconscious" can be grasped and adequately expounded upon in a methodical way only after the prior analysis of "being conscious" [Bewusstheit]. Since our first task here is to make thematic the elementary essence of the always overlooked universal-subjective givenness of the world, to loosen the rigid fundamental posture of our naïve-natural life-world attitude (living straightforwardly toward things), to grasp things and the world itself in the alteration of subjective relativities as unity-constructions through subjective syntheses—in short, since it is a matter of the ABC's of intentional analysis, not even the basic features of the long methodical path from the intentional elementary analyses to the *intentional* theory of the "unconscious" can be sketched here.

One will be quick to raise the objection that setting up the problematics of the "unconscious" as intentional problematics is a questionable methodical prejudice right from the start, representing, as it were, the attempt to interpret the "un-conscious" according to the methodical means for understanding consciousness. Has one not thus made a prior decision that the unconscious is somehow obscured consciousness, consciousness that

1. Biemel's note: "The following appendix was written by Eugen Fink in 1936 for the *Crisis* and is published with his permission." The text appears in the German version as "Beilage XXI," pp. 473–75.

[385]

can be awakened, a preliminary form or after-image of consciousness, i.e., something that can ultimately be traced back to consciousness? Does one not thus have, in respect to the life of subjectivity, the preconceived opinion that life and consciousness are the same? But is it not the ever growing tendency of "depth psychology," modern biology, etc. (and also of the realistic and irrationalistic philosophies of the present) to conceive of consciousness as a [mere] stratum of the concrete man and to oppose to it other dimensions of life not traceable to consciousness? Is it not a typical preconceived opinion of all "idealism" that the "spirit," the "soul," "consciousness," makes up the full being of man; whereas we are gradually progressing more and more, through a "depth psychology" that is certified by its therapeutic successes, through the results of modern biology, etc., toward the insight that the sphere of consciousness, the domain of idealistic philosophy, ultimately represents a *derivative* [*fundierte*] *dimension of "life"*?

This objection, which is raised in many variations against the so-called "consciousness-idealism of phenomenology," is based on a fundamental philosophical *naïveté*. This is not the place to criticize the "mythical" theories set up on the basis of an obscure empirical procedure about the true essence of life (announcing itself in the phenomena of the "unconscious"), be it the naturalistic mechanism of the "libido" or some other "dynamics" of drives and instincts. The naïveté we refer to consists, before all theory-construction about the unconscious, in an *omission*. One thinks one is already acquainted with what the "conscious," or consciousness, is and dismisses the task of first making into a prior subject matter the concept against which any science of the unconscious must demarcate its subject matter, i.e., precisely that of consciousness. But because one does not know what consciousness is, one misses in principle the point of departure of a science of the "unconscious." Naturally, when we are awake, we always know and are acquainted with what is commonly meant by "consciousness." It is in a certain sense what is closest to us: we see things, think about something, desire something, judge, etc. Just this typical familiarity and pregivenness of "consciousness" in its rough articulation (which suffices for everyday life) as acts, actions, experiences [*Akte, Handlungen, Erlebnisse*], etc.—just this familiarity gives rise to the illusion that consciousness is something immediately given. The intentional analytics of phenomenology, however, destroys the illusion of the "immediate givenness of consciousness" and leads one into a science of a new sort that is difficult to sustain, where one gradually learns to see and to grasp for the first time what consciousness is. And if one has worked one's way through the long paths of intentional analytics to an understanding of "consciousness," one can never again wish to expound on the problematics of the "unconscious" from the naïve point of view, dealing as it does with consciousness and the unconscious as if they were familiar everyday things. For the unconscious, too, as well as for consciousness, there exists the *illusion* of everyday, given immediacy: we are all familiar, after all, with the phenomena of sleep, of fainting, of being overtaken by obscure driving forces, creative states, and the like. The naïveté of the current theory of the "unconscious" consists in the fact that it engrosses itself in these interesting phenomena which are pregiven in everyday life, undertakes an inductive empirical inquiry, proposes constructive "explanations," and is tacitly guided all along by a naïve and dogmatic *implicit theory about consciousness* of which it always makes use in spite of its demarcation [of these phenomena] from phenomena of consciousness, which are also taken in their everyday familiarity.

As long as the exposition of the problem of the unconscious is determined by such an implicit theory of consciousness, it is in principle philosophically naïve. Only *after* an *explicit* analysis of consciousness can the problem of the unconscious be posed at all. But only in the working mastery of this problem will it be revealed whether or not the "unconscious" can be treated according to the methodical means of the intentional analysis.

Appendix IX:
Denial of Scientific Philosophy. Necessity
of Reflection. The Reflection [Must Be]
Historical. How Is History Required? [1]

PHILOSOPHY AS SCIENCE, as serious, rigorous, indeed
apodictically rigorous, science—*the dream is over.* To be sure,
the man who has once tasted of the fruits of philosophy, has
become acquainted with its systems, and has then unhesitatingly
admired these as among the highest goods of culture can no
longer let philosophy and philosophizing alone. Some regard the
philosophies as art works of great artistic spirits and consider
philosophy "as such" to have the unity of an art. Others oppose
philosophy to the sciences in another way, such that it stands on
a plane with religion, into which we have grown historically.
What religious faith, as long as it is still a living faith, renders
certain, as God and divinely revealed truth, is something metaphysically transcendent; it transcends the world, which is the
subject matter of scientific knowledge, as its ultimate ground of
being, and this ultimate ground contains the absolute norms
under which we place our human existence in the world. Philosophy once thought of itself as the science of the totality of what
is. Thus even if philosophy itself drew the distinction between
the world, as the totality of what exists finitely, and God, as the
principle uniting the infinity of finite things (and then as an
infinite superpersonality), it thought itself capable of knowing
scientifically the metaphysical principle and the world through
this principle. Whatever it later substituted in the way of world-
transcending, metaphysical [principles], however it conceived of
the unity of the absolute, it thought all too long that scientific

1. Biemel's note: "Summer 1935." The text appears in the German edition as "Beilage XXVIII," pp. 508–13.

[389]

paths could lead to the transcendent, the absolute, the metaphysical. According to this, an alliance of science and religion was also possible, as in medieval [philosophy, which claimed] [2] to be able to bring religious faith and scientific reason into complete harmony. But these times are over—such is the generally reigning opinion of such people. A powerful and constantly growing current of philosophy which renounces scientific discipline, like the current of religious disbelief, is inundating European humanity.

The conviction has certainly become dominant that philosophy is a task for man as struggling for his existence [*Existenz*], man who has raised himself to autonomy in the European cultural development and sees himself as standing, thanks to the sciences, within the horizon of the infinities—and of the destinies these involve. The world-reflection of autonomous man necessarily leads to the transcendent as something which is unknowable and cannot be practically mastered. Man is capable only of arriving, by starting from his own position, from his horizons of knowledge and feeling, at certain conjectures and thereby of forming for himself certain ways of believing which, as his world-view, offer him a personal evidence for conjectures and for norms of action under the guidance of the conjecturally believed absolute. Such a posture also provides groups of men who bear within themselves a similar original direction with something like common understanding and mutual advancement.

A world-view is thus essentially an individual accomplishment, a sort of personal religious faith; but it is distinguished from traditional faith, that of revealed religion, through the fact that it makes no claim to an unconditioned truth binding for all men and communicable to all men: just as scientific truth about the absolute is not possible, so it is impossible to establish a world-view truth which is totally valid for each human being. Any such claim would mean that knowledge upon rational—i.e., scientific—grounds was possible about the absolute and its relation to man.

Philosophy is in danger, i.e., its future is endangered; should this not give a special sense to the question of the present task of philosophy, as a question posed in such a time [as was described above]?

Throughout the millennia, or rather in the repeatedly re-

2. Biemel's interpolation.

newed epochs of living and again reviving philosophy, the belief
was sustained—therein, after all, consisted its existence
[*Existenz*]—in the possibility and sometimes the successful realization of philosophy—in the form of systems and their
"schools." What sustained the belief, however, when the systems
changed, when the schools could not be unified through the
unification of convictions? Therein lay a failure which could not
remain concealed. What sustained the consciousness of a necessary task which was taken up personally and existentially because it had to be taken up, [understood] at the same time as *one*
consciousness of fulfilling, in taking over its realization as a
personal necessity, a superpersonal necessity, a task for humanity intentionally implied in one's own life-task?

What can bind us to our goal? Is it only the foolhardiness of
striving toward a goal which is beautiful but only vaguely possible, one which is not definitely impossible but still, in the end,
imaginary, one which gradually, after the experience of millennia, finally begins to bear a very great inductive probability of
being unattainable? Or does what appears from the outside to be
a failure, and on the whole actually is one, bring with it a certain
evidence of practical possibility and necessity, as the evidence of
an imperfect, one-sided, partial success, but still a success in this
failure?

However, if such an evidence ever was alive, in our time at
any rate it has become weak, has lost its vitality. Surely, if
philosophy has a unified sense involving a legitimate, necessary
task, such evidence must exist as the evident consciousness of a
project, even if imperfectly clear, which is on the way [toward
fulfillment] in all the attempts of the great systems, at least in
individual directions, whereas in other directions criticism is
justified. Only by engrossing ourselves in the revitalized content
of the traditional systems can we feel this evidence; and if we
penetrate them, interrogate them, the sense of the task of philosophy can become clear.

There is no doubt, then, that we must engross ourselves in
historical considerations if we are to be able to understand ourselves as philosophers and understand what philosophy is to
become through us. It is no longer sufficient to grasp, in the
midst of the naïve pressure of life and activity, so to speak,
though out of the existential depths of personality, at certain
working problems we have run up against in our naïve development, to treat of them with our working partners, with those
who, in the same course of a living tradition, have run up

against the same problems. This suffices no longer in the dangerous situation in which today's philosophy knows itself to be—
must know, must admit to itself, in order to secure a future
threatened by the suggestive force of the "spirit of the time."

To the philosopher and to a generation of philosophers, acting responsibly in a human and cultural space, there accrue, also
deriving from this cultural space, responsibilities and corresponding actions. It is the same here as it is generally for men in
times of danger. For the sake of the life-task that has been taken
up, in times of danger one must first let these very tasks alone
and do what will make a normal life possible again in the future.
The effect will generally be such that the total life-situation, and
with it the original life-tasks, has been changed or in the end has
even become fully without an object. *Thus reflection is required
in every sense* in order to right ourselves.

The historical reflection we have in mind here concerns our
existence [*Existenz*] as philosophers and, correlatively, the existence of philosophy, which, for its part, *is* through our philosophical existence.*

The situation is complicated. *Every philosopher "takes something from the history"* of past philosophers, from past philosophical writings—just as he has at his disposal, from the present
philosophical environment, the works that have most recently
been added and put in circulation, takes up those that have just
appeared, and, what is possible only in the case [of the present],
makes more or less use of the possibility of entering into a
personal exchange of ideas with still living fellow philosophers.

The philosopher "takes something from history": Now history is after all not before us like a warehouse containing its
assembled wares, such that everyone can convince himself of the
existence of these wares as being not dreamed-up, not illusory,
but actually tangible and secure in their being and being-such.
Even the documents themselves, the works of the philosophers
or the reports about them as literary facts, are not simply

* Here we can also say more simply and, at the same time, in
preliminarily generalizing way: The reflection in question is a particular case of that self-reflection in which man as a person seeks to
reflect upon the ultimate sense of his existence [*Dasein*]. We must
distinguish between a broader and a narrower concept of self-
reflection [*Selbstbesinnung*]: pure ego-reflection [*Ichreflexion*] and
reflection upon the whole life of the ego as ego; and reflection [*Besin-
nung*] in the pregnant sense of inquiring back into the sense or teleological essence of the ego.

themselves there [before us] as if they were present and always perceivable things. That is, what is thinglike about them is not yet the document that a given reader understands as a philosophical work or as a report, since what is present in a thinglike way is a bearer of significations for him. But this is the way he accepts it; and right away it can become questionable whether this is really a matter of a literary transmission or whether it is false, whether it is a poetic transformation containing a kernel of historical actuality, etc. The reader, the philosophical one who thinks for himself, is not moved by a concern for scientific history (for whole epochs this was completely excluded); he takes up uncritically what is offered to him as a fact of transmission and lets himself be motivated by what he reads into it theoretically, by "the" Platonic, Aristotelian philosophy, etc. One takes hold of this set, another of that set, of literary documents that are available to him or to his time generally; and if he receives from Plato, for example, even quite decisive impulses, so that one later counts him among the Platonists, perhaps he has never, in the crowded course of his philosophical life-work, had the time, the possibility, or the desire to study all the Platonic or supposedly Platonic writings, not to speak of the reports or critiques of other thinkers which have an indirect relation to the Platonic philosophy and elucidate it.

He reads as one who has gone through a philosophical education in his time, who has himself become a philosopher and has perhaps already made a literary appearance; he reads and naturally understands what he reads from the standpoint of his own thoughts; he apperceives Plato in his own way, on the basis of the "perception" of his already developed concepts, methods, convictions. Through this apperception he gains something new, further developing himself as a philosopher; and, in an analogous way, taking up and interpreting other philosophical writings, he becomes a different philosopher. If he reads Plato again after a time, Plato takes on a new face for him, and the new Plato, and other authors newly understood by him, motivate him anew, etc.

Now in our epoch everyone has in his [3] surrounding world, in the practical realm of general availability, a science of history, and in particular a scientific history of philosophy; or rather, belonging as a preliminary stage to general history itself and to every sort of special history is a scientific preliminary interpreta-

3. Reading *in seiner* for *seine*.

tion and critique of the literary and other documentation of the historical past—which is our past and that of the historian who belongs within our "we." Once again: *What is,* what must be, *the significance of this for the philosopher who thinks for himself?* Is the work lost that he, unconcerned about scientific historical study, has done under the guidance of, through the use of, his "unhistorical," untrue Plato, etc.?

What kind of "poetic invention" [*Dichtung*], what kind of historical interpretation is this? What kind is appropriate, and to what extent, to help us? How must we carry it on, even beyond our philosophizing life, in order to clarify our unclear consciousness of our *telos?*

Never was this clarification more urgently needed than in our time; for millennia philosophy could advance in naïve theorization; through naïvely developed concepts it could pose naïve problems, develop, define, and pursue them with naïve methodology. The naïve, but in itself unclear, certainty concerning its goal was questioned skeptically from the beginning, to be sure; but no matter how much even skepticism intervened in a motivating way in the course of philosophy, the validity of the sense of philosophy's end remained continuously unbroken; theoretical results attained had in each case the force of serious and confirmed accomplishment even if they later succumbed to the criticism of successors.

Let us be more precise. I know, of course, what I am striving for under the title of philosophy, as the goal and field of my work. And yet I do not know. What autonomous thinker has ever been satisfied with this, his "knowledge"? For what autonomous thinker, in his philosophizing life, has "philosophy" ever ceased to be an enigma? Everyone has the sense of philosophy's end, to whose realization his life is devoted; everyone has certain formulae, expressed in definitions; but only secondary thinkers, who in truth should not be called philosophers, are consoled by their definitions, beating to death with their word-concepts the problematic *telos* of philosophizing. In that obscure "knowledge," and in the word-concepts of the formulae, the historical is concealed; it is, according to its own proper sense, the spiritual inheritance of him who philosophizes; and in the same way, obviously, he understands the others in whose company, in critical friendship and enmity, he philosophizes. And in philosophizing he is also in company with himself as he earlier understood and did philosophy; and he knows that, in the process, historical tradition, as he understood it and used it, entered into him in a motivating way and as a spiritual sediment. His historical picture, in part made by himself and in part taken over, his "poetic invention of the history of philosophy," has not and does not remain fixed—that he knows; and yet every "invention" serves him and can serve him in understanding himself and his aim, and his own aim in relation to that of others and their "inventions," their aims, and finally what it is that is common to all, which makes up philosophy "as such" as a unitary *telos* and makes the systems attempts at its fulfillment for us all, for us [who are] at the same time in company with the philosophers of the past (in the various ways we have been able to invent them for ourselves).

Appendix X:
Fink's Outline for the Continuation of the Crisis[1]

1. The *genuine* universality of the psychological epochē

THE MISUNDERSTANDING of [this] universality has already been cleared up. Thus now, before the transition from psychology to transcendental philosophy, the genuine universal epochē of psychology must be brought out. It is nothing other than an epochē in respect to *world*-validity. Thus once again, analysis of world-consciousness and its manner of implying individual consciousness as subject matter. But the psychologist cannot universally bracket the horizon-validity of world-consciousness at will in connection with persons that interest him psychologically; rather, there is an order which belongs to the consistency of the world-epochē. He can only begin *with himself,* with his conscious life (under the epochē of its world-validity); only from his own point of view does he have others in the genuine psychological attitude. Thus a psychology that has come to a self-understanding of the attitude which makes it possible (of the universal epochē in the genuine sense) can begin in no other way than by being first a *psychology of the psychologist.* The illusion disappears that one can begin at will with any person at all. The genuinely universal epochē of psychology destroys the *illusion of the mutual externality of souls:* the mutual

1. Biemel's note: "This appendix comprises the proposal Fink gave to Husserl before Easter 1936 (?)" It should be noted that the train of thought in the first parts of this sketch is already incorporated into the last sections of the *Crisis* text. The text appears in the German edition as "Beilage XXIX," pp. 514–16.

internality which extends out from the psychologist determines the course of the psychological investigation.

2. The paradox of psychology

The genuine universal epochē as epochē of world-consciousness is the clarified final form of the sought-after psychological "abstraction" (as complement to the natural abstraction). But is it still an "abstraction"? Is the soul a complementary (though independent) aspect of the concrete human being? What is the ontic meaning of the "soul" that is laid bare by the genuine universal epochē? Psychology *begins* as a special science alongside others on the *ground of the pregiven world*. In the clarification of the method peculiar to it, however, i.e., in the explicit performance of the genuine universal epochē, it suspends the *presupposition of the world-ground* that was posited in its understanding of its own beginning; it divests itself of the ground on which it established itself; it becomes *groundless* by its own efforts. But this "groundlessness" exhibits the paradox of psychology. What kind of "inwardness" *is* that of world-meaning life? Where does it belong, actually? When the psychologist works, he has no world-ground; but when he *reflects,* he falls back into the *situation of his first approach:* psychology counts for him as a science of a definite region of what is. In this tension between the working situation of the psychologist and his falling-back through self-interpretation based on the horizon of understanding connected with his "first approach," in the antinomy between psychology establishing itself on the world-ground and psychology divesting itself of the world-ground, lies the "crux."

3. The resolution of the paradox

When psychology not only "brackets," through the genuine universal epochē, the world-consciousness that bears psychology itself in its first approach, but also makes this a *subject of analysis* in its own right, and this in such a way that it traces all pregiven "crude" articulations of the meaning life—the act-intentionalities and the easily demonstrable horizon-intentionalities—back to constituting functions that lie deeper: then it also becomes involved in an analysis of the constitutive function of world-consciousness. In other words, it not only practices the epoché in respect to world-consciousness, but in this posture of epoché it also investigates its *constitutive origin*. World-consciousness can then never again be an "opaque ground"; psychology sees through its own first approach "upon the world-ground" in its meaning-bestowing origins. With this, psychology suspends itself: it leads into *transcendental phenomenology*.

4. Characterization of the relation between psychology and phenomenology (the relation of the two "attitudes" to each other)

Basically there is no psychology that could remain psychology. Once the method of disclosing *intentionality* has been found, then, "consistent with the matter itself," the analytic way from the pregiven unities to the truly constituting depths of intentional life and thus to the transcendental dimension will be further pursued. *Psychology must flow into transcendental philosophy.*

In spite of this there always exists a difference between psychology and phenomenology, even after traversing the way from psychology to transcendental philosophy. Psychology is not a "mere preliminary stage" of phenomenology, caught in a reflection on its first approach: it is that as a *stage of the way* to phenomenology. But when it has traversed this way, when it has "flowed out," even then there is a difference between the two.

The interplay between the two attitudes

The problem-area is characterized by the problematics of *self-apperception*. All transcendental "self"-constitution is a placing of the constituting life into the thematic context of the constituted structures. Even after the transcendental reduction, subjectivity does not cease objectifying itself as man among fellow men and things; it is just that this continuing self-constitution is now a transcendentally elucidated process.

The horizon of *constituted self-objectification* (even when transcendentally "transparent") determines the legitimate problem-sphere of psychology after its self-dissolution into phenomenology: it now becomes a *thematically limited phenomenological sphere of problems* but one in which, in turn, everything nevertheless "belongs" (the problem of "flowing in"). Transcendental philosophy has, as opposed to the limited horizon of psychology that is bound to the scope of self-objectification (after the reduction), the truly *absolute horizon.*

Fourth part of the treatise

The idea of all sciences being taken back into the unity of transcendental philosophy.

1. Psychology and psychophysics or biology as illustrations of the relation between legitimately limited mundane problematics and phenomenology.

2. The descriptive sciences of nature (their a priori as "ontology of the life-world") and the phenomenology of idealization.

3. The "unity" of science as the unity of a universal correlative-system.

The phenomenological concept of metaphysics.

Fifth part

The indispensable task of philosophy: humanity's responsibility for itself.

Index